# AUDIENCE RATINGS:

# RADIO, TELEVISION, AND CABLE

### Revised Student Edition

# COMMUNICATION TEXTBOOK SERIES

Jennings Bryant—Editor

## Broadcasting

James Fletcher—Advisor

BEVILLE • Audience Ratings: Radio,
Television, Cable
(Revised Student Edition)

# AUDIENCE RATINGS:

# RADIO, TELEVISION, AND CABLE

Revised Student Edition
including a complete account
of Peoplemeter Developments

## Hugh Malcolm Beville, Jr.

**LEA** LAWRENCE ERLBAUM ASSOCIATES, PUBLISHERS
1988   Hillsdale, New Jersey                    Hove and London

Lawrence Erlbaum Associates, Inc., Publishers
365 Broadway
Hillsdale, New Jersey 07642

**Library of Congress Cataloging-in-Publication Data**

Beville, Hugh Malcolm—1988.
Audience ratings.

(Communication)
Bibliography: p.
Includes index.
   1. Radio programs—Rating.   2. Television programs—
Rating.   I. Title.   II. Communication (Hillsdale, N.J.)
HE8689.7.A8B46   1988       384.54′3       88-432
ISBN 0-8058-0175-8
ISBN 0-8058-0174-X (pbk.)

Printed in the United States of America
10  9  8  7  6  5  4

*To my wife, Eleanor*

# Contents

# Foreword

This volume fills a widespread and long-felt need for an authoritative reference work on broadcast ratings. Because of rating's influence over programming and advertising, there is a high degree of interest in broadcast ratings in many quarters: businessmen, marketers, advertisers,program producers as well as the broadcast and cable industries themselves. Washington officials, Wall Street analysts, writers and journalists, and all people have a stake in the procedures and outcome of ratings surveys. Yet no authoritative source exists.

Information supplied by each ratings company is limited to its specific ongoing or past services whereas books that refer to ratings devote no more than a chapter to the subject.

The academic community in the fields of telecommunications, marketing, and advertising lack a significant source book. Those entering the fields of electronic media, advertising, and other media have no place to turn for a background on ratings. Few professionals in the fields of broadcasting or advertising are aware of how ratings developed and why and how the present systems came to be. Hugh M. Beville, Jr., has called on over a half century of personal experience in broadcast research to put this account into print as a lasting contribution and reference work.

The book is outlined in a relatively straightforward manner. First comes the historical development of radio and ratio ratings. Chapter 3 deals with television ratings, which directly drew on radio experience. The treatment is largely by company because, initially at least, every major rating service advocated and used a unique technique. Chapter 4 deals with a comparative analysis of methodologies, drawing on many of the significant methodological studies carred out by rating services and industry groups. The next chapters deal with two areas that have mushroomed in importance in the past five years—qualitative and cable audience measurements. In Chapter 7 current utilization of ratings is discussed from the viewpoint of the users—broadcasters, spot representatives, agencies and advertisers, and program producers. The following two chapters cover public and governmental concerns with ratings and attempts to meet the many criticisms and complaints about ratings and their role in programming. Chapter 10 summarizes the lessons learned, while Chapter 11 looks ahead to future trends, especially as related to the oncoming era of new technologies.

# Preface

Programs are the heart of broadcasting, while sales provide the muscle. Ratings with their feedback element are the nerve system that largely controls what is broadcast.

In 1987, broadcasting and cable were part of a $25 billion industry. A pervasive element influencing all aspects of the electronic media is the audience rating. It is difficult to imagine a successful system of free commercial broadcasting without this important feedback. The ratings report the size and composition of the audience that is reached by a given program, station, or schedule of commercial announcements. These data are crucial to the activities of broadcasting management, sales representatives, program producers, advertisers and their agencies, writers, performers, and their agents. More important, from a public standpoint, the rating expectation for any program under consideration is a major component in network and station decisions as to what programs will survive and when and where they should be scheduled.

Ratings are a powerful force in broadcasting and telecommunications. They determine the price that will be paid for programs and the pay that performers will receive. They govern the rates that advertisers will pay for 60-second or 30-second or smaller commercial units in and around each program. Ratings determine stations' audience and rank order in their market, and to a large degree they dictate the profitability of broadcasting stations and their value when put up for sale. The salary and bonus compensation of key network and station officials are also governed by ratings success. Ratings results ultimately determine whether top management and program and news management in television and radio broadcast organizations will retain their jobs, be promoted, or demoted.

In the final analysis, the simple twist of the wrist (or push of the button) of people switching their sets on and off or tuning from station to station provides the single most important piece of information about audience behavior.

## Why Ratings?

The importance that ratings have in today's broadcasting has developed over time as the extent, frequency, and rapidity of ratings results increased and as the cost of broadcasting spiraled. Nevertheless, the essential considerations underlying its development were present from the time the first rating service was envisioned in 1929. Five major factors generated a climate favorable to ratings growth:

1. Broadcasting produced an intangible service. At its beginning it was a new, exciting, almost mystical phenomenon based on unseen waves shooting through the atmosphere at the speed of light. No purchase record was created by the user. There were no newsstand sales or home delivery subscriptions, no box office, no gate receipts. For advertisers there were no pages to scan, no dummies to critique, no tearsheets to prove actual appearance, and no publisher's statement or Audit Bureau of Circulation to establish number of distribution copies. Even today, when we have both video and radio recordings of actual broadcasts, to a large degree the ratings books with their complete competitive schedule and detailed audience figures are the industry's primary record of performance and the basis for a vast spectrum of decisions at every level of management.

2. Tuning to broadcast programs was free and simple. As the choice widened, radio listeners selected music of various types, comedy, drama, news, sports, or serials. Freedom to tune in or out, and to switch stations at any instant, gave the audience a tremendous power, especially if programmers could somehow track that mass activity. One might say that every home with a radio or TV set is like a voting booth where informed choices are being made constantly—dial changes are executed, unacceptable programs are tuned out—all with a simple physical act. Broadcasting was the ultimate in democratic communication— listening to an opera performance cost no more than tuning in to a pop singer's latest album; watching the Superbowl is no more expensive than viewing a debate on a proposed local nuclear power plant.

3. Originally the advertiser, by his purchase of time and program separately, became his own program producer. His concern was, therefore, centered on the specific audience of his program and on its competitive success in a particular time period. Radio was unlike print media, where measurements of exposure to a company's particular advertisements were sketchy at best. Once pioneering research had proved that adequate broadcast program audience measurement was possible, advertisers and agencies pushed for such surveys to report on results of their own and their competitors' efforts.

Even today, when the rule is purchase of announcement availabilities rather than entire time periods of programs, the advertiser (and advertising agency) is fundamentally most concerned with the degree to which the audience target has been reached with the advertiser's particular schedule of commercials. What is happening to the medium at large is of secondary interest.

4. Because of its unique temporal quality, the broadcast audience is relatively easy to measure by acceptable survey techniques. A program's audience is assembled at a particular time; the program can normally be heard or seen only during the period of the broadcast. Listening and viewing habits are keyed to individual living patterns and are guided by various printed program schedules. Unlike other mass media, radio and TV audience measurement is greatly simplified, considerably more accurate, and vastly more affordable.

5. The physical range of radio broadcasting was unpredictable, especially in its first two decades, before the broadcast spectrum bulged with stations. The geographic area in which an individual radio station was received could be enormous (WLW, Cincinnati, called itself the "Nation's Station" with only a modicum of puffery). Furthermore, atmospheric conditions so controlled radio reception that audience potential varied (sometimes widely) by the hour, by the day, and by the season of the year. Clear channel stations were given frequency monopolies at night to enable them to cover wide rural areas that lacked local stations, while regional and local channels served more restricted areas.

It was inevitable that advertisers who were paying commercial broadcasting's bills in the late 1920s should be strongly interested in a method to measure what they were gettng for their money. It was, therefore, a relatively easy task for Archibald M. Crossley, in 1929, to interest them in sponsoring a somewhat revolutionary new research technique: sample recall telephone interviews on a continuous basis to record home listening behavior.

From the date of the first Crossley survey, over 50 years ago, the general principles of the ratings survey field have not changed:

1. Services are owned and operated by private entrepreneurs.

2. They are syndicated to as many users as possible in order to spread costs.

3. They use sampling procedures, whatever technique is used to collect audience data.

4. In preparing their reports, they require and receive a substantial amount of data about program schedules from stations and networks.

5. They report two fundamental numbers:

(a) Ratings—the percentage of all radio or television households or persons within a demographic group in the survey area who view a specific program or station.

(b) Share—during a specific time period the percentage of the total audience (households or persons using radio or TV) that tuned to a particular program or station during that period (program rating divided by sum of all ratings for time period).

Over the past 50 years, numerous innovations and refinements have been introduced with the inauguration of metered panels and diary keeping being perhaps the most significant. Nevertheless, as the story of ratings unfolds, one must conclude that the techniques pioneered in the first two decades have served and still serve the industry well.

Whether future new techniques will be successful is conjectural. One thing seems certain: There can be no perfect rating service. That means that ratings users are provided with rough estimates by crude tools. Ratings users should know as much as possible about the frailties and limitations of those tools as they go about using them in decision making. I hope that this book contributes to the users' enlightenment.

### Audience Measurement: Only One Aspect of Broadcast Research

Today's fields of market, media, communications, and public opinion research are so complex that some explanation is required to properly position the subject of this book—broadcast and cable ratings. From a marketing standpoint, media research deals with effective use of major advertising media: electronic (radio, television, cable), print (newspapers, magazines, and trade journals), outdoor, and direct mail.

A major element in media research is audience measurement, which is generally carried out by syndicated services. Normally, for broadcast ratings, the medium pays a substantial part of the cost of these services, which now totals over $160 million annually. The combined agency and advertiser share of costs today is around 15 percent.

Audience measurement, although it receives a large portion of the research expenditures of both buyer and seller, is by no means the only type of research in the broadcast media field. Agencies spend considerable time and money on various forms of "copy tests" of TV and radio commercials. A number of different techniques are available for this purpose, but they are not the subject of this book. Nor will we deal at all with the various research approaches to the pretesting of program concepts, pilots, casting, and so on.

Prior to the emergence of projectable ratings, networks and stations expended substantial effort in the 1930s in surveying the number of radio families, the hour-by-hour use of radio, and the geographical coverage of stations. Although referred to in those situations where such research affected ratings development, no comprehensive discussion is provided on those studies. Measuring the sales effectiveness of broadcasting has been a constant challenge, and many such studies have been undertaken in the past. Neither are those covered in this volume.

This book does discuss research projects that have been designed as methodology tests of existing or proposed rating techniques. Otherwise, our concern is solely with the regularly conducted and published estimates of audience size and program (or station) ratings, conducted by syndicated services and available to any user (station, network, program producer, advertiser, advertising agency, spot representative, buying service, and so on) at a cost stipulated by a published rate card.

This book not only documents the growth and research behind today's audience measurement infrastructure but it gives personal highlights of the early pioneers. The ratings business has always involved a limited number of key players, and the interaction of human factors has provided a somewhat dramatic story that I wanted to include. I joined the National Broadcasting Company as a statistician in March 1930, the month in which the first ratings survey was conducted. NBC, with two networks, was the dominant element in all broadcasting, so every aspiring researcher or rating service entrepreneur had to see us. No new development escaped our attention. There is hardly a person mentioned in the book whom I did not know personally and with whom I did not have a professional (and in some cases, personal) relationship.

I was instrumental in encouraging new services by initial subscription support, for Hooper in both radio and television, for Trendex, for Seiler's American Research Bureau and for TVQ, and budgeted for the NBC Cumulative Radio Audience Measurement project, forerunner of Radio's All Dimension Audience Report. I served on, and was often chairman of, virtually every significant industry activity organized to evaluate or test ratings methodologies—National Association of Broadcasters Research Committee, All-Radio Methodology Study, Advertising Research Foundation committees, Committee on Nationwide Television Audience Measurement, Committee on Local Television and Radio Audience Measurement, and Broadcast Ratings Council.

As a result, I have been intimately involved in ratings throughout a professional lifetime of over 50 years. What I didn't know firsthand I learned from the principle players by personal or telephone interview, letters, or exchanges of informal notes, as this book was written. Thus, my statements are based on confirming interviews with persons involved. If there is any subjective bias in my reporting, it is attributable to my position as a broadcast executive. I make no claim to viewing the field from the angle of a ratings supplier or a buyer of broadcast time.

This revised edition fills the gap between Spring 1984 when the original edition was finished, and January 1988. This period has witnessed the most dramatic developments in television ratings in forty years, Nielsen's Television Index (NTI) was the dominant monopoly power in network television until 1983, when AGB PLC, a British research company, advanced a bold plan for a U.S. peoplemeter service to be performed with larger samples and at lower costs than Nielsen's. Nielsen responded by starting to test its own peoplemeter on an extensive scale. The race was on, with the result that as of September 1987 there are two national competitive peoplemeter services operating, Nielsen and AGB Research.

Despite widespread industry acceptance, there are those, especially the national TV networks, who are dissatisfied with various aspects of peoplemeters.

Meanwhile two other companies, ScanAmerica and Roger Percy, are working just offstage to perfect peoplemeter services with added features. All of these developments are covered in Chapter XI.

There had also been major changes in qualitative ratings as well as local radio ratings. These, plus other updating (especially in Appendix C, for example), are the significant revisions in this volume. Of particular help in this revision were Lee Morganlander of Nielsen, Bob Hoffman of AGB, and Jim Spaeth of Scan-America.

My account of the early history was aided by George Gallup, Darrell Lucas, and Frank Stanton. Others who contributed to the historical events of which I did not have firsthand knowledge include CAB—Archibald M. Crossley, John Karol, and James Ward; Hooper—Fred Kenkel, Gordon Buck, David Dole, Frank Stisser; CBS Diaries—Harper Carraine, Charles Smith, Sam Barton; Audience Surveys—Eugene Katz; Pulse—Sydney and Lawrence Roslow; Trendex—Edward Hynes and Robert Rogers (also for Hooperatings); Nielsen—Arthur C. Nielsen, Sr., Henry Rahmel, William Swigert, Gale Metzger, David Traylor, Marie Austin, Kenneth Mogensen, Edward Schillmoeller, Ruth Betzer, and William Behana; Arbitron—James Seiler, Rupert Ridgeway, James Rupp, William McClenaghan, Peter Langhoff, Norman Hecht, Theodore Shaker, A. J. Aurichio, Shelley Cagner; TRAC VII—Richard Lysacker and Leslie Frankel; RAM—John Patton; RADOX—Albert Sindlinger; Sindlinger—Albert Sindlinger and Gerald Glasser; RADAR—Thomas Coffin, Catherine Coholan Mansfield, William Rubens, Gerald Glasser, Gale Metzger, Miriam Murphy; Birch—Thomas Birch.

Unfortunately, countless others who assisted me with information and suggestions must go unmentioned here, but I thank them for their contributions. Special thanks go to Doris Katz, the peerless NBC Research Librarian who cheerfully supplied any and every figure, date, or fact that I could not come up with elsewhere, and Betty Brinkerhoff, who labored loyally and tirelessly in preparing the manuscript for publication.

Four people read the entire book, and special thanks go to them also: Dr. Thomas Coffin of NBC Research was an ardent supporter, adviser, and frank critic; Dr. Samuel Tuchman of NBC Corporate Planning particularly provided advice on the book's structure; Dr. Lawrence Myers, Professor of Broadcasting,

Syracuse University Newhouse School, gave helpful suggestions about historical and technical aspects; Dr. Jennings Bryant of Houston University contributed to language clarification and organization.

The sympathy and support of my loving wife, Eleanor, was of crucial impor- tance in bringing this book to fruition. I am most grateful for her many sacrifices to a struggling author.

Hugh M. Beville, Jr.

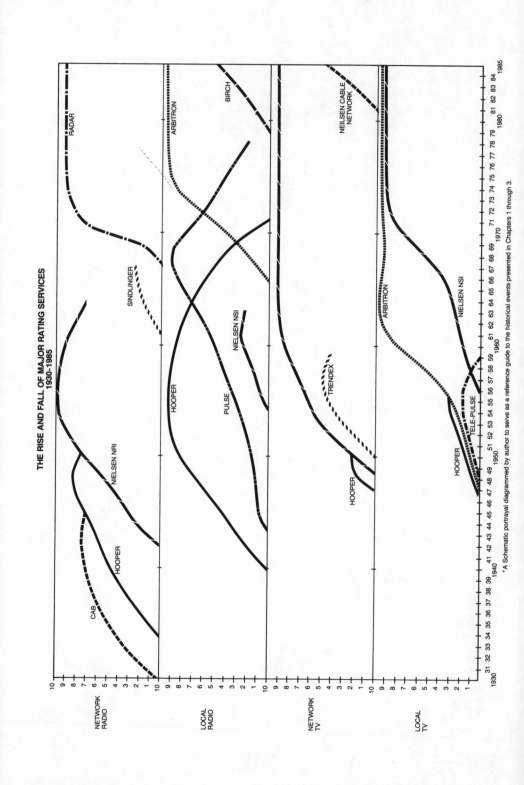

THE RISE AND FALL OF MAJOR RATING SERVICES
1930-1985

*A Schematic portrayal diagrammed by author to serve as a reference guide to the historical events presented in Chapters 1 through 3.

# 1 Radio Services— Pre-TV (1930–1946)

## I. HOW IT ALL BEGAN

The early 1920s were a period of relative calm in American society. Life was simple, and the country had returned to the isolationism that for a long time had been interrupted by World War I. The 1920 presidential election of conservative Republican Warren G. Harding officially ended Woodrow Wilson's dream of active U.S. involvement in postwar world affairs.

The political turning point of November 1920 was shared with another less visible event. Little attention was paid at first to the fact that Westinghouse radio station KDKA had broadcast the Harding-Cox election returns on November 2, 1920. However, public interest in radio rapidly increased as scores and then hundreds of stations sprang up across the land. As daily schedules were diversified and lengthened, radio "suddenly symbolized a coming age of enlightenment. It was seen as leading to the fulfillment of democracy. . . . It would link rich and poor, young and old. It would end the isolation of rural life. It would unite the nation."[1] We can readily appreciate today that Harding's election in 1920 had nowhere near the impact on the future of American life as did the broadcast of the election returns on KDKA. The electronic age had arrived.

Unless one lived through this period, it is difficult indeed to visualize what public excitement this miraculous device created. (The dazzling emergence of television in post-World War II America was a relatively pallid performance compared with the phenomenon of radio.) Home conveniences such as electricity and telephone service and mechanical marvels like automobiles and phonographs were widely used then, but they were by no means universal. There were no electric refrigerators or oil burners, no supermarkets or rental cars, no bus routes

1

or airlines. The Harvard undergraduate paid $200 a year tuition plus another $300 for room and board. The New York Times cost 2¢. Men wore felt hats in winter, straw skimmers in summer; women wore corsets all year round; the brassiere had not yet been invented; and the computer was decades in the future.

This was the America that now suddenly found that speech and music could inexplicably be transmitted over the air right into their homes. The power of invisible voice transmission hitherto limited to gods and ghosts was now in human hands. Barriers of distance evaporated as people dialed through the night to "pull in" stations from thousands of miles away. At first, earphones and sets powered by crystals or storage batteries were required for home reception. However, separate loudspeakers and normal electrical current soon came into play, and public interest soared. When Stromberg Carlson, Atwater Kent, General Electric (GE), Radio Corporation of America (RCA), and others introduced self-contained radio sets with consoles priced at around $200 (equivalent to over $1000 in 1984 dollars), millions of American families acquired a radio receiver.

The public excitement provided by this miraculous radio medium of mass communication was soon to be matched by advertiser enthusiasm. The initial sponsored broadcast over WEAF, New York (now WNBC) was a late-afternoon, 10-minute period on August 28, 1932, for which the Queensborough Corporation paid $50 to promote its Jackson Heights apartments. After William H. Rankin of the Rankin Advertising Agency tried radio promotion successfully for a beauty product, advertiser and agency interest picked up. The early straight promotional talks were replaced in 1923 by the introduction of musical groups, such as the Cliquot Club Eskimos, the Ipana Troubadours, and the A & P Gypsies, dedicated to publicizing trade names with no sales message. One writer accounted for the rapid acceptance of sponsored broadcasts this way: "An accident of history— the fact that commercial radio began simultaneously with the post-World War I breakup of Victorian social attitudes—this profoundly affected the development of broadcasting in America."[2]

In 1923, American Telephone & Telegraph (AT&T) began experimenting with networking WEAF programs to stations in Boston, Washington, Philadelphia, Schenectady, Providence, and Hartford over existing intercity telephone lines. By July 1924, a network of 16 stations stretching as far west as Minneapolis, Kansas City, Davenport, Iowa, and Dallas was being set up. An internal AT&T staff study estimated it would reach 53 percent of the U.S. population and 62 percent of U.S. radio sets. By 1925, scores of advertisers used network radio, and the number increased significantly after the formation of NBC in November 1926, based on the AT&T lineup, known as the Red Network. In January 1927, NBC acquired the smaller Westinghouse chain of five stations, with WJZ (now WABC), New York, as the "flagship" station. The latter group was known as the Blue Network (predecessor of today's ABC) and was expanded to parallel the Red Network. The CBS radio network came into being in 1928.

The new medium was on the threshold of becoming a major national communications force.

Advertisers who at first had treated radio as an experimental venture (similar to their recent interest in cable TV) were ready now to grant its potential for creating sales. There was one major drawback: Pioneer radio lacked any measurement of its unseen audience. Much had to be taken on faith. How many families had radio? What areas were served by various stations? When did people listen? What programs were people listening to? And especially what is the size of my program's audience? Who is actually listening?

## Early Attempts at Determining the Audience

The first effort to provide solid data came when NBC commissioned Dr. Daniel Starch, a Harvard professor and pioneer market research consultant, to conduct an extensive survey east of the Rockies in March/April 1928. Over 17,000 personal interviews in 105 cities and towns and in 68 rural counties showed that 34.6 percent of the families owned a radio, a penetration that if projected to the total United States (including the unsurveyed area) would yield 9,640,000 total radio families.[3] Although this was a valuable benchmark, by the time the study was released in early 1929 NBC was estimating there were more than 11 million radio families. The Starch study did nothing to measure listening patterns insofar as stations and programs were concerned, so it had a minimal impact on the advertising world.

Strong evidence of radio's grip on its audience was evident in such a national phenomenon as the nightly suspension of all normal activities for the 7:00 P.M. "Amos 'n' Andy" broadcast. In order to get patrons to the first show at local motion picture theaters, the program was piped in before the movie.

Audience mail indicated significant audience response, but such nonsystematic feedback was inconclusive because much of it was in response to over-the-air offers of such material as autographed photos of the star, a free sample of the product, a booklet, or some premium (early forms of what today is termed "hyping"). One use of mail was to plot a station's coverage pattern but even that was unreliable because no trustworthy data on radio ownership by counties was available. Only when the 1930 census provided such figures (in 1932) could letters per thousand radio families be calculated for coverage purposes.

Nevertheless, lacking any other yardstick, the number of fan letters for stars was an important clue to the unparalleled audience response that radio generated. NBC received 1 million letters in 1929, 2 million in 1930. However, such a crude feedback mechanism was not in the league with the circulation statements issued by the Audit Bureau of Circulation for the print media. Consequently, publishers and many in advertising were not convinced that radio should be considered a serious medium. Nevertheless, in 1929, 200 advertisers used NBC, a figure double that in 1928. By 1930 the client count went to 263 while the network's gross sales soared over 50 percent to $22 million.

More and more members of the Association of National Advertisers (ANA) were concerned with the degree to which radio time purchases had to be made on faith, with no way to evaluate either the network's performance or the size of audience to the program developed by their advertising agency. Claims by networks and stations varied widely, and documentation was flimsy or non-existent—but relief was on the way.

## II.   1930—THE CURTAIN RISES:
## THE COOPERATIVE ANALYSIS OF BROADCASTING
## AND TELEPHONE RECALL INTERVIEWS

On February 7, 1930, a fateful meeting was held at the Yale Club in New York. The advertising executives present were prospective participants in a survey of radio program audiences due to go into the field in March of that year. Archibald M. Crossley, head of a market research firm which had developed the survey plan with the assistance of the Association of National Advertisers (ANA), proposed that the survey be supported basically by advertisers. He agreed to undertake financing and responsibility if the ANA would give him its endorsement, which it did. The Cooperative Analysis of Broadcasting (CAB) thus inaugurated its 16-year run. The world of advertising would never be the same again. By creating advertiser confidence in the audience delivery of radio, the CAB ensured rapid growth in future radio investments, heralding the electronic media era.

In March 1930, CAB field interviewing inaugurated a 12-month study in 50 cities with three 4-month comprehensive reports, each covering 17,000 user radio families. Each telephone call was to cover the previous 24 hours, determining when sets were used, who listened, what programs and stations were heard, and what programs were preferred. Advertisers agreed to pay $70 per month ($60 if an ANA member). In the first year 49 advertisers subscribed, producing a revenue of $33,045. The cost was about 37¢ per telephone call.

Archibald Crossley's introduction to the problems of measuring radio audiences came from Sam H. Giellerup, an executive with Frank Seaman Advertising. Giellerup in 1927 asked Crossley to check on which radio stations in the purchased network of one of his clients, Davis Baking Powder Co., actually carried the program. This was done via household telephone interviews. Consequently, when Giellerup approached Crossley early in 1929 for a somewhat similar effort for another client, Eastman Kodak, Crossley persuaded him to go further and try to determine what percentage of the radio families had heard the Kodak program.

Carleton Healy, Eastman Kodak's advertising manager, was enthusiastic about the amount of radio audience information Crossley's survey produced. Healy described it at a meeting of the ANA, where considerable interest was generated, resulting in Crossley's receiving about a dozen radio audience assignments from individual clients. Meanwhile, Giellerup, in a magazine article, had proposed a subscription measurement service supported by advertisers.[4]

In mid 1929, Crossley added a Harvard graduate to his New York staff who had previously served as an occasional Crossley interviewer. John Karol quickly discerned the significance of audience measurement for radio and urged Crossley to move into the field aggressively because of its growth potential and Crossley's strong starting base. Crossley and Karol then met with A. E. Hasse, managing director, and A. L. Lehman of the staff of the Association of National Advertisers to explore the ANA's interest. Lehman suggested that a compilation of Crossley findings from his various individual surveys would be a useful basis for determining the direction of further steps.

Crossley and Karol then prepared a report, "The Advertiser Looks at Radio," which was widely distributed by the ANA in late 1929. The 102-page report, based on 31,000 interviews, contained information on the potential radio audience (60 percent of set owners used a set sometime during an evening), the popularity of individual programs and program types, audience variation by hours and by cities, and so on. It did much to show advertisers what Crossley's telephone technique could do if employed on a continuous basis.

Events moved quickly. In November 1929, Crossley presented a detailed operating proposal for a year's study to be spread over each of the next 12 months to Sam Conybeare, advertising manager of Armstrong Cork and chairman of the ANA Radio Committee. The total cost was to be $1800 per month. Conybeare offered the proposal to the ANA Radio Committee, but it was rejected. However, the ANA promised its endorsement if Crossley would go ahead with the proposal independently, assuming all financial risks. Crossley did and by the end of January 1930 he had secured enough subscriptions to cover his budget. The meeting on February 7, 1930 provided final joint subscriber suggestions and official ANA endorsement. Crossley's suggestion for appointing a liaison committee of subscribers was accepted, and the initial interviewing began one month later.

Although the Association of National Advertisers stopped short of commissioning Crossley to conduct the Cooperative Analysis of Broadcasting, it maintained a deep proprietary interest in the project. When the rating service was later chosen to receive the prestigious Harvard Advertising Award for outstanding research, the formal award was made to the ANA.

The ANA's willingness to participate to this degree in a somewhat speculative media research effort reflected the strong need of its members for audience measurement of a new medium that experience showed had vast potential as an advertising tool. Market research was still in its infancy, public opinion polling was unknown, and sampling techniques were crude and considered untrustworthy by many in advertising. For the ANA to participate in the formation of the Audit Bureau of Circulation in 1914 on a tripartite basis (advertisers, agencies, and publishers) was one thing; to unilaterally take on a continuous media audience measurement system using sample telephone calls was another. It was a bold pioneering move that set standards and precedents for all advertising research.

Initially, only advertisers were accepted as clients. Although a number of agency representatives attended the historic Yale Club meeting of February 7, 1930, they were not solicited as subscribers. However, a year later agency subscriptions were accepted, and by the end of the third year agencies were paying about two-thirds of the total budget, which had remained constant. Crossley's initial concerns about the degree to which advertisers would continue when their agencies became subscribers were valid. Compared with the original 49 advertiser subscribers, the third year showed 21 advertisers and 18 agencies, while in the fourth year advertiser subscribers dropped to 17 and agencies rose to 27. Networks were not accepted as subscribers at that time.

In an effort to find new revenue sources, on October 5, 1932, Crossley submitted to the ANA a report entitled "Detailed Recommendations to the Governing Committee Regarding Network and Station Participation." The report was based on experimental work for several radio stations and a written offer of $10,000 from NBC toward such costs, with the understanding that another $15,000 would be made available.

Crossley's proposal for doing network and station geographical audience studies was not acceptable to the ANA. Instead, in October 1933, a membership corporation was organized to take over all contracts and assets of the Cooperative Analysis of Broadcasting, and A. W. Lehman of the ANA staff was appointed its executive director. Crossley, Inc. was commissioned to perform the survey work.

Although many subscribers were opposed to it and Crossley was reluctant to accept it, this new arrangement had several advantages for both Crossley and the ANA. Crossley, Inc. was relieved of the problem of sales and certain service aspects. Crossley had always been more interested in his market and opinion research activities. This freed him of some responsibility for the administration of the radio rating service, which by now was less challenging to him than it had been intitally when the techniques and procedures were being introduced.

Insofar as the ANA and the CAB Governing Committee were concerned, it assured them of continued control over the service. This meant that it would be safe from the threatened broadcaster influence inherent in Crossley's 1932 expansion proposal. At the same time, the new organization might be able to do something about the popular penchant for referring to the CAB's output as "Crossley ratings," a practice frowned on by the ANA.

It did not take long for "ratingitis" to appear on Madison Avenue, Michigan Avenue, and Sunset Boulevard. First, such trade journals as *Variety* began disclosing and discussing Crossley ratings. Then the gossip columnists (Walter Winchell and Ed Sullivan) picked up the practice, soon to be emulated by newspaper radio editors and columnists. The CAB was a faceless abstraction, but Crossley was the creator of the ratings. Even among advertisers and agencies the audience numbers were "Crossley ratings." Despite the CAB Governing Committee's unhappiness, nothing could halt this trend, the new administrative structure included.

Archibald Crossley played no part in promoting his name in the trade and press. Nevertheless, he is the first to admit that the publicity benefited his market and opinion research business as well as generated custom radio surveys. Inasmuch as the rating service was never very profitable (and often showed losses), he considered the unsought publicity a major recompense for his extensive and continuous effort.

As we see in Section IV, the next entrant in the radio ratings field was a man of a different stripe, a man eager to have his name attached to rating numbers.

## III. COOPERATIVE ANALYSIS OF BROADCASTING DEVELOPMENTS: 1930–1946

A look at the CAB service following its first report shows these highlights:[5]

1931   The second-year survey expanded into many more interview points: 49 station cities and 98 towns and villages remote from stations. Fifty-three percent of the telephone subscribers surveyed owned radios with Arlington, Massachusetts at a high of 77 percent and Natchez, Mississippi at a low of 12 percent. The CAB estimated that out of 66 million total listeners, an advertiser, with a single evening network program, could average 3 million but go as high as 8 million. New programs were reported to start with a rating[6] of about 5 but if successful could rise to 20 or 25 in six months. "Amos 'n' Andy" was tops, with a 38 rating.

1932   The sample design was drastically altered. In contrast to interviewing in small towns and villages, the survey now concentrated in cities each of which was served by the NBC Red, NBC Blue, and CBS networks. Thus, the concept of ratings as a relatively pure program measure, unaffected by station coverage and varying lineups, was initiated. Since no ratings were truly projectable to actual audience size until the late 1940s, a strong case could be made for considering ratings as strictly a gauge of relative program popularity.

1933   Thirty-nine cities of "fairly equal" network competition were used, with a total of 75,030 telephone calls. Audience size by socioeconomic groups (determined by rent and occupation) was instituted.

1934–
1935    Radio ownership among telephone subscribers was up to 96%, but only 31% of the nation's families had telephones.

1935–
1936    Surveying was now reduced to 33 cities served by all networks. The day-part method that Crossley proposed (to reduce memory loss) was introduced. Instead of covering the entire preceding day's listening in one call, separate calls were made at four periods of the day: At 12:15 interviewers covered listening up to noon; at 5:15, listening from noon to 5:00 P.M.; at 8:15, listening from 5:00 to 8:00 P.M. At 9:00 the following morning listening data for the previous evening after 8:00 P.M. was collected. Total day-part samples were close to a quarter million annually.

As we see in the following section, the CAB service was facing its first competitor: the Clark–Hooper service, which in the fall of 1934 introduced the coincidental telephone call technique (reporting listening as of the minute of the phone call). It seems likely that Crossley's day-part refinement in recall interviewing was partly a response to the Clark–Hooper claims of greater accuracy through immediacy; it was CAB's first step toward the ultimate adoption of the coincidental technique a decade later.

1937    NBC and CBS were accepted as subscribers but without representation on the CAB governing board. During this period D. P. Smelser, research director of Procter & Gamble, was chairman of that board and wielded great influence in molding CAB policies and procedures.

1938–
1939    The problem of representation of nontelephone homes became a major concern of the CAB in 1938. In 1929, there had been relatively few radio owners among nontelephone households, but now the penetration of radio ownership went far beyond telephone homes. Crossley's random call data showed Class D homes (the lowest socio-economic group) with only one-fourth the number of telephones needed to properly reflect it in his sample. The solution was to move to a quota sample to get the proper proportion of Class D homes in the total. Crossley indicated that "now over one-half of the calls were made in the lower income groups instead of less than one-quarter."

1940–
1941    In a further step toward immediacy, the listening day was now divided into eight parts (instead of the four inaugurated in 1935). Calls were made five minutes after the hours of 11 A.M. and 1, 3, 5, 7, and 9 P.M. Each interviewer covered listening for the previous two hours. Calls at 9:05 A.M. covered both after-9:00 P.M. activity the previous evening and pre-9:00 A.M. listening the current morning.

1942–
1943    The "overlap method" was introduced, utilizing 32 sets of interviews per day (compared with the original four and later eight day parts). The procedure covered each half hour, by interviews at four different times. For example, 1:00–1:30 P.M. listening would be covered by four calls obtaining two-hour records made at 1:30, 2:00, 2:30, and 3:00 P.M. The purpose of this methodological change was to average the time span between listening activity and interview to 75 minutes on a consistent basis for all time periods. The CAB emphasized that it was measuring "conscious program impressions," in contrast to Hooper's coincidental ratings, which tended to be higher.

1943    Crossley recognized the need for a true national cross-sectional survey that could be validly projected to U.S. totals. He developed a plan that would employ personal interviews and telephone calls and cover small towns and rural areas, calling it the Full Program Coincidental. The estimated annual cost was $384,000, which he considered within reasonable limits, but the CAB Governing Committee did not accept it. Had it succeeded, it might well have changed the outcome of the survival contest with Hooper and later with Nielsen.

1944–
1945    The CAB overlap method apparently failed to give the service a viable competitive tool with which to fend off Hooper's steady gains in acceptance. Despite some members who favored its so-called conscious impression ratings, in 1944 the CAB Governing Committee decided to meet Hooper's competition head on by adopting his coincidental technique. At the same time, apparently to differentiate its product somewhat by implying greater projectability, the CAB abandoned its equal network coverage concept (which Hooper also used) and increased its survey scope to include 81 cities of 50,000 population or over, divided into four city-size groups. A cautionary note stated: "The ratings cannot be projected to total U.S. population since they do not include data for cities under 50,000, rural or farm calls or nontelephone homes." As valid as such warnings were, they were universally ignored. CAB ratings from 81 cities were the most representative available. True projectable ratings were four years in the future, and there was only one way to estimate national radio audiences: use CAB ratings based on 81 cities or Hooper ratings based on 36 cities with equal network service or some "do-it-yourself" formula for merging the two.

1945–
1946    As the CAB completed 15 years of service to the advertising and broadcasting industries, it faced several serious problems. Even though network subscribers were now providing a major portion of its funds, advertisers

and agencies retained control of the Board of Governors. Financial problems had existed for several years, and there was indebtedness to Crossley for past work. The Hooper service was less expensive and was gaining wider acceptance all the time. A. C. Nielsen's meter service, which promised ultimately to produce projectable U.S. ratings on a daily basis, was expanded to an area comprising 63 percent of U.S. households and it was becoming more widely used.

Now that the CAB had adopted Hooper's coincidental telephone technique, it could be assumed that the ratings would be reasonably close, even though the areas covered were not the same. Actually, Hooper showed higher radio usage, and thus higher ratings on the average, of 20 percent.

## The CAB's Final Downfall

Late in 1945 Dr. Hans Zeisel of the McCann-Erickson research department conducted an intensive study to determine the cause of the consistent CAB-Hooper difference. The details of the research appear in Appendix D, but the conclusions were inescapably bad for the CAB. The study found that three factors operated to create the 20 percent higher ratings reported by Hooper:

1. The Hooper interviewer waited for six rings before classifying a home as unoccupied (and not listening); the CAB interviewer stopped after four rings.
2. CAB used an unsatisfactory system of handling listeners who did not or could not identify the program turned on.
3. CAB and Hooper used different statistical treatments of "busy" homes.

The Zeisel findings were presented at a meeting of the Radio Executives Club on February 7, 1946, by Marion Harper, Jr., then vice president for research (later president) of McCann-Erickson. The findings proved to be the thunderbolt that felled the CAB. Nielsen made a competitive speech on March 21, extolling the superiority of his Nielsen Television Index (NTI) meter-based service over the CAB and Hooper ratings. The CAB asked a three-person committee for recommendations. The committee concluded in a report issued in April 1946: "the present CAB rating service should not be continued because it does not meet the specifications of an ideal rating service." The CAB governors met with Hooper and Nielsen and then polled the membership. By mid May the CAB membership voted to continue.

At a May meeting, the Board of Governors, then headed by Bernard (Ben) Duffy, president of Batten, Barton, Durstine & Osborn, with each of the four radio network members represented, voted on whether the CAB should continue. The board favored continuation, but at least three networks said they would withdraw and that proved the fatal financial blow, because by this time networks supplied a major portion of the revenue. A deal was quickly made with Hooper on June 17, 1946, to take over serving CAB subscribers, effective July 31.

After 16 years, the effort to produce a ratings service by a committee of users proved no match for the efforts of private entrepreneurs Hooper and Nielsen. The first round was over; there was one more to go.

## IV. C. E. HOOPER AND THE TELEPHONE COINCIDENTAL

"Were you listening to the radio just now?" This is the way the Clark–Hooper interviewers began their short telephone interview in 1934. The next questions were: "To what program were you listening, please?" "Over what station is that program coming?" The simplicity of the questions, the immediacy represented by data collected at the moment the person was listening, the relative randomness of sampling, and the elimination of all but a limited noncompletion problem (busy signals and refusals) were significant elements favoring the coincidental telephone interview method over the 24-hour recall interview then used by the Cooperative Analysis of Broadcasting.

In the fall of 1934, the new research firm of Clark–Hooper Inc. launched the first syndicated coincidental survey conducted in 16 cities. It was financed by a subscriber group of magazine publishers who were feeling the competitive heat of radio and who became convinced that the ratings provided by the CAB service overstated the audience of network radio programs. Early that year, Montgomery Clark and C. E. Hooper had left the Daniel Starch research organization to set up their own shop to produce what they considered an improved survey of magazine ad readership.

The group of magazine executives who encouraged them to measure radio in competition with the CAB was led by Don Parsons, promotion director of *McCall's* magazine. Parsons urged Hooper to produce a more valid measurement of radio audiences that would "start with total number of sets as 100 percent and then show the number of people not at home and at home but not listening, followed by the percentage of sets tuned in and the division of listeners according to programs—the reporting to show program ratings as percentages of total sets rather than merely of the identified listening audience."[7] The first Clark–Hooper ratings showed a significantly lower level than those presented by the CAB for most programs.

Although Hooper was the foremost exponent and practitioner of the coincidental telephone technique for 20 years, he was not its inventor. Just who was is a matter of some mystery. George Gallup employed personal coincidentals for radio surveys at Drake University from 1929 to 1931. He set up a countrywide system for conducting telephone coincidentals soon after he joined Young &

Rubicam (Y&R) as director of research in July 1932.[8] Hooper often acknowledged the assistance he received from Gallup while making his initial plans. When Hooper's service became established, Gallup abandoned the private Y&R effort.

Some attribute the first coincidental telephone technique to either Percival White or Pauline Arnold, early market researchers. Both were conducting coincidentals in the early 1930s.[9] Pauline Arnold conducted a nationwide coincidental phone survey of daytime listening for NBC in April 1934.

The first published coincidental survey results appear to be the product of a study conducted in the early summer of 1932 in Boston. Sponsored by the Yankee Network, the study involved 12,404 telephone interviews. The survey was planned by John Karol, and the results were tabulated by Walter Mann, a market researcher. A parallel study under similar auspices was conducted later that summer in Providence, Rhode Island. Thus, a number of researchers pioneered the telephone coincidental technique.

Hooper's contributions to the coincidental technique were (1) to establish an "available audience" (which meant the percentage of households with someone at home and awake; in other words, any home that answered his interviewer's call) and (2) to develop a method of prorating "busies" and refusals (which were in the available audience). (The technical details of these contributions are discussed in Chapter 4.)

Once the first Clark–Hooper radio report had emerged, Hooper began to sell it to advertisers, agencies, and networks. He was aware that publisher support was unlikely to continue for long and that he was bucking an entrenched "establishment" operation in the CAB, with its support by the ANA and the American Association of Advertising Agencies, and the track record of four years of Crossley surveying. Progress was slow, but he found early support from the networks. The radio networks had not been accepted as subscribers by the ANA-dominated Cooperative Analysis of Broadcasting, which wanted no part of media influence (at that time). Despite the fact that CAB reports were discreetly circulated and analyzed at network offices, their public use was forbidden. No such restrictions were attached to the Clark–Hooper data. Moreover, network researchers were convinced that despite the smaller rating numbers produced for most programs, the coincidental was a more accurate and valid measurement tool.

After working harmoniously with Clark for four years, Hooper decided to go it alone. He saw a great future for radio measurement, while Clark was more interested in the print field. Despite the fact that radio represented only one-fifth of the company's billings, Hooper was willing to risk the loss of his share of the magazine business to concentrate on radio with his own small staff of nine employees. In 1938 C. E. Hooper, Inc. opened its doors and the Hooper ratings era began.

As noted earlier, the press tended to refer to the "Crossley ratings" and "Crossley points" when reporting CAB information about radio stars and programs. Since the CAB Board of Governors frowned on and discouraged use of

Crossley's name, the charismatic Hooper realized that here was a vacuum to be filled. He had a natural flair for publicity, and whereas the CAB style was secretive, Hooper's style was the opposite. He assured himself of continuous press coverage by releasing every month the First Fifteen highest-rating evening programs (and later the Top Ten Daytime Shows). Not only the trade press but columnists and radio editors were quick to quote the Hooper standings and to trace the trend of top performers. Unlike Crossley, Hooper was not interested in market, opinion, and other forms of commercial research. His niche was radio and he became one of its best-known industry figures. Known far and wide as "Hoop," his ratings became "Hooperatings" and he welcomed becoming the butt of many jokes and cartoons. Hooper claimed to be doing "audience measurement," not research.

By 1938 the Hooperating service covered 32 cities with station affiliates of the three networks. The number of calls in each was roughly representative of the city's size, with a minimum for the smaller cities. Daytime ratings were introduced.

Analysis of the five questions from the interview could yield much data on audience behavior: households with people at home and awake (available audience), sets in use, hours of listening, network program ratings and share of audience, composition of the audience, audience trends by time period, day, month, and year, and sponsor identification.

Up to this point, syndicated rating survey activity had been confined to national network programs. What little had been done at the local level was especially commissioned, as the Yankee Network 1932 studies had been. Hooper saw an opportunity to produce local ratings by combining interviews in a metropolitan area over three or four months. The samples were thin, but he promised improvement if stations would support the service. Attending the 1940 NAB convention in San Francisco, Hooper presented his package to as many station managers as he could. In 1946, when he sold his network rating service to Nielsen, C. E. Hooper, Inc. maintained a flourishing and growing local radio market business.

In 1941 Dr. Matthew N. Chappell, a Columbia University psychology professor, was retained by Hooper as a consultant. Chappell examined the CAB and Hooper's methods and ratings figures and his analysis revealed that a major problem affecting the telephone recall was the "no answers." In the coincidental technique, this became a "not at home" in the sample base, while the Crossley system ignored it. Chappell thoroughly explored the inherent memory variable in a 24-hour recall. (For details, see Appendix D.)

Professor Darrell B. Lucas of New York University further examined Chappell's findings. In 1942 he wrote to the Cooperative Analysis of Broadcasting outlining the weaknesses of the recall technique. To Lucas, the fact that the daypart recall always rated less popular shows below the coincidental level was a fatal flaw. He reasoned that the coincidental "average audience" by definition must be smaller than the recall "total audience" assuming total recall. Unquestionably, the Chappell/Lucas findings were a potent factor in the CAB's decision to go first to the overlap method in 1942 and ultimately to the coincidental technique in 1944.

During World War II, Hooper's position in the ratings field became steadily more secure. He instituted another common-sense innovation: the ratings pocketpiece, which quickly became a fixture in the network rating field. For more than a decade, ratings reports had appeared in a conventional 8½" × 11" booklet (although Hooper's were in a horizontal form rather than the vertical form adopted by the CAB). Hooper realized that these reports, although useful for research analysts at networks and agencies, were too cumbersome and detailed to receive much executive attention. New packaging was needed, and in 1943 he brought out an eight-page 3" × 6" green pocketpiece with a page for each night's network schedule (with sponsor's name) including the latest rating and share and the change from the previous report. It was small and convenient to carry in an inside suit pocket where it could be easily referred to. Hooper subscriber executives quickly adopted the Hooper pocketpiece, which became a Madison Avenue status symbol.

With the publication in 1944 of Chappell and Hooper's "Radio Audience Measurement," ratings service competition intensified. While Hooper gained ground over the CAB, a new competitor—A. C. Nielsen, with his mechanical meter system—was slowly but surely gaining acceptance. Hooper's greatest days of glory were still ahead, however.

The immediate post-World War II period (1946–1950) was the most eventful in the history of radio ratings (as well as in the radio industry). As we stated, the Cooperative Analysis of Broadcasting, after 16 years, folded in July 1946. Hooper acquired and agreed to service all CAB accounts.

C. E. Hooper and his Hooperatings were now preeminent, a supremacy that was confirmed by several milestones of radio programming. In October 1946, Bing Crosby, in a contract with Philco, in order to obtain the right to prerecord his ABC show (all network programs were then live), agreed that his program would have to go live if the Hooperating dropped below 12. After an opening rating of 24, Crosby dropped successively to 18.3, 15.1, and 12.2. A hasty infusion of bigger-name guest stars saved Crosby from going live.[10] A later instance was William S. Paley's deal to move Jack Benny, network radio's No. 1 program, from NBC to CBS in January 1949. Said Robert Metz: "The only way Benny's sponsor, the American Tobacco Company, would go along with the switch was if Paley guaranteed them $3000 for every point that Jack Benny fell below his Hooper rating at NBC—$3000 per point per week. At that time Benny's Hooper rating was a formidable 24 plus, but Paley never had to make any payments."[11] *The Saturday Evening Post,* then a top weekly magazine, carried an article (November 22, 1947) by Collie Small about Hooper entitled "The Biggest Man in Radio," stating: "He makes 10,000,000 telephone calls a year and radio's top councils plot their course by his charts."

Nevertheless, Hooper could not and did not rest on his laurels. His radio measurement was faced with two serious problems:

1. The continued expansion of the Nielsen Audimeter service, which by 1947 sampled 68 percent of U.S. radio homes and was targeting 97 percent coverage by 1948. This would provide the industry with day-long, minute-by-minute meter data on a truly projectable basis for the first time.

2. The rapid growth of television, which was most pronounced in telephone households in major cities where Hooper's measurements were taken. This meant that Hooperatings were now understating national radio audiences, because an abnormally high proportion of his respondents had TV and had therefore drastically reduced their radio usage.

Where it had been an accepted practice to project Hooperatings to produce national audience estimates, this was no longer even remotely justified, because the Hooper universe no longer approximated total U.S. radio. The Federal Communications Commission had put a freeze on television expansion (pending development of today's allocation system), so that between September 1948 and April 1952 TV service was limited to 63 markets. Hooper operated in the local call area of 36 cities, 34 of which had one or more TV stations (only Hartford and Portland, Oregon, were without local TV). Added to the problem of asymmetrical geographic TV growth was the question of what to do about television audience measurement, which Hooper was being pressured to produce.

Hooper recognized his strategic weakness in the coming face-off with archrival Nielsen over U.S. projectable audience figures and set out to find his own answer. His attention focused on listener diaries, of which he had some knowledge from work done by CBS beginning in 1940. As early as 1945, Hooper disclosed work on what later became Projectable U.S. Hooperatings. In early 1946 Hooper hired Gordon Buck to head up the Area Surveys Division of C. E. Hooper, Inc. Buck had about 5 years of diary experience with Industrial Surveys and provided Hooper with the expertise he needed to get started. However, the two disagreed over Hooper's proposed use of diary results, and Buck resigned in October 1946. Hooper then hired David Dole, who had no diary experience but had worked for 10 years in radio at the Henri Hurst and McDonald Advertising agency in Chicago and placed him in charge of the U.S. Hooperatings production.

U.S. Hooperatings were designed to merge the results of two techniques—coincidental telephone interviews and diaries—to produce projectable national ratings and audience figures. Hooper's formula was:

$$\frac{94 \text{ city coincidental ratings}}{94 \text{ city diary ratings}} = \frac{\text{U.S. Hooperatings}}{\text{U.S. diary ratings}}$$

In other words, U.S. diary quarter-hour figures were converted to the coincidental average-minute base by the ratio of coincidental and diary ratings for each program in 94 cities. Hooper was wedded to the coincidental average-minute concept and was adamantly opposed to publishing pure diary figures, which he distrusted because they were self-administered.

The first U.S. Hooperating study was conducted in January–February 1948 with a total of 1,734,000 coincidental telephone calls and 4800 household diaries mailed out (about 2000 returned). A one-time-per-week half-hour program was covered by 12,780 coincidental calls, a 5-day daytime quarter hour by 17,475 calls. Three diaries (one for each radio set) were furnished each home. Projections were made to the latest available (1946) estimate of U.S. radio homes— 33,998,000. This study was released in April 1948 and met with limited acceptance. (Three shows were reported reaching more than eight million homes: "Fibber McGee and Molly," "Charlie McCarthy," and "The Jack Benny Show.") For the first time Hooper was able to provide U.S. audience figures in terms of number of homes.

Hooper was ahead with projectables but could he stay there? He originally planned three studies a year; however, the second was not done until January– February 1948. It used a mailing of 6000 diaries, with names and addresses supplied by the Hooper-Holmes Bureau. Dole reports that the usable diary return was 2436. A third survey was conducted later in 1949, but by that time Hooper's attention was on other matters.

In September 1949, Nielsen announced that he would issue four reports a month, an attempt to speed ratings data to subscribers and overcome one of Hooper's greatest advantages—fast delivery. Nielsen had achieved his 97 percent geographic coverage of U.S. homes and was gaining clients. CBS canceled the Hooperating service to rely on Nielsen. Hooper's profits were tumbling fast, and since the service had never accumulated a financial reserve, drastic action had to be taken.

Arthur C. Nielsen had on several previous occasions suggested a buyout of Hooperatings and had offered $250,000 for it in 1938.[12] Now, in December 1949, there were indications of a Nielsen–Hooper deal in the making. By January 1950, the two parties confirmed discussions, and the official announcement came in early March.

The price paid for U.S. Radio and Television Hooperatings was said to have been between $500,000 and $750,000. Hooper retained his City Hooperatings (radio and TV), his Area Coverage Indexes, and Sales Impact ratings. C. E. Hooper, Inc. could not reenter the national rating field for 5 years, and Hooper personally agreed to a 10-year ban. Both companies reported losing money on ratings at the time (a fact more than likely attributable to their efforts to launch viable television measurements with limited client support).

Hooper denied that he was quitting the field. He insisted that because of the manner of TV growth, only local market ratings were meaningful and that he could continue interviewing in 100 cities. *Time* magazine quoted him as saying: "We rode network radio up, now we're letting someone else ride it down."[13] Hooper hoped to carry on the battle on his own ground, but few of his former clients were interested in that approach. For a time Hooper toyed with an instantaneous Hooperecorder as well as other new products, but none of them readily absorbed his restless nature.

# V.  A. C. NIELSEN AND THE METER

Radio broadcasting had introduced the electronic age on a broad scale, so what could be more fitting than an electronic solution to the problem of measuring radio audience. The idea of metering the tuning of radio sets goes back as far as the telephone recall interview and the coincidental telephone method.

Claude E. Robinson, then a student at Columbia University, applied on November 7, 1929, for a U.S. patent on a meter device he had invented. In the patent application, after a short description of objectives, are these paragraphs:

> It is the object of the present invention to provide a device for producing a record indicating the wavelengths or frequencies to which a receiver has been tuned when it is turned on, the time of day when it is turned on and the length of time it is turned on.

> It is another object of the invention to record the time during which a receiving set is operated and more particularly the wavelengths to which one or more receiving sets are tuned during the time that they are operated.

> It is a further object of the invention to provide for scientifically measuring the broadcast listener response by making a comparative record of the wavelengths of broadcasting stations to which each of a plurality of receiving sets is tuned over a selected period of time. By staking out a geographical or population for a survey, and taking a radio census to determine who the radio listeners are, and then providing radio receiving sets equipped with tuning recorders for a selected sample of these listeners, a comparative record will be made which will be a scientific measurement of listener response. The relative popularity of programs being broadcast from different broadcasting stations will be recorded. The record will show the length of time during which each set is tuned to each wavelength, the hour of the day during which each set is operated and the various programs that the set is tuned to receive.

Certainly this indicates that Robinson had a complete understanding of the use of his meter as an audience measurement instrument. The third paragraph of the foregoing extract could be a brief description of either of today's local meter services (with TV substituted for radio).

However, nothing tangible came of the Robinson patent. According to George Gallup, Robinson, who later was Gallup's partner in opinion research, was so hard up for money to complete college that he sold his patent to RCA for a few hundred dollars. Oddly, RCA seems not to have appreciated the value of the meter as a practical device. There is no evidence that RCA made any attempt to develop Robinson's meter or even to call it to the attention of its broadcasting subsidiary, NBC.[14]

## The Elder–Woodruff Audimeter

The meter that is now known as the Nielsen Audimeter had its beginnings with Robert Elder, marketing instructor at Massachusetts Institute of Technology. In the winter of 1933–1934, Elder had become involved in the problem of measuring radio's effectiveness as an advertising medium because of interest expressed by Grafton Perkins, advertising manager of Lever Brothers, and by CBS vice president Paul Kesten. Elder had conducted two mail surveys, one in 1930 and another in 1931, both published by CBS under the title "Does Radio Sell Goods?" Postcard questionnaires yielding product use data for radio and nonradio households were the base for strong affirmative conclusions regarding the aural medium's sales power.[15]

Elder reports that these studies got him "really hipped on the idea that the effectiveness of advertising could be measured if we could be just smart enough to figure out how to do it."[16] The crude technique he had used would not work because radio ownership was becoming virtually universal. The obvious answer "was to isolate regular listeners to a program, occasional listeners, and nonlisteners and to make running measurements of the brand-buying habits of these groups . . . for comparison with their program-listening habits. And the most accurate method appeared to be electronic measurement of radio listening and diaries or home inventories of product usage." Elder made such a proposal to Paul Kesten of CBS in 1932.

In the winter of 1933–1934, a pair of MIT seniors seeking a senior research project expanded on Elder's concept and started to design an electrical instrument to accomplish their goal. Their engineering background was not adequate, so they sought help from Elder, who was by then assistant professor of engineering and business administration, and Louis F. Woodruff, an associate professor of electrical engineering at MIT. The two professors agreed to supervise the student's project, with Woodruff concentrating on instrument design and Elder on a technique for using it. A single crude instrument (which was on a par with the Wright brothers' first successful flying machine) was built and tried on several sets with the graphs laboriously decoded.

Woodruff became intrigued with the development of a commercially feasible meter based on Elder's encouragement that there was a market need for the meter data. Together the two professors financed construction of half a dozen experimental models, which were attached to friends' radios for testing and gradual modification. Elder describes the instrument that they finally concluded would work dependably:

It worked this way: an eccentric cam was attached to the tuning shaft of the radio set, and connected by a Bowden wire to a stylus mounted above a perforated tape passing over a sprocket actuated by a synchronous electric motor. The stylus moved laterally in either direction as the tuning dial turned to change the wavelength, and the tape moved continuously horizontally with time. The stylus was brought into contact with the tape magnetically when the set was turned on. When installing the device on a set, the set was successively tuned to each clearly received station across the dial and the position of the stylus mark on the tape noted with the call letters of the station. Finally the time of starting the tape was noted exactly. Originally, we tried a paper tape and a pencil-lead stylus, but this did not work dependably. After much searching we found a red paper tape with a thin white wax coating (I think low density polyethylene, but I didn't know much about plastics then). That, with a sharp metal stylus, produced a clear sharp mark that left us differentiate stations that were quite close together. This material was made by the Haloid Company. (It was long before the birth of Xerox.)[17]

The worst problem encountered in operating the model was having the current interrupted so that the time record was destroyed. This happened most frequently when the Audimeter plug was disconnected but also took place with blown fuses or power blackouts. An arrangement to lock plugs into wall outlets solved the problem to some degree.

When Elder instituted a patent search, he discovered that RCA had been issued a patent (June 5, 1934) for the Robinson device that interfered with the Audimeter. After several negotiating sessions, Elder received a letter from RCA patent attorneys "essentially giving us a royalty-free license to make and use a limited number of instruments." Elder coined the name Audimeter, and he and Woodruff trademarked it.

Elder and Woodruff filed for their basic patent on August 17, 1936 and received it on October 10, 1939.

## First Commercial Use of the Audimeter

According to Elder, the first commercial use of the Audimeter was in the fall of 1935 after John Karol, CBS research director, who was acquainted with the Elder–Woodruff invention, "suggested to John Shepard (owner of WNAC, Boston) that a survey with our instrument might be useful." The survey was conducted for and at the expense of Shepard, who also owned other New England stations and operated the regional Yankee Network.[18] A total of 110 Audimeters costing about $100 each were employed.

The Boston survey got quite a bit of publicity and resulted in interest from Paul Stewart, a market researcher who knew Elder. Stewart (formerly with the U.S. Department of Commerce and later a partner in Stewart-Douglas, management consultants) was then employed by the New York engineering/management consulting firm Anderson-Nichols. Anderson quickly agreed to a contract to take over the Audimeters for a New York area study for station WOR. Anderson-Nichols ran into many difficulties, however, and the survey was never completed.

## Nielsen Acquires Audimeter

In the spring of 1936, Elder spoke at a meeting of the Market Research Council held at the Yale Club in New York. Arthur C. Nielsen had been urged by several major advertising clients of his marketing service to attend the luncheon, so he was present with an associate, Beverly Murphy, later chairman of Campbell Soup Company.

Nielsen, who had established a successful market research business with his Drug and Food Indexes, was impressed enough to begin negotiating immediately for the Audimeter. As an electrical engineer, Nielsen quickly recognized both the advantages of meter measurement and the shortcomings of the existing Audimeter. Moreover, as an experienced market researcher he realized the need for a substantial number of meters to produce radio ratings with a commercially acceptable degree of statistical accuracy and the need for careful and accurate analysis of the meter records. A a businessman he was acutely aware of the need for a substantial capital investment. (Little did Nielsen appreciate, at that time, how large that investment would become.) Therefore, he proposed that the Nielsen Company acquire ownership of the Audimeter realizing that much work needed to be done.

A deal was worked out with Elder and Woodruff and signed in the spring of 1936. The two men signed over the existing stock of meters, the patent applications that had been filed, and the trademark rights to the name Audimeter. Nielsen paid the legal and patent costs incurred by the inventors and a modest sum for the work they had done and the cost of the instruments (which was repaid to John Shepard, who had financed the 1935 Boston survey). Nielsen agreed to pay Elder and Woodruff 15 percent of the pretax profits of the business done based on the patents transferred. The two professors agreed to do consulting work on an agreed hourly rate. Most of the consulting was done by Woodruff because Elder joined Lever Brothers as manager of market research in 1937. The Audimeter inventors never actually collected royalties under the contract, because the patents expired while the Nielsen Radio Index still showed red ink. In 1962 Nielsen made them a single payment of $25,000 (Woodruff had died in 1960, so his share went to his executor).

Elder had always considered the Audimeter and its record of viewing as a means to an end—determining advertising effectiveness—rather than as an end in itself. In fact, he commented: "I think that television broadcasting suffers greatly from the misuse of the NTI and for that reason I am not too happy about my part in getting it started."[19] He went on to describe techniques used at Lever Brothers in the years 1938–1945 to determine the varying sales effectiveness of their sponsored programs and others as well. Nielsen shared Elder's enthusiasm for such use of the Radio Index by tying it to consumer usage pantry surveys. However, early efforts in this direction proved that obtaining reliable information on low-consumption items required sample sizes well beyond economic possibilities. Eventually, this concept of the Audimeter gave way to its near universal acceptance as an excellent source of audience data when installed in a continuous panel. The vast variety of data available from such an operation is detailed in Chapter 7.

Once the Audimeter was acquired, Nielsen launched a major research and development effort under Hugh Rusch, a Nielsen vice president. This encompassed the Audimeter itself (especially timing and recording aspects); field techniques for sampling and gaining family acceptance; editing, keypunching, and tabulating of tapes; determining and recording household purchases, and a host of legal problems associated with a continuous panel. In Nielsen's words: "The difficulty which became apparent very quickly was that an average of over 40 percent of the households used experimentally suffered one or more power outages in the four-week interval used for measurements, and the Audimeter had not been designed to take account of such outages which, of course, rendered unacceptable the graphic records produced by the meters. A tremendous amount of executive and technical time and effort—and money—were expended over a long time interval before we succeeded in developing methods which solved the power outage problem."[20]

Fortunately for Nielsen, his Food and Drug Indexes (founded in 1934 and 1933, respectively) were becoming widely accepted and furnished a cash flow that could be tapped for funding the Audimeter project. In 1938, by which time the Audimeter had been substantially redesigned, what was called the Chicago pilot was launched as a full-scale field test involving a 200-home sample. The sample was divided into two areas fanning out from Chicago—one through Wisconsin in the direction of Minneapolis, the other southeast across Indiana toward Cincinnati. This was intended to encompass all kinds of household meter situations—urban, small cities, towns, rural villages, and farms. The pilot was operated for four years, during which time the Audimeter was refined; means were developed for hooking up the many types of receivers in use and by which field and recovery and editing procedures could be tried and evaluated.

In December 1942, despite wartime equipment shortages, Nielsen went commercial with an 800-home sample in the east central portion of the United States—an area accounting for approximately 25 percent of households. Acceptance was limited for a service predicated on such limited geography, but by 1945 the service had acquired 47 subscribers, mostly large advertisers and the networks. The pantry inventory was an attraction for advertisers and, coupled with his reputation and credibility with sponsors, Nielsen developed a strong position in the rating field. His service provided analytic value not possible elsewhere, and all knew he was working toward a national projectable service. At that time, reports were generated monthly (covering 4 weeks), geared to tape collections by field workers. Report delivery was originally 12 weeks after close of the measured month, but this was gradually reduced to 10 and then 8 weeks.

In 1946, when the end of World War II made it possible to obtain additional Audimeters, Nielsen Radio Index (NRI) coverage was expanded to 63 percent of all U.S. homes. The sample covered all areas except the following: New

England and virtually all of the Middle Atlantic, Southeast, Mid-South, Plains, and Rocky Mountain states. A total of 1300 Audimeters were placed in 1100 homes. Nielsen was now ready to compete head on with the Cooperative Analysis of Broadcasting and C. E. Hooper. In a speech, Nielsen explained that his company had spent nearly 10 years and $2 million to refine the original Audimeter "to a point where it produces accurate results under all conditions . . . . and to get the instrument into successful production on a quantity basis and at a reasonable cost."[21] He cited the exhaustive 4-year pilot test, which had eliminated "most of the hazards usually encountered in the inauguration of a highly technical business" before launching the NRI service in 1942. "While coverage of the remaining areas is *definitely planned,*" he said, "the present area is considered sufficiently representative to provide a sound basis for solving" a number of major problems (especially those related to national network programs).

Nielsen then detailed the characteristics of the NRI service and the types of information furnished. He next launched into an item-by-item comparison with the coincidental services (Hooper and the CAB) on accuracy of basic data, sample size, sample quality, diagnostic potential, sales effectiveness measurement, and delivery speed. Nielsen's speech was delivered only 6 weeks after one given by Marion Harper, referred to earlier, comparing CAB unfavorably with Hooper in executing the coincidental technique.

Nielsen, recognizing that the CAB's existence was precarious, on April 12, 1946, addressed to all CAB governors a letter to which was attached a printed copy of his speech "New Facts about Radio Research." Nielsen believed that "discontinuance of CAB ratings service, accompanied by endorsement of Nielsen Radio Index by the CAB governors would give the industry—promptly—the 'ideal' radio research service" recommended by its three-man committee. Nielsen issued both his letter and the printed speech to the industry and the press with the explanation that "at last we feel obliged . . . to speak publicly, and with complete frankness, on the whole subject of radio research." Thus, a month before the demise of the CAB, Nielsen was throwing down the gauntlet to Hooper, who he doubtless suspected would win round one. Round two had already begun, and Nielsen was now going to use the press in much the way Hooper had been doing for years. About this time Nielsen began releasing lists of top-rated shows, another move to elbow Hooper out of center stage.

In April 1949, when the NRI was expanded to cover 97 percent of U.S.homes (only the Mountain time zone was excluded on the basis of extreme field costs), Nielsen had achieved his long-sought objective of national projectable ratings. Hooper had beaten him to this goal by publishing his first U.S. Hooperatings study a year earlier; but Hooper's technique was not widely accepted, and he did not complete a second survey until April 1949. So now Hooper's ratings were in direct competition with Nielsen's. Nielsen won handily because he had a continuous meter service that operated around the clock, 48 weeks a year. Hooper's somewhat jerrybuilt combination of coincidentals and diaries was not truly competitive. Combined with the troubles he had with his regular 36-city monthly service because of the incursion of television in his sample cities, Hooper now knew he was beaten. Nielsen started discussions with Hooper in the fall of 1949 and by March 1950 had closed the deal to acquire Hooper's national radio and television services.

The industry once again (as between 1930 and 1934) had a single national radio rating service, something for which many spokesmen had often pleaded. In eight years Nielsen, the third starter, had outdistanced Crossley and Hooper and stood alone on the national radio ratings field. One outcome was a sharp increase in Nielsen's rates to networks, which nearly doubled in 1951 to cover increase in sample size to 1500 homes and speedier delivery. (CBS' rates went from $56,000 to $100,000.)

The field was now becoming more complex. The emergence of many more local radio stations and the growth of spot radio had increased the market for local ratings, and there Hooper was still supreme. In addition, the Pulse, a new local service developed by its president Dr. Sydney Roslow, was getting under way. Automobile and portable radio sets were steadily increasing the volume of out-of-home listening (unmeasurable by Audimeter). The household was no longer a fully satisfactory unit of radio measurement. Advertisers' attention was turning to demographic analysis. Then there was that new electronic medium— television—whose spiraling growth was captivating agencies and advertisers. Nielsen, as a result of the Hooper deal, had already positioned himself well to be the industry's national service, but because of the FCC freeze on new stations, local ratings were assuming even greater importance in TV than in radio. Perhaps Hooper was right: Could it be that he had sold Nielsen "a dead horse," as he asserted?

## VI.   THE MEN WHO MADE THE RATINGS: CROSSLEY, HOOPER, AND NIELSEN

Probably few fields of commercial activity owe their development to such a small coterie of individuals as does broadcast audience measurement. Archibald M. Crossley, C. E. Hooper, and Arthur C. Nielsen each made major contributions to ratings in their determination to see a particular methodology established and used in a field that after 1934 became highly competitive.

These three pioneers, although close in age, differed widely in personality and temperament. Nevertheless, they shared certain qualities that not only con- tributed to their professional success but also benefited the ratings field. They were men of integrity, intellect, vision, and persistence, who placed a high value on professional ethics and entrepreneurial independence. They were rugged inno- vators who started their own businesses from scratch. Each fought hard, in his own way, to generate audience measurements that they believed were superior to those produced by other techniques. Their high moral standards were perhaps their greatest legacy to the ratings field. Such healthy competition resulted in advances and modifications to the advantage of users. Radio was a new medium introducing new aspects of time and space into communications; market research was in its infancy; public opinion polling was virtually unheard of; and models for syndicated audience measurement services were nonexistent.

Crossley and Hooper in particular maintained a warm personal relationship during the competitive years in which Hooper emerged victorious. Crossley, always more interested in market and public opinion research than in the CAB radio service, delegated much of the radio operation to assistants. Moreover, his relationship with the Cooperative Analysis of Broadcasting deprived him of the freedom to exercise his judgment and to meet competitive thrusts from Hooper. One can only speculate whether the developments of the 1930s and 1940s would have been more favorable to Crossley had he controlled his service completely, rather than having to bow to decisions of the CAB Board of Governors.

In contrast to Crossley, always a low-key, fatherly type figure, Hooper was a truly charismatic individual: handsome, debonair, exuberant, and witty, a man of infectious enthusiasm, a great salesman with a natural flair for public relations and showmanship. He had scores of industry friends from coast to coast with whom he shared his love of outdoor sports. Members of his organization were part of the "Hooper family," and he maintained a parochial interest in their personal lives. Radio research was Hooper's forté, and he worked constantly to put his service on top, even though he was bucking the "establishment"—the tripartite (ANA, 4A's, Network) nonprofit Cooperative Analysis of Broadcasting.

Arthur Nielsen, on the other hand, was a professional electrical engineer whose philosophy about audience surveying was that it should be an observation of specific action by consumers, rather than answers to questions where human elements could influence results. Before tackling radio, he had built a successful market research business measuring the retail movement of drug and grocery brands by regular store audits. In contrast to Hooper's ebullient personality, Nielsen, although equally articulate, was scholarly and reserved in demeanor. He graduated from the University of Wisconsin School of Engineering with a scholastic grade average never equaled. Thoroughness and attention to detail were hallmarks of Nielsen's approach. Whereas an agreement with Hooper could be closed over lunch with a handshake, contract discussions with Nielsen often resembled a labor-management negotiation. Whereas Hooper loved flying and took planes whenever possible, Nielsen, who also traveled thousands of miles a year, never flew because of the higher rate of fatalities in air travel.

Both Hooper and Nielsen were excellent salesmen but used diametrically opposite approaches. Hooper would take one issue, simplify it to his advantage, and play the results hard in the press and in personal solicitation. Nielsen, on the other hand, always presented an exhaustive (and to the recipient sometimes exhausting) array of facts and carefully reasoned (and numbered) arguments.

Nielsen focused his atention on the advertiser as the key client; Hooper's greatest efforts were directed to agencies, where he was widely known and liked. Crossley had no need to sell his ratings; the CAB handled that, and Crossley's contact with users was negligible. He was more concerned with measurement method-ology and became willing to consider the merits of other techniques.

In contrast to the bond between Crossley and Hooper, the relationship between Hooper and Nielsen was one of coolness and increasingly tense rivalry. During much of the time between 1934 and 1946, Hooper was the underdog. Then, just as he was able to enjoy an unchallenged position as "The Biggest Man in Radio,"[22] Nielsen began to threaten with his meter service.

The slow but thorough development of the national projectable meter ratings finally gave Nielsen the edge needed for victory. His methodology, financial position, organization and widespread industry acceptance rendered him nearly invincible. The ratings conflict that had lasted for nearly two decades ended at last in 1950, with Nielsen victorious.

These three men had dominated radio ratings for 20 years: from March 1930 when Crossley conducted the first rating survey, using telephone recall, through the rise and fall of Hooper and his coincidental technique, to the final ascendancy of Nielsen's Audimeter service with the Hooper–Nielsen deal of March 1950. The industry had progressed from surveys that provided only crude "ratings," showing relative popularity of programs in limited areas, to a national sample providing projectable estimates in millions of households.

But radio ratings were not to settle down; several new factors would see to that. Television would rapidly draw advertising dollars and rating attention away from radio to the new medium. The mushrooming growth of car radios and the miniaturization of portable radios created a sizable and growing out-of-home audience not measurable by the Audimeter. The advent of thousands of new AM and FM radio stations provided a greater need and more opportunity for *local* radio rating services. Hooper expected to capitalize on that development.

None of the 1930s trio is still active in the ratings field; only one is living. Crossley, who abandoned the field in 1946 to concentrate in market and opinion research, is retired, but his firm, Crossley Surveys, Inc., continues to operate. Hooper died on December 15, 1954, killed instantly when he slipped and fell into an unguarded airplane propeller while duck hunting. His name still lives in the firm of Starch-INRA-Hooper.

Arthur Nielsen, Sr., the last to remain active, died in June 1980 after a long illness. From the mid 1960s, he left television ratings to others and concentrated on expanding his company's overseas research activities and on diversifying at home. The A. C. Nielsen Co.—by far the nation's leading market research firm, with annual revenues over $600 million—merged with Dun & Bradstreet in 1984.

Nielsen made more contributions to market and media research that are widely recognized but several are not often appreciated. He firmly believed that quality research was expensive (by the cost structure standards of the day) and that clients should be prepared to pay the full price (and yield the supplier a reasonable profit). Nielsen's prices were always higher than those of any competitor, and long-term, ironclad contracts were required. Therefore, subscriber top management was invariably involved in Nielsen negotiations. By this approach Nielsen assured that his company would prosper and that funds for experimentation and new service developments were available to cope with improved technology.

A second (and somewhat corollary) Nielsen principle was that his research results should reach top management. He recognized that relatively low-level research directors were seldom able to get the attention of presidents and operating vice presidents. Therefore, at least once annually, Nielsen would ask clients for an audience with all involved top executives, at which he would present a lengthy presentation on NRI results, including many special Nielsen analyses.

These presentations were his way of ensuring that top management was cognizant of the depth of the valuable data in NRI reports, which justified the high expense for the service. Nielsen's detailed presentations became a hallmark of the Nielsen services throughout the industry.

The broadcasting industry owes much to Crossley, Hooper, and Nielsen: Just how much would take volumes to record. The foregoing brief look into their personalities and methods provides readers some understanding of their immensely important personal roles in pioneering the broadcast ratings field.

## NOTES

1. Eric Barnouw, *The Sponsor* (New York: Oxford University Press, 1978), p. 12.
2. Ibid, p. 26.
3. Daniel Starch, *A Study of Radio Broadcasting Based Exclusively on Personal Interviews with Families in the United States East of the Rocky Mountains,* New York: National Broadcasting Company, April 1928.
4. S. H. Giellerup, "It's Time we Took the 'Blue Sky' Out of the Air," *Advertising and Selling,* Vol. XIII, No. 13, October 16, 1929, p. 19. Giellerup's proposal was for an all-county mail survey to determine station listening rather than program audiences.
5. The primary source for changes in CAB service details between 1930 and 1946 was "The Public Wants," an unpublished manuscript by Archibald M. Crossley dated March 1979.
6. The base (100 percent) for these ratings was the total number of telephone households contacted for interviews. Nonrespondents were eliminated.
7. Frank W. Nye, *"Hoop" of Hooperatings* (Norwalk, Conn.: privately printed, 1957).
8. George Gallup, letter to the author dated December 28, 1977.

9. Nye, *"Hoop" of Hooperatings,* p. 7. "Pauline Arnold used the coincidental telephone method at least three years before Hoop talked it over with Gallup and adopted it. Her husband, Mr. Percival White, devised the name and christened it." (Miss Arnold and Mr. White merged their research business into the Market Research Corp. of America, Inc. in 1934. Also cited in a letter to the author from Matilda White Riley, daughter of Percival White, dated June 11, 1978. F. Hillis Lumley, a pioneer radio researcher, describes a telephone and personal interview conducted in Omaha, Nebraska, in the spring of 1931. "Habits of the Radio Audience," *Journal of Applied Psychology XVII,* 1933, p. 29.

10. Nye, *"Hoop" of Hooperatings,* p. 80.

11. Robert Metz, *Reflections in a Bloodshot Eye* (New York: Playboy Press, 1975).

12. Nye, *"Hoop" of Hooperatings,* p. 56.

13. *Time,* March 13, 1950, p. 64.

14. This is somewhat conjectural. The RCA Patent Department says that all records were destroyed. The writer joined NBC in early 1930 and is certain that it never came to the attention of the NBC research staff.

15. Columbia Broadcasting System, "Does Radio Sell Goods?", promotional pamphlet.

16. Robert Elder, letter to the author dated February 8, 1978.

17. Ibid.

18. Recall that Shepard was the sponsor of the first published commercial coincidental survey, conducted in 1932 (see Section IV).

19. Robert Elder letter of February 8, 1978. This letter plus others from Elder and a meeting with him in Tucson, Arizona, in November 1978 form the basis for much of this section.

20. A. C. Nielsen, letter to the author dated February 1978.

21. A. C. Nielsen, address to the Radio Executives Club of New York, March 21, 1946.

22. *Saturday Evening Post,* title of an article published in the issue of November 22, 1947.

# 2

# Radio Services—Post-TV (1946–1987)

## I. EARLY RADIO DIARIES—PRE-TV (CBS, HOOPER, SEILER)

A written diary of a family's or person's listening experience for a complete week, returned by mail, was long a measurement technique without an advocate. Unlike the telephone recall, the telephone coincidental, the meter, and the roster recall, no syndicated radio diary service emerged to market this technique.

James Seiler, an early pioneer of the diary technique for radio, used that experience in developing the household television diary he employed when he formed the American Research Bureau (ARB) in September 1949. Seiler thereby joined those individuals who championed their individual technique, but it was not until 1967 that ARB began its syndicated radio diary service.

The diary requires the respondent (either individual or household member) to enter his or her listening activity throughout a prescribed time period in a booklet supplied by the rating service. Most diaries are kept for 7 days, but there are variants from 1 to 14 days. Diary keepers can be recruited by mail, telephone, or personal interview or in combinations of these approaches.

The diary, because it is self-administered, has never been accepted as being on a par with the coincidental or the meter in terms of accuracy. People can forget to record all listening or make entries well after the listening event and commit errors in time, program name, channel number, or call letters. Errors of commission are also possible, in which the respondent fills in the diary either ahead of time or after the fact with "usually tuned programs" rather than actual behavior. The possibility that diary keepers want to please or "look good" can influence their entries, a conditioning element that is less prevalent in most other techniques.

Nevertheless, the diary technique had been used in one form or another for individual radio studies over many years. The first on record was a national diary study conducted for NBC by Pauline Arnold (later, partner with her husband, Percival White, in the Market Research Corporation of America) in April 1934 and published in August 1935 under the title "Sales Begin When Programs Begin." This was really an activity diary kept by a sample of 3042 housewives. The diary recorded—by half-hour periods 8:00 A.M. to 5:00 P.M. for an entire week—the listening of household members plus the housewife's other activities (whether accompanied by listening or not) such as preparing meals, doing laundry, housekeeping, shopping). The purpose was to demonstrate a significant level of daytime listening by housewives, and that listening often accompanied or preceded activities in which advertisers' products were used (soaps, cleansers, food, etc.). Audience data by half hours for men, women, and children were published.[1]

## Wayne University Research Project, 1938

Professor Garnet R. Garrison[2] of Wayne University conducted a survey in 1938 using a "listener's table," which comprised three sheets for a day (divided into six-hour time frames), each sheet broken down into quarter hours. The 21 sheets were provided to families to record stations, programs, and listeners as they listened. The study was carried out by students at the elementary, secondary, and college levels of Detroit public schools. This was an early and crude form of the diary.

## CBS—Industrial Surveys 1940–1948

No further use of the diary seems to have been made until an experiment in 1940 done by Industrial Surveys in Oak Park, Illinois, under commission from CBS. Industrial Surveys was a small market research firm that had been established in Chicago in 1937 by Sam Barton.

CBS had been utilizing a mail ballot for annual network coverage surveys, and Frank Stanton, then research director and later president of CBS, engaged Industrial Surveys to handle the mailing and tabulating for the 1939 study. Between 1938 and 1940, Barton and CBS research executives John Churchill, Harper Carraine, and Charles Smith developed an improved procedure called the Controlled Mail Ballot technique introduced by CBS in the fifth series of station listening areas, in 1940.

Eight controls raised response level to 75 percent for U.S. returns representing a cross section of U.S. radio families: (1) ballot personally addressed, first class; (2) all postage prepaid; (3) a small gift with first mailing; (4) adequate instructions for full family cooperation; (5) postcard "Thank You" 48 hours after questionnaire mailing; (6) follow-up on nonresponders after two weeks; (7) further follow-up with premiums; and (8) return of incomplete ballots with additional instructions. It was the combined CBS–Industrial Surveys experience with this mail ballot to determine *station* listening patterns that led to the experimentation with diaries to obtain *program* listening data. Stanton wanted listening audience data for early mornings, late evenings, and weekends, which were not available from coincidental Hooperatings. Samuel Gill, a pioneer radio researcher, conducted pilot roster studies for CBS in 1940.

After Barton's tests proved that the diary procedure worked, the first full use of the diary technique for program audience measurement was carried out for CBS in Washington in the fall of 1942.[3] Then CBS commissioned Industrial Surveys to conduct diary studies in all five of its company-owned radio markets. Each study involved the station's entire coverage area, with nontelephone as well as telephone homes included (thus going well beyond Hooper's measurement universe).[4] CBS, in releasing the results in May 1943, strongly stressed the diagnostic aspects of the results: the ability to chart audience flow from program to program, audience turnover ratios, audience composition, and lead-in/lead-out factors. CBS envisioned the diary studies primarily as internal program tools and urged its affiliates to "apply the technique in their own surveys."[5]

Mail placement was used in all CBS diary studies before the spring of 1947.[6] The network research department explained its 1947 switch to personal interviews saying that the interviews:

1. Obtained a more representative sample—lower socioeconomic families and "nonradio fans" can be more readily recruited.
2. Improved the quality of diary returns—interviewers can show family representative how the sample diary is to be kept.
3. Obtained more information and greater accuracy—interviewer can probe.
4. Field work can begin on shorter notice—3 weeks versus 16.

In 1947 CBS used Benson and Benson, a market research firm of Princeton, New Jersey, for its interviewing work. The original sample for each station area was 1200 families, of which about 1000 returned completed diaries by mail. From these 1000, Benson and Benson selected 750 cases that represented the radio families in the area based on six factors: geography, family size, occupation of family head, home ownership, race, and hours of listening. A ruled, closed-end diary was used, asking for station call letters by quarter hours, with four demographic factors—men, women, and children 12 to 18 and 5 to 11—provided.

## Eugene Katz—Audience Surveys Inc., 1946—1947

An early convert to the listener diary was Eugene Katz, then president of the Katz station representative firm. His experience in the Office of War Information during World War II had interested him in survey research. Katz learned about the CBS pioneer diary experiments from Sam Barton of Industrial Surveys and decided that they offered an enormous asset to help broadcast stations understand program listening phenomena by analysis of audience turnover, inheritance, and so on. He hired Robert Salk, one of the researchers who had worked on the early CBS studies, and organized a subsidiary, Audience Surveys, Inc., to conduct station diary studies on a custom basis. These studies cost $12,000 to $15,000 each, but the operation never broke even, and it was liquidated after several years (although Salk subsequently carried on some studies as an independent consultant). But like the CBS effort, Audience Surveys was not syndicated so as to provide for sharing of costs. Whereas CBS could afford such studies on a custom basis for major market stations, others could not. Syndicated radio ratings based on diaries were still in the future.

In 1945 and 1947 Dr. Charles Sandage, University of Illinois professor, conducted individual listener radio diary studies in three central Illinois counties.

## U.S. Hooperatings, 1948–1949

The experience of C. E. Hooper in use of diaries to produce U.S. Hooperatings was described in Chapter 1. In these 1948 and 1949 surveys, the diary rating value from the U.S. cross-sectional survey served the purpose only of adjusting the coincidental average rating in 94 cities. As Hooper said: "The function of the diary in producing final results is merely to serve as a device in establishing relationships between those areas that can be reached by telephone and the country as a whole which *cannot* be reached practically by telephone."[7]

U.S. Hooperatings were never widely accepted by the trade because Nielsen's national projectable meter ratings on an ongoing regular basis appeared in 1949. Thus the first attempt by a syndicated service to utilize diaries to measure radio listening ended in failure, not necessarily, however, because of rejection of the diary technique itself. In fact, some of Hooper's staff and critics found fault with his decision to adjust coincidental findings rather than use straight diary results.

## Seiler and Radio Diaries

In 1946, Seiler, research director of NBC-owned station WRC in Washington, D.C., became familiar with the CBS and Hooper diary experience but was convinced that the proper role for diaries in radio was to measure individual, not total household, listening. With the aid of the NBC Research Department, a pilot project using a probability sample of total population was developed and conducted in Washington in February–March 1948.

Unfortunately, no great interest was aroused by this pioneering venture in technique and demographic measurement, probably because all eyes were then on the brilliant new star—television. It was only after 20 years of local radio measurement by Hooper and Pulse that the personal open-ended diary was finally launched by the American Research Bureau as a local radio service. Today the open-ended diary dominates the local radio rating field (see Section VII). Moreover, the household diary technique, so long frowned on, is the preeminent local television market measurement tool.

## II.  PULSE AND THE PERSONAL
## INTERVIEW ROSTER RECALL[8]

In the 1930s the conventional "approved" manner of conducting market and media sample surveys was the personal interview. Crossley with his telephone recall procedure and Hooper with the telephone coincidental were bold pioneers who recognized the intrinsic merits of interviewing by using the rapidly expanding telephone system, which was reaching an ever-increasing share of the U.S. population. Nevertheless, the personal interview had many merits (and adherents), and most special studies of radio audience dimensions, aside from syndicated ratings, used some form of personal interview. That included such surveys as the CBS annual Starch studies of total radio listening by individual half hours throughout the day and the NBC Summer vs. Winter listening study of 1935.

In 1940 and 1941, Dr. Sydney Roslow, a psychologist who had worked at the Psychological Corporation (a research company largely composed of academic social scientists), experimented with the roster recall technique. This consisted of using a roster (complete daily schedule) of all programs broadcast on local stations the previous day as an aid to people's recall ability. A "time-line" association between daily pursuits and listening was followed to aid respondents' memory. Several advertising agencies had experimented with the technique, and the Psychological Corporation had used it in a study commissioned by WBEN, Buffalo, New York, in 1939.

Roslow's pilot work and encouragement from a number of people in radio research (e.g., noted sociologist Paul Lazarsfeld) convinced him that he should concentrate on radio rather than market research in developing the small company he had formed in 1940. He was particularly impressed by the likelihood of bias in Hooper's local market telephone coincidental service in New York. Sidney Fishman, then research director of WNEW, a nonnetwork station, was convinced that popular music and ethnic stations (in those days Italian, Yiddish, and Polish) were shortchanged because resident phone subscription was below 50 percent of radio ownership, and ethnic respondents could not or would not cooperate in telephone interviews.

The first official New York Pulse report covered the period October–November, 1941. Its subscribers were WCBS (then WABC), WNBC (then WEAF), WNEW, WOR, and N. W. Ayer (whose research director, Bill Rickets, had been one of the experimenters with aided recall). The sample was 300 completed interviews for each day, 2100 for the week. However, the day was divided into three day parts, with equivalent samples for each. The reaction was mixed;

agency media researchers saw little purpose in challenging the Hooper coincidentals.

World War II interrupted Pulse's progress because, in January 1942, Roslow joined the Program Surveys Division of the Department of Agriculture in Washington; Mrs. Roslow carried on the business as a caretaker in his absence. Two large studies were done for WCAU, Philadelphia, in 1944–1945. Shortly thereafter Roslow added Boston, Chicago, Cincinnati, and Richmond to his roster of regular subscribers. It was generally the nonnetwork pop-music and the network owned and operated stations that took the lead in supporting Pulse in major markets. Advertising agencies and "old-line" network affiliates resisted and stuck with Hooper.

Nevertheless, Pulse expanded gradually until it became the dominant local radio service. Several factors accounted for this growing acceptance. Pulse's personal interview roster recall procedure included *all* radio listening, for all hours, including automobile and other out-of-home listening for *all* homes (including nontelephone). Hooper's coincidentals were limited to in-home listening in telephone households during the hours 8:00 A.M. to 10:30 P.M. Pulse also offered more in demographic detail, whereas the Hooper service was largely limited to household ratings and shares for day parts. Moreover, Pulse was unaffected by the competition that involved the big three—CAB, Hooper, and Nielsen—and by the problems of TV bias in telephone-only samples.

At the time of the Harris Committee[9] hearings in early 1963, Sydney Roslow stated that Pulse was publishing reports on 250 radio markets and had as clients 150 advertising agencies and 650 radio stations. Roslow reported that the Washington, D.C., survey for November–December 1962 was based on 3330 roster interviews, 1495 not-at-home contacts (unoccupied homes), and 1291 house-to-house coincidental interviews, with the sample distributed in 49 separate clusters. At that time, Pulse used the personal interview coincidental and 15-minute recall to secure about 20 percent of its data. As demographic data became more important, as did audience figures for black and Hispanic stations, Pulse was in the best position to provide them. Later Pulse added broad weekly cumulative figures based on unaided recall.

After hitting a peak in the 1960s, Pulse experienced a steady decline in the 1970s. Various explanations have been advanced to account for the supplanting of Pulse by Arbitron as the paramount and eventually sole local radio service. Sydney Roslow attributed it to the following factors: (1) agency acceptance of the diary technique for measuring television audience and their subsequent acceptance of the ARB personal diary method for radio; (2) the fact that radio was not profitable enough for agencies to afford more than one service; and (3) Arbitron, with its Control Data Corporation parent, had greater computer power and expertise to provide speedier service and special tabulations faster and cheaper. Laurence Roslow, former vice president of Pulse, believes that the industry All-Radio Methodology Study (ARMS; see Appendix D), while giving the Pulse technique good marks, legitimized the ARB diary method, introduced in 1967. The latter had a competitive economic advantage, obtaining a week's record with each diary and mailing diaries to measure areas outside of the metropolitan area, the limited universe used by Hooper and Pulse.

In the 1970s, Pulse also had to adjust to changing radio listening patterns brought about by the increased number of radio stations, including FM. The program roster was replaced by a station roster as the interviewing aid, a move Roslow says was in keeping with changed listening habits but that weakened the amount of respondent aid. Delivery speed was an important factor, too: Pulse covered eight weeks and often had difficulty in completing its interviewing quota on schedule. Another aspect was ARB's simultaneous "sweep" of all markets, which agencies had embraced based on TV experience. As cumulative weekly ratings and various demographics became more important selling tools, many stations became convinced that the diary, with whatever deficiencies it might have, was superior to week-long recall in Pulse's personal interviews. Laurence Roslow also believes that stations that were relatively well rated in Arbitron (beautiful music, talk, news) were more aggressive in selling to agencies than stations rated better by Pulse (rock and ethnic formats), so that diaries became the accepted methodology.

The Pulse downtrend had been accelerating during the early 1970s. Various management changes in 1975 and 1976 sealed Pulse's fate. Dr. Sydney Roslow, who owned and controlled the business, retired to Florida in 1975 and named his son, Richard, as president. In 1976, two veteran Pulse officials, Laurence Roslow (nephew of Sydney and its first full-time employee), who had directed all operations, and George Sternberg (Sydney Roslow's brother-in-law), sales manager, left the organization. There was no way that Richard (and his younger brother, Peter) could turn Pulse around. In April 1978, after 37 years, Pulse stopped operations. Arbitron was now supreme and unchallenged in local radio measurement, and despite various potential competitors remained so until the emergence of the Birch service.

## III.  NIELSEN'S RADIO SERVICES, 1946–1964

Prior to 1945 the Nielsen company farmed out technical Audimeter development projects. Early that year Henry Rahmel, a newly hired, MIT-trained electronics engineer with eight years of agency experience, mustered enough courage to recommend that the Nielsen company "either find a better meter or discontinue NRI."[10] Much to his surprise, A. C. Nielsen agreed and assigned Rahmel the task of developing a new meter. Rahmel organized an engineering group that year. This group improved the recording device and electronic means of measuring set tuning so that better than 90 percent usable information was obtained.

A device measuring variable radio-band widths and dial positions and yielding digital (instead of analog) outputs was developed.

A major breakthrough was the development of the Mailable Tape Audimeter, using 35mm film in a small mailable cartridge suitable for changing and mailing by the sample household. Installation of this Audimeter began in 1949 and was completed for the entire sample by 1954. The household was compensated on the spot when two quarters automatically popped out into the cooperator's hand as the new tape cartridge was inserted to replace the completed one, which was mailed to Nielsen in Chicago for processing. This mailable Audimeter model permitted great improvement in speed of reporting (time lag reduced from 12 to 8 weeks) at reduced cost. This meter could record four receivers (radio or television) in the form of binary codes on the single film. The film record was suitable for automatic reading by a flying spot scanner for data entry to a computer.

Another technological advance came from the outside in the form of the computer. Arthur Nielsen first recognized computer potential for ratings production at the close of World War II. In 1949 he contracted with Mauchly and Eckert, the inventors of ENIAC (the first electronic digital computer in the United States, built in 1946 to calculate artillery firing tables), for the first commercial UNIVAC computer they would manufacture. Mauchly and Eckert, however, lacked the financial resources to complete the contract, and eventually Remington Rand took over UNIVAC. General Leslie R. Groves (of Manhattan Project fame), now in charge of the computer project for Remington Rand, said costs had been underestimated by the inventors. Nielsen would either have to pay considerably more or accept a return of the 80 percent already paid down on the contract, which Nielsen reluctantly did.[11] The first computer installed by Nielsen was a 650 IBM in 1954. The Nielsen media group obtained its own computer, a UNIVAC, in 1959.

By 1945, Nielsen also realized that marketing a media measurement service such as NRI required a different strategy than he had used so successfully with his store audit indexes, for which the advertiser was the target. Most advertisers relied on their advertising agencies to make media plans and decisions. Consequently, they expected their agencies to purchase and use the NRI service with minimal financial support out of their own pocket. Nielsen's initial policy had been to sell his radio service only to networks and advertisers, with agencies of clients receiving limited data. Therefore, Nielsen's approach was not working; he needed experienced "outsider" assistance, and he hired two new executives to provide it. Norwood Weaver and Charles Wolcott both had backgrounds in advertising and research. Wolcott especially contributed "many useful suggestions to Nielsen about sales practices and packaging the service. He—more than any single individual—was responsible for changing Nielsen's mind about offering NRI to ad agencies."[12]

Arthur Nielsen, like Hooper, distrusted the accuracy of listener or viewer diary measurements. He believed that respondents failed to fill them out as they listened. On the other hand, rising client demand for "people data" forced him to consider a diary service auxiliary to the NRI meter service to provide data on network program audiences by sex and age. He assigned the engineering group the problem of developing a reminder mechanism to accompany diaries. The result was the Recordimeter, a device placed on top of or adjacent to each household radio receiver and wired to the set. The Recordimeter had two functions: (1) to remind diary keepers to make entries current (by three short light flashes plus three short buzzes each half hour) and (2) to provide a measurement basis for rejecting diaries that materially overstated or understated tuning as measured by the meter. The rejection procedure was based on a Veeder Counter, a device that was much like the odometer on a car speedometer, which aggregated the hours of set usage during each day the diary was kept. Respondents, by entering the daily and weekly beginning and ending figures on the diary, provided a basis for a crude verification of the level of diary-entered usage of that particular set. If Nielsen's standards were not met, the diary in question was discarded.

## NSI Service

Once the Recordimeter was developed in 1954, Nielsen inaugurated the Nielsen Station Index (NSI) to include both radio and TV audience measurement for households recruited by personal calls. Reports averaged eight weeks of field work. The first six markets scheduled were Los Angeles, Philadelphia, San Francisco, Boston, Chicago, and Seattle. Early in 1955 the first two reports (Los Angeles and Philadelphia) were released.

In the fall of 1955 NSI launched its service in the 30 top U.S. markets with these unique features:

1. Measurement of entire coverage area.
2. All-household sample frame.
3. Personally placed diaries; call-backs where needed.
4. Recordimeter-controlled, closed-end diaries.
5. Exclusive NSI area market-by-market (DMA).
6. Eight-week averages.
7. Four-week reach and frequency estimates.
8. Radio and TV measured in same households.

Audience demographics were initially composed of men, women, teens, and children but age groups were gradually introduced and expanded. To accommodate client demographic needs, larger samples were introduced.

In 1957 and 1958 NSI added 24 more markets, but without the Recordimeter. Further extensions occurred in 1959—77 markets; 1960—146 markets; and 1961—219 markets. In 1962 Nielsen discontinued quarter-hour ratings because of declining radio listening levels and the rapidly increasing number of radio stations.

This cost many client cancellations, which sparked the NSI decision to abandon radio. Not only was television seriously diminishing prime-time radio audiences, but the advent of automobile and portable receivers, plus many new independent stations, was rapidly changing basic radio listening patterns.

In 1963 the local radio service was discontinued. The TV aspect had always been the major interest, and Nielsen's radio ratings had never been able to compete with the more widely used Hooper and Pulse data. Sample size, delivery speed, and price were all negative factors.

## The Rise and Fall of the Nielsen Radio Index

With his buyout of Hooper in March 1950, Arthur Nielsen became king of radio ratings. He had long aspired to that position and had worked tirelessly to achieve it. It proved to be a position that lasted fewer years than anyone then imagined it would.

During those years, however, Nielsen made a series of major moves to overcome the two greatest shortcomings of the NRI national service: slow delivery and lack of people data. Delivery was speeded by the technological breakthrough perfected by the Nielsen development laboratory in the mid 1940s: the mailable film cartridge described earlier in this section. The second major innovation—to introduce demographic data as a supplement to household meter figures—was the Recordimeter, which was incorporated in Nielsen's National Audience Composition (NAC) service, which started as a sister service to NRI, in 1954. A parallel sample panel of 2400 households, selected like the NRI sample, furnished the information on a basis of 800 keeping a 1-week diary 13 times a year. The NAC demographic data on a base of 1600 for 2 weeks (the NRI reporting period) were published for 38 weeks a year, not the 50 used in the NRI.

In 1954, along with the development of the home-set Recordimeter, one was developed for car radios. This made it possible for Nielsen to add an automobile listening component to the NRI household ratings. Unfortunately, Nielsen's auto-plus measurement was developed on a small sample, not for individual programs, but for broad day-part averages. Thus it was a crude add-on measurement, but it served its purpose for a time. Although it covered only a portion of the mounting out-of-home audience, it temporarily assuaged restive industry clients.

By the early 1960s the skyrocketing growth of television and Nielsen's heavy stake in the future of that medium, plus the growing problems of measuring radio audiences accurately, caused serious concern about the future of NRI, both at the Nielsen Company and among major clients such as networks. Nielsen, who had entered radio audience measurement in 1936 because of advertiser interest and pressure, was well attuned to the diminishing interest in radio on the part of these same major companies in 1963. That was the year that the local radio service was abandoned, and the handwriting was on the wall. Finally, there was the matter of personal pride and corporate image. The Nielsen Company had not fared too well in the congressional committee hearings of 1963; in fact, the Nielsen Company, as top dog, had been the investigators' prime target. In explaining his decision to drop the NRI, Nielsen wrote:[13]

> As you know, the company which I founded, and which bears my name, has recently been lambasted unmercifully by broadcasters, and others. I feel that a rather substantial portion of the criticism was predicated on the limitations (actual and/or alleged) in the techniques we are using for *radio*, both network and local; since we were losing money on these services and saw no prospect of ever eliminating the losses, I felt that we could not justify to our stockholders a course which would have continued to subject us to criticism which tends to damage our professional reputation. . . . I'm sure you know that the outcome of our long effort in radio has been a great personal disappointment to me. . . .

The Nielsen Company from time to time still reviews the situation regarding possibly reentering radio measurement. A recent examination took place in the fall of 1980, when several national networks attempted to convince Nielsen management that it should again measure radio audiences. The answer, however, was "no," as it has been ever since 1964.

## IV.  THE C. E. HOOPER LOCAL COINCIDENTAL RADIO SERVICE

### Post-TV (1946–1971)

The Hooper local radio service continued after the Nielsen deal and did indeed thrive for a time, as Hooper had predicted. Radio reports for over 100 markets were produced, but they were limited to sets in use and shares on a day-part basis for 7:00 A.M. to 7:00 P.M. (no one was interested in radio during TV's prime time).

Hooper modified the coincidental questions to include television as well as radio usage (with the two media alternated in first position). Thus he could acquire data for both services in a single interview. In 1949 Hooper instituted another basic change with the introduction of a coincidental—immediate (15-minute) recall method using a "duplex-coincidental" interview, which omitted the traditional men, women, or children question as well as "what was advertised."[14] It became clear that telephone interviews would tend to shortchange radio audiences because the telephone sample was heavily skewed toward TV ownership. Radio industry confidence in the service was gradually undermined as Pulse capitalized on its ability to measure a sample including nontelephone households. Nevertheless, Fred Kenkel, who retired as executive vice president of Hooper in 1961, says that at that time "we had a greater income from many more station subscribers than ever before in Hooper history."[15] By the time of the 1963 Harris Committee hearings, however, Hooper's regular syndicated service covered only 60 markets, with others on a custom basis.

Frank Stisser, who became president of C. E. Hooper, Inc. in 1958, sold the company to what then became Starch-INRA-Hooper in 1969. During the late 1960s, Pulse had surged ahead as the primary ratings guide because of Hooper's competitive disadvantages. Stisser recognized the need for a new approach to measurement of the total radio audience and wanted funds to develop a new service (which in effect ARB was then also launching). Stisser left the new organization in March 1971 out of disappointment that his development proposals failed to receive management support. For all practical purposes, the Hooper syndicated radio rating service was no more. Starch-INRA-Hooper still offer coincidental audience measurement services (using the Hooper name), but only a few stations are users on a custom basis.

No syndicated radio rating service employs the telephone coincidental technique today. Cost is undoubtedly a factor, because labor and telephone costs are no longer at the levels they were in the 1930s and 1940s. However, other factors (such as out-of-home radio listening, late-night audiences, and need for cumulative ratings) are at issue; these are discussed in Chapter 4.

The telephone coincidental does, however, play a very important role in the ratings field. The technique is simple, relatively easy to conduct, speedy, and lends itself to use for measuring single programs or quickly assessing the effects of talent or time-period changes on a special-order basis. Its use on a custom basis by stations and research services is widespread in radio and TV as well as in cable measurements (see Chapter 6).

As we discuss in Chapter 4, this method, despite its limitations, often serves as a benchmark in methodological surveys when employing refinements in the form of the so-called Industry Sponsored Research (ISR) Coincidental. With its high response rate and low error factor, this type of coincidental is given high marks for validity and thus is a good reality yardstick against which other techniques can be gauged.


## V.  SINDLINGER TELEPHONE RECALL—1962–1967

After the Cooperative Analysis of Broadcasting abandoned telephone recalls in favor of a clone of Hooper's coincidental method in 1944, this recall technique fell into disuse. Sydney Roslow used personal recall in Pulse, but this was accompanied by a complete roster of local program schedules as a memory aid to respondents.

Unaided telephone recall, therefore, had not been used in radio measurement for 18 years when Robert Pauley, president of the ABC Radio Network, induced Albert Sindlinger to institute a syndicated service for network radio in July 1962. Sindlinger (following his out-of-court settlement with Nielsen over RADOX in

1952; see Chapter 3), had entered the custom market and economic research field based on use of continuous telephone interviewing. Topics reported on included buying intentions for durables, readership of daily and Sunday newspapers in major markets, brand use of over 100 household products. After starting in 1959 with limited TV measurement, Sindlinger had increased it to a daily service in 1961. Some of his clients (such as DuPont and Ford) ordered checks on radio and TV audience trends for internal evaluation (with no privileges of promotional use or public release.) Early in 1961 Sindlinger announced a TV service using telephone recall and large samples (see Chapter 3).

When a confrontation developed between ABC Radio and Nielsen over NRI's inability to measure out-of-home audiences accurately, Pauley abandoned Nielsen and appealed to Sindlinger to enter the radio field. Because he had an ongoing service, Sindlinger agreed. They were both sure that Nielsen would soon quit radio and that the other networks and agencies and advertisers would welcome a national service that (1) measured out-of-home as well as in-home listening, (2) used not households but people (12 years and older) as the unit of measurement, and (3) was based on significantly larger and continuous sampling. For example, the Sidlinger Radio Activity Service (RAS) report for September 1962 was based on a sample of 16,313 (7680 males and 8633 females) out of 21,600 attempts for Monday–Friday average data. The survey plan involved:

- Daily attempts (776), 5400 weekly, covering 287 U.S. sample counties.
- Permanent employees (388) who worked an average of 21 hours per week.
- Centralized, monitored calling, continuous seven days a week, year round.
- Interviewers alternating survey questionnaires (radio and other surveys) 15 minutes per interview.
- Sindlinger's "call-back-feedback" system on no-answers: all numbers dialed six times on scheduled day; if no answer, number is recalled on same day of week two weeks later, with repeat calls until answered.
- Male–female balance maintained.
- Separate Monday–Friday projections.
- No weighting factors used.

Sindlinger was then using an IBM 1620 computer with 40K memory to turn out reports quickly.

For the next five years Sindlinger was the sole radio network rating service. But few users were very happy with the service, and agency acceptance was difficult to achieve. The networks at first believed Sindlinger's figures to be unrealistically high, but when they came down markedly several years later, their confidence was further shaken. Sindlinger, while collecting $750,000 annually from the four radio networks, was losing money, because agency interest in radio networks declined as their audiences diminished in the face of new competition (TV and many new local AM and FM stations).

In July 1963 Sindlinger's RAS was the subject of an evaluation by Dr. Gerald J. Glasser, professor of business statistics at New York University (who had been retained by William Rubens, NBC director of audience measurement). Dr. Glasser's report[16] had several comments of significance. He viewed favorably the people–rating concept as preferable to the household measures for most purposes. Nevertheless, he pointed out that a "rating for individuals will be numerically lower than a rating for households that counts a household in the radio audience if at least one individual member of the household is in the audience." Sindlinger's measurement was a total audience measurement for 15-minute units.

After cautioning about possible biases from use of listed telephone households, Glasser mildly criticized several features of the RAS, on which he strongly urged methodological testing. Interviewers were given more telephone numbers than the number of completions specified, so they had some leeway in selecting numbers to call. The selection of individuals within a household was determined mostly on the basis of availability. If a female answered, the interviewer asked to speak to a male 12 years or older. This Glasser contended was unsatisfactory "from a theoretical standpoint" because "the plan should call for the selection of individuals by a probability-sampling design." On Glasser's advice, NBC's Cumulative Radio Audience Measurement (CRAM) and the subsequent Radio's All Dimension Audience Report (RADAR) surveys introduced this probability feature into telephone recall radio measurement in 1965 and 1966 (see Section VI, following).

A major element in Sindlinger's daily recall technique was his "call-back, feedback" system of dealing with nonresponses (refusals, busies, and language difficulties). Glasser characterized the six-call-back rule as "commendable" but raised questions about the degree to which field interviewers adhered to the schedule. While Sindlinger's reported experience was that 50 percent of original no-answers became completed interviews two weeks later, that does not overcome the nonresponse bias for the original period called. Glasser concluded that: "The use of the feedback plan is likely to provide better results than doing nothing about non-response. In essence, however, the plan is a substitutional technique in the sense that any not-at-home households are being replaced and represented in the sample by households that are available." He advocated an analysis of the plan "from the standpoint of mathematical statistics" to determine under what conditions a feedback system may actually be expected to provide some gain in the accuracy of survey results."[17] (Note, however, that the feedback system would perhaps be more acceptable for most of Sindlinger's market- and business-related interviewing, where the "time-sample" element is not the factor it is for radio measurement.)

The industry's experience with Sindlinger's service was not a blissful one, but he introduced (or reintroduced) several commendable features:

1. Serious efforts to overcome a major weakness—nonresponse—in resuscitating the telephone recall interview (which had disappeared in 1949).
2. The use of persons, rather than households, as the base sampling and reporting unit. This was not a unique idea, but it had never before been used in syndicated audience measurement.
3. Continuous interviewing 365 days a year so that the service results competed with the output of meters in coverage of network schedules.
4. Considerably larger samples than any previous radio measurements.

In the first quarter of 1967 Sindlinger dropped the Radio Network Service in a comprehensive corporate reorganization to get into the black. By that time, however, the radio networks had a new horse in the stable, ready to approach the starting gate: RADAR.

## VI.   RADAR: THE COMMITTEE METHODOLOGY—
## 1962–1984

### Daily Personal Telephone Recall

The gap in network radio ratings left by Nielsen's withdrawal from the field in June 1964 had not been satisfactorily filled by the Sindlinger service, at least not in the opinion of several networks. In the words of one radio researcher, they faced a paradox in "that all the attributes which were assuring radio's survival in a television world—radio's compactness, its mobility, economy, ubiquity, and diversity—these were the very factors that were progressively making the radio medium more and more of a nightmare to measure."[18]

At the NBC research department this problem had been a major concern as early as 1962, before NRI folded. The two existing syndicated services (Nielsen measurements of houehold listening by meter and Sindlinger measurements of personal listening by telephone recall) showed disappointing correlation even when adjustments were made for the known differences in base and method. An intensive search was instituted for a better method of measuring radio: a method designed to measure *all* listening, by *all* persons, *accurately* on a weekly cumulative as well as an average quarter-hour basis.[19] The objective was to develop a method credible to networks, agencies, and advertisers, one that would generate confidence and acceptance of radio audience figures. NBC first launched a telephone coincidental survey that (1) interviewed everyone in the home and (2) arranged for recall interviews to contact all not-at-home persons to secure reports of out-of-home listening at the time of original coincidental. Thus a combination method was employed: For at-home family members the measure was coincidental; for members away at time of original call a recall measure relied on the individual's memory of his or her activity at the moment of the *original* sample call. The findings in the March 1963 national experiment, conducted by Trendex, with usable data from 90 percent of sample homes, showed that whereas Nielsen understated radio audiences, Sindlinger then overstated them. More important to future efforts was learning how to handle some problems involved in radio audience measurement.

The problem of measuring radio's cumulative audience was now addressed by NBC. Alternate ways of obtaining an individual respondent's cooperation over a full seven-day period were tested in a small-scale Cleveland pilot test early in 1964. Daily telephone recall of the selected respondent was tried and resulted in twice the cooperation rate of typical diary procedures.

The NBC Radio Network then decided to make a major commitment of resources to develop a new radio survey method that would produce cumulative audience data for individuals and would evaluate recent Sindlinger radio usage levels, which had dropped drastically since 1963.

The Trendex study that followed in April 1965 was in fact two surveys:

1. An augmented coincidental (like the 1963 study) limited to six one-hour time periods. This provided a criterion or benchmark of maximum accuracy against which to check the results of the recall study (which provided much more extensive listening data than could be obtained by coincidental means).

2. A daily telephone recall survey in which each person selected was interviewed *every* day for seven days to produce round the clock quarter-hour and cumulative numbers. This procedure in effect provided the advantages of a diary while avoiding some of the problems of diaries, in that control of making the entries was in the hands of the interviewer rather than the respondent.

To construct the sample, every tenth number in a Trendex list of 100,000 telephone homes (controlled by geographic region and city size) was selected. Up to six calls were made to obtain family composition data. This listening provided 27,000 names of individuals, which (after stratification for family size and demographic composition) were sampled on an every-eleventh-person basis for participation in the daily telephone recall study. Usable listening information was obtained from 71 percent of the selected sample of 2474 persons as a result of the multiple follow-up efforts.

The results of this study, known as CRAM (Cumulative Radio Audience Measurement), successfully solved the problem of repetitive daily callbacks to a sample of individuals). It was the first radio cumulative survey of individual listeners ever conducted. The contributions of CRAM were: (1) the development of a successful technique for achieving a probability sample of individuals and (2) the successful implementation of a recruitment and daily call-back procedure to obtain seven full days of listening data (in home and out) in order to produce valid weekly cumulative figures. NBC published the 1965 CRAM study in 1966 and presented it widely as a new and more accurate way to measure network radio audiences. Moreover, approaches were inaugurated to generate support by other radio networks for a continuous service of the CRAM type.

RADAR (Radio's All Dimension Audience Report) was born in June 1966 when research representatives of the four radio networks formed a steering committee[20] to design a new joint survey. Dr. Gerald Glasser, professor of business statistics at New York University, was engaged as consultant. Dr. Glasser's guidelines for the study, dated November 3, 1966, proposed a probability sample that could facilitate computation of standard errors. His other recommendations included consideration of random-digit dialing in preference to telephone lists (the first such proposal in broadcast audience measurement).

Brand Rating Research Inc. was selected for the field work, and the initial RADAR study was launched in the spring of 1967, using a design somewhat improved over the pioneer CRAM. The prelisting was carried out by personal interviews in 1200 separate interviewing clusters, one of the most widely dispersed samples every used in commercial research. Prelisting secured 87 percent completion; 78 percent of these supplied full-week data. The recall-coincidental comparisons were more reassuring than had been the case in CRAM, so the validity of the call-back procedure appeared established.

The 1967 RADAR report was followed by two more in 1968 and two in 1969 and on an annual basis in 1970 and 1971 by Brand Rating Research. In each of the latter two years, Statistical Research Inc., a research firm founded early in 1969 by Dr. Glasser and Gale Metzger, former research director for the Nielsen Media Division, took over more of the sample selection work. The network sponsors in 1972 shifted the entire RADAR project to Statistical Research Inc. SRI introduced a variety of improvements in the methodology. The most noteworthy was the employment of random-digit dialing rather than telephone directory listings. Random-digit dialing (RDD) employs computer-generated telephone numbers based on telephone company central office assignments. This procedure not only produces a statistically random sample but also ensures that unlisted and newly connected subscribers are included. It is a major improvement because it removes a serious bias in listed telephone samples: the tendency to underrepresent young, mobile, ethnic families.[21]

Another significant SRI contribution was the use of centrally supervised telephone interviewing using rigid supervisory controls of daily recall interviews. At first 18 locations were used but gradual reductions lead to use of only SRI's own WATS telephone center.

The measurement period progressed over the years from a 2-week interval in 1972 to continuous measurement (48 weeks) in 1983. The sample size increased from 4000 to 6000 respondents over the same period of time. In 1976 RADAR began issuing two reports a year (spring and fall), with each report composed of the two most recent studies' averages.

SRI's approximate 74 percent rate of response for the tabulated RADAR study is the highest among standard ongoing broadcast audience measurements, and the results have been consistent over the years. Since 1973 SRI has collected commercial and program clearance data from subscribing networks and merged that data with respondent quarter-hour listening information to produce each report. A person listening to a station during a quarter hour in which a network commercial is carried is considered to be in that commercial audience. SRI is currently processing more than two million clearance records for each RADAR report. To check on the accuracy of the clearance information, SRI conducts a monitoring study with a sample of stations for each network.

RADAR On-Line offers direct client access to RADAR network audience information, via computer, and provides immediate tabulations to network audience data. Tabulations include analyses of published data, multiweek reach and frequency, network duplication analyses, and optimization plans. Other additions have included expanded demographic breakouts, socioeconomic variables, and special analyses including postanalysis. SRI now processes clearances for an advertiser's specific commercials to provide estimates for a specific network schedule.

## VII.   ARBITRON—LOCAL MARKET RADIO SERVICE

James Seiler, director of research for NBC-owned WRC, Washington, D.C., in 1947, had advocated that: (1) Radio audience measurement should be switched from the sets-in-use concept used by Hooper coincidentals and Nielsen meters to ratings on number of persons; and (2) diary studies be used as the most economical way to provide such measurements.[22] A successful pilot test of Seiler's proposal was financed by the NBC research department in February-March 1948. A response rate of 90.5 percent of all names selected by probability methods showed what could be done with good controls and supervision.[23] This pioneer radio survey was not followed up, because measuring television audiences became a bigger challenge. Seiler became immersed in use of household diaries for TV measurement and formed the American Research Bureau[24] in September 1949 to institute a syndicated TV rating service. Consequently, it was not until 1967 that a syndicated service utilizing individual radio diaries was launched, by ARB. That diary service is now the preeminent measurement of local market radio and represents a major arm of Arbitron's audience survey activities. Probably this 19-year hiatus in the implementation of a personal radio diary service stemmed from two developments: (1) the rapid growth of television, which diverted Seiler's efforts to the TV household diary, to the formation of the ARB, and involvement with meter developments and (2) the entry into the field of Pulse, Sindlinger, and RADAR services, all of which provided radio audience data on a "people" basis.

With Nielsen out of local and network radio measurement, Hooper declining in significance because of inability to cover away-from-home listening data, and Sindlinger abandoning network radio ratings, a substantial void existed in the local radio medium in 1967. Only Pulse was offering available local service. At the ARB, which had begun radio experiments before Seiler departed as president in September 1964, William McClenaghan, assistant research head, saw an opportunity to launch a local market radio service using open-end personal radio diaries. He convinced the new president, George Dick, that he should back the effort (which ultimately proved a heavy drain on ARB profits before success was achieved). These diaries were placed much like television diaries, using preparatory telephone interviews. However, instead of receiving a household diary for each set, *each person* in the household received an individual diary. These were open-ended diaries with a page for each day of the week. (An open-ended diary is one that is not ruled and contains no printed time divisions; the listener-respondent fills it in as he or she listens, whether in or out of home.)

The radio-only diary had been tested by ARB in an extensive pilot survey in Detroit, conducted in February 1964 and designed to compare radio listening estimates obtained by the individual diary (multimedia and radio only) with estimates obtained by more widely accepted techniques (telephone coincidental and telephone recall). (Appendix D gives further details about this study.) Although the study had serious limitations (including very low cooperation and response rates), its conclusion was clearly that "if the radio-only diary were used, it would show inflated levels of household exposure" when average-minute comparisons with telephone coincidentals were developed. Based on these results, ARB pursued a multimedia diary study in 5 markets in April 1964 and added 10 markets in 1965. However, serious radio-industry resistance developed to a multimedia measurement in which newspaper, magazine, and television exposure would be recorded along with radio listening. Much of this revolved around the relatively low levels of out-of-home listening developed by the multimedia diary. When Peter Langhoff replaced George Dick as ARB president in 1966, he quickly arranged a test of degrees of attentiveness, which demonstrated that hearing was "a major factor in total radio audience . . . respondent failure to list incidental listening or hearing might be a major failing of the multimedia method." In addition, the All Radio Methodology Study (ARMS) had given poor marks to multimedia measurement but radio-only diaries scored well. The radio-only ARB diary service was launched in the fall of 1966, with 28 markets surveyed.

The ARB Radio Local Market Service was accredited by the Broadcast Rating Council (BRC) in 1968 and showed slow but steady gains in competition with the Pulse. In the opinion of McClenaghan, who headed ARB's radio service, the major breakthrough came in 1971 and 1972, when ethnic interviewing and weighting systems were introduced. The special interviewing designed for blacks provided that an ARB interviewer call each day and record the previous day's listening in each family member's diary. For Spanish-speaking areas, personal interviews were used to place and explain the use of bilingual diaries. The interviewers returned at week's end, when they could ensure that the diary had been properly completed.

For years, ethnic radio stations, the Broadcast Rating Council, and others had expressed concern over the limitations of diaries in measuring blacks and Hispanics, because problems of literacy, language, and culture led to extremely low response ratios from those groups. Nevertheless, serious attention to its ethnic problems was finally galvanized at ARB in 1971 by a suit filed against the company by station WDAS, Philadelphia, claiming that business losses were due to faulty survey results. The weakness of ARB in this area had been a strong selling point for Pulse, with its personal interview daily recall technique. With ARB's adoption of the new procedures, advertising agencies that had previously supported only Pulse now accepted ARB.

The American Research Bureau continued to improve and expand its radio service. One example is the advent of a form of random-digit dialing to bring nonlisted telephone subscribers into the sample. The nonlisted (voluntary unlisted plus new numbers) account for about 40 percent of all subscribers in some major markets. All test studies show that nonlisted subscribers are younger, more ethnic, and listen more than listed people, so the Arbitron move is a trend toward a better sample. At present the Arbitron technique, called Expanded Sample Frame (ESF), is employed in the metropolitan areas of all markets served. A second major advance came in 1981 with completion of a massive and expensive replication study to determine with greater precision the estimated standard error for Arbitron's radio ratings. Implementation of these results took place in the fall of 1981.

Another improvement was Arbitron's move to replace monthly surveys with quarterly ones in all radio markets in 1982. This followed testing of the procedure over a two-year period in several markets. The prime objective was to spread interviewing over three months and thus produce a more representative report. The opportunity and incentive for special promotions and programming to hype ratings, and the effect of unusual weather and local events on results are severely curtailed.

Beginning in early 1982, Arbitron implemented new procedures for handling black respondents. Replacing the telephone retrieval technique introduced in 1971, Arbitron went back to a diary for blacks, using a Differential Survey Treatment (DST). The DST, which provided added premiums and follow-up reminder telephone calls, raised the black response rate to a level not far from that for whites. The same technique was introduced for Hispanics' listening in place of personally placed diaries, the procedure that had been in use since 1972.

This meant that nontelephone Hispanic households in high-density Spanish areas were no longer included.

In July 1984, Arbitron inaugurated its Arbitrends system in the top 23 markets. Arbitrends utilizes a station's IBM-XT computer to deliver Arbitron report data. "Before the books are even printed Arbitron can do the averaging, trending, and analyses"[25] that stations need. This makes possible not only the quarterly report but a rolling average report that combines the most recent three months. The station subscriber can select the data and form it finds most useful; the proper data will be downloaded from computer to computer.

Beginning in 1986, all nonethnic households not accorded DST were sent a presurvey letter enclosing $1 and a follow-up letter during the survey with a $1 household premium. To households identified as having a male 18–24, a $2 premium was sent to each household member. The average market response rate (percent of potential individuals in-tab) rose to 43 percent in the Fall 1986 survey.

As of mid-1987, Arbitron measured 259 radio markets, 130 twice a year, and 79 four times annually.[26] Arbitrends is available to all subscribers in the latter group.

## VIII.  THE BIRCH REPORT

Arbitron maintained uncontested dominance in syndicated local radio audience measurement after Pulse ceased operations in April 1978. A number of potential challengers appeared at various times, but none achieved much industry support or real staying power until Thomas Birch founded Radio Marketing Research in the early 1980s.

While a college student, Birch began his radio career working as a part-time disc jockey for several Rochester stations. After graduation, Birch moved south and honed his interest in audience call-out research as an aid to music programming at several stations.

In 1975 a system he developed for KMOA, Oklahoma City, for tracking market shares and results from music call-out research was launched with two other participating stations, one providing important computer access. The experiment worked, and when Birch moved to Miami in 1978 he followed the same procedure. Soon, other cities wanted the service, and Birch, who by now had also acquired computer expertise, decided in 1979 to launch a rating service.

At first it was largely a programming tool, but Birch purchased one of the first microcomputers available and reprogrammed the service for sales as well. By the fall of 1980, Birch was serving 18 markets with a monthly service and began adding experienced executives to his staff.

Birch's acquisition of all Mediatrend subscribers from Media Statistics in March 1982 (following James Seiler's death) gave a tremendous boost to the service. Mediatrend used a similar technique and was easily absorbed. Seiler had major market subscribers, which Birch needed badly.

In September 1984 Birch made a significant move toward becoming a viable Arbitron competitor when he hired two former Arbitron executives, Richard Weinstein as President and William Livek as Executive Vice President. They shifted Birch strategy to focus on agency use of the service as primary buying service. Their initial success came with Kenyon and Eckhardt and BBDO, and soon others followed and station subscriptions mushroomed.

In July 1986 Birch acquired added capital when United Dutch Publishing (VNU) acquired a significant minority interest in the firm. Weinstein left at that time, and Livek moved up to President and Chief Operating Officer; Birch, as chairman, is CEO. As of April 1987 the company served 230 markets with its standard reports.

The Birch technique is a telephone interview to obtain by recall the listening activity of one designated person per sample per household for the past 24 hours. The interviewer probes for start and stop times, location, and station heard for each listening period with day parts 6:00 A.M.–10:00 A.M. and 10:00 A.M.–3:00 P.M. today and 7:00 P.M.–midnight the previous night.

Weekly cumulative figures, developed by formula, were added to the quarterly reports in 1984. The formula involves asking "yesterday listeners" what stations they had listened to the day before (done by day part). "Knowing the percentage who listened on both days, says Birch, permits projecting audience estimates to the full week, using an algorithm developed by James Yergin, former Group W research executive, from a diary study."[27] The methodology involved has yet to receive wide technical acceptance. Birch applied for accreditation from the Electronic Media Rating Council.

For its sample, Birch uses the A. C. Nielsen probability Total Telephone Frame listing developed for the Nielsen Station Index (see page 74). Predesignated households selected at random from the TTF listing are called during evening hours. A single respondent in each household is selected, using the "last birthday" technique. No other household member is eligible. Three calls are made to reach households and three to track down designated respondents. These follow-ups mean that completion often occurs on a day other than that for which the original selection was made. Birch claims 61 percent response.

Weighting procedures include design weights to compensate for different size households and for various groupings of days in reports. Sample balancing is also used for ethnic, age-sex, and county location factors. Ratings, shares, and cumes are reported on an average quarter-hour and/or day-part basis.

The basic Birch report is the monthly/quarterly service. The quarterly reports are detailed (100 or more pages), covering average quarter-hour, daily, and weekly cumulatives by day parts and demographic groups in addition to location of listening (home, automobile, other) and limited product usage results. Monthly reports are really a composite of the latest two months of interviewing (March/April, for example). A Birch advantage is speedy delivery—two weeks after the close of the interviewing period.

The Birch report, like Burke and Sindlinger, went back to the original day-after unaided telephone recall interview methodology pioneered by Archibald Crossley in 1929, despite evidence over the years (CAB-Hooper comparisons, 1934–1944; ARMS, 1964–1965) that the technique possessed two serious shortcomings. As an instrument for recording personal radio activity, an unannounced recall interview invariably produces faulty information: Some listening is not recalled while in other cases usual patterns (not actually followed yesterday because of either personal or station program changes) are erroneously reported. This memory bias tends to depress overall listening levels. The second serious biasing factor are the unanswered telephone numbers from the original sample selection. There is no possible way to account satisfactorily for this group; discarding them and substituting answerers tends to raise listening because heavy not-at-homes are omitted from the sample base. Reinterviews that may be completed on days other than that initially predesignated are in effect used as substitutes for sample respondents predesignated for the later day but unreached on that date.

Birch's significant headway toward becoming an established "second service" to Arbitron is based on such features as a single random interviewee in each household, monitored data collection in three Birch interview centers, and claims of higher response rates than Arbitron. Other factors are lower cost, monthly data, two-week delivery, and qualitative data. The product and service data cover 20 categories over three months' interviewing (see Chapter 5 for further details).

## IX. OTHER RADIO SERVICES 1930–1982

The previous sections presented a synopsis of the radio rating services that, at one time or another, were in the mainstream of industry use (i.e., services widely employed in evaluation of audience delivery by networks and stations, advertisers and agencies). There were many other aspirants for such a place in audience measurement. Some were only ideas, never actually tried; others operated on a contract basis in regional areas. A small number got to a pilot stage and floundered; a handful actually became for a time marginally viable as supplements to the major operations. Producing a truly comprehensive list of all such efforts is beyond the scope of this book. Nevertheless, some are noteworthy or interesting because they lend additional texture to the scroll or because of what their failure contributes to our understanding of what has not worked, as well as what has. Moreover, some innovations went into the deep freeze, only to emerge later when the marketplace accepted them.

The two major groups of interest are (1) various efforts to produce a meter measurement service to compete with A. C. Nielsen and (2) a number of entrants in the radio field seeking to offer an option to Arbitron, which enjoyed a near monopoly status after the demise of the Pulse in May 1978.

## IAMS (Instantaneous Audience Measurement Service)

Under the direction of Dr. Peter Goldmark, a CBS development engineer, and with the active input and support of CBS president Dr. Frank Stanton (formerly its research director), the CBS Engineering Research and Development Laboratory developed IAMS in 1947. Stemming from the radar work of World War II, the Instantaneous Audience Measurement Service was designed to report continuously for a sample on a minute-to-minute basis at the very moment of listening. Audience size data was then recorded on tape as fast as it took a radio signal to go from central control point and return from an installed home. It was comprised of:

• A high-frequency audio signal of very brief duration (a few millionths of a second) transmitted in all directions from an existing standard radio station in the area.

• Throughout the area, a cross-sectional sample of households, equipped with a transponder the size of a portable typewriter, automatically signaled by ultra short wave from the control point once each minute, reporting whether the radio is in use and the station to which it is tuned.

• The tape recorder within the central location produces minute-by-minute sets in use, station shares, and ratings, using an electronic binary computer capable of counting 250,000 units per second.

The IAMS device provided for a nine-way breakdown of the sample homes (e.g., three socioeconomic levels and three geographic locations) so that the "who and where" of audience could be ascertained. The costs of recruiting and equipping such a sample would be substantial.

Stanton envisioned IAMS as ancillary to the Nielsen Radio Index. Its primary plus would be speed: instant results versus months-old reports from NRI. Standing alone, IAMS was really not much better than the results of a coincidental telephone survey available within 12 hours of program air time. Its distinctive virtues (aside from the use of radio waves rather than the telephone lines involved in other proposals) would be the ability to cover nontelephone and nonmetropolitan homes not surveyed in coincidentals. CBS never implemented the IAMS system, nor was there any great interest in its introduction. Hooper was still going strong, while Nielsen was moving rapidly to complete national coverage and to decrease delivery lag by use of mailable cartridges.

## Sindlinger's RADOX

The earliest serious challenge to Nielsen's dominant position in meter audience calibration came from RADOX, a system invented by naval Commander Harold R. Reiss and developed by Alfred Sindlinger, a lifelong friend of Reiss. Although

Nielsen had demonstrated an instantaneous rating panel of 24 homes in the New York area using telephone lines connected to a central office, in 1946, this had been in the nature of a provocative look at the future.

Therefore, when Sindlinger inaugurated the RADOX service in Philadelphia in September 1948, after many months of preparatory work, it represented broadcasting's first instantaneous service. Alfred Politz, a prominent market researcher, designed the sample, which was targeted at 500 persons, but it took many months for that total to be reached. The operation covered all radio and TV station activity between 8:00 A.M. and 10:00 P.M. for seven radio and three TV stations. Reports were teletyped to clients daily.

The RADOX system matched the audio signal being received in the home set (transmitted by a transponder attached to the set) with the output of all local stations every two and a half minutes. In the initial installation, this was done manually; employees did the matching with headsets having one earpiece tuned to each signal. Reiss had designed an electronic matching device, but its use awaited an expected influx of new capital. According to Sindlinger, this capital was to come from a group of private investors that included Ralph Bard, former undersecretary of the Navy.

The challenge to Nielsen's meter monopoly was too real to be taken lightly. Charles Wolcott, a top executive of A. C. Nielsen wrote to Mr. Nielsen: "I fail to see how we can turn our backs on the possibility that RADOX could complicate our situation—that is, if RADOX continues to develop, we are no longer exclusively the proud possessors of measurement by electronic means.[28] It did not take Nielsen long to move. RADOX was vulnerable on two fronts—patent and finance—and each front was quickly attacked. Regarding patents, it turned out that both parties had patent applications pending, and the U.S. Patent Office ultimately declared that an "interference" existed. Nielsen's major thrust, Sindlinger maintained, was to use the cloudy patent situation to chill the interest of the investor group in any financing help for RADOX. In April 1950, Sindlinger & Co. sued A. C. Nielsen, Inc. in federal court, alleging that the following factors existed:

1. Illegal use of a confused patent situation.
2. Interference with investors and potential clients.
3. Monopolistic practices and restraint of trade.

Possible damages were limited to $1 million. An out-of-court settlement was reached in January 1952, prior to court trial. Sindlinger & Co. gave up all patent rights to RADOX and cleared the Nielsen patent. In return for this, and for abandoning the damage suit, Nielsen paid Sindlinger & Co. $75,000 plus costs. Sindlinger agreed that if RADOX were continued he would pay 30¢ per month for each wired home in the sample.

Since 1952 the only challenges to Nielsen's meter dominance have come in television from Arbitron (see Chapter 3), first in 1957–1961 and then beginning anew in 1976.

## DAX

An all-electronic system named Data Accurately Cross-Checked (DAX) was proposed for radio by Dr. Sydney Roslow of Pulse in July 1954. DAX was an invention of William Horn, with assistance from Dr. John Ragazzi of Columbia University. The device used ordinary telephone lines to send data to a master control all-electronic calculator that recorded minute-by-minute set usage. Each home unit could accommodate four or more sets and utilized transistors and printed circuits. Only a pilot hookup of six TV sets was reported; Pulse lacked the resources to pursue the development.

## Radio Ratings Initiatives, 1964–1982

The past decade has seen a multitude of attempts to challenge the largely monopolistic position held by the Arbitron Ratings Company diary service in the local market radio field. The list of aspirants include large and small research entities. Nevertheless, as of April 1987, there is only a single survivor, the Birch report. Mediatrend (by Media Statistics), Trendex, TRAC-7 (Audits and Surveys), Burke, and RAM all failed. All of these actually produced reports, some like Media Statistics over a long period, others such as Trendex and TRAC-7 hardly beyond the pilot stage. The interesting aspect of these developments is that, with the exception of RAM, which used a one-day diary, all employed some form of telephone recall—the original Crossley CAB methodology pioneered in 1930 and after 1940 used only by Sindlinger from 1962 to 1967. As we see in Chapter 4, the limitations of this technique, which neither Crossley nor Sindlinger could successfully overcome, are still present. Only RADAR, which is in effect a different technique, found the solution to the two major problems of recall—memory loss and statistical base. Birch is trying hard but still has to pass a true research test.

## Mediatrend—A Service of Media Statistics

When in September 1964 James Seiler was abruptly released as president of American Research Bureau, he made some fast decisions. A group of five loyal ARB executives (all of whom supported Seiler's efforts to buy ARB back from CEIR) joined him to start a new venture in the ratings field. Media Statistics Inc. was organized in November, 1964 and plans were designed to establish a new rating service in 1965.

A large-scale methodology test was conducted in New York in March 1965 to validate a two-media (radio and TV) diary. The test left many questions unanswered, but Media Statistics pushed ahead with the new service. It involved weekly cumulative figures, expanded demographics, and the opportunity to determine cross-media audience patterns. Starting in 15 markets in the fall of 1965, Media Statistics signed up 40 agencies and seemed on the way to a successful future. But ARB (Arbitron), which had tentatively flirted with the multimedia diary concept, switched to use of a separate personal radio diary in 1966. This had broadcast support because of its higher ratings, and Media Statistics in July 1967 forswore its plans to launch a major new rating service and sold its subscriber contracts to ARB.

Seiler then began developing a stable of flexible services that could serve some need for just about any radio station in the country,[29] services that consisted of local surveys using telephone recall. Areas covered could be cities or parts or groups of counties, with sample sizes varying for reports.

Out of this activity, Media Statistics developed its Mediatrend reports. Unlike the customized studies (largely used in medium-sized and small markets), Mediatrend was a regular monthly syndicated service covering a number of major markets. In each metropolitan area, a sample of 500 to 1000 persons aged 12 and over were interviewed each month with a 24-hour recall radio questionnaire. Reports, delivered one week after fieldwork completion, included a 6:00 A.M. to 12 midnight share (Monday to Friday), daily cumulative figures, breakdowns by day parts, and demographics. This service was never designed nor sold as a stand-alone rating service but as a supplement to Arbitron, which issued reports only two to four times yearly for these markets. Mediatrend was used for program tracking and as a predictor for Arbitron's next rating book.

When James Seiler died suddenly in January 1982, the future of Media Statistics was cloudy. Seiler and Thomas Birch had already held preliminary discussions about a possible joining of interests. Now Birch moved in with an offer to take over the firm's radio client contracts, much as Seiler had at one time taken over Hooper's clients. John Landreth, Seiler's successor as head of Media Statistics, was left free to continue custom studies and research in areas such as video cassette recorders (VCR) and cable. Media Statistics would collect a percentage of the revenue produced by the ongoing Mediatrend contracts taken over. Media Statistics went out of business in January 1984.

## TRAC-7

Radio broadcasters, in the love-hate relationship typical of station attitudes toward ratings services, were especially disenchanted with the Arbitron syndicated radio service in the mid 1970s. The demise of Pulse, having bequeathed Arbitron a virtual monopoly, made stations feel "locked in," their entire fate in the hands of an outside service that was replete with shortcomings. Arbitron's surveys were generally conducted only once or twice a year, and poor numbers—due perhaps to a statistical bounce based on small sample—could clobber a station's sales and profits for months to come. Dissatisfaction with Arbitron was also based on the perception of large, unexplained, and often temporary changes in audience position. Disenchantment with the diary procedure sometimes resulted from visits to Arbitron's operational center in Beltsville, Maryland, to review actual diaries used in tabulation. Improperly filled-out diaries, illegible and incon‐ sistent entries, and weak editing procedures were criticized. Some wanted more marketing data to help radio stations compete with newspapers.

In 1977, under the leadership of the Radio Advertising Bureau and with support from the National Association of Broadcasters, a determined effort was launched to develop an acceptable method of measuring local radio station audi‐ ences through telephone interviewing. Equal importance was given to average quarter-hour and weekly cumulative audience estimates. Audits and Surveys, Inc. was engaged to carry out the necessary methodological testing and feasibility study.

Audits and Surveys, Inc. started by reviewing past studies using the one-interview, seven-day recall and focused on cumulative measurements with new questioning techniques. The results of this feasibility study led to the design of a proposed new radio ratings service christened TRAC-7.

The Audits and Surveys feasibility study had clearly indicated that weekly recall (up to 168 hours) produced vast understatements and inaccuracies because of memory loss and people's tendency to report average experience, forgetting actual behavior during the past week. If accurate weekly cumulatives were to be obtained, they had to come from an individual-day buildup such as the diary or the RADAR procedure provided. TRAC-7 followed the latter as a model.

Upon completion of the Audits and Surveys study,[30] the Radio Advertising Bureau (RAB) asked for bids from research companies to implement a ratings service. RAB, however, quickly withdrew from further participation for legal reasons, but it strongly encouraged Audits and Surveys to launch the service it proposed. Broadcast stations and groups associated with the RAB promised subscription support. As a result, Audits and Surveys announced in the spring of 1978 that it would inaugurate the TRAC-7 service in October embodying these features:

• Computer-assisted telephone interviewing (CATI) utilizing computer ter‐ minals in centralized locations. All instructions came to the interviewer from the computers, and all inputs went directly to the computer.
• Sample of one person per household (12 years or older) randomly drawn from all telephone households in metropolitan, DMA, and total station area coverage and projection to those households.
• Sample (division)—65 percent of respondents/25 percent of interviewing

days devoted to single-day, 24-hour listening records for average quarter-hour and daily cumulatives; thirty-five percent of respondents/75 percent of interviewing days provided 24-hour listening records collected on each of seven days to obtain average quarter-hour, daily, and weekly cumulatives.

• An original and six follow-up call-backs were made to reach designated households. Interviewing was conducted continuously 12 weeks per quarter.

• Quarterly reports total sample size of 7225 daily and 3700 weekly.

With the endorsement of the RAB, TRAC-7 quickly signed $700,000 in business and started the service in October 1978, with the 20 top markets scheduled for coverage within a year. There were some glitches in the CATI system and reports were delayed, and that lost Audits and Surveys important momentum in its competitive battle with Burke Broadcast Research, which entered the field almost simultaneously with a cheaper telephone recall methodology. TRAC-7, with its many quality features, was more expensive than both Arbitron and Burke. The latter, with smaller samples, only two call-backs, and cumulatives reported by a single seven-day recall interview, was the least expensive service.

Audits and Surveys management viewed Burke's entry as the "spoiler"— without it they felt confident that TRAC-7 would have succeeded.[31] With Burke active, many prospects withheld decisions in order to compare results before deciding whether to accept a new service or retain Arbitron or both. Some promised station support did not materialize, and, facing continued losses, Audits and Surveys suspended TRAC-7 in June 1979.

## Burke Broadcast Research

Burke International Research Corporation of Cincinnati is among the leading market and media research firms in the United States. Burke scores on recall of TV commercials obtained by telephone interviews are widely used by advertisers and agencies as a form of copy registration. Burke's decision to enter radio ratings research, a new field for them, was probably prompted by several circumstances. The single Arbitron service was surely a major factor but so was the radio industry's determined search for a telephone recall system (a field in which Burke held great experience and expertise). Also timely was the availability of Harry Bolger, formerly director of development for A. C. Nielsen, who had attempted to interest the Nielsen company in reentering the radio audience measurement field. Bolger was hired to head the Burke Broadcast Research (BBR) service in 1977.

The Burke methodology bore many characteristics in common with TRAC-7: 24-hour telephone recall, one respondent per household, inclusion in sample of nonlisted telephone households, continuous interviewing, quarterly reports, top 20 markets scheduled, all interviewing done by employees of the service,

service start about October 1, 1978, computer tape comparable to quarterly report available.

Relative to TRAC-7, Burke suffered from several comparative weaknesses: Weekly cumulative audience estimates were based on a separate set of interviews during which seven-day recall was employed; the Burke "plus 1" technique of bringing nonlisted households into the sample is not true random-digit dialing (RDD) as practiced by Audits and Surveys; sample sizes were lower than those of TRAC-7 with greater sampling errors; and Burke carried limitations in sample balancing and in product usage data provided. Burke's advantages were more markets in the beginning (10 in October 1978, 10 more in January 1979) and availability of individual respondent data via an on-line system. Burke's methodology had been tested on a limited scale in Cincinnati in the spring of 1978.

In the head-to-head competition for subscribers, Burke fared second best, because Audits and Surveys had the longer record of involvement and the TRAC-7 technique had industry endorsement. In reality, it was an impossible situation for both firms in a field where the viability of even one new radio service was questionable. Burke reports showed average quarter-hour and weekly cumulative figures higher than those of Arbitron or TRAC-7, a development that cast some doubt on the methodology employed. Burke suspended operations for seven weeks during the summer of 1979, hoping to obtain more contracts after TRAC-7 withdrew. When this proved unrewarding and the outlook for a profitable operation faded, the service was folded with publication of the October–December 1979 quarterly reports.

### RAM (Radio Audience Measurement)

The RAM ratings service, founded by Jack McCoy, originated with McCoy's interest in research for radio programming purposes, especially record selection and rotation. Arbitron data were not precise nor frequent enough, and McCoy, combining his programming and computer talents, initiated a one-day diary that secured listening data plus music preferences and product information. At first, this was a supplement to his program consulting work, but in 1976 the RAM rating service was organized in San Diego. McCoy was president and John Patton, marketing director (later vice president).

RAM grew rapidly in individual station acceptance in medium-sized markets in the West and South. However, the service obtained no support from important station groups nor much acceptance in the top 20 markets. Here it was not only competing against heavily entrenched Arbitron but several new and vigorous competitors (Burke and TRAC-7), which had set their sights on penetrating major markets first—the reverse of RAM's strategy. Nevertheless, by June 1978 RAM claimed subscribers in 63 markets (including all top 50). In 1979, Donald Cole, a West Coast investor and entrepreneur, acquired RAM from McCoy as an investment for a reputed payment of $1.5 million, and John Patton moved up from marketing vice president to president. Many management changes were needed—better quality control, budget, and financial systems, etc.—but essentially the business was overextended, growth had disappeared, and capital was vanishing quickly. When it became obvious that Burke was going to leave the field, Cole and Patton attempted to fashion some sort of merger or takeover but found no interest on Burke's part. A last desperate and completely unsuccessful effort was made in mid 1980 to interest a number of major station groups in acquiring a stake in RAM as an Arbitron competitor. Following this strikeout, Cole sold what was left of RAM back to McCoy for whatever use he could make of it in the music consulting activity he had continued.[32]

The RAM technique consisted of several major basic elements: (1) a one-day personal pocket-size diary with instructions on the front, qualitative questions on the back, and the double-spread rules with spaces for all radio listening; (2) 50 weeks of data were collected daily, thus permitting weekly and monthly, as well as 13-week, data composited to cover the last three months; and (3) returned diaries were entered on the computer immediately—flash ratings were available within 90 hours. A major plus was control and weighting of sample by zip codes, important in extensive metropolitan areas with heavily populated counties such as New York and Los Angeles.

RAM secured its sample households from Metro Mail tapes, and a preplacement computer-generated datagram was sent to each household. Interviewers made up to five calls to reach each designated household. When reached the callee was asked to supply names of all family members so a diary could be sent for each. A placement call prompting respondents was made the day the diaries should arrive at the household.

RAM, like the other services that emerged in 1978 in an effort to share the radio ratings field with Arbitron, was partially a victim of bad timing. After a period of complete Arbitron dominance, it was too confusing for the radio industry, relatively unsophisticated as it was in research, to deal with three new competitors at once. When the Birch report came into the picture after TRAC-7, Burke, Ram, and Mediatrend left, it fared far better as a viable Arbitron rival.

## TRACE (Traffic Radio Audience Coincidental Enumeration)

The TRACE radio service was inaugurated in Honolulu, Hawaii, in 1952 by Survey and Marketing Services (SMS). M. D. Myers, owner of SMS, originated the plan to measure automobile radio listening by a coincidental technique and combine the car data with home listening data obtained by conventional telephone coincidental interviews. Interviewers were stationed at key intersections on main routes throughout the Honolulu metropolitan area during morning and evening rush hours.

Points selected had either stop signs or traffic lights, providing an opportunity for the interviewer to note (1) if the radio was on, and (2) the number of occupants in the car (men/women/children). By observation or question, the station tuned in was ascertainable. The results were issued in a report that presented in-home and automobile results separately.

Seven Honolulu stations subscribed, and Myers tried to expand the service to California in 1962–1963, but experiments in several cities were not successful in gaining support.[33] TRACE went through several ownership changes and eventually suspended operations in 1973.

The traffic interview procedure worked well in Honolulu's mild climate in the 1950s and 1960s because car windows were generally open; air conditioning was not then in use.

The TRACE service successfully served a special local market need. It was a carefully conducted survey operation and enjoyed accreditation by the Broadcast Rating Council for a number of years.


# NOTES


1. A parallel coincidental telephone survey was conducted in over 94,000 homes to develop listening data. Inasmuch as the results were somewhat inconsistent with the diary sample, they were not released. In 1934, telephone household penetration was only 31 percent nationally, and telephone interviews were limited to local call areas and were thus not comparable to mailed diaries. Moreover, there is an essential difference between the diary's half-hour listening unit and the average-minute measure produced by the coincidental.
2. Garnet R. Garrison, "Research in Educational Broadcasting," Report of a Work-Study Group, Hugh Beville, chairman, *Education on the Air 1940*, p. 333.
3. Lawrence Myers, Jr., "An Examination of Television Audience Measurement Methods and an Application of Sequential Analysis to the Telephone Interview Method," doctoral thesis, Syracuse University, June 1956.
4. Matthew N. Chappell and C. E. Hooper state: "The method is designed for one week in length rather than for continuous operation." (New York: Stephen Daye, 1944, p. 22.)
5. *Variety*, May 12, 1943, p. 33.
6. *The CBS Listener Diary, an Area Measurement of Station and Program Listening* (New York: Columbia Broadcasting System Inc, July 1948).
7. *U.S. Hooperatings, Winter 1948* (New York: C. E. Hooper, Inc. 1950).
8. Although Pulse started a rating service in New York in 1941, the com-

pany's emergence as a commercial factor was not felt until after 1945 because of the wartime hiatus. Therefore, the Pulse account is positioned in this chapter.

9. Special Subcommittee on Investigations of the Committee on Interstate and Foreign Commerce, House of Representatives (both chaired by Representative Oren Harris of Arkansas).

10. Henry Rahmel, letter to the author, December 18, 1980.

11. Ibid.

12. Henry Rahmel, letter to the author, June 14, 1984.

13. Arthur C. Nielsen, Sr., letter to the author, April 5, 1964.

14. Lawrence Myers, Jr., "An Examination of Television Audience Measurement Methods and an Application of Sequential Analysis to the Telephone Interview Method." PhD dissertation, Syracuse University, 1956.

15. Fred H. Kenkel, letter to the author, February 20, 1978.

16. Gerald J. Glasser, Evaluation of the Sindlinger Radio Activity Service, 1963 Report.

17. Ibid.

18. Harper L. Carraine, director, CBS Radio Division Research, in an undated document attached to a letter to the author dated April 18, 1973.

19. The NBC research department effort was headed by Dr. Thomas Coffin, director of research, with William Rubens, director of audience measurement, spearheading the early studies. Paul Klein succeeded Rubens in the work performed by Trendex for the CRAM study. Cathy Coholan Mansfield and later Marshall Dickman were involved in pilot testing.

20. The committee consisted of Josh Mayberry, director of research, ABC Radio Network; Harper Carraine, director of radio research, CBS Broadcast Group; Lucille A. Stern, director of research, Mutual Broadcasting; and two NBC participants, Dr. Thomas Coffin, vice president—research, and Marshall Dickman, manager, radio audience measurement.

21. The RDD technique is described by Sanford Cooper in "Random Sampling by Telephone—An Improved Subject," *Journal of Marketing Research,* 1964. A complete treatment is provided in Glasser and Metzger, "Random Digit Dialing as a Method of Telephone Sampling" *Journal of Marketing Research,* February 1972, pp. 59–64.

22. James W. Seiler, "Ratings on Individual Basis Are Urged," *Broadcasting,* May 12, 1947. Undoubtedly the first to use the individual rather than family diary was Professor C. H. Sandage, University of Illinois, who conducted three single-county studies in central Illinois in 1945 and 1946 using a weekly personal closed-end diary.

23. H. M. Beville, Jr., "Surveying Radio Listeners by Use of a Probability Sample," *Journal of Marketing,* October 1949, p. 39.

24. The American Research Bureau became Arbitron in 1973.

25. *Arbitrends, Computer Delivered Radio Market Information*, Arbitron ratings booklet (undated).
26. Ridgeway letter of July 3, 1984.
27. "Spot Report," *Radio/Television Age*, April 30, 1984, p. 101.
28. Charles Wolcott, letter to A. C. Nielsen, Sr. of October 7, 1949.
29. A major nonrating activity of Media Statistics during the 1970s was the conduct of "ascertainment" surveys to determine the needs and interests of communities, as then required of new station applicants by the Federal Communications Commission.
30. Feasibility Study of Telephone Measurement of Radio Using Varying Numbers of Interviews per Person, conducted under sponsorship of the Radio Advertising Bureau and the National Association of Broadcasters, June–September 1977—Survey Division Audits and Surveys, Inc.
31. Richard Lysaker, president, Audits and Surveys, interview with the author of December 28, 1982.
32. Account based on telephone interviews with John Patton in April–May 1983.
33. *Broadcasting*, August 27, 1962.

# 3

# Television Services
# (1946–1987)

## I. INTRODUCTION

RCA/NBC introduced commercial television in the United States at the New York World's Fair in 1939, but its budding growth was halted by World War II. NBC managed to keep its New York station, WNBT, running on an abbreviated schedule of evening programs during the war to serve the few thousands of sets in use in the area. Several other stations also supplied limited service. No newspapers furnished TV listings, so NBC offered to mail its weekly schedule regularly to anyone requesting it. The postcard program listing was arranged for mail-back, with boxes for people to check which programs they had viewed and a few lines for comments or suggestions.

This, then, became the basis for the first crude TV ratings. The simple feedback worked fine under the circumstances and was a useful tool to programmers. Nevertheless, if telelvision was to become an accepted advertising vehicle, better audience measurement would be necessary and it was logical to build such measurements on the established principles and technologies tested in radio.[1]

## II. TELEVISION COINCIDENTALS:
## HOOPER AND TRENDEX

C. E. Hooper, who had emerged at the head of the radio ratings field in the mid 1940s was the logical service to handle television audience measurement. Unlike Nielsen's meter, Hooper's telephone instrument was usable for a few hours an evening on a periodic basis in a few markets, an ideal arrangement because the rating service could be expanded in hours, frequency, and geography to match the growth of the medium as well as industry need and support. Moreover, because he was making thousands of coincidental calls every day, Hooper was in good position to develop a list of television set owners.

Nevertheless, early in 1947 Hooper showed no interest in TV ratings; at the time he was thoroughly immersed in trying to get his U.S. radio ratings launched to beat Nielsen in the race for nationwide projectable ratings. Moreover, Hooper, still a deep-dyed radio fan, was skeptical that television would go over with the public—a view shared by many in advertising at the time. NBC had what it considered a trump card to play to induce Hooper to start a New York TV service—its list of set owners, which was now growing each week by new requests as well as by names of new set purchasers received from the New York RCA distributor. A list of 20,000 set owners was enough to give any researcher a start on a New York ratings service.

The author invited Dr. Peter Langhoff, newly appointed research vice president of Young and Rubicam, to join him in an appeal to Hooper to initiate television Hooperatings. Hooper could have the NBC list and their immediate subscriber support; or NBC and Y&R would jointly undertake to interest another firm in entering the TV rating field. Even this threat failed to produce a commitment from Hooper. It was obvious that his reluctance was partly due to a lack of enthusiasm for television. The situation changed dramatically when Hooper saw his first Yankee baseball game telecast on a brand-new model 10-inch RCA set. Being the sports buff he was, Hooper now enthusiastically accepted the offer, and by the end of the year was ready to start a New York rating service for television. Coincidental calls would be confined to evening hours, but diaries would also be used to develop overall viewing, reception quality, and the like.

Hooper's TV service was expanded during 1948 and 1949 as set sales soared and new stations emerged in all major cities. Unfortunately, Hooper never saw that television was the big future of broadcasting. Had he retained network TV when he sold the radio service to Nielsen in early 1950, he could have prospered. Instead, the day after the deal was announced Hooper held a press conference in which he said that "to make the deal attractive [we] threw in the national television ratings."[2] Hooper had almost scornfully thrown away the ticket to the future of his company.

C. E. Hooper, Inc. continued in the local TV field after the Nielsen deal and until Hooper's death in December 1954. In 1955 the firm, then headed by James Knipe, sold the local TV service to the American Research Bureau. Fred Kenkel, then executive vice president, wrote, "I believe if we had held out a little longer, TV Hooperatings would have gained greater acceptance. The very day before the deal was signed, we received subscriptions from leading stations in three cities. . . ."[3] C. E. Hooper, Inc. was now limited to local radio, but for years it collected income paid off by the ARB deal. Daniel Starch and staff acquired the company in 1969.[4] Now known as Starch-INRA-Hooper, the firm offers audience measurement services on a custom basis to stations but does not supply a regular syndicated service.

## Trendex

If Hooper didn't see the potential for television in 1950, there were some in his company who did. At a champagne party that Hooper gave his staff to celebrate his "victory" over Nielsen, two of his key employees immediately began developing their own new TV service to do telephone coincidentals: Trendex. Edward G. Hynes, Jr. and Robert B. Rogers had joined Hooper in late 1945 after World War II. Their experience there complemented each other ideally: Hynes worked in sales out of New York; Rogers headed production in Norwalk, Connecticut.

Soon after starting Trendex as a replacement for Hooper's TV service, in June 1950, Hynes and Rogers were encouraged by NBC and CBS to inaugurate a regular syndicated coincidental service. This was started as a 10-city operation in 1950 but quickly expanded to 27 markets for a program popularity report measuring network audiences under equal opportunities of viewing (where all three national networks had local outlets). In June 1961, because Nielsen's speeded-up Audimeter service precluded the networks' need for regular overnight coincidentals, Trendex discontinued its syndicated service. For many years thereafter, however, networks purchased overnight Trendex coincidental ratings to get readings on each fall's revised program schedule and at times when new series schedule changes or specials were launched.

Trendex throve because it was fast, flexible, and relatively inexpensive. The three networks were especially addicted to Trendex numbers because overnight reports on new shows were imperative. This provided a number of weeks of competitive ratings for program evaluation before the first NTI report was received. (Nielsen reports covered two weeks and had a six-week delivery schedule; a rating for a September 15 broadcast was not received until November 1.) Trendex reports were generally based on 1000 coincidental dialings per half-hour time period.

As the heir to the Hooper tradition, Trendex carried on its syndicated coincidental service until the basic limitations of the technique could no longer compete with projectable meter data covering all time periods and delivered with reasonable speed. Henceforth the telephone coincidental technique would be confined to custom surveys and validation measurements. Trendex continued in business, doing a variety of regular and custom surveys using telephone interviews.

## III.  ARBITRON AND THE VIEWER DIARY

No technique for measuring audiences has had a checkered career to match that of the listener diary. Ironically, it was the advent of television that sparked widespread acceptance of the household diary as a valid measurement tool and led to the success of the American Research Bureau (now Arbitron Ratings Co.), first and foremost syndicator to employ diaries. As we saw in Chapter 2, the radio household diary had been well developed by CBS in the 1940s and had been utilized by Hooper in U.S. Hooperatings in 1948 and 1949. Although James Seiler, when he was director of research at station WRC, Washington, D.C., in 1947 and 1948, had conducted several surveys using personal radio diaries, these efforts took a back seat with the rapid emergence of television and its need for household audience numbers.

Seiler produced his first household diary study for WNBW (the Washington NBC-owned station, now WRC-TV) in 1947 and continued these surveys on a quarterly basis. Other local TV stations became interested and began participating by sharing NBC's costs. Seiler, still an employee of NBC, managed the studies during 1948 and early 1949. At that time, he decided to set up his own survey business and obtained NBC's permission to use the name American Research Bureau, the identification used by interviewers with respondents in the original diary work.

Seiler formed the American Research Bureau as an independent proprietorship in September 1949. Based on previously obtained commitments, surveys were conducted that month in Washington, Baltimore, and Philadelphia. In October, New York was added, followed by Cleveland and Chicago in 1950. Support for ARB developed slowly, but overhead was low (half an office in the National Press Building and three employees), and the company remained afloat. Seiler attributed his survival to the low TV penetration at the time (about 15 percent in the above markets). Hooper and Pulse were the big local market radio ratings services, but their regular sampling activity did not yield enough TV households to provide much measurement potential. The ARB, on the other hand, used a random telephone sample to obtain several hundred TV homes needed for its diary survey of a week's viewing.

The Nielsen–Hooper deal of March 1950 left Hooper in the local market for both radio and television. However, despite his pioneering start in TV, Hooper never was able to achieve a strong position in the medium. Perhaps it was partly due to his long love affair with radio and lack of trust in television's future. On the other hand, Seiler's view is probably correct: More substantive factors were at work. The diary was a more economical tool per unit of information collected, because one diary measured every quarter hour of the week. Its sample distribution could readily be expanded to cover the entire station areas at the small added cost of one or two toll calls per diary. Moreover, it provided many of the analytic possibilities of household meter records: the opportunity for audience flow analysis on a common sample and for cumulative audience computations of program and commercial combinations. Later, audience composition data gave diaries a strong unique dimension of their own.

One of Seiler's first moves proved crucial to achieving his ambition to provide a uniform service in all TV markets. In the early 1950s there were no truly national networks because the American Telephone & Telegraph coaxial cable did not extend to the West Coast. As a result, television on the West Coast grew up largely as separate local operations. In Los Angeles, where there were seven very high frequency (VHF) stations competing, a diary service called Tele-Que had been inaugurated in 1947 by a young research company named for its principal officers: Joseph Coffin, Henry Clay, and Roger Cooper. After numerous discussions, Seiler arranged a merger and the reports were combined in 1951. This gave ARB local reports for Los Angeles, San Francisco, and San Diego; an office on the West Coast to complement the newly established New York office; and a coterie of talented Tele-Que research executives, who played important roles in the growth of the ARB for several decades: John Landreth, Roger Cooper, Henry Clay, and R. R. Ridgeway.

What exactly did ARB offer? An early report, one for Washington covering the week of May 11–17, 1949, is typical. A sample of 455 diaries was placed, and 364 or 80 percent were recovered and usable. Random calls to local telephone subscribers were placed to secure the TV-owning sample. TV homes were selected at random from manufacturer warranty lists outside of the local telephone zone, but within the metropolitan area. Ratings were reported on a quarter-hour basis beginning whenever the first program appeared on any of the four local stations. On weekdays, this was at 5:00 P.M. with "Howdy Doody," an early children's show with ratings around 30 at 5:30. Ratings of 65 were credited to Milton Berle and Ed Sullivan, while Arthur Godfrey (a former top local radio personality) came in with 55 to 60 for his two CBS shows. Shares for these shows, not shown in the report, were 80 to 90. Baseball drew a 40 rating on Tuesday evening and on Saturday afternoon, while "Crusade in Europe" hit 50 at 9:00 P.M. Thursday.

ARB added to its list of markets through the early 1950s. Then in 1955 the Hooper local TV service was taken over in a deal by which ARB supplied its diary reports to Hooper subscribers and paid C. E. Hooper, Inc. 50 percent of the revenue received from those subscribers for 10 years.

In 1957, cramped for space to accommodate a rapidly growing staff, Seiler moved to larger quarters in Beltsville, Maryland. (After several building expansions there, Arbitron in 1979 found it necessary to acquire additional executive office space in nearby Laurel, Maryland.)

By 1961, ARB was measuring every U.S. TV market and twice annually producing national sweeps (measurement in all markets simultaneously). Clients, numbering in the hundreds, included stations, representatives, networks, advertisers, and agencies. The basic techniques remained the same except for greatly increased demographics (there were none in 1950) and computerization.

On June 30, 1961, ARB merged with CEIR, a highly successful Washington computer usage firm headed by Dr. Herbert Robinson. A British economist, Robinson held government liaison posts in Washington during World War II. As the war ended, he saw the potential of the emerging computer for handling the vast array of jobs generated by the Washington bureaucracy. Having spotted this need, Robinson became, in effect, a service bureau to handle the computational needs of the U.S. government on a highly profitable contract basis. CEIR (Committee for Economic and Industrial Research) was formed in 1950 and was incredibly successful for a decade. Then, gradually, as computers became more competitive and computer service spread, federal agencies began acquiring their own hardware and software. The future of CEIR was threatened.

In 1961 Robinson proposed a takeover of ARB to offset this loss, with payment to be made in CEIR stock, then selling (over the counter) at 65. Seiler, who controlled virtually all ARB shares, accepted the offer along with a three-year contract as president. This, for one who had built a successful and profitable firm from scratch, proved to be a disastrous business decision. Seiler reported that "CEIR had financial and other problems and was of limited help to ARB." By the time the three-year employment contract expired, the stock price had fallen to single-digit levels, and relations with Robinson were strained. Seiler and associates proposed buying ARB back, but on September 1, 1964, Robinson peremptorily replaced Seiler with George Dick as ARB president.

This move proved as disastrous for CEIR as the sale of ARB had been for Seiler. The first result was that the entire top echelon of ARB executives left to join Seiler in a new firm, Media Statistics. The group included virtually all the executives who had contributed to the success of ARB as a rating service and as a useful tool to the industry.[5]

It developed that Dick, whose experience had been primarily with computers, was totally inexperienced in his new position. His contacts with ARB staff and with clients and prospects quickly disclosed his ignorance of the television business and of ratings research. Within two years ARB went from an $800,000 profit to a $600,000 loss. In May 1966, Robinson replaced Dick as president with Dr. Peter Langhoff, who for 18 years had been vice president for research at Young & Rubicam. In 1967 CEIR and American Research Bureau were acquired by Control Data Corporation, a major computer manufacturer.

Langhoff moved to strengthen the ARB staff, which had not yet recovered from the loss of key executives to Media Statistics. In July 1967, a large delegation of agency and other research people met at a conclave at which several new ARB features were announced, the most significant being the addition of product use data. As a result, ARB, which had slipped seriously behind Nielsen's NSI in sales, recovered the lead it had held when Seiler was in charge. Unfortunately, however, Langhoff was not as successful in wooing broadcast stations as he had been with advertising agencies, where he was known personally and respected for his research credentials. The latter did not impress TV station managers, who found Langhoff's understanding of their problems scant and his manner austere. In Langhoff's view, their major complaint was that the numbers were too low (which they were, relative to Nielsen's).

By the fall of 1970, ARB was in serious trouble; broadcasters (especially such major station groups as Taft, Storer, Cox, Corinthian, and Avco) were withholding contract renewals to the tune of $2 million on an annual basis. At this point Robert Price, the vice president of Control Data overseeing American Research Bureau operations, accepted a proposal from Seiler to act as a consultant in breaking the logjam. Seiler made one condition: that product usage data be removed from the ARB diary and reports. He knew that many broadcasters and station representatives believed that, in collecting this added information, ARB was adversely affecting its cooperation rate and television levels. At least, comparisons with Nielsen seemed to point in that direction. With Price's consent, Seiler and his staff went to work on a commission basis to recoup the lost contracts for ARB. All but $200,000 of that $2 million at stake was brought in by the efforts of Seiler and Media Statistics executives.[6] In 1971 ARB moved further to parallel Nielsen's diary by adopting the closed-end format (with quarter-hour page rulings). Langhoff, however, who had opposed the CDC-Seiler agreement, was now finished as ARB president. Control Data moved him to take over Ticketron and various computer activities related to state-run lotteries.

In 1972 Theodore (Ted) Shaker became president of Arbitron. With a background of many years in broadcast sales and management, Shaker, although not a researcher, supplied the knowledge of and rapport with the broadcasting field that neither of his past two predecessors could boast.

Unlike the Nielsen organization, which trains and builds from within and grooms executives for higher posts by long service, Arbitron's experience has often been one of substantial turnover among production chiefs, heads of research, product managers and service directors.

One of Shaker's innovations was to change the company's name from American Research Bureau to Arbitron in 1973. The Arbitron name, originally attached to ARB's meter service in 1957, became the name of the total service and eventually of the company. The change was believed essential because ethnic group cooperation was threatened by a belief that American Research Bureau must be a government agency. Thus, a name originally adopted because its quasi-official sound might aid response was now scrapped for the opposite reason— a subtle comment on the composition and values of our changing society. But Shaker's penchant for name changes went a step further. In 1982 Arbitron became officially The Arbitron Ratings Company, with the intention of more clearly positioning its activities with respondents.

## Arbitron and the Meter

While the Nielsen Company was generally known as the meter master because of its long dominance in the national picture with NRI and NTI, James Seiler was not content to surrender a meter monopoly to this strong competitor. In 1957 Arbitron got a jump on that competitor by launching an instantaneous meter service of about 300 specially telephone wired households in the 17 county New

York metropolitan area. Day-after results were delivered to local station sub-scribers. Seiler's move was well received by an industry that felt competition would make the Neilsen Company more nimble and a little easier to deal with. Seiler announced plans to expand his service to other major markets.

Nielsen responded as he had with RADOX (see Chapter 2). The first move was to institute a competitive instantaneous service in New York, which was inaugurated in 1959. Seiler's financial status was not vulnerable, but his patent position was. Under Henry Rahmel's technical leadership, the A. C. Nielsen Company had acquired patents on every conceivable means of metering. Sind-linger had discovered this in 1952; now Seiler learned the same lesson. Shortly after CEIR took over Arbitron, an agreement was reached in October 1961 whereby Nielsen granted Arbitron rights to use its receiver monitoring equipment by agreeing to pay Nielsen 5 percent of the net selling price of the salable data. Nielsen's penchant for technical, legal, and financial detail paid off again.

After beating Nielsen in New York by two years, it became evident to Shaker, immediately after he became president, that Arbitron's instantaneous meter service had fatal flaws. The meter was beset with technical problems in keeping abreast of rapidly advancing technology built into home television receivers. The sample deteriorated because of these technical limitations and a lack of a statistically sound replacement procedure. A final sore point for Shaker was the royalty payment to Nielsen. Shaker decided to fold the service in 1972, but he did not lose interest in developing a meter that would be in every way competitive with Nielsen. He first wanted to compete in major local markets, but he never lost sight of the idea that at some time in the future the opportunity for a competitive national meter service might present itself.

Shaker turned to Melpar, a small, highly regarded electronics firm, to develop a meter to Arbitron's specifications. Melpar, a subsidiary of E-Systems, delivered meters in 1974 that proved to be defective in field operation. Since they failed to meet agreed specifications, Arbitron sued for breach of contract and reached an out-of-court settlement, with E-Systems paying Arbitron $5.5 million cash damages in March 1981.

Meanwhile Arbitron and the parent Control Data Corporation set about uti-lizing CDC in-house expertise and acquired patents on new technology to build the present Arbitron instantaneous meter. The present local meter services were inaugurated in 1976 with meters manufactured by CDC. Arbitron then not only matched but at times surpassed Nielsen, with local TV market installations in 13 top markets as of mid 1987. Arbitron's aggressiveness forced Nielsen to also expand into these new markets. NSI finally pulled ahead of Arbitron by one in 1986. Arbitron's early start received a negative reaction from established network affiliates, which resisted meters because they benefit least (compared to inde-pendents and cable) from meter measurement. The result has been a significant number of holdouts and a spiteful tendency to sign with Nielsen when its service became operable. Arbitron therefore failed to gain a big advantage by being first with the meters in a market. Nevertheless by May 1987 Arbitron claimed 65 stations and 300 advertising agencies using its meter services nationwide.

Despite changes in ownership, management, executives, and name, Arbitron has held a major share of the local market TV service against strong Nielsen competition. It is considered to be even with Nielsen although Arbitron has a slight edge through a stronger position in regional advertising centers.

Arbitron has been an innovator in many TV ratings developments: total survey areas (1959), simultaneous sweeps (1959), projected persons estimates (1960), cable controls (1964), Spanish-language diary (1965), the Area of Dominant Influence (ADI) concept (1966), sample balancing (1969), and many additions and refinements in report design and content, plus ancillary reports such as the Television Markets and Rankings Guide, Syndicated Program Analyses, Network Program Analyses, and Television USA, a day-part summary of all TV markets. Arbitron Information on Demand (AID) provides all hard-copy data and much greater detail through tapes and computer access. Arbitron led the way in the use of geodemographic data, at first with PRIZM, and then with Donnelley's Cluster Plus (See Chapter V for descriptions of these tools). The latter, linked to product data from Simmons Market Research Bureau (SMRB), is marketed as Product Target AID. Station subscribers can use on-line microprocessors to develop ratings data, zeroing in on their prime prospects.

Arbitron television handled the problems of low response and underrepresentation in ethnic homes in the same manner as Arbitron radio with one exception: For Hispanic households, where diaries were placed by personal interview (1967–1983), television used Spanish-language diaries and radio used bilingual diaries. The Differential Survey Treatment (DST) was introduced in 1982–1983 for blacks and Hispanics. This uses heavy money premiums to induce cooperation in younger households so that ethnic response rates nearly parallel those for whites.

In October 1984, Arbitron Ratings Company and Burke Marketing Services finalized an agreement to work together on a new syndicated rating service called ScanAmerica. Arbitron's parent corporation, Control Data Corporation, had acquired a minority interest in Burke Marketing with an option to purchase the remainder of Burke after five years. ScanAmerica is an electronic meter system that measures television viewing of individuals as well as product purchases made within the measured household. (See Chapter 11 for recent peoplemeter developments.)

## IV.  NIELSEN TV SERVICES 1947–1987

A. C. Nielsen, in his deal with Hooper in January 1950, demonstrated the shrewd approach that characterized his phenomenal business success over the years.[7] When Nielsen was ostensibly bargaining to get Hooper out of the national radio measurement field, he linked to his proposal the acquisition of Hooper's stripling network TV service, the only viable one at the time. Nielsen was certain that television held the future of broadcasting; the mercurial Hooper was still a radio fan, convinced that local audience measurements would dominate in the future because of TV's spotty growth. When Hooper "just threw in the national television ratings" (his own words), he handed Nielsen the passkey to the future: uncontested dominance of network television measurement that has continued unabated for over three decades. Although Nielsen had inaugurated a local meter TV service in the New York market in August 1949, it was restricted in sample size to the limited number of households in the NRI sample that acquired television sets.

## National Television Index (NTI)

Following the Hooper acquisition, Nielsen ran a joint Nielsen–Hooper national service from March to August 1950. The NTI metered sample grew from 214 to 290 installed households (a subsample of NRI's 1500 sample). This supplied TV usage by time periods. Each program's share of audience was determined by Hooper's coincidental telephone calls in 405 households per city within 50 miles of 42 U.S. cities. Program ratings, a product of NTI households using television (HUT) and Hooper shares, were expressed as a percentage of TV households in cities where the program was broadcast on a program station area (PSA) basis. Monthly reports were issued based on two alternate weeks measured.

Beginning in September 1950, NTI reports were based solely on Nielsen sample data. Ratings were still produced on a PSA basis, and sample size rose rapidly: in the fall of 1951—450; 1952—600; 1953—700. In the fall of 1953 the PSA rating basis was abandoned in favor of a program station basis (PSB), in which the denominator became the ability of NTI households to receive one or more stations carrying the program (according to Nielsen field check), rather than arbitrary definition by market. There were comparable levels between PSA and PSB.

In the early television years, when many markets had only one or two local stations, network lineups were more important than program popularity in developing high audience ratings. In October 1951 Nielsen instituted a new service based on an NTI subsample made up of nine markets that had a full-time VHF affiliate for each of the three TV networks. Known as the Multi-Network Area (MNA) report, this became the standard measure of program popularity under relatively equal competitive conditions.[8] An additional value was that it could be produced more quickly than the national pocketpiece (approximately a week ahead) and was therefore greatly valued for trend spotting. Other markets were added as they qualified; by 1960 the report included 70 markets.

By July 1960 Nielsen began reporting ratings based on total U.S. TV households.[9] Station and network facilities had increased to the point where the average network program could be viewed by well over 90 percent of all U.S. TV households, and sample size had reached 1100 homes installed.

During 1964 and 1965, following the Harris committee hearings, NTI converted to a new sample based on 1960 census data and added the Mountain Time Zone. Also, a systematic sample was built in to ensure that no homes remained in the sample over five years. By the summer of 1965, the installed sample size was 1150 households, a figure that gradually increased to 1250 by 1982.

Regarding Audimeter technology, Nielsen's great stride occurred in 1973 with the introduction of the Storage Instantaneous Audimeter (SIA), which provided day-after ratings for local market services in New York and Los Angeles and 48-hour ratings for national network TV shows. The SIA instrument records all set usage and holds the data in storage ready for retrieval from Nielsen's main computer center in Dunedin, Florida. Sample homes are connected by a special telephone line so that the data can be collected at any time, but it is usually done between 2:00 A.M. and 6:00 A.M. daily. Instant processing enables the computer to furnish client subscribers with local figures by 9:00 A.M. via their own terminal. Network ratings require an extra day because of the necessity of verifying station lineups. NTI ratings were now available 52 weeks a year.

Since 1977 Nielsen has been gradually automating the network station procedure with its Automated Measurement of Lineups (AMOL). AMOL employs digital coding of all network program episodes transmitted in one of the vertical blanking intervals[10] of the television picture. In 1984 this procedure was used for all three TV networks but not for all affiliated stations. It permits Nielsen to know automatically and instantly what stations carried each network program sent out. AMOL will further improve speed and accuracy of network ratings when it is 100 percent operable.

In 1975 NTI began rating programs of less than five minutes' duration, and all programs were rated to the nearest minute (rather than the nearest five minutes). Since 1977 a number of useful secondary and summary publications have been introduced: the NTI Planners Report, with year-to-year and seasonal comparisons; the NTI Network Prime Time Feature Film Directory, with ratings for all films aired since September 1961; special releases covering holiday viewing; miniseries cumulatives; and the NTI Cable Status Report.

In 1983, the greatest change in the Nielsen Television Index in two decades occurred. The demands of superstations (such as Ted Turner's WTBS, Atlanta) and the requirements of satellite cable networks induced Nielsen to increase its sample from 1250 to 1700 metered households. The 450 new households were added in increments of 50 through the year. Priority was given to the 150 households in the new sample that were cable subscribers. That group was added to WTBS and cable network reports in October 1982.

## National Audience Composition (NAC)

A full description of the Nielsen NAC service is discussed in Chapter 2, Section III, where the Recordimeter and the sample are detailed. This service, which paralleled NRI and NTI beginning in 1954, was devised to furnish the demographic (people) data not produced by a meter. After the demise of the NRI service in 1964, NAC became a television-only service ancillary to NTI. In 1966, a forced three-year sample turnover was instituted for the NAC panel (compared to five years for Audimeter homes, where minimal work is involved for sample household members). Improved delivery for NTI/NAC persons data was introduced in 1968. In 1970, the NAC report sample size was increased from one-quarter to one-third of the total panel each week. There are 39 NAC measured weeks annually, and each panel household keeps an Audilog record for 13 weeks. In 1980-1981, 89 percent of installed sample homes returned usable diaries (one or more days). Nineteen out of 26 issues of the NTI pocketpiece annually include demographic data from NAC. New computational procedures introduced in 1974 enabled personal data to be used on "households with any" of 14 demographic categories for NAC on the same basis as NTI. At the same time, audience analysis for persons by age and sex within market breaks was made available.

## Nielsen Station Index (NSI)

The Nielsen Recordimeter-based NSI local market television service was launched simultaneously with the radio service in 1954; see Chapter 2, Section III for details of its growth until 1963, when the local radio service was discontinued. NSI-Radio and TV were sold as individual services, although most clients bought both. Separate diaries were provided for each set used. Sample sizes varied initially by market from 150 for smaller metropolitan markets to several hundred in larger markets where areas beyond the metro were included (a Nielsen first). The NSI service, starting with 6 markets, expanded to 30 by fall of 1955. In 1957–1958, expansion continued with 24 additional markets but without the Recordimeter. Further additions of diary-only markets brought the total to 219 markets by 1961.

When the local radio service was discontinued by 1963, the NSI TV service was completely revamped to meet Arbitron competition: eight-week reports were discontinued in favor of four weeks; computer-selected samples from listed telephone frames were used; sample recruitment was concentrated in interview centers, where supervised employees placed WATS calls, and samples were increased. Control for CATV (community antenna TV) was initiated.

Between 1965 and 1984, the following developments took place: Additional demographic data and many new TV stations doubled the size of market reports to an average of about 100 pages; reports are delivered 21 days after measurement (versus 36 days before); reports are often ahead of delivery schedule (as opposed to previous frequent delays of up to 7 days). Actual calendar production days were cut in half—from 24 days to 12—due to more powerful automation, better printing facilities, and more efficient staff.

In the fall of 1976, NSI introduced Total Telephone Frame (TTF), the addition of unlisted telephone households by use of random-digit dialing (RDD), in 14 metropolitan areas. The TFF procedure was expanded to 68 markets by 1978, and by 1980 it covered the entire sample universe.

NSI tried several approaches to the problem of adequately representing black and Hispanic households in NSI in-tab samples. Prior to the inclusion of unlisted telephone households in 1967, separate socioeconomic units of central city hard-core poverty areas were geographically defined by U.S. statistical data and sampled as separate cells. Spanish-language diaries were introduced, and Spanish-speaking interviewers were used in placement. A major overhaul in this area took place in 1978 when socioeconomic control areas were abandoned in favor of increased monetary incentives and midweek call-backs to bring ethnic response up.

## NSI Instantaneous Audimeter TV Service

NSI's entry into the local meter service began in New York, with the first printed report released in February 1960. Each sample household in the New York metropolitan area was connected by leased telephone line so that Audimeter tuning data could be transmitted to a central computer. The meter, of course, provided only households levels: demographic details still came from diaries. It was not until 1970 that a second market—Los Angeles—was so equipped. In 1973, SIA equipment was installed in these two markets, sample sizes were increased to 500 each in 1975, and Chicago was added in 1976. By 1984, NSI had added six additional metered markets. Arbitron began in 1982 to match and surpass Nielsen in meter-equipped markets. At first Nielsen, under station pressure, vacillated about meeting the Arbitron challenge. However, key agencies favorable to meter measurement induced NSI to meet the competitive thrust and match Arbitron market by market. Later Nielsen gained a slight margin when by mid 1987 the score was Nielsen 14 and Arbitron 13.

In 1984 Nielsen, in response to the projected entry of British AGB Research into the United States with people meters (Section 4, this Chapter and Chapter 11 for peoplemeter developments) began a national test of the Nielsen people meter (with push buttons for family members to record viewing). Such a device, if workable in households, could replace diary based demographics in meter services. Another 1984 development was the acquisition of A.C. Nielsen, Inc. by

Dun and Bradstreet, a move not expected to affect the course of the company's activities.

## V.   AGB RESEARCH PLC

A new entrant in the U.S. television measurement field appeared in 1982 in the form of AGB Research PLC, an English firm. AGB, with a significant success record in using meters in Europe and elsewhere, has now staked out the United States and especially the Nielsen national service as its target.

AGB Research PLC started in business as Audits of Great Britain, founded in 1962 by three former executives of the Attwood organization: G. B. Audley, D. A. Brown, and D. M. Wharrie. At that time, Attwood was a dominant factor in British market and media research and held the contract for the meter service used by commercial television in the United Kingdom. The fledgling AGB concentrated on continuous panel market research, store audits, and in-home grocery audits until 1968. Then, with a newly designed meter, it supplanted Attwood by winning the contract for the U.K. meter service, a contract negotiated by the Joint Industry Committee for Television Advertising Research, a tripartite organization of broadcasters, advertisers, and agencies.

Later, as AGB grew, it acquired Attwood as a subsidiary. In 1981, the British Broadcasting Corporation's noncommercial television network joined the sponsoring group, and the name was changed to Broadcasters Audience Research Board.

At present, AGB has 3200 meters in Great Britain and also conducts meter services in Germany, Ireland, Holland, Italy, France, Hong Kong, and the Philippines. Several of these were acquired local services and so are not using the standard form of AGB meter.

AGB's big meter push has come in the area of "people meters," in which a household push-button device allows each family member to indicate when he or she is viewing. Such meters have been successfully employed in Ireland, Holland, Italy, and Germany (the former Teleskopie service acquired by AGB in 1982). AGB has introduced them in Great Britain, where their plan called for the entire panel of 4000 to have people meters by September 1984. AGB has also experimented extensively with an "electronic diary," a sophisticated device in which a viewer not only records viewing by a light pen instead of a push-button, but can record his or her opinon on the program (and other matters) and register product use data.

### U.S. Presence and Plans

Early in 1982, AGB acquired National Family Opinion (NFO), a national survey organization based in Toledo, Ohio, for $9 million. In mid 1982, AGB announced its intention to enter the U.S. television audience field with its meter. AGB then proposed in 1983 to conduct a market test of its advanced meter system. At the same time, AGB announced that it had contracted to purchase a majority interest in Information and Analysis, a New York firm established in 1978 by Norman Hecht, formerly Arbitron Television vice president. This company would now become the nucleus of the AGB media operations in the United States (as NFO had become the U.S. market research arm). Hecht would continue to head the newly constituted unit, yet to be named.

The U.S. test proposed by AGB involved a one-city (Boston) public trial validation of the people measurement devices over an eight-month period beginning in fall 1984. Two matched panels of 200 households each are employed. Panels A and B test the push-button "People Meter," and B uses the electronic diary type during the final two months. Panel A employs only the set meter during the first two months as an accepted industry benchmark. Telephone coincidentals are to provide validation.

AGB proposed that the cost of this study, $1,050,000 (which includes no AGB overhead or profits), be user financed. The plan was kicked off with impressive equipment demonstrations, and AGB announced sufficient success in the financing effort to go forward. Industry support has come from advertisers, agencies, broadcast networks, and cable interests.

## What AGB Offers

The goal is a national service based on 5000 to 7000 metered households and 13,000 to 18,000 people participants, at a cost of 50 percent to 65 percent of Nielsen's charges. The Boston test is a bold bid to involve industry elements in financially supporting a test of a competitor for the Nielsen NTI service. AGB offers the following incentives:

- An overall lower-cost meter operation than Nielsen's, permitting a larger national sample at a significant saving.
- A thoroughly tested electronic meter system with integrated people meters, eliminating all diary adjustments, limitations, and costs.

## Why the Test?

AGB is a relatively unknown organization in this country. It must demonstrate not only the technical ability of its equipment but the willingness of Americans to cooperate daily in pushing buttons in an accurate manner. Whereas set meters are out of sight (and mind, probably), the daily presence of buttons to push (or light pens to use) could become a boring chore, could condition people's viewing patterns, and could create security problems because of the visibility of the equipment. Will recruitment rates be further eroded when the push-button task is added? U.S. research people are not entirely persuaded by evidence of their success in other countries where cultural values and viewing choices are quite different.


## AGB's U.S. Future

AGB executives state that they are in the United States to stay. They believe that their service is superior to Nielsen's and are confident that they can seriously challenge Nielsen's long monopoly of the TV national measurement business. AGB's foreign success has come largely by their acceptance by industry organizations rather than individual users. Their inexperience in marketing to U.S. media and their unfamiliarity with the immensely complex television industry in the United States raise questions that only time can answer. AGB, with better than $100 million sales annually, has the financial muscle to challenge Nielsen head-on (See Chapter 11 for recent peoplemeter developments.)


# VI.   OTHER TV SERVICES

Any discussion of the early development of television ratings services would be imcomplete without briefly referring to some of the early entrants in the field that failed. Videodex, Pulse, and Sindlinger were the most prominent of this group. None of them achieved widespread acceptance, and they were little used in the mainstream of television programming, buying, and selling at the national level.


## Videodex

Videodex was established in Chicago as a local television rating service in 1949, before the city had network coaxial cable connection. Like ARB, it used a viewer diary. Conducted by Jay and Graham Research Inc., Videodex won local and regional acceptance in the Chicago area and in 1950 announced expansion to a national sample of 9000, to include all 63 television markets in the country. Sample distribution was weighted up for markets where local reports would be issued in addition to national network ratings figures. The Videodex technique and service were in many respects similar to ARB's with certain differences. In diary form Videodex asked for demographics information from men, women, teenagers, and children 12 and under; their opinion of the program watched, whether it was excellent, good, or fair; and their opinion of the commercials, whether they were interesting, neutral, or irritating. The Videodex sample consisted of a stable panel—the same household reported seven consecutive months (with first month's diary not tabulated because of "conditioning"). Names from manufacturers' warranty cards were used, with recruitment by mail and telephone follow-up.

During its operational lifetime, Videodex made several adjustments in technique, but the service never attained the industry acceptance accorded its diary competitor, ARB. In January 1958, Videodex claimed that it covered all TV markets, with samples in each of 250 to 600 homes, but the national service was discontinued in November 1958 when all subscribers had abandoned it.[11] As Seiler expanded in coverage, subscribers, and agency acceptance in the late 1950s, Videodex also dissolved as a syndicated local service of any significance. At the time of the congressional hearings on ratings in 1963, Videodex had become a small operation of seven people (then headquartered in New York) doing custom surveys for spot TV advertisers. After the disastrous showing it made in the Harris hearings, Videodex, never more than a fringe for practical purposes, was no longer a factor.

## Tele-Pulse

Pulse, Dr. Sydney Roslow's personal interview day-after roster recall survey system, entered the television field in New York in 1948. In 1949 the Tele-Pulse service was reporting television audience estimates in New York, Chicago, Philadelphia, and Cincinnati. Costs were relatively high because with few TV sets in use, locating television households involved many wasted personal calls. Television was then only in operation in the afternoon and evening, and a single roster recall interview was made early the next day. This was considered acceptable then because of the impact and memorability of TV programs in those early days of the medium. And the viewer would be quite knowledgeable about any set usage by others the previous day.

Later, Roslow changed the interview schedule to (1) shorten the lapse in time between respondent's viewing and his or her reporting to a Pulse interviewer and (2) make certain that all family members had an opportunity to report on evening program viewing. Various combinations were tried, with interviewing taking place between 4:00 P.M. and 8:00 P.M. covering a portion of the present day or evening (7:00 P.M. to midnight) of the preceding day. This involved separate day-part samples. A variant for smaller markets was a single interview between 6:00 P.M. and 9:00 P.M. that covered telelvision activities from 7:00 A.M. to 6:00 P.M. that day and from 6:00 P.M. to midnight the previous evening.

Surveys were generally conducted during the first 7 days each month. Results were reported about 30 days later. Sample sizes, originally about 200 per quarter hour, were expanded as the service grew.

The Tele-Pulse service expanded to 40 TV markets in 1952 and 70 in 1954, a growth closely paralleling Pulse's somewhat higher radio market entry curve. Tele-Pulse competed in the local field on a fairly even basis with American Research Bureau's diary and Hooper's coincidental services through the early

1950s. Then in 1955 the competitive picture changed drastically. Following Hooper's death in December 1954, ARB bought out the Hooper coincidental service and gradually folded it up while acquiring its client list. The same year Nielsen entered the local ratings field with a combination radio and television service (both in same sample households) in 30 markets using the diary-Recordimeter technique. Tele-Pulse could not withstand the combined competitive pressure of a greatly strengthened ARB and the marketing clout of the Nielsen organization. Tele-Pulse's major deficiency was its geographic limitation to metropolitan areas, whereas both ARB and Nielsen could survey entire station coverage areas, which were enlarging with station transmission improvements. From 1956 on, Tele-Pulse quickly declined; for all practical purposes it was out of the field by 1958 and ceased operations in 1960.

## Telerad System (1956)

In April 1956, a West Coast group introduced Telerad,[12] a system that had many of the characteristics of the CBS 1947 IAMS radio development. The group comprised Robert Miller, a marketing professor, University of Southern California; George Wood, engineer; Gerald Katz, statistician of the Hughes Aircraft Corp.; and Benjamin Potts, vice president and general manager of the Lennen and Newell advertising agency in Los Angeles. Potts planned to devote full time to promoting and securing financial backing for a national sample of 20,000 for Telerad. A prototype unit had been completed by the Behlman Engineering Laboratory, Burbank, California.

The Telerad system consisted of a local central communications center located near major TV transmitters. This center was equipped with a battery of electronic computers for each program channel in the area. It transmitted a high-frequency synchronizing signal to Telerad reporter units attached to a sample of home receivers. At 30-second intervals, the recorder unit would transmit set usage and channel tuned. Special FCC allocation would be necessary; sharing of UHF frequencies was suggested. No further information ever reached the public about Telerad, which embodied all the limitations ascribed to IAMS (Chapter 2, Section IX).

## TPI Ratings Inc. (1958)

TPI (Television-Personal Interview) was organized by M. A. Wallach Research, Inc. to conduct ratings studies. Encouraged, promoted, and partially financed by George J. Abrams, vice president and advertising director of Revlon Inc., researcher Miles Wallach inaugurated the use of personal coincidental interviewing together with telephone coincidentals on a matched sample using the same questionnaire. The first pilot test was conducted in Syracuse, New York, during the week of March 9, 1958, using a team of more than 50 interviewers. Despite adverse weather, the 5000 personal interviews (matched by 5000 telephone coincidental interviews) were conducted from 10 A.M. to 11 P.M., including mealtime hours.

Personal and telephone coincidental ratings were close, but comparisons with Arbitron's February report showed that the diary figures were substantially higher. Especially affected were prime-time periods, in which Arbitron sets in use registered 50 percent higher than did the coincidental average. The telephone coincidental generally produced higher ratings except for some daytime periods.

Abrams, who was chairman of the Radio-TV Committee of the Association of National Advertisers (ANA), presented details of the Syracuse test at an ANA meeting late in March 1958. *Broadcasting*[13] reported that the "reaction was stone cold among highly placed researchers in agency and network echelons." Nevertheless, there was sufficient advertiser interest that Ford, Chrysler, and *Reader's Digest* joined Revlon in a study that year, which Wallach presented to an ANA meeting in November. Based on a 6,000-interview survey in three cities, Wallach seemed prepared to reject the telephone coincidental in favor of "in-house interviewing." He stressed that current rating services overstated audiences by about 30 percent, that they did not help advertisers reach the best prospects, and that advertisers were not doing a good selling job. A few other individual studies were completed but TPI faded quickly as a serious rating entry.


## Sindlinger (1961–1962)

Albert Sindlinger inaugurated a national television rating service in January 1961. Following his settlement with Nielsen over RADOX in 1952 (see Chapter 2, Section IX), Sindlinger had been conducting large-scale national marketing studies for such major clients as duPont, Ford, and other manufacturers. These companies were interested in Sindlinger's idea for a TV rating service with qualitative data (income, occupation, and education) as well as demographic breakdowns based on interviews with individuals, not households. There were 1600 in the daily sample and reports covered evening viewing by networks. Sindlinger hoped that his people data, qualitative factors, and fast continuous service would be welcomed.

The Sindlinger Television Service hoped to recoup a large part of its cost by sale of qualitative data to advertisers, so ratings data for broadcasters was relatively inexpensive. The service never caught on, in Sindlinger's opinion because in using people as a base the ratings were lower than those produced on the traditional household base. When Sindlinger inaugurated his radio network service in September 1962, he dropped the TV product, while continuing radio for five years (see Chapter 2, Section V).

## Tanner Engineering Co. (1964)

Conversations in the hallways and suites among delegates to the NAB convention at the Stevens Hotel in Chicago, April 6–8, 1964, were dominated by a single topic: a panel truck equipped with rotating antennas and electromagnetic scanning gear, which could detect and record all TV set usage within a 300-yard range as the truck cruised at speeds of 5 to 50 miles per hour. Most broadcast station owners, managers, and executives had much more confidence in electronic technology than in ratings produced by sample interviews. Consequently, the Tanner Engineering Co. display was quickly accepted at face value as the solution to the audience measurement problem.

The technique, called Tanner Electronic Survey Tabulation (TEST), had been developed by James L. Tanner, a young San Diego inventor with some broadcast experience. Tanner stressed that similar earlier proposals had depended on the TV sets' local oscillator radiation, whereas his system picked up, magnetically, the horizontal scanning signal radiating from sets in operation. Equipment in the truck compared radiated signals from sets with TV station signals (received via a separate loop antenna) to determine the channel tuned in. Up to 3500 sets could be counted per half hour. Data were recorded on tape and transmitted periodically to a computer center. Equipped trucks cost $15,000 to $20,000.

Tanner did not plan to set up a rating service; he merely offered his system and equipment on a lease basis to interested research companies. Unfortunately, mechanical problems with the truck prevented field demonstrations following the convention.

Researchers quickly pointed out that the system had no record of untuned sets, and therefore all that could be produced were "share of audience" figures. Moreover, there was little virtue in touring around to pick up average-minute figures for different times from block to block. It might be better to use fixed locations with known parameters. Engineers questioned the use of the system near apartment houses or for older, weaker sets. Then the cost seemed prohibitive; a national service would require a minimum of several hundred trucks, which would mean a multimillion-dollar investment for field equipment alone.

The number of research and economic questions surrounding the Tanner technique apparently were never seriously addressed. No research company ever acquired a Tanner truck, and as far as public record is concerned, no practical use was ever made of TEST.

## NOTES

1. Shortly after returning from Army service to rejoin NBC as research director in 1945, the author developed, with NBC president Niles Trammell, a three-pronged research strategy for TV development: regular

reporting of TV sets in use by market, acceptable syndicated programs ratings, and sales effectiveness surveys.

2. Hindsight is wonderful: Hooper was in a weak bargaining position because his business was going deeply into the red. He was willing to do anything to save it from bankruptcy.

3. Fred Kenkel, letter to the author dated April 18, 1978.

4. An interesting historical twist: C. E. Hooper had started his media research career with Daniel Starch, an association he severed to go into business with Clark in 1934.

5. Seiler told the author in 1980 that because ARB was then so dominant (with an 80 percent share of local TV business), he received a telephone call from Arthur Nielsen, Sr. the very day of his release by Robinson, proposing discussions on a merger or other joint arrangement with NSI. Nielsen Sr. was now dead so no confirmation was possible. Arthur Nielsen, Jr. had no recollection of such a proposal and believed it a misunderstanding of an offer to discuss employment of Seiler by Nielsen.

6. This account is largely based on interviews with James Seiler and some other confirmation.

7. And which, along with the more profitable market index services, led to the amassing of a considerable fortune. Arthur C. Nielsen, Jr., his principal heir, is annually included in the *Fortune* list of the 500 wealthiest Americans.

8. Local competitive conditions were not the same then as today. Common antenna farms were rare (Empire State building, Mt. Wilson, Calif.), so site location gave many early pioneers an advantage. The station's age and the character of local programming were significant pluses, which network shows inherited.

9. Note that although the base for ratings had been TV households in the area in which the program could be received, it was always possible to translate a PSA or PSB rating into a U.S. rating by multiplying the reported rating by the percentage of station coverage (which is grounded on total U.S. TV households).

10. A vertical blanking interval is the split-second time between the individual pictures that make up the TV picture seen on the screen. Only highly sophisticated instruments can read the discrete code that appears there for every network program broadcast.

11. *Part 2, Broadcast Ratings, Hearings before a Subcommittee of the Committee on Interstate and Foreign Commerce, House of Representatives, 88th Congress, on the Methodology, Accuracy, and Use of Ratings in Broadcasting*, pp. 534–537.

12. Based on "Instantaneous Rating System Claim Made by West Coast Agency Executive," *Broadcasting*, April 23, 1956, p. 50.

13. *Broadcasting*, March 31, 1958.

# 4

## Rating Methodologies: A Comparative Examination

### I. INTRODUCTION

The average rating user, when queried as to what he or she wants most from ratings, will probably respond "accuracy," meaning numbers that are free from errors or trustworthy for decision making. On the other hand, we know that all ratings by their very nature are estimates and are therefore subject to errors and variations of several types. The question then becomes not one of absolute accuracy but of relative accuracy. How much accuracy can be obtained at what cost? The expense must be related to the monetary exposure of the decision involved.

Broadcast ratings have employed a wide range of techniques over the years. As we saw in Chapter 1, radio's two first syndicated services the early 1930s—the Cooperative Analysis of Broadcasting (CAB) using recall and the Hooper coincidentals—both employed telephone interviewing. In the mid 1940s, the Nielsen Audimeter won acceptance, and roster recall utilizing personal interviews was introduced by Pulse.

The success of direct mail in the conduct of station coverage surveys in the 1930s led CBS to experiment with mail diaries in the early 1940s. This prompted the adoption of the mail diary by American Research Bureau in 1948 and later by Nielsen for local market reports.

Today the emphasis is on meters (which register set usage and station tuning) as well as respondent diaries (either household or personal). Other techniques and variants of these basic methods have been used. However, the only successful new methodology currently in use is RADAR, which utilizes a carefully selected panel of individuals who are interviewed daily by telephone for a week to obtain personal listening data on a recall basis for the previous day.

CAB utilized telephone recall methods until 1944. Recognizing that memory loss played a role in recall, CAB gradually reduced the recall period while maintaining that it measured "attentive listening," by which it meant listening that entailed a "conscious impression." Hooper's coincidental telephone method measured listening at the moment of call (with no memory factor) but could produce only "average minute" ratings, which were significantly lower than CAB's recall estimates.[1] Nielsen's meter measured set tuning, not listening per se. Nevertheless, the Audimeter could yield average audience as well as total audience figures for programs of varying length (assuming set tuning was equivalent to audience). It is clear that the operational definition of audience was modified to suit the instrument used in survey data collection.

Audience definition was finally resolved to some degree when the Advertising Research Foundation in 1954 adopted set tuning as the best basis for household audience measurement. On the other hand, today's diary methods emphasize "viewing" and "listening" individuals—but the precise definition of action recorded is really left to the judgment of the diary keeper who makes the entry. If a person works for eight hours in a store or restaurant where the radio is constantly on, is he or she a listener for those eight hours? If three family members are in the room with a TV set on, the quality of viewing attention may vary greatly from the teenager doing homework, to the person serving a meal, to the tired worker relaxing with a beer. How can any technique reflect these differences in degree of attentiveness?

There are no easy answers to the most elemental aspect of validity in ratings: Who should be included as listening and viewing audience? Psychologists can debate this issue, but industry ratings services and users take a realistic attitude. The operational definitions used in meter, diary, and telephone surveys are reasonably well accepted and understood (as are some of the major differences). Since trends are based on common definitions, the issue is not critical in most ratings use, and other factors appear to be more significant contributors to variations in results between rating techniques.

## Some Basic Considerations

Before discussing the possible error in audience measurement, we should focus on the statistical definition of two concepts related to accuracy: validity and reliability.

### Validity

Validity is the degree to which the measurement actually fully and precisely measures the attribute of interest (television viewing or radio listening—in our case, the reality of audience behavior). In order to establish the degree of validity that may be attached to any measurement technique, it is necessary to deal with two factors: definition of audience and criteria of validity.

*Definition of Audience.*   The station manager or agency time buyer who wants an audience size number for decision making rarely considers that there may be several ways to define audience. As we saw in earlier chapters, during the radio ratings heyday, the three principal competitors each espoused a methodology that employed a different definition of "audience." Searching for true validity becomes somewhat difficult without a universally accepted standard definition of viewing and listening.

*Criteria of Validity.*   At present, industry researchers lean strongly toward a coincidental telephone procedure measuring set tuning and individuals' presence in the room as the yardstick or criterion for evaluating the effectiveness of other techniques. The particular coincidental method employed for evaluative studies is a far cry from that used by Hooper (and many others over the years). The present method was originally developed by Statistical Research Inc. for the Committee for National Television Audience Measurement (CONTAM) in 1967 but has since been used by other industry research groups involved with methodology.[2] This procedure, known as the Industry Sponsored Research (ISR) coincidental, has the following advantages:

- Probability sample of all telephone households achieved by random-digit dialing.
- High response rate (due to intensive follow-up procedures) and the fact that reasonable assumptions for nonresponse can be made.
- No memory factor involved (except for fractional group of "busy telephones").
- Quality of sampling and interviewing highly controlled and monitored at central call locations.

The limitations delineated below are significant but not crucial (at least for television):

- Only in-home audience is measurable.
- Only hours from 7:00 A.M. to 11:00 P.M. can be included.
- No nontelephone households (about 5 percent of total U.S. television owners) can be included.
- Only average audience data are obtained (neither average quarter hour, total program audience, nor any cumulative ratings are directly obtainable).

The ISR coincidental has been extremely valuable as a validity criterion (yardstick of reality) for checking television ratings (limited to in-home measurement).

## Reliability

To the researcher, reliability is the degree to which a particular sample measurement will produce the same results that would be obtained by a complete census utilizing the same methodology under exactly comparable conditions. "Same results" means within statistical tolerance levels associated with a particular sample size. We discuss reliability in detail shortly in connection with sampling procedure. For now, it is sufficient to note that sampling error exists in every survey, that it is measurable if probability sampling is employed, that it can be sizable when small samples are involved, and that the size of the market or universe being measured is not a determining factor.

*Nonresponse.*   Whereas we must be concerned with response errors (either of commission or omission) in dealing with the instrument, in assessing field procedures we have two general types of errors: nonresponse and operational errors. Nonresponse errors are errors that can occur because not all selected sample households or persons are actually reached or heard from. A high standard for completed respondent records in tabulation is 75 percent of the original designated sample. This is seldom attained; the usual result in ratings measurement is about 50 percent. With only half the sample actually measured, ratings could be badly biased if nonrespondents differed greatly from respondents in viewing or listening behavior. Fortunately, with the exception of black and Hispanic groups and programs and stations directed to those two ethnic categories the nonresponse bias has been shown to be of minimal nature. Nonrespondents tend to view and listen in patterns essentially similar to respondents.

*Operational Errors.*   Whereas sampling errors can be measured with a relatively high degree of accuracy (assuming probability design), and response and nonresponse errors can be isolated and estimated by methodological research, there are two errors that are most insidious because they can create unknown biases: the errors of omission and commission associated with any human activity. These operational errors can occur at any stage of the planning, fieldwork, and data processing of a rating survey.

*Fieldwork.*   Errors can be made in sample selection or in implementing sample procedures at the home office. Interviewers may fail to follow faithfully instructions for sampling or interviewing. Even under the most stringent training, supervision, and quality control, it is virtually impossible to eliminate variation in fieldworkers' approach and performance. Incompatibility between interviewer and respondent is bound to occur in certain cases. Some people want to please the interviewer while others want to get rid of the prober as quickly as possible. When personal interviewing is involved, these problems are magnified, because an interviewer's appearance (sex, race, dress, grooming, etc.) and manner can be critical factors in the degree of cooperation obtained and perhaps can influence answers as well. Language problems can seriously impede satisfactory interviews in any methodology.

Many of these factors are eliminated or reduced in significance with telephone interviews. Moreover, today much telephone fieldwork is done from centralized call points using WATS lines. Here interviewers can be trained, supervised and monitored to ensure uniformity in questionnaire usage, in efforts to overcome nonresponse, and in probing for completeness.

In diary surveys, the initial telephone call to recruit cooperators is most important. Inasmuch as the diary is self-administered, the problem of proper entry of data is transferred to the respondent. Clear, understandable, written instructions are required.

Meters remove many of the human elements that create problems with other techniques but introduce their own unique opportunities for operational miscues. Certain types of TV sets require unusual connection devices to take metering, and some viewing may be missed or improperly identified until adequate connections are made. Newly purchased sets (which normally get heavy usage) may not be connected for weeks after purchase, household data collection devices may not be adequate to record all viewing, and so on.

*Data Processing.*   Converting questionnaires or diaries to computerized data creates many opportunities for human error. Shortcomings of editing manuals and failure to refer to or properly interpret the manuals is one potential error source. Other errors are possible when editors miscode and terminal operators produce faults. The advent of computers and various electronic checks has substantially reduced human error potential, but it still exists. And, of course, an error in a computer program can be even more serious because it is repetitive and usually difficult to detect.

Processing meter data, which is transmitted by electronic impulse over wires directly to the computer, is almost free of error potential. Nevertheless, there are still chances for error in such activities as weighting, cable penetration, combining diary and meter data, time zone aberrations, and the like.

Rating companies exert great effort to minimize the occurrence and effect of operational errors. Thorough training and effective supervision are employed. Controls of various kinds can spot many errors. Verification of fieldwork on a sample basis and comparison of individual interviewers' work to norms help to maintain quality performance. In Chapter 9 we discuss the role of the Electronic Media Rating Council (EMRC) in auditing accredited rating services. EMRC's audits, conducted by certified public accounting firms, place major emphasis on detection and correction of operational errors in the system.

To sum up, this discussion has covered four types of errors with which any sample survey must cope:

1. *Response errors*—the misreporting of initial data by respondents due to faulty memory, misunderstanding of instructions or questions, or conditioning.

The latter could involve people's entering "usually listened to" programs in a diary (regardless of actual behavior), or it could originate with a desire to please or to "look good" by reporting untrue behavior. The physical presence of diaries or meter devices requiring respondent action might increase or decrease or even change respondent's use of a medium.

2. *Nonresponse errors*—errors introduced because not all preselected sample households or individuals cooperate in supplying needed data. In most radio and television survey efforts, the response rate is about 50 percent. This raises the prospect of serious bias if the respondents are greatly different from the non-responding sample half in respect to viewing or listening behavior.

3. *Operational errors*—errors can be committed throughout the processing of data from interviewers entering data in a wrong column or transposing figures from respondents, to computer errors in a weighting program traceable to "bugs" in the software.

4. *Sample error*—the one error that is mathematically measurable, provided probability sampling principles are followed. It is related directly to the sample size and can be lowered by costly sample size increases.

It is well to keep these possibilities of error in mind as we examine the various ratings methodologies individually.

## II.  WHAT IS A METHODOLOGY?

Insofar as broadcasting ratings are concerned, a methodology is a combination of four factors, any one of which can affect the accuracy of the final ratings figures:

1. *The instrument*—the questionnaire, diary, or mechanical meter that records the original viewing or listening data and the accompanying material and instructions that determine how certain responses are recorded.

2. *The data collection procedures*—personal interview, telephone, mail, meter with cartridge or leased line, interactive cable; interviewer training, control, and supervision; verification procedures, etc.

3. *The sample design*—universe, basic frame, randomness, sampling error (statistical reliability), degree to which sample plan is achieved, nonresponse and its effects.

4. *Operational and administrative procedures*—procedures used in processing data, standards for handling of ambiguous and incomplete responses, weighting, projections, printing, report composition, quality control.

The industry mainly thinks and talks about methodologies in terms of the instrument (meter, diary, etc.) without considering all the differences that may exist between individual services.

At present, although Arbitron and Nielsen both produce television diary measurements for individual markets, there are some noteworthy variations in their procedures:

• Whereas both make preliminary telephone calls to sample households prior to mailing diaries, Arbitron largely uses local interviewers calling from their homes, whereas Nielsen employs three centers from which such calls are placed over WATS lines by supervised interviewers.

• Arbitron and Nielsen use different incentive and follow-up procedures to induce ethnic household members to respond.

• Nielsen and Arbitron differ considerably in the sample balancing and weighting procedures employed to offset differential response rates from various geographical and demographic strata in the sample.

Similar technical differences exist within survey companies. Nielsen, in collecting diary data for its National Audience Composition (NAC) service, utilizes a fixed panel selected in the same manner as its Nielsen Television Index (NTI) national meter service. A Recordimeter on each TV set in the panel household serves as a control device to verify diary total viewing. No such controls are imposed in Nielsen Station Index (NSI) local services where diary and meter data are combined to produce a person's estimates.

In Arbitron's case, "closed-end" household diaries are used for television, whereas radio measurement is achieved by an "open-end" personal diary.

Clearly, one must be aware of such specifics when comparing or using individual rating services. Identifying a survey as diary or meter, Nielsen or Arbitron is not enough. All salient features of a particular service must be understood by users in order to evaluate its output properly.[3] Numerous combinations and refinements of basic elements are possible, and many are employed. Moreover, changes are constantly being implemented. Diary services have used not only the conventional one-week diary record but a one-day diary (RAM) and a two-week diary (Simmons Market Research Bureau[4]). Arbitron and Nielsen use different sampling procedures for their competitive meter services.

This section examines each of the four basic methodological elements. Nevertheless, one must recognize that any individual service puts them together in its own manner. Moreover, in execution, much depends on the caliber, skill, training, experience, and supervision of fieldworkers and data processors. Verification routines and quality control checks are indispensable to ensure that techniques are employed according to design.

As we look closely at the technical aspects of rating methodology, it must be with the firm knowledge that (1) all ratings are estimates; (2) there is no perfect (100 percent accurate) rating system to produce those estimates; and (3) ratings, which are measurements of the recent past, are used primarily to predict future performance.

Before analyzing individual methodologies, let's take a closer look at the four elements chosen for their description.

## The Instrument

Instruments for recording television and radio usage vary from the three or four questions asked in a conventional coincidental telephone call to an extremely complex electronic meter capable of discriminating and recording usage of any of television's 80 channels plus up to 100 cable television channels. Self-administered diaries comprise a major element of rating efforts today because they are flexible and report much information at relatively low unit cost compared to competitive techniques. Because respondents must clearly understand how to record data, the design of rating diaries receives constant attention from services. Simplicity for participant and data processor and low mailing cost are primary factors. Determining what questions to include in the initial recruitment interview and in the diary itself is a problem affecting cost (telephone time) and/or response.

The major aspect of the instrument is that it is the key to the validity of the measurement. If it fails to record accurately the reality of the listening or viewing behavior sought, nothing else in the process can overcome this fundamental flaw. No subsequent editing, weighting, or manipulation of data can "put Humpty Dumpty together again." On the other hand, the degree of accuracy of the instrument is one of the most difficult of all aspects to achieve and to verify.

## The Collection Procedures

Where interviewers are used (telephone coincidentals and recall, personal interviews, diary placement, meter recruitment), great effort is necessary to recruit, screen, train, and supervise quality workers. The most difficult to oversee is the personal interviewer, who to a great degree is working on his or her own with minimum supervision. The interviewer must not only implement a somewhat complex plan of household (and probably household member) sampling (which could necessitate call-backs) but is required to gain maximum cooperation in filling out a lengthy questionnaire or gaining respondent's consent to become a panel member in a continuing meter or diary service for several years. Obviously, personal interviewing demands special personalities, skills, and training. Control over fraud and security against personal bias are more difficult to achieve than in other techniques.

Those who interview from their homes—either for coincidental, recall questionnaire, or diary placement—are the next most independent and hence share some of the problems of the personal interviewer. Studies show wide differences in response rate (and rating data) between individual telephone interviewers working in the same area with comparable samples.

The trend toward centralized interviewing call-out centers has overcome many personnel problems because on-the-spot training, supervision, control, and monitoring are imposed. Shortcuts, sloppiness, or interview problems can be detected and corrected quickly. Response rate, data completeness, and quality are likely to be better than for household interviewing. For example, partially completed interviews are sometimes a problem because assumptions must be made during editing. Close supervision during interviewing can reduce this problem and contribute to improved accuracy. Use of computer-assisted consumer interviews employing a CRT display hooked up to a computer offers promise of greater interview control and on-the-spot computer editing, which improves data accuracy.

## Sampling

Every college statistical course discusses sampling principles and practices, and dozens of books have been written for every level of readership. Nevertheless, sampling and sample error remain among the least understood aspects of rating methodology.

Martin Mayer once postulated[5] that an almost ideal rating service could be conducted by a staff of "well-trained, reasonably intelligent, highly responsible ghosts." The ghosts would drift unseen through the walls of sample homes and observe and record TV viewing by family members. Data could be transmitted immediately by extrasensory means.

Mayer, unfortunately, failed to point out that even with a ghostly operation there would still be errors attached to the estimates produced. These have to do with the sampling aspects of data collection. Two elements are involved: (1) the sampling frame used and (2) the statistical error associated with the sample results.

*Sample Frame.*   The National Association of Broadcasters' "Standard Definition of Broadcast Research Terms"[6] says: "A frame provides a working definition of the statistical population in a study, and a means of access to the elementary units selected for study." In practice, however, a frame may be subject to various imperfections such as incompleteness, or duplication, or both.

Whereas ratings actually seek to produce estimates that are projectable to all radio- or television-owning households in some well-defined geographic area, a convenient, up-to-date list of such households does not exist. If it did, such a list would be an ideal "sample frame." Lacking such a list, most early radio and TV ratings used the latest telephone directory as a frame. Telephone recall, telephone coincidental, and diary surveys all relied on samples of listed telephone households to represent all TV or radio households. On the other hand, meter household samples come from carefully drawn probability samples of all households, employing complete prelisting of randomly selected small areas. Meter samples are not subject to the problem (unlisted telephone and nontelephone households) inherent in using telephone lists.

*Variability—Statistical Sampling Error.*   Leaving aside sample frame problems, all estimates (ratings and projected audience numbers) based on sample surveys contain a characteristic known as sampling error. Unlike other potential errors referred to, the sampling error for a sample drawn so that each unit has a known chance of selection can be readily computed. This universally accepted statistical measure of sample error is called a standard error.

With the aid of the theory of probability, standard error enables one to calculate the probabilities of sampling errors for ratings of various sizes. The approximate formulas for such computations appear in ratings books.

Basically, when using a probability sample and a fixed design, statistical sample error for ratings is a function of sample size and is not determined by the size of the market or population measured. For example, it takes a sample of 1200 households to measure the San Francisco market with the same precision as 1200 households used in a national ratings service.

*Computing Statistical Sampling Error.*   If a sample is drawn on a probability basis—that is, with each unit of the sample having a known chance of being selected—mathematics can determine the size of the statistical error. Assume that we are surveying a metropolitan area with 500 diaries to obtain estimated TV household ratings. Our survey may show Program XYZ with a rating of 21 (21 percent of all households in sample reported viewing Program XYZ). We could select a second 500 sample in precisely the same manner during the same week that would report a rating of 19; a third might say 22, and so on. Let's assume that in reality a complete census showed the true rating to be 20. The individual sample findings were all within the margin of error to be expected under these circumstances. Any one of the figures (21, 19, 22) would be as good an estimate as any other.[7] When Program XYZ's 21 rating is compared with others, it must be recognized that this is indeed an estimate, not a precise number (as will the others be, also). And when the next rating report shows Program XYZ at 24, that is no guarantee that its audience has grown even though a number comparison shows households up by a substantial percent. This may well be nothing but a statistical variation (as might a rating drop to 18). That is why ratings analysts work with trends or rolling averages. Examining a series of ratings tells the story, not any single observation.

*Reducing Standard Error.*   While sample size is not, in itself, necessarily the sole determinant of the size of a standard error, when all other elements of a survey procedure are the same, an increase in the sample size will decrease the standard error. However, the relative decrease will not be directly proportional to the relative increase in sample size. For most sampling plans, to reduce a standard error by 50 percent requires a quadrupling of sample size.

*Relative Standard Error.* Relative standard error is the ratio of the estimated standard error of a rating to the size of the rating itself. For example, a rating of 10 with an estimated standard error of 3 has a relative standard error of 30 percent. Since standard errors vary with the size of the rating or audience estimate involved, the relative standard error is, for comparative purposes, a more meaningful measure of the reliability of audience estimates.

In any ratings report, the relative standard error figures will vary widely. HUT (households using TV) figures and station ratings figures for broad dayparts will have the lowest standard error (and therefore be the most reliable statistically). On the other hand, individual quarter-hour program ratings for small demographic groups such as teenage girls, children 6 to 11, or females 15 to 24 years old will have significantly larger relative standard errors. In general, high ratings have smaller relative standard errors than low ratings in the same demographic column.

Agencies buying schedules on numerous stations in scores of markets get the benefit of higher reliability in averaging many individual ratings. On the other hand, stations must cope with high relative error in comparing single programs with local competition or from one report to another.

## Operational and Administrative Procedures

High quality in all operational and administrative procedures is the principal bulwark against processing errors. These errors can occur at any point from the initial sampling and data collection to the numbers printed in the final rating "book."

Fieldwork, when not performed under supervision in interviewing centers, must be verified on a random basis. The proportion so checked normally varies from 5 to 15 percent of the sample total. Verification should be done as soon after the the interview as possible to ascertain if (1) the interview was actually conducted in the manner and at the time reported and (2) the information provided corresponded to that reported by the interviewer.

Interview or diary data, at the processing center, passes through edit routines that translate respondent data to symbols used in entering them for electronic data processing. Edit manuals and experienced special editors are available for consultation by editors. In entering data, only tolerable ranges of responses may be permitted by the computer system (stations receivable in the area, for example). Verifying the work of new employees is often a valuable safeguard and guide to training needs.

There are several types of operational errors connected with meter services. As panel homes acquire replacement or added sets or become cable subscribers, their status may not be updated for many weeks. Malfunctioning meters can usually be detected, but until they are corrected the homes represented are dropped from the sample. This could create bias. Constant policing of the panel is necessary.

Computer programs that control data tabulation can develop "bugs" whenever they are rewritten to reflect a revision in the questionnaire or the report format. Internal "methods groups" and "computer auditors" are essential safeguards against computer error, which potentially could affect many figures over time, in hundreds of reports.

Claims are often made that new technologies such as CRT (cathode ray tube) systems will provide automated interviewing systems that remove any possible error from an interviewer's recording of response. Such systems are not error free and must be subjected to "old-fashioned checking, monitoring and verifying."[8]

## III.   INDIVIDUAL METHODOLOGIES

In the following analysis of individual methodologies, we emphasize techniques as presently practiced by ongoing services or, in the case of methodologies not currently in operation, how they have been employed in their most recent commercial application. The order of the various rating methodologies is discussed as follows:

1. ISR telephone coincidental.
2. Conventional telephone coincidental.
3. The telephone recall (unaided).
4. RADAR (Radio's All Dimension Audience Research).
5. Weekly TV household diary (closed end).
6. Nielsen Audience Composition (NAC) Service.
7. Personal radio diary (open end).
8. Special diary procedures—one day, two weeks, etc.
9. The electronic meter.
10. Personal roster recall (Pulse).
11. Personal interview—coincidental.

Our primary focus is identifying key elements in each technique so that the reader will understand the strengths and weaknesses of each. The rating services are constantly being revised or modified in some respect. Anyone seeking up-to-date information should request it from individual services. (See Appendix B for rating service information.)

## ISR Telephone Coincidental

We introduce our discussion of individual methodologies by describing one that is not in regular use by any rating service: the Industry Sponsored Research (ISR) telephone coincidental developed and refined by CONTAM (Commitee on National TV Audience Measurement) and COLTRAM (Committee on Local TV and Radio Audience Measurement). This technique has been thoroughly tested and used as a reality yardstick for several methodological studies.

Statistical Research, Inc. was responsible for the industry surveys and contributed greatly to the refinements in the coincidental technique to develop the ISR coincidental. A telephone coincidental survey determines television or radio activity coincident with the time the telephone rang (thus, if a set should be turned off to permit someone to answer the telephone, it would nevertheless be counted as "in use" for survey purposes).

### The Instrument

This is a straightforward one-page questionnaire asking the following questions:

- Is this (telephone number)?
- How many television sets are in the household?
- Where are the television sets located?
- How many set(s) were on or off when the telephone first rang?
- If off, is the set currently in working order?
- What program and channel was on each set in use when the telephone rang?
- What is the age and sex of all persons in the room with each tuned set (including visitors)?
- Limited classification data:
  Age and sex of all persons living in household.
  Age and sex of head of household.
  Race.
  Listed versus nonlisted telephone status.
  Number of different telephone numbers in household.

### Collection Procedures

Prior experience with telephone interviews, preferably with coincidental surveys and a minimum of four hours in training, including two hours of practice calling, are required of all interviewers. Calls are placed from one or two central locations with maximum supervision and monitoring capability. Direct telephone line monitoring of all interviewing takes place constantly on a sample basis to ensure uniformity and to detect deviations from script or procedures.

Telephone number call assignments are designated for specific minutes, since timing on a coincidental survey is an important variable to control. Digital clocks, easily readable from calling stations, enable interviewers to register exact time. Virtually all calls are placed within one minute of the predesignated time.

The initial call to each sample unit includes up to two dialings of eight rings each. In addition, busy lines are given a second dialing within one minute of the predesignated time. All initial coincidental calls that result in a busy line, no answer, refusal, or language problems are recalled later that day and when necessary on subsequent days. Up to five attempts are made every day up to seven days following the initial call. Initial refusals and language problems are similarly called.

When contacted on follow-up, sample households are interviewed following a questionnaire similar to that used initially in order to ascertain television activity *at the time of the original call* (which obviously involves recall) and to determine TV set ownership and household demographics. In one study virtually all interviews with initial "busy lines" and "refusals" and nearly 90 percent of the initial "no answers" were completed within 24 hours of the initial call. Total response rate approached 94 percent.

## The Sample

Since the ISR coincidental has been used in a variety of "yardstick" situations (comparisons with meters and with diaries for both national and local TV rating services), there is no one standard sample method. However, we find the following procedures utilized, in several New York stations rating committee surveys, to obtain a high-quality independent measure of household audience.[9]

A random-digit dial (RDD) sample was utilized to include unlisted as well as listed telephone households. Essentially, RDD involves using computers to generate four-digit random telephone numbers for all working central offices (the first three digits) within the survey area. In the 17-county New York metropolitan area, there were approximately 1200 working central offices. Using tables of random numbers, five or six random four-digit numbers were generated for each central office number. In later studies, computer runs of possible numbers were compared with listed numbers to reveal what number banks are in use so that unused blocks can be eliminated. On a systematic basis, the computer then selects every *n*th number for interviewer assignment.

At this point, the interviewer does not know whether the number to be called is a nonworking number or a household, a business, or an institution that falls outside of the household sample frame. Therefore, a preliminary screening question precedes administering the questionnaire.

## Operational Procedures

The rigid routine for multiple calls and follow-up interviews used in ISR coincidentals is not one associated with conventional coincidental surveys. In one ISR study[10]—CONTAM No. 4, for example—more than 30 attempts were made to contact one sample unit. The hard core group averaged more than 17 attempts each. Special efforts are made at interviewing centers to apply a checklist of 18 elements as soon after each dialing as possible.[11] In this way, supervisors can inform interviewers about errors and omissions on a timely basis. Checks are incorporated to assure that set tuning is credited to the correct station. In this study, unidentified stations averaged 2.5 percent.

Weighting to equalize time and to compensate for geographic population estimates is applied. There is also a down-weighting for households that have more than one telephone number and thus a greater chance of inclusion in the sample.

Coincidental HUT values are computed as the ratio of estimated households reporting one or more sets on to estimated television households. In constructing these estimates, coincidental information was used where available (e.g., for contacted and interviewed households). For refusals, busy lines, and refusal/ language problems, television ownership and usage projections for each group were based on the information obtained in the follow-up interviews.

Persons Using Television (PUT) values for a given age/sex category are computed as the ratio of estimated number of such persons reported in the television audience to the total number in the category universe. Estimated number of persons are calculated as estimated HUT times the number of estimated viewers per tuned household, times the estimate of television households in the survey area.

Estimated viewers per tuned household are calculated as the sum of adjusted viewers per tuned household (VPTH) values for 13 age/sex groups. The adjustment is achieved by multiplying VPTH values from the sample by a ratio of persons per household in each category for the population, to a comparable figure from the sample.[12]

### Summary: ISR Telephone Coincidental

The Industry Sponsored Research telephone coincidental is a carefully done, rigorous procedure that produces valid data while achieving an imposing 90 percent response. Its cost is from 5 to 10 times that of a normal coincidental. It is, therefore, not employed frequently, but it is recognized as the preeminent measurement "standard value" or reality yardstick by which other techniques can be tested. We use it as a point of reference to analyze other rating methodologies. (ISR strengths and limitations were given in the introduction of this chapter.)

## The Conventional Telephone Coincidental

Compared to the ISR coincidental just described, the conventional coincidental is a simple methodology that makes assumptions, not call-backs.

### The Instrument

In 1934, C. E. Hooper decided that the way to find out what people were listening to was to call them and ask them what they were tuned to at that moment. He used an extremely uncomplicated approach. His procedure specified these questions in each interview:

Introduction:    "This is the Radio Research Bureau."

Question 1:    "What were you listening to on the radio when the telephone rang?"

Question 2a:    "What station is that program broadcast over?" (asked if program name is given in answer to Question 1.

Question 2b:    "What program is that station broadcasting?" asked if station call letters are given in answer to Question 1).

Question 3:    "What product is advertised by this program?"

Close:    "Thank you. Goodbye."

Later, other questions were added to the Hooper coincidental interview, but the principal questions, as just worded, were used consistently and fiercely defended by Hooper over many years, even though critics had some reservations about them.

One criticism was about the first question; it had two limitations: (1) it assumed that every respondent owned a radio and (2) more serious, it assumed that the radio was in use. The critics claimed that these two elements could bias replies. The respondent might feel he or she should be listening and could stretch the truth a bit if the set had recently been turned off or was about to be turned on.

Nevertheless, Hooper stuck with the above question procedure except that he soon added a fourth question:

Question 4:    "Please tell me how many men, women, and children, including yourself, were listening to the radio when the telephone rang."

During radio's early days, the procedure worked well. There was a single family set in the living room and thus no problem in ascertaining who was present when the set was on. As to who is in fact a program listener, Chappell and Hooper state, "The respondent knows whether or not he considers himself to be a program listener. He is the only one who can have this knowledge. If he views himself as a listener, he says so."[13] Yet the Hooper process allowed the respondent to determine whether or not other family members present "are listening." Once again, the listening definition is modified by operational facility.

When the Cooperative Analysis of Broadcasting (CAB) abandoned the telephone recall in favor of coincidental interviewing in 1944, they used a somewhat different questionnaire.

With the advent of television, we find that Trendex, the foremost commercial coincidental practitioner for TV, used these questions:

1. "Do you have a television set?"
2. "Were you or anyone in your home watching TV just now?" If yes:
3. "What program or channel?"
4. "How many men, women, or children under eighteen were viewing?"

5. "Who selected the program?"

In 1957 Trendex recognized the multi-set growth by adding the following questions:

"All together, how many TV sets do you have in your home?" If two or more:

"Is anyone in your home watching the other TV?" If yes: "What program or channel is tuned in?"

"How many men, women, or children under eighteen are watching that TV?"

### Collection Procedures

Most telephone coincidental surveys are conducted by interviewers calling from their own homes, a pattern that was followed from the beginning because it was inexpensive, flexible, and efficient. The simplicity of the instrument required little training, and home workers at first could use their own unlimited-service phones to make all calls required in a local area at no added telephone expense. Interviewers could be recruited through local ads, church and social service groups, and word of mouth.

Since interviewing was not continuous but limited to one week a month for such standard services as Hooper and Trendex, no office space was required. Interviewers carried out certain minimum tabulation chores and mailed the results in each day after the fieldwork was completed. On occasion, when so-called overnight ratings were required, the data were telephoned or telegraphed to rating headquarters late at night so that results were deliverable by 10:00 A.M. on the following morning.

Interviewers were paid on the basis of number of calls attempted or completed. Verification checks to keep interviewers honest were conducted either by local supervisors or the home office.

Today's telephone charges have rendered some of the original procedure obsolete. "Unlimited service" no longer exists for most home subscribers. Furthermore, with many women now in the full-time or part-time work force, recruiting interviewers is more difficult and costs are higher. The paperwork problems of handling payments with present-day governmental requirements is considerable. More significant is the fact that, when centralized interviewing is used, interviewer performance follows prescribed approaches more closely, and yields more uniform results. Setting up central interviewing points utilizing WATS lines makes possible better training, closer supervision, and continuous monitoring, with shortcomings quickly corrected.

Even when a family sample and straightforward interview is involved, different interviewers produce results that differ more than can be expected from sampling variations. This can be due to interviewers deviating from the script or otherwise failing to ask questions according to instructions. Moreover, even when the script is followed, personal mannerisms of speech, diction, accent, and tone of voice may influence responses significantly. One controlled study showed that even on such a basic factor as multiset TV households, supervised interviewers reported a 15 percent higher level than in-home callers.[14]

A similar situation arises in respect to number of dialings employed. In CONTAM Study #4, average television usage was reported as 52.4 when five rings were used (assuming that no answers meant that TV households had the set off). When eight rings are allowed and then another eight rings a minute later, plus other adjustments based on assumptions about no-answers, busies, and refusals (and language problems), households using television (HUT) levels rose 4.4 points (8.4 percent) to 56.8. Higher degrees of effort and use of different assumptions about households giving incomplete information yield higher HUT levels. Even higher television usage was reported when information from follow-up interviews on no-answers, busies, and refusals (and language problems) were included.

### Comparison: ISR and Conventional Coincidental Procedures

The traditional treatment compared to the ISR treatment is shown below:

|  | *ISR* | *Conventional* |
|---|---|---|
| Dialing/Rings | 8 plus 8 | 5–6 |
| No-answers | | |
| TV ownership | Determined by follow-up | Assume same percentage as among cooperators |
| Set use | Determined by follow-up if reached by following day. Otherwise assume same percentage as original no-answers reached by following day. | Assume set off |
| Disconnects | Discarded from sample when found on original or follow-up call | Discarded from sample (original call) |
| Business phones | Discarded from sample when found on original or follow-up call | Discarded from sample (original call) |
| Non TV households | Discarded from sample when found on original or follow-up call | Discarded from sample (original call) |

Busy lines[15]

| | | |
|---|---|---|
| TV ownership | Determined by follow-up | Assume same percentage as among cooperators |
| Set use | Determined by follow-up if reached by following day. Otherwise same percentage as original busies reached on follow-up | Assume same percentage as among cooperators |

Refusals (and language problems)[15]

| | | |
|---|---|---|
| TV ownership | Determined by follow-up. For follow-up refusals use same percentage as among original refusals that cooperated on follow-up | Assume same proportion as among cooperators |
| Set use | Determined by follow-up if reached by following day. Otherwise assume same percentage as original refusals that cooperated on follow-up | Assume same proportion as among cooperators |

The classic assumption of early coincidental proponents that a "no answer" (after 4 to 6 rings) meant no one was at home and thus no listening or viewing has been proven wrong by ISR surveys. In one case, recalls the next day showed that about 5 percent of the "no answers" were indeed occupied households that for various reasons failed to answer the original telephone call (even after 16 rings). About 10 percent of no-answers were, in fact, disconnected telephones and thus out of the sample. This was determined because on a subsequent call an operator indicated that the number was disconnected or a check with the telephone company brought such a reply. Using the normal assumption that a no-answer means a household with no one at home or using TV can therefore reduce rating levels artificially.

### The Sample

One prime asset of the telephone coincidental for many years was the comparative ease of drawing a relatively unbiased sample from the telephone directory. The directory contains a consistent number of names per page, so that the total population represented could be easily determined. In most cases businesses, institutions, and other nonhousehold listings can be identified and omitted at the outset. Using random number tables or a systematic selection of numbers per page can secure an operational sample quickly. The numbers transposed to interviewers' call sheets with space for notations and call results completed the task.

Such telephone samples avoid the cluster problems associated with personal interviews. Adequate geographic distribution within the local call area is assured. (At one time, it cost no more to call someone in a suburb than someone in a downtown apartment.) Limitations stem from phone directories being out of date (so some subscribers are not properly listed) and the large number of unlisted telephone subscribers in recent years. Although the national average for nonlisted is estimated at 20 percent, a much higher ratio prevails in all major markets. In Los Angeles and New York the figure appears to be higher than 40 percent, but exact data are unavailable.

The introduction of random-digit dialing in the ISR coincidental overcame the possible bias introduced by growing numbers of unlisted telephone house-holds. This extension of the sample frame represented a major breakthrough. However, the true probability aspect of RDD sampling has been lost by improperly characterized "random-digit type samples." These utilize telephone directory numbers to which some uniform digit is added: 1 or 5, for example. This, of course, produces a sample with some unlisted households, although the proba-bility is determined by the listed households. Therefore, new exchanges or new number blocks (not appearing in the directory) would have no chance of inclusion, and thus true probability is destroyed.

### Operational Procedure

Conventional coincidentals are set up and run off in many instances with little care and attention to detail. The lack of call-backs (as associated with ISR coincidentals) means that many assumptions must be made about no-answers, busies, and refusals. For example CONTAM, reporting on a series of three studies in 1969 and 1970, calculated the proportion of calls requiring assumptions to vary from 31 to 45 percent when simulated conventional coincidental practices were employed, whereas the carefully done ISR coincidental necessitated assumptions in only 8 to 10 percent of all calls after the intensive call-backs that produced hard information.

The flexibility as to date, time period, and area to be covered, plus the speed with which special surveys can be mounted, represent unique advantages for the telephone coincidental. Results can be quickly called in from the field (or handled under centralized interviewing). Thus, they can be made available to the user within hours—faster even than by meters.

The single most important factor affecting audience estimates is the effort expended in contacting designated sample telephone numbers. The fewer assump-tions needed, the more data obtained directly from sample households, the more accurate the estimates are likely to be. Moreover, better procedures tend to raise ratings over those produced by sloppy methods, which may overlook audience.

## Summary:    Conventional Telephone Coincidental

The telephone coincidental as conventionally carried out employing the latest telephone directory has many virtues as a technique for measuring radio, television, and cable audience.

### STRENGTHS

- It can be focused on a single program or block of programs.
- It can be set up quickly with results reported speedily.
- Cooperation rate is relatively high.
- Accuracy of data is superior because no memory factor is involved.
- Demographic data can be obtained.
- A relatively unbiased sample of listed telephone households can be readily drawn.
- Nonresponse is relatively low.
- The sample can be tailored to cover an area on a nonclustered basis.
- Limited training and supervision are required to reach minimum performance standards.
- Overall expense may be less than other alternatives because measurement can be targeted to specific programs, time periods, or areas.
- Repeat surveys for trend analysis can be established on any meaningful schedule for specific time periods or programs.

### WEAKNESSES

- Does not cover nonlisted telephone households—a major factor in large markets or where ethnic audiences are significant. (Of course, this deficiency can be corrected by using more expensive random-digit dialing.)
- Ratings figures are not generally projectable to the entire numerical coverage areas of stations or networks.
- It produces only average-minute data; no cumulative numbers are possible.
- It cannot cover periods from 10:30 P.M. to 7:30 A.M.
- It covers only in-home audience behavior.
- It is relatively costly on a per-measured-unit basis.

Overall, the conventional telephone coincidental stacks up well. It has a built-in flexibility not associated with meters, diaries, or recall surveys. Its greatest virtue is its ability to track trends over time on a ratings or share basis. It can be improved in quality by add-ons such as RDD, additional rings, and follow-up of no-answers and busies to reduce inaccurate assumptions. It has proved especially useful as a means of measuring audiences for cable-originated programs in local franchise areas for specific time periods.

## The Telephone Recall

The telephone recall, the forerunner of all ratings techniques, was first launched in 1930 by Archibald Crossley for the pioneer Cooperative Analysis of Broadcasting (and abandoned in 1944 in favor of coincidental telephone interviewing). Except for a brief unsuccessful effort by Albert Sindlinger in 1961–62 the telephone recall has not been used for television. In 1962 Sindlinger switched to radio with a syndicated network service lasting five years. In the past decade, this methodology has come to the fore from time to time under various names, including Mediastat, Burke (1978–1979), and TRAC 7 (1977–1978). The latest telephone recall proponent is Birch, a Miami-based company that has developed an ongoing monthly radio service in a large number of markets. (See Chapter 2 for details of these services.)

Basically, telephone recall surveys involve a telephone interview in which the respondent is asked to recall all radio listening (or television viewing) yesterday or for 24 hours preceding the call. On occasion, telephone recall data are used to supplement coincidental results (after 10:30 P.M. and before 7:30 A.M.) or diaries (for ethnic groups). Many mutations of the methodology are possible; in the following examination of the essential details we outline only several typical examples.

### The Instrument

The original CAB daily recall questionnaire asked for information about:

- The hours during which the radio set was in use the previous day.
- The programs that were heard during those hours.
- The station from which the programs were broadcast.
- Who was listening.

The Birch Report in 1984 was using a five-page questionnaire.

### Collection Procedures

Recall interviewing requires broader skills than coincidentals, where memory is not a factor. The average interview may last 10 minutes (compared with one or two for a coincidental), so greater effort is necessary to maintain respondent interest and to minimize nonresponse. Probing is crucial to jog the interviewee's memory. On the other hand, it cannot prompt or suggest listening behavior, programs, or stations by name. Biasing comments by interviewers should not be tolerated but are difficult to control except in centralized interviewing.

Usually the respondent is followed through the day on the basis of his or her personal activity: rising, dressing, eating, commuting, shopping, etc., to determine when he or she might have been exposed to radio—not necessarily the respondent's own. Then, more detailed probing concerns stations heard—which are often identified by call letters, frequency, program, personality, on-air slogan, or type of format. By carefully reviewing the person's daily route step by step, the previous day's listening pattern is constructed.

Recently, telephone recall surveys have been attempting to secure weekly cumulative data by adding questions such as: What other stations have you heard for at least five minutes during the past seven days? Any others? Information secured in this fashion would appear to have extremely limited validity and questionable value. Until properly conducted validation studies can be produced to support such procedures, cumulative figures derived in this manner must bear a large question mark. An ingenious approach to solving the cumulative problem was adopted by Birch in 1984. In some recall interviews, data for two days are secured. This is then extrapolated to a weekly basis predicated on relationships determined from test diary studies. This approach has not been widely accepted by the research community, pending further validation and testing.

## The Sample

The same initial sample considerations applicable to the telephone coincidental apply to the telephone recall. Most studies utilize the directory list directly or modify it somewhat to bring nonlisted homes into the sample. Random-digit dialing could be used but would add to cost and probably reduce cooperation rate. In contrast to the early CAB concern with radio household measurement, all recent uses of telephone recall have measured individual listening. The methods used to select the household member to be interviewed vary widely and create significant opportunity for bias. The simplest approach is to talk to the person who answers the phone. This is guaranteed to overrepresent teens and undersample men. Since men are the most difficult to reach, Sindlinger had interviewers always ask for a male if one was at home. A more acceptable approach is to (1) prelist all family members from oldest to youngest (within the age brackets to be surveyed, (2) arrange a satisfactory time to call that person back if he/she is not at home.

A more troublesome problem related to recall samples is how to handle no-answers. In many cases, such nonresponse is ignored and other replacement households are called. It is hardly likely that the replacement is like the originally designated household in most respects. Difficult-to-reach households are generally (1) smaller, with fewer young children, (2) more affluent (more people working, more cars, etc.), and (3) younger (more mobile). Properly representing these population elements requires repeated call-backs on the initial day and later (but to obtain data for the original interview day).

Efforts to overcome this deficiency in the recall method have been only marginally successful at best. Whereas the nature of the coincidental enables certain assumptions to be made about no-answers, that is not possible with recall; the household or person unreachable today could have been in yesterday's audience that you are measuring. The likelihood on the average is that ignoring no-answers will eliminate the more "not at home" people and produce an upward bias in ratings.

### Operational Procedures

As a substantially more complex methodology than the coincidental, the telephone recall increases the need for care and quality control. Interviewer instructions and training are more demanding. Administration and recording of selection of individuals and call-back attempts require more exacting monitoring and paperwork.

Once completed interviews reach the tabulating center, a series of questions arises to plague the data processors. Interviewer handwriting may be indecipherable, station identifications may be obscure or contradictory, some interviews may be incomplete. In only a few cases is it possible to recontact the interviewer, who is a contract worker. Manuals and editors must be consulted. Arbitrary rules and decisions prevail.

Unless interviewing is supervised and monitored from central call locations, there is a need for a significant level (5 to 10 percent) of verification of field interviews. This is to protect against both fraud and sloppiness. It should focus on interviewer manner and efficiency as well as on the substance being reported and recorded.

### Summary: The Telephone Recall

The telephone recall methodology, despite major deficiencies in its sample base and memory loss problems, seems destined to play a continuing role in radio audience measurement. In a greatly revised and improved form, RADAR employs telephone recall, but that improved technique is described separately in the following section. The strengths and weaknesses of the conventional telephone recall are as follows:

**STRENGTHS**
- It provides out-of-home as well as in-home listening or viewing.
- It produces data at a relatively low cost per unit.
- A relatively unbiased sample of listed telephone households can be drawn readily.
- The sample can be drawn on a nonclustered basis and tailored to cover a specific area.
- It can cover all parts of each day surveyed (including early morning and late night).

**WEAKNESSES**

- It is heavily dependent for accuracy on respondent's memory.
- There is no satisfactory way to deal with nonresponse, therefore it raises serious questions about possible bias toward overstating listening/viewing.
- It does not cover nonlisted homes (a deficiency that can be overcome by random-digit dialing, at greater expense).
- It produces no acceptable weekly cumulative data.

## RADAR (Radio's All Dimension Audience Research)

In Chapter 2 we traced the development of RADAR, which has been the industry-accepted radio network service since 1967. Dr. Gerald Glasser served as statistical consultant for the network committee that patterned this syndicated survey on the earlier CRAM survey, pioneered by NBC. After Statistical Research Inc. (SRI) was organized by Glasser and Gale Metzger in early 1969, this firm played an increasing role in producing RADAR surveys. Its first contribution was to introduce random-digit dialing (RDD) in August 1969, and by 1972 SRI had taken over all RADAR planning and production functions.

The national networks had three major goals in their development of RADAR, a telephone recall survey that (1) eliminated the usual nonresponse problems, (2) yielded valid weekly cumulative data, and (3) was truly projectable. RADAR appears to meet those requirements satisfactorily.

### The Instrument

The actual questionnaire used is a booklet, with the first page containing detailed questions about the respondent. This is followed by ruled pages for each day of the week to be completed on the basis of the repeated daily calls for the previous 24 hours of listening.

### Collection Procedure

The first phase is for the interviewer to call the preselected number, determine if it is a household (not a business or institution), and obtain a listing of all household members from oldest to youngest. The person to be part of the sample is then selected by random procedure.

The initial telephone contact with the predesignated person is made by the interviewer a week before the survey period begins. The purpose of this call is for the interviewer to introduce herself or himself, explain the nature of the survey, try to elicit the respondent's cooperation, and determine what is the best time of day for the daily call about radio listening in the previous 24 hours. A premium gift is sent to the respondent immediately. Every effort is made to establish a friendly rapport but at the same time maintain a businesslike relationship.

Daily calls are made at the agreed-on time; each day the interviewer confirms the time for the next day's contact. The interviewer, strictly following the instructions and the questionnaire, starts with the respondent's activity and listening at the time on the preceding day last reported and proceeds by quarter hour.

### The Sample

To preselect sample households, RADAR uses random-digit dialing with a few minor modifications. The first field step is for the interviewer to reach an assigned telephone number. Once that is done, the first screening takes place as follows:

- All businesses, institutions, and other nonhouseholds are discarded.
- Disconnects and nonworking numbers are removed.
- No-answers, busies, refusals, or language problems are designated for follow-up. This follow-up starts immediately and is continued for 72 hours.

In every household reached, the interviewer administers the person-selection process designed to assure probability selection.

### Operational Procedures

All interviewing is centralized in one calling center equipped for monitoring interviewing work without the interviewers' knowledge of when it is being done. Interviewers are all experienced in telephone work and are given two days' training and practice interviewing before working on a survey. The incentive system is well planned; consisting of several phases, it is rigorously implemented to a schedule related to telephone contacts with respondents.

Supervisors carefully monitor interviews, completed work, and assignment sheets to ensure adherence to procedures and standards. Since deviations are quickly detected, they can be readily corrected. In this way editing problems are kept to a minimum.

In a limited number of cases when information for one or two days is missing (usually the last two days of the week), SRI uses ascription methods to complete the weekly record for tabulation.

### Summary: RADAR

As conducted by Statistical Research Inc., RADAR is a quality operation in all steps, especially as compared with conventional telephone recall surveys. Nevertheless, it is not without its limitations. Those relative to slow delivery of data are due to be relieved by client computer access via RADAR ON LINE.)

**STRENGTHS**
- RADAR approaches true probability samples closer than any other measurement of individual media exposure.

- Its completion rate of 70 percent plus is the highest of any syndicated rating service.
- RADAR interviews 48 weeks a year.
- Its valid weekly cumulative radio listening data are produced for each respondent.
- Network lineup information is employed to provide accurate program and commercial audiences.
- Out-of-home listening is probably reported relatively well.
- A high degree of centralized control assures quality procedures throughout.

### WEAKNESSES
- Memory loss can still be a factor, even with expert probing.
- Conditioning of respondents is possible. With a clear knowledge that his/ her listening will be reported and recorded each day, the respondent could be influenced unconsciously, possibly in the direction of more or different listening than might otherwise occur.
- Reports are relatively slow in delivery (3 months following interviewing close).
- Only two reports yearly, each combining the most recent 48 weeks of interviewing.
- It is very expensive per unit of measured listening.

## Weekly TV Household Diary (Closed End)

The TV household diary, a self-administered record of viewing by household members, is the most widely employed survey method in commercial research. It is used by both Arbitron and Nielsen (NSI) for all local market reports, even those with meter services. Approximately one million such diaries are tabulated by the two services annually, and a total of 2000 individual-market, four-week reports are sent to subscribers. Inasmuch as the response rate averages about 45 to 50 percent, this means that well over two million weekly TV household diaries are mailed annually. The diaries used are "closed end," having horizontal rulings to indicate every quarter hour throughout each day of the week covered. ("Open-end" diaries are unruled.)

### The Instrument

The basic elements of a weekly diary are these: (1) an easily understood explanation of how to keep the diary, what to record immediately and what to record as viewing takes place during the survey week; (2) certain classification data about the household, family members, county of residence, number of TV sets, cable status, etc.; (3) blank pages ruled to provide space for entry of program name, channel number, and call letters for viewing during the week; and (4) numbered columns in which to indicate what household members watched each program entered.

### Collection Procedures

Sample households are called two weeks in advance by service interviewers, and strong efforts are made to gain consent of the respondent to become a diary keeper for a week. At this time, the interviewer determines the number of TV sets in the household and tells the respondent that a diary will be sent for each set and that it is to remain with the set so that any member can readily enter viewing data. Even viewing by visitors should be recorded.

Diaries are mailed to sample homes by first-class mail one week before the start of the survey week. All sample homes receive diaries, even those that initially refused to cooperate. Experience shows that on average about 30 percent of these initial nonresponse households will then cooperate and complete diaries. Overall response quality is improved—at least minimally—by this contribution.

A token payment, conventionally $1 per diary, goes out with the mailing. Usually a telephone call is made the day before the diary week starts, to make certain the diaries arrived, to answer any question respondent may have, and to alert the household to the task ahead. Another call is generally made midweek of the diary-keeping period to answer questions and to remind the household to see the diary-keeping through to conclusion. At week's end the diary becomes a postage-paid self-mailer that is easy to post. Diary weeks start on Wednesday (Arbitron) or Thursday (Nielsen).

### The Sample

For many years, diary samples were drawn like telephone coincidental and recall survey samples—from telephone directories (or from telephone lists computerized by Metromail for mailing-list purposes). With the advent of random-digit dialing (RDD), however, both Nielsen and Arbitron moved to introduce this new technique, especially in areas of heavy ethnic concentration shown to be high in unlisted telephones. Today, Nielsen NSI and Arbitron use a form of RDD in all sample areas.

Because with RDD the interviewer must call numbers rather than names from directories, and because unlisted households are by definition normally trying to avoid unwanted phone calls, the introduction of RDD procedures has brought somewhat lowered cooperation rates. The difference in average cooperation rates between listed and qualified unlisted households is about 8 percentage points. (NSI in July 1981 showed 50 percent versus 42 percent).

### Operational Procedures

Although diary systems are self-administered by viewers, to a great degree their success depends on the skill and persuasiveness of the interviewer, the form and amount of incentive provided, and the ease of filling out and mailing the diary. Both services constantly work on these elements, testing new variants, in order to offset a gradual decline in cooperation generally experienced in public opinion and market research surveys.

One major difference between services is that Nielsen interviewers operate from five call-out centers where uniform training and supervision is possible. Arbitron handles about 17 percent of its interviewing from a central location, but the remainder is done by a widespread field staff working from home. A high degree of verification is therefore necessary with the latter group.

Another variation between Arbitron and Nielsen is in the weighting procedures they employ. Arbitron first stratifies on broad geography (metropolitan area, area of dominant influence (ADI), and total station area), then sample balances on households and demographics separately. Nielsen uses 17 demographic categories for NSI weighting. Both use race, county, and some form of cable cells.

Each market report is a composite of four consecutive individual diary weeks. Four national four-week sweeps when all markets are surveyed simultaneously are scheduled in October–November, January–February, April–May, and July. Report delivery takes place about four weeks after the end of the survey period.

## Summary: Weekly TV Household Diary (Closed End)

As the workhorse of television ratings, the closed-end household diary has important advantages and disadvantages.

### STRENGTHS

- It is relatively inexpensive in terms of the scope and volume of data produced on household and demographic group viewing. (Respondent does the recording, mails the diary back, saving interviewer costs.)
- It provides many demographic breakouts as well as household data.
- It provides average quarter-hour and various other day-part combinations, 6:00 A.M.–midnight up to weekly cumulatives derived from the same source.
- There are significant geographic breaks produced—metropolitan, ADI/DMA, total station area.
- Reports are available with sufficient frequency to provide trend data important to many users.
- Diaries are open to inspection by subscribers, thus providing a feedback link unavailable in other methodologies.

### WEAKNESSES

- Failure of respondents to record all in-home viewing produces a possible bias and understatement of audience to certain stations and programs.
- Viewing by children, teens, and young males tends to be underreported.
- Conditioning element plus tendency to report "usual viewing" creates further bias potential.
- Relatively low response rate (40 to 50 percent) indicates possible bias in results: Responders tend to view slightly more than nonresponders, for example.

- Where nonlisted telephones are not included in the sample there is a further risk of biased results because nonlisted households tend to be younger, larger, more mobile, and more frequently at-home, all factors associated with heavy viewing households.
- Serious problems arise in dealing with poorly educated and foreign-born respondents where communication is difficult and response is low. (See the following section on special ethnic procedures now in effect.)
- Respondent fatigue may affect reporting accuracy and response rates the latter part of week.
- The limited number of weeks presently surveyed in sweeps each year (16) invites hyping, the practice of scheduling the best movies and specials and promoting them heavily so that normal ratings numbers may be distorted.

For all household members to keep an accurate record of viewing on several television sets is a challenging task indeed. Clearly, memory will often be called on to ensure completion of viewing in previous periods including accurate entries for all the family members present. Errors of omission and commission are to be expected; for example, viewing in so-called fringe times (5–8 P.M. and after 11 P.M. daily) is generally understated in diary surveys. Respondents will sometimes indicate viewing of regularly scheduled programs even when they have been preempted.

## Nielsen Audience Composition (NAC) Service

When Arthur Nielsen in 1954 faced up to the fact that Audimeter records of household tuning were not meeting the industry's audience measurement needs, he was confronted with a serious dilemma. For many years he had scorned diaries, saying: "The diary technique involves serious and basic inaccuracies."[16]

Therefore, adoption of a straight viewing diary was for him an unacceptable solution to audience composition measurement. His engineering mind required that some mechanism be introduced (1) to jog the laggard record keeper to produce entries on schedule as listening occurred and (2) to measure set usage so that diaries that were seriously deficient in entries could be rejected.

### The Instrument

The Nielsen laboratory created an automatic electrical reminder and verifying device known as the Recordimeter. This instrument was installed in a national panel of households selected by the same sampling and recruitment techniques as the NTI Audimeters. This second panel would periodically keep a weekly diary called an Audilog.

Two devices in tandem comprise the Audilog instrument. The Recordimeter is an electrical device that is attached to a TV receiver and operates when the set is turned on. First, it flashes a light signal (accompanied by a buzzer) every

15 minutes to remind viewers to make entries in the Audilog. (An on-off switch enables panel members to turn off the buzzer but not the light.) Second, it records, on a counter device, the accumulated number of hours of that set's usage (in the same fashion as the odometer on an automobile speedometer). Each day the total set usage reading, as shown by this verifier, is entered in the Audilog.

The Audilog is a closed-end weekly diary similar in form to that used in local market reports, but it needs little data about how to keep the diary or household characteristics (other than changes) because the Audilog keepers are part of an ongoing, personally recruited panel. The principal additional element is provision for the cooperating household to enter the verifier meter numbers for each day of the diary week.

Nielsen believes that the use of Recordimeters significantly improves the quality of demographic data obtained. It provides a reminder to diary keepers to reduce the amount of entries made on a recall basis. Moreover, the presence of the verifier hour count not only provides a basis for rejection of aberrant diaries but also plays an important psychological role in producing more conscientious diary keeping, because the respondent knows of the checking role of the Audilog.

### Collection Procedures

Audilogs are distributed and collected by mail. Nielsen field representatives can, if necessary, make personal calls, and the operations center in Dunedin, Florida, can telephone if problems arise.

### The Sample

Unlike conventional diary surveys, which use one-time-only telephone samples, the NAC Audilog operation is designed to parallel in every way the Nielsen Television Index sample. The sampling process used is described under NTI (Chapter 3) and is not repeated here. Since it is drawn from a probability prelisting, it includes nontelephone as well as telephone homes.

Nielsen reports that approximately 50 percent of the "primary" predesignated households become cooperators. A total of 2500 sample households comprises the NAC at any one time. The average survey reports are based on approximately 800 households. The sample is completely turned over every three years (versus five years for NTI meter households).

### Operational Procedures

As an ongoing panel operation, the NAC survey is administered in much the same manner as the NTI service; in fact, its results are reported as an integral part of that service. The same Nielsen headquarters and field staffs run both surveys.

Each NAC household maintains diary records for 13 weeks, one-third of the total 2500 households comprising each sample used to provide demographic data for 39 weeks.

Any Audilog in which the total amount of viewing reported differs significantly from the set hour count is rejected. Nielsen establishes its own standards for such rejection. A habitual offender in this regard would be removed from the panel and replaced.

NAC data is published as part of NTI pocket piece reports 19 times per year (out of the 24 biweekly reports issued). The NTI meter survey supplies the household rating and share levels; NAC data on audience composition are then applied to the meter-generated audience ratings for each program and time period.

### Summary: Nielsen Audience Composition Service

The Nielsen NAC service is unique among diary services for several reasons. It is supplemental to a meter service (NTI); it employs a patented reminder–verifier—the Recordimeter; it uses a fixed continuing panel; and the sampling is performed on an area probability basis. Its function is not to produce household rating levels but audience composition for viewing households as determined by the NTI Audimeter. Nevertheless, the growing importance of people data makes the NAC service crucial to the Nielsen NTI numbers.

#### STRENGTHS

• The Recordimeter, regardless of its limitations, undoubtedly serves a useful function as a reminder and a verifying device.

• It has a high response rate (89 percent usable for one or more days in 1980-1981).

• The verifying feature results in rejection of Audilogs that overreport or underreport set usage.

• The verification check can be a psychological factor inducing more constant diary keeping.

• The carefully drawn fixed sample is of better quality than can be afforded in one-time-only surveys. It includes nontelephone and nonlisted telephone households.

• The use of an experienced panel assumes better diary keeping than is produced in conventional diary surveys, where poor handwriting, failure to follow instructions, and cryptic entries give headaches to diary editors.

• Use of meter measurement of households as the base for demographic projections from NAC helps to overcome some normal diary deficiencies.

• Adjustment of NAC persons' data to NTI (meter) data is based on viewing households for NTI and NAC, which have persons in specific age/sex categories (whereas local diary/meter projections ignore such distinctions between households).[17]

**WEAKNESSES**

• Some errors in diary recording (based on habitual rather than actual behavior or failure to enter all viewing) are still to be expected even with the Recordimeter.

• Conditioning of respondents is always a possibility, especially when the panel household become "experts" because they are expected to provide completed weekly Audilog records, on time, 13 weeks a year over a three-year period.

• Security against fraudulent practices is always more serious when fixed panels are employed. Respondents can become known to others and also become conscious of the value of their contribution to a small sample.

Unquestionably, NAC serves its purpose well; it overcomes the Audimeter's major deficiency—its inability to provide "people data." NAC's cost is such that after an early introductory use that was abandoned in 1958, it has not been used by Nielsen in local metered markets. Here, conventional diary sample data provide the demographic component to the meter's household members.

## Personal Radio Diary

In contrast to the *closed-end* weekly TV household diary (employing ruled time periods on each daily page), local radio measurement is dominated by the *open-end* personal diary. Arbitron radio service has used this technique since its inception in 1967. From time to time, minor revisions have been introduced in the Arbitron radio diary, but it remains essentially the same research tool originally introduced.

### The Instrument

The diary consists of a 6″ × 3″ booklet designed to be carried by the respondent in pocket or purse, with a page for recording each day's listening. No horizontal time rulings are provided. A respondent writes in his or her listening experience using his or her own hourly designation. Vertical lines try to establish whether listening is done on AM or FM stations, in home or out of home, in the car, or other places.

Instructions ask respondent to list for each entry time listened (on and off) and station (call letters and/or dial position). Classification data requested include sex and age, working status, etc.

### Collection Procedures

Selected diary sample homes are called weeks in advance of survey to enlist cooperation and ascertain how many family members ages 12 and over are at home and eligible to receive diaries. Unlike the practice in television, where diaries are mailed to all sample households including original noncooperators, in radio Arbitron mails diaries only to participating respondents. Since an individual diary must be sent for each household member, there is no way to handle the problem when the initial respondent refuses cooperation. Mailing a random number of diaries would greatly increase the possibility of fraudulent diary entries and returns.

The individual diaries are returned directly to Arbitron in Beltsville, Maryland, where tabulation takes place.

### The Sample

The sample is drawn in the same manner as for Arbitron television. Metromail telephone listings from directories is the basic frame but it is supplemented by RDD in the metropolitan area of major markets in order to bring nonlisted households into the sample. Within each agreeing sample household, a diary is provided for every member 12 and over.

### Operational Procedures

As in the case of its TV operations, Arbitron makes its calls to sample households using interviewers working at home. Only a fraction of such calls emanate from a central location, the Beltsville operations center. Mid week calls are placed to each household to answer questions, to remind diary keepers to keep at it and to mail promptly at week's end. Arbitron's Differential Survey Treatment (DST) procedure calls for $5 payments to all individuals in certain household categories that are traditionally underreported (young black males).

Editing problems for radio are more difficult than for TV. Individual idiosyncrasies in writing and recording show up on a personal diary. Many more radio than TV stations are receivable in a market, and they frequently change call letters, slogans, and formats and sometimes dial positions. Industry committees work closely with Arbitron to aid its efforts to ensure that insofar as possible all legitimately reported listening is tabulated and properly attributed to individual stations.

Following many years of measuring four weeks per survey, as in TV, Arbitron radio, after testing in several markets, went to a 12-week survey period in 1981. Two sweeps per year, spring and fall, are normal.

### Summary: Personal Radio Diary (Open End)

The open-end unstructured personal diary appears to work reasonably well for radio, especially since so much listening (about 40 percent on average, higher for young adults) is done out of the home.

**STRENGTHS**

- The personal diary provides a record of listening in cars, offices, and other work places, restaurants, stores, etc. in addition to the home.

- Direct demographic sample is not tied to household base (except for sample selection purposes).
- Weekly cumulative ratings are provided.
- It is a reasonably inexpensive technique for a difficult measurement job.

### WEAKNESSES

- As in all diary surveys, there is the question of omitted listening and inaccurate entries in a self-administered instrument.
- Response rate is around 40 percent on average but in certain markets dips to rather low levels—occasionally under 30 percent.
- Cooperation among several important audience segments is particularly low. Most serious are adult males under 35, especially blacks and Hispanics. Special procedures are used by Arbitron to handle these problems.
- Editing handwritten entries—call letters, dial positions, and station slogans—is particularly difficult in radio.

Up to now, no higher-quality survey technique affordable by local market radio has come into being.

## Special Diary Procedures

The foregoing discussion of diaries has dealt with present-day standard weekly formats used by existing rating companies. Note, however, that a wide range of surveys has been made with diaries kept by respondents from one day to two weeks. For example, the Radio Audience Measurement (RAM) service in 1976–1978 (see Chapter 2, Section IX) used one-day diaries with radio listening data on the inside double page and other varied questions (product use, record preferences, life-style) on the back. The Television Audience Assessment (TAA) study of 1982 successfully used one-day mail in diaries to collect evening household television viewing records over a two-week period (see Chapter 5). The Simmons Market Research Bureau uses a two-week diary to develop TV viewing data employed as part of the extensive array of annual surveys on magazine audiences and product (service) usage (see Chapter 5).

These various diary procedures have not been subjected to the steady use and rigorous methodological testing associated with weekly television and radio diaries. Results of such tests as have been made have been inconsistent. It is consequently not possible to generalize about strengths and weaknesses. RAM, for example, accepted any one-day record received. TAA required consistent daily mailing if the respondent's diaries were to be tabulated.

Assuming there was equal care taken in sampling and recruiting, we could expect higher response rates and higher costs with daily as compared to weekly diaries. Keeping two-week diaries may reduce cooperation as well as cost per quarter hour of audience data. In the 1965 All-Radio Methodology Study (ARMS, see Appendix D), several forms of daily diary reporting were tested, with disappointing results.

## The Electronic Meter

In Chapter 1, we saw that one of the very first efforts at a measurement instrument for radio audiences was a pioneer meter invented in 1929. The Audimeter, originated in 1934, was taken over in 1936 by Arthur C. Nielsen, Sr. He developed it into a commercial audience measurement tool. The Nielsen Radio Index (NRI) incubated slowly because of the need for refinement in the design of the original instrument to meet actual in-home operating conditions and the problem of manufacturing and installing meters during World War II. By 1949, however, NRI had become the dominant radio rating service because of the wealth of information it could deliver. The Nielsen meter was quickly adapted to television in 1950, and all Nielsen radio service was abandoned in 1964. No meter has been used for radio since that date, nor is one likely to be used considering the nature of today's widely dispersed listening patterns.

As we know, other meters were developed and proposed at various times, but it was not until Arbitron came out with its successful New York instantaneous meter service in 1957 that the Nielsen Company faced the challenge of a competitive and financially viable meter service. Nielsen NSI launched an instantaneous service of its own in New York in 1959. The original Arbitron service was discontinued in 1972 because of technical and sampling problems but was reintroduced with a newly designed meter in 1976.

### The Instrument

When researchers speak of survey "instruments," they rarely envisage anything like the present-day sophisticated instantaneous electronic meters used in TV audience research. Today's instruments cost over $1000 each, not counting wiring, installation, and home office data collection costs. Setting up a local meter service with a sample panel of 300 installed households in a major market involves expenses well beyond $1 million. The general configuration of meters today is similar. It is a far cry from the original Nielsen Audimeter, with which a field man had to call on each sample household every two weeks to pick up the paper tape record and insert a new tape (a procedure later replaced by mailable film cartridges).

### Collection Procedures

Today's meters record time, television set on or off, channel number tuned every minute and transmit the data to a home storage unit. It is stored here until accessed by the central office computer, usually between 2:00 A.M.and 6:00 A.M. on the following day. This necessitates a leased line to the home, which enables the central office computer to dial automatically and switch from home to home in the sample, to aggregate data for ratings results to report to clients.

## The Sample

Sampling is especially important in the meter technique for several reasons. The meter panel is fixed, with annual turnover (planned and random) averaging perhaps 25 percent annually. Many households retain the meter installation for the full five years that current policy considers maximum. Meticulous care in the selection and recruitment is therefore a fundamental necessity. There is no opportunity to correct problem situations as there is when each periodic survey uses a fresh sample.

A second characteristic of meter samples is their relatively small size—300 to 500 in individual market areas. Again, there must be careful, unbiased selection procedures and a minimum of nonresponse. Fortunately, because meters are an expensive methodology, the money (and time) to do first-rate sampling is available. Therefore, nontelephone homes, nonlisted homes, cable TV homes, multiset households, and newly constructed household units (including remodeled units) tend to get proper representation. If this were not so, corrective procedures would be lengthy and expensive. Repeated efforts to recruit predesignated households help Nielsen to keep household cooperation at levels close to 50 percent; Arbitron slightly lower.

Nielsen and Arbitron employ somewhat different approaches to the sampling problem. Arbitron applies greater stratification to various sampling steps and also uses post meter result sample balancing, which Nielsen frowns on.

Nielsen employs a probability sample for national and local meter services based on geographic area representation. For the NTI–NAC national sample, a total of 363 urban counties representing 41 percent of U.S. households are classified as "must counties." The remainder are then stratified in such a manner that a representative sample is selected. Within selected counties, minor civil divisions are similarly stratified so that selections can be made on a probability basis. Then block statistics are employed (with updatings for new construction and demolition of dwelling units). Finally, an enumeration is made by a Nielsen fieldworker of all dwelling units on a preselected block. From this enumeration a random selection calls up the unit to be contacted as the "basic" respondent household. If this household cannot be recruited after several efforts, a local substitution is made. The only control over that substitution is that, in addition to being on the preselected block, the household must match the characteristics of the unrecruited basic household as to child/no child and cable status. If the substitute household later moves, a renewed effort is made to obtain the original "basic"; if unsuccessful, then the new family in the substitute household is targeted.

Several steps are involved in selecting Arbitron's Meter Panel sample. First is the creation of a master (parent sample) to represent all housing units in the ADI. Second is drawing a subset of housing units from the parent sample to form a predesignated sample for recruitment. The third step relates to ongoing maintenance procedures and control of the demographic composition of the installed Meter Panel sample.

The housing units in Arbitron's parent sample are selected by use of the "half-open interval" form of area probability sampling, in which a special sample frame created by Metromail is employed for selecting sample field locations. All housing units have an equal chance of inclusion (regardless of whether they were included in the original Metromail sampling frame). In selecting its sample of field locations, Arbitron uses stratification on eight factors (population density, region, county, cable penetration, ethnic composition, family income, household size, and percent of employed women) to help ensure samples proportionate to population demographics.

Geodemographic stratification is used in the initial sample selections of the Meter Panel. Out of this procedure comes the initial Meter Panel predesignated first sample selections and a series of initially drawn alternative selections. The latter are used when the predesignated selections are uninstallable due to "no TV," "industry connection," "household refusal," etc. For ongoing maintenance (as turnover takes place), the demographic composition of the Meter Panel is controlled to meet target objectives for basic demographic groupings.

As a final step "to minimize biases and random fluctuations in the demographics of the daily in-tab sample," Arbitron uses a poststratification technique called "sample balancing," geared to three factors: region, race, and age of head of the household.

### Operational Procedures

Incentives for household panel members include payment of all legitimate service charges to maintain TV sets in operating condition and various premium gifts for loyal participation in the survey. In some cases periodic newsletters are sent out to make cooperators aware of the significance of their efforts, to reiterate security aspects and to engender a feeling of mutual trust with the rating service.

Some turnover of sample homes occurs from households moving and leaving the sample. Nevertheless, it is standard practice to turn over all sample households every five years. Intricate sample design steps are taken to make these turnover installations on a random basis while trying not to seriously affect trends from the past samples.

Local meter services deliver rating data to Arbitron and Nielsen subscribers by 9 A.M. the day following the broadcast. In the NTI network operation, the national meter results reach subscribers one day later.

Sample households are queried periodically from the central office computer to ensure that the system is in working order. If problems appear, field personnel are dispatched as quickly as possible, and depending on the circumstances the home may be temporarily removed from the sample.

### Summary: The Electronic Meter

The meter, with its freedom from many of the potential human errors associated with other systems, has earned a permanent position in TV audience measurement, for many reasons.

### STRENGTHS

- The wealth of data provided. It records every day minute by minute throughout the year. Every type of measurement unit can be covered: specific minutes, average minute, average quarter hours, and total program audience daily, weekly, or four-week cumulative household ratings.
- Speed of delivery. Rating and share data go to clients in printout form within 24 to 48 hours. Many clients have computerized results sent directly to their own computers.
- Analytic possibilities on a household basis are unlimited: lead-in, lead-out analyses, duplication and unduplicated reach figures for campaigns or flights, etc. Working through a third party (to preserve household anonymity), special analyses can be ordered on the household-by-household level.
- Mechanical reporting eliminates chance of bias or error involved in human recording by either interviewer or in-home cooperator.
- Produces more accurate ratings for independent stations and cable networks.
- Carefully drawn probability sample can produce better representation of nontelephone homes and ethnic groups than what comes from telephone-based samples.
- Furnishes a household base for demographic projections from diary results thus overcoming certain diary weaknesses.

### WEAKNESSES

- The possibility of conditioning in respondent household. Having a meter in your household for five years could have a biasing effect on viewing, however slight or unconscious, on certain family members.
- No data produced on individual viewing. This must be collected by diaries and combined with household meter results, a procedure that preserves many of the weaknesses of diaries as people measurements.
- Expense severely limits sample size. In New York, for example, diary services employ independent samples of 2500 six or eight times a year in the 17-county metropolitan area; meter services use 500 households, which turn over about 25 percent annually.
- Security can be a serious problem. In any continuous panel, the identity of members can become known; efforts to induce fraudulent behavior are not unknown.
- Problems of metering all sets in multiset households sometimes are economically insoluble because of technical and/or practical problems (portables, built-ins, etc.). The two services differ in how such cases are treated.

All factors considered, it must be accepted that the meter methodology offers the most complete information and possibly the closest to accuracy (on items of set usage activity) of any technique in regular use. Its results have been proven in a number of methodology tests to closely approximate those produced by the Industry Sponsored Research coincidentals, the generally accepted standard of evaluation. Since it can be and generally is supplemented by diary-based demographic data adjusted to the meter household base, one of the most serious limitations of the meter can be overcome although with concern for accuracy of persons data. Biases indigenous to the diary (e.g., inadequate representation of young adults and children) may be perpetuated even though HUT levels and station shares shift with the meter. The Nielsen NAC service has long tried to compensate for this. Arbitron has recently instituted a corrective refinement in local metered markets. The respective samples are segmented into three groups on a child and household-head age basis, so that the meter-diary combination can be made separately for each.

### Peoplemeters (See Chapter 11 for recent peoplemeter developments)

This is a device that calls for cooperating panel household members to punch buttons on a control panel to indicate their presence during a broadcast. Each family member has his own numbered button. AGB, Nielsen, and Arbitron all have entries in the field. We do not discuss the peoplemeter in depth here because no conclusions about its efficacy can be presented at this writing. However, it is informative to ponder the following comments of John A. Dimling, then executive director, Electronic Media Rating Council:

> For a people meter to work, however, several conditions must be satisfied: first, the fact that respondents are watching television must be communicated to the electronic system; second, communicating this fact should not change the respondent's viewing behavior from what it would have been if the respondent's viewing was not being measured; third, the first two conditions should be met without reducing response rates to unacceptably low levels. I must confess that since most people meters require some conscious action by respondents whenever the respondent views television, I am a bit skeptical about whether both these conditions can be met over an extended period of time, as they must be if the cost is to be kept in line. I have always felt one clear advantage of the meter was that it required no action by the household, and in fact could be forgotten by members of the household. There is also one additional potential problem with personal meters—if the equipment used to collect data is conspicuous, it may be more difficult to maintain the confidentiality of the sample.[18]

### Personal Roster Recall (Pulse)

The only methodology to be practiced by a single survey service was the aided recall personal interview developed by Pulse in the 1940s. Originally a local radio measurement, Pulse's technique involved an up-to-date roster of all programs scheduled by radio stations in the survey area for the rating period. Pulse interviewers carried these rosters from door to door to aid interviewees in recalling listening for the previous 24 hours.

## The Instrument

In addition to the roster, the Pulse interviewer carried a one-page questionnaire on which to register replies to classification and demographic questions about the household and its members To help prompt respondents' memories, they were interviewed about the previous day's activities along a "time line" that ran from getting up to going to sleep at night. Completed questionnaires were turned in to the supervisor daily.

## Collection Procedures

Pulse by its nature as a personal interview service involved the largest field staff of any rating service. Contract firms were employed on a local or regional basis to recruit, train, and supervise interviewers, originally at about 25¢ per interview.

## The Sample

Drawing and implementing an unbiased personal interview sample with recall questions poses some of the most difficult problems in rating research. Unlike mail or telephone techniques, which can select homes on a completely random and unclustered basis, personal interviews, for economic reasons, demand geographic clustering. Pulse sought about 10 interviews in each cluster. From a statistical standpoint, such samples are less efficient than those that involve no clustering.

Pulse tried several devices for randomly determining the starting point for interviewing in the metropolitan area. One was a transparent grid overlay with etched horizontal and vertical rules. Thus random start points on city maps could be determined by using random grid squares. In later years, Pulse used Metromail (the same organization employed by Arbitron and Nielsen for diary sample names) to select random household addresses from their listed telephone compilation—one number for each cluster. Interviewers were sent to that street address with instructions to start interviewing at the next residence (to the west, east, etc.).

To handle the not-at-home problem, Sydney Roslow adapted a procedure developed by Alfred Politz and W. R. Simmons known as a "nights-at-home" adjustment.[19] The principle asserts that there is a differential probability of a household being at home on any given evening. Therefore, respondents were asked how many evenings they had been at home during the previous week. On the basis of this response, weighting was assigned to the interview: the once-a-week household was weighted seven times the value of the every-night-at-homer (because he or she represented six others not contacted whereas interviewers would always catch one of the latter group). Others received weights commensurate with their response. Although not a perfect solution, at least Pulse recognized the problem and by nights-at-home adjustment compensated for a serious sample bias in recall surveys.

## Operational Procedures

The principal operational problem associated with the personal interview method is the element of control. Of all techniques, this is the one in which results are most likely to be affected by interviewer performance and where deviations are most difficult to detect. Personal interviewers pounding the pavement in all kinds of weather, ringing doorbells, and cajoling busy respondents, have a very difficult task. They often must enter neighborhoods that are possibly unsafe, especially after dark. They must be trained to follow the household selection plan strictly and to interview all family members if possible, avoiding any leading or biasing comments or actions. A friendly but businesslike approach is needed if the interviewer is to complete quotas without influencing the respondents.

Verifying the interviewer's work is imperative, because the pressures and hazards of the work can induce fraudulent questionnaire completion and other forms of "cheating." Pulse required 20 percent verification by local supervisors, followed by verification calls from the main office in New York.

Bad weather and illness can frequently delay interviewers' work. In cases where fieldwork was rejected because of poorly completed questionnaires or suspected cheating, resurveys required extra time. As a result, Pulse reports often covered days or weeks following those originally scheduled and were frequently delivered late.

By its nature, the personal interview approach is somewhat cumbersome and time consuming. To systematize the flow of data and computations, Pulse, a relatively small organization, found it economical to spread the work over the year rather than measure only in sweep periods.

## Summary: Personal Roster Recall

The personal roster (interview-aided) recall ratings technique lived and died with Pulse. Some radio broadcasters still mourn the passing of this bulwark service of the 1960s, but a review of its strengths and weaknesses may show why it expired. The method had achieved good marks in the ARMS Methodological Study of 1965 (see Appendix D), but the increase in number of stations and the changes in listening patterns created new problems. Greater emphasis on cumulative data and intensified field survey problems put Pulse at a disadvantage relative to Arbitron's personal diary technique.

### STRENGTHS

- Sample includes all households, including listed and unlisted telephone subscribers and nontelephone.
- Personal contact may improve rapport and encourage conscientious reporting.
- Presence of family members together can help each person's recall of the previous day's behavioral and listening patterns. Language problems are overcome because younger members usually speak English.

WEAKNESSES

- Sampling involves clustering, which reduces statistical efficiency of the survey.
- Subcontracting to local research firms gives little home office control over interviewer selection or training.
- Interviewer control and security against cheating and shortcuts are difficult to maintain because of their large numbers and geographical dispersion.
- Difficult field conditions such as heavy rain and snow, off-limits luxury apartments, dangerous high-crime urban neighborhoods create problems in sample completion on schedule, or at all.
- The nights-at-home adjustment does not completely offset the possible bias created by nonresponse of not-at-homes.
- There is greater possibility that interviewing in a face-to-face situation may influence or bias results because of interviewer's sex, dress, manner, speech, race etc., than in telephone surveys.
- Weekly cumulative ratings were based on questions about "other stations listened to" and are unlikely to be very accurate.
- The degree of memory aid in a station roster is probably of small account; reporting errors due to memory factors could be large.

## Personal Interview—Coincidental

Although George Gallup experimented with the personal coincidental procedure at Drake University in 1928, its use by national or local syndicated services has been extremely limited.

In 1958, as reported in Chapter 3, the Telephone-Personal Interview (TPI) service conducted surveys in three cities using a combination of telephone and personal coincidentals. Results were somewhat inconsistent. Although the propounder of the method, Miles Wallach, insisted that the results proved that any diary results exaggerated TV viewing levels, the service received no advertiser support after the pilot studies.

One national media service employed personal interview coincidentals in a survey of major consumer advertising media. In 1966, Politz Media Service (PMS) measured issue audience and advertising-page exposure for 12 major magazines. In addition, that survey also determined "average minute" household usage of television on a coincidental basis at the start of the interview. The 1966 PMS study employed a rigorous probability sampling design, with tightly controlled interviewing. A U.S. cross-sectional sample was designated for interviewing on each of the 56 consecutive survey days. Interviewer visits to respondent households were randomly timed within specified interviewing hours.[21]

Between November 1969 and 1979, Clapp and Mayne, a market research firm in San Juan, Puerto Rico, conducted a personal coincidental study of TV viewing there. Known as the Television Audience Profile, this service measured television audiences throughout the island for its initial sponsor, WAPA TV,

Channel 4. A sample quota system ensured that geographical dispersion was matched for each half-hour period. Interviewers' starting points and routes were specified in advance. Surveys were conducted over a four-week period four times each year. Personal coincidental samples totaled from 50,000 (at the beginning) to 30,000 (at the end, when costs necessitated reductions). Ratings and projections were provided for households and normal age-sex breakdowns. The service was discontinued because stations were unhappy with the variability in figures from one half hour to another, a result of the relatively small samples affordable.[22]

### Summary: Personal Interview—Coincidental

Inasmuch as the personal interview coincidental method has been used only in limited studies and has never been subjected to the rigorous investigations and comparative studies accorded more widely used techniques, there is little to say about its pros and cons. Many of the strengths and weaknesses of telephone coincidentals would apply, except that:

- Personal coincidental surveys cannot be set up as flexibly.
- Sampling and training/supervising a field staff become much more difficult.
- Sampling must be of a cluster type, losing efficiency.
- Costs are significantly higher.
- Response rates may be lower because people shy away from talking (or even opening doors) to strangers.

Its principal advantage over telephone coincidentals is that it covers non-telephone households. In low telephone penetration areas (which in some cases are low labor cost regions), it may be viable and considerably more representative.

## Cost Factors

Cost is a major consideration in determining what methodology to use in a syndicated rating service. The service, to be viable, has to be reasonably structured so that users will pay enough to meet overall expenses. Evaluating cost elements for various methodologies includes the following considerations:

1. Costs for individual methodologies may vary widely depending on quality (control, verification, interviewing training and standards, etc.), editing and computing efficiency, overhead allocation, response rate, and the like.

2. Costs (and cost relationships) change over time. New and more complex meters may be needed to handle cable and VCRs; postage or telephone rates may change drastically.

3. Much depends on whether daily, weekly, monthly, quarterly, or semiannual reports are specified, and in what detail, by program hours, geographic

areas, demographic breaks, etc. Are computer tapes to be furnished with on-line access for special tabulations? Is out-of-home as well as in-home activity to be measured?

4. Existing services (like Detroit automakers) guard many details of their cost structure from the prying eyes of competitors and clients.

Variations over five to one have been noted in bids on specific rating projects, the differences being accounted for by such factors as specially trained interviewers versus straight subcontracting of fieldwork; centralized and supervised interviewing using WATS lines versus local independent interviewers working from homes; follow-up interviews, mailings, and enhanced incentives versus limited contact and payment to respondents; and use of preprepared diary forms that respondents can answer by filling in boxes versus writing-in listening or viewing data.

We have seen that the coincidental telephone method, which reigned supreme for a decade, is no longer a viable technique for syndicated services. There are historical reasons for this. When C. E. Hooper started in 1934, and throughout the heyday of his successful service, there were no telephone charges to be paid. Interviewers were housewives calling from their home phones, which had telephone company "unlimited service" for local areas. The interviewer did her own sampling by using a systematic skip interval throughout the local directory. No significant nonlisted problem existed. With only five questions asked, no special training was required. Interviewers mailed in simple tabulations of their interview results on a daily basis.

Only one week a month was studied and only a limited number of time periods—nothing before 10:00 A.M. or after 11:00 P.M. (EST). Interviews were limited to 36 metropolitan areas; results were not projectable—they were a comparative index of listening behavior.

To exist today, such a service should have (1) supervised centralized interviewing, (2) use of WATS lines to call throughout the United States, (3) a sampling design based on random-digit dialing to include unlisted numbers, (4) an acceptable method to apportion busies and nonresponses, and (5) a computer program to produce projected houehold and people data. The deficiencies relative to hourly restrictions, out-of-home listening, and any cumulative data (on the quarter hour, hour, day, or week), while unimportant in the 1930s, would make such a service completely uncompetitive today not only in terms of costs but also utility.

In looking at meters, we would expect cost factors to vary as Nielsen went from personal tape pickup to mailable film cartridges to the SIA on-line instantaneous system using leased telephone lines. Now AGB maintains that leased lines may not be necessary for its meters. If so, meter service economics will be drastically altered.

One generality is that there can be good (and expensive) or poor (and cheap) implementation of any methodology. The differences within a given technique's execution can be as great as those between methodologies. Another consideration is that weekly diary techniques have built-in efficiencies because each can provide much raw data recorded by the respondent. It would take many telephone calls to collect the same information using either coincidental or day-after recall. Moreover, neither of those provides the acceptable weekly cumulative figures widely used today.

## Conclusion

There is no perfect or ideal way to measure electronic media audiences, nor will there ever be. In addition to methodological considerations, factors such as frequency, continuity, sample size, market coverage, and delivery speed also must be considered in designing a syndicated service. Techniques such as the meter are not useful in radio with its vast out-of-home audience component. The telephone coincidental has value for radio and cable for special purposes but shares the in-household limitations of the meter.

Any technique may be done well or done badly. One meter service or one diary service may be superior to its competitors because of rigorous quality controls and careful execution of every step in the process. Nevertheless, from a practical standpoint, one must consider the performance of various services pragmatically. Improvements in meter and diary measurement have been made by both major services. Competition forces each to match the other's advances. Since they compete successfully side by side, we feel justified in evaluating them on the basis of "the state of the art."

The number of subscribers who will share the cost is a major element in a service's success. For example, Nielsen can look to many prospects to purchase the NTI national reports: networks, agencies, national advertisers, film and program producers, buying services, industry organizations, and groups involved in advertising, lobbying, and dealing with broadcast networks. Contrast that potential with a rating service designed to serve a cable system in a single franchise area. There is only one cable operator to pay the bill; local advertisers are unlikely to share costs. This means that the financial means for quality measurement is available for a syndicated national network service whereas the financial returns a rating service can expect from local cable will be minuscule for years to come. There is no escaping the realities of the marketplace, which can often be as decisive as methodology can.

All techniques are tools for the professional research analyst. What is necessary is to recognize that audience measurement is a complex, sophisticated field of consumer research, which must be in the hands of properly trained professionals. Only they can ensure that a reasonable qualitative level is appreciated and demanded.

## NOTES

1. CAB could deal with telephone no-answers only by excluding them (and consequent substitution). Hooper assumed a no-answer meant that no one was listening, that no one was believed to be at home at the time of the call. Also, CAB measured total audience, which was, by definition, larger than the coincidental's average audience.

2. New York Stations Ratings Committee and the Committee on Local Television and Radio Measurement (COLTRAM). See Appendix D for a digest of these studies, especially "How Good Is the Television Diary Technique?" a study conducted for COLTRAM by Statistical Research, Inc. in 1975.

3. The Electronic Media Rating Council (EMRC), for example, does not accredit companies or methodologies. Each individual service must be separately accredited and audited; Nielsen has four and Arbitron three with EMRC accreditation. Each also has nonaccredited services.

4. The Radio Advertising Bureau Goals Committee has experimented with diaries to produce four-week cumulative data.

5. Martin Mayer, *"The Intelligent Man's Guide to Broadcast Ratings"* (New York: Advertising Research Foundation, 1962).

6. *Standard Definitions of Broadcast Research Terms* (National Association of Broadcasters, Washington, D.C., 1970).

7. The expected variability range for a rating of 21 would be from 19 to 23 in 67 percent of such samples; in 33 percent, the rating would probably be below 19 or above 23. There is a 95 percent probability that the sample value would fall between 17 and 25. See Appendix D, CONTAM study no. 1, for further details on sample error.

8. Gale D. Metzger, president, Statistical Research, Inc., "A Plea to End Sloppy Research," *Advertising Age,* October 26, 1981, p. 52.

9. *A Study of Television Usage in the New York Metropolitan Area* (Westfield N.J.: Statistical Research, Inc., May 1971), p. 23.

10. "How Good Are Television Ratings? (continued . . . .)", report on a special CONTAM study (no. 4) conducted in April 1969 and presented at the Advertising Research Foundation annual conference, October 14, 1969.

11. These include: Did coincidental interviewer make two attempts on no-answers and busies? Did they go through operator on nonconnects? Were changed numbers in same code area called immediately?

12. The three preceding paragraphs are based largely on the Technical Appendix of "How Good Is the Television Diary Technique?" a study conducted by Statistical Research, Inc. in consultation with COLTRAM and published by the National Association of Broadcasters, Washington, D.C., fall, 1976.

13. Matthew N. Chappell and C. E. Hooper, *Radio Audience Measurement* (New York: Stephen Daye, 1944), p. 65.
14. "How Good Are Television Ratings? (continued . . .)", October 14, 1969.
15. Dr. Lawrence Myers, professor of broadcasting, S. I. Newhouse School of Public Communications, Syracuse University, in comments to the author dated April 29, 1984, expressed his professional opinion that busies and refusals should be handled like disconnects and discarded. Industry research practitioners do not agree.
16. Arthur C. Nielsen, *Television Audience Research for Great Britain* (Chicago, Ill.: A. C. Nielsen Company Limited (Oxford), 1955), p. 73.
17. In 1984 Arbitron introduced for its metered markets a somewhat refined method of "marrying" diary demographics to household data.
18. John A. Dimling, "Why Existing Methodologies?" Researching the Electronic Media II, Advertising Research Foundation Key Issues Workshop, December 15, 1983.
19. Alfred Politz and Willard Simmons, "An Attempt to Get the 'Not at Homes' into the Sample Without Callbacks," *Journal of American Statistical Association*, XLIV, 1944, p. 10.
20. See Albert Blankenship, *Professional Telephone Surveys* (New York: McGraw-Hill, 1979). Blankenship's summary of the telephone's advantages over personal interviews includes (1) higher completion rates, (2) complete avoidance of the Green River ordinance (the need for a permit or license), (3) greater level of cooperation, (4) dispersed samples, (5) high interviewing accuracy, (6) decrease in interviewer bias, (7) increased interviewer morale, (8) virtual elimination of cheating, (9) proper selection of respondents, and (10) no third-party (family member) influence.
21. This description comes from "Electronic Test of In-Home TV Viewing among Those Families Who Fail to Respond to the Doorbell," Advertising Research Foundation Arrowhead Study No. 8, 1968.
22. This account of the Television Audience Profile was provided the author by Ms. Jackie Da Costa in a personal interview on July 6, 1984. Ms. Da Costa, while senior vice president at the Ted Bates agency, New York, acted as consultant to Clapp and Mayne in designing the TAP project in Puerto Rico.

# 5

# Qualitative Versus
# Quantitative Ratings

## I. INTRODUCTION

A frequently expressed criticism of broadcast ratings is that they are quantitative and not qualitative. Ratings are limited to reporting binary (yes/no) set user actions: (1) electing to turn on a receiver and (2) choosing (or not choosing) any one of many programs available by a flick of the tuning dial (or the push of a button). Such crude data may suffice for the advertiser's commercial purposes, but it is hardly the basis on which intelligent decisions about programming can be made, according to the detractors of ratings. This complaint is most often heard when network programs are canceled despite the existence of a highly articulate group of fans as with "Twilight Zone" and "Star Trek." Some in public TV likewise maintain that commercial rating measurement is not sufficient for its needs, that audience size alone is an inadequate evaluation of whether public television is reaching its more exacting programming objectives.

There are several complexities to the concept of qualitative ratings that are not found in conventional audience size measurements. Quantitative measurement is relatively simple and clear: The numbers—whether household or demographic ratings or share of audience projections, national or local—are developed by syndicated services using standardized and readily understood terms. When told that "Hill Street Blues" on Thursday at 10:00 P.M. last week achieved a share of 29.5 nationally, 22.6 in Philadelphia, and 31.8 in San Francisco, the meaning is clear (and even more so when trends of all available weekly shares are followed).

Moreover, broadcast quantitative measurements report (as accurately as the technique permits) the *actual viewing behavior* of the household or person in the sample. The meter, the diary, and the telephone coincidental or recall all seek this goal: an objective recording of what took place. And the survey data are reasonably projectable to known total population estimates.

Once we move into the qualitative field, the researcher often must rely on verbalizations of people's attitudes and opinions. There are no single, well-understood standards of quality that are universally accepted. Even those who have devoted most effort to this area are far from agreement as to the meaning of "qualitative."

Nevertheless, qualitative ratings have been getting more attention in recent years and may be about to become a significant supplement to quantitative ratings. In the past they have had their ups and downs, and the prognosis for the current crop of services is by no means all positive. Some will indubitably fail while others may merge. However, there seems now to be sufficient market interest on the part of stations and agencies and advertisers to warrant a modest growth in the near future. The emergence of cable and other new video media, with emphasis on "narrowcasting"—programming to selective audiences—is likely to further stimulate growth of certain forms of qualitative measurement.

Foundations, academics, media critics, and many in public television believe that the quantitative services used in commercial TV are seriously deficient in defining audience reaction. As a result, there has emerged a substantial push to initiate some form of syndicated qualitative ratings.

The notion that head counting should be supplemented by qualitative data is far from new. In the 1950's, Nielsen unsuccessfully tried to launch a product-use adjunct to the Nielsen Radio Index national meter panel service. Arbitron (then the American Research Bureau) included product use data for 15 categories along with its ratings between 1967 and 1971. This feature was eliminated because of subscriber resistance, which resulted from their belief that more time consuming diary keeping (1) lowered respondent cooperation levels and (2) reduced the accuracy of viewing response data. An industry-sponsored research study by Statistical Research, Inc. (SRI) concluded that, as a buying guide, diary-produced demographic data were probably more useful than product use information.

Frequently overlooked is the fact that a national syndicated qualitative rating service has existed since 1958. TVQ, a mail survey of a 1500 sample of U.S. TV households, publishes seven reports annually, giving viewers' assessment of programs on a "liking" scale. In 1979, Roger Percy's Vox Box service was established to provide many detailed analyses of viewers' reactions to programs and commercials, but has had little industry acceptance.

The recent trend has been to develop ongoing syndicated qualitative services that would roughly parallel Arbitron and Nielsen network and local rating report books. Thus far there is minimal evidence that the marketplace will support such services outside of a few top markets. Of the present contenders, those with the best chance to succeed are services ancillary to existing audience data operations.

The keen interest of cable program services in qualitative measures promises some support from the new video medium.

## Defining "Qualitative"

A major stumbling block in discussing qualitative ratings is that there is little unanimity among advocates on what to measure. Even those most interested in this area are far from agreement as to what "qualitative" means. Do they want to measure: the quality of the program, the degree of satisfaction or involvement it creates, or the quality of the audience reached (in relation to a selected audience target)?

In 1980, the Corporation for Public Broadcasting, which has in recent years pioneered in this field, concluded:

> Unfortunately, the principal proponents of qualitative television ratings (qualitative research providers, media reform groups, foundations) have not extended the definition of qualitative television research much further. Customarily, one is told that qualitative program ratings will supplement traditional measures of audience size and composition and tell us 'something more' about the nature of the viewer's response to programming. Usually undefined in such statements, however, are the specific qualitative research variables, the specific program evaluation criteria which the new ratings system will measure.[1]

The following list provides some of the answers given to the question: "What kind of qualitative rating do you want?"

• More detailed demographic information as to occupation, income, education, and working status (for women).

• Data on personal and household ownership of cars, boats, and usage of products, participation in sports, vacation and business travel, second homes, etc.

• Which viewers actually see the commercials, how many exposures they receive, which viewers are likely to buy, and why.

• Classification of viewers by life-style psychographics, psychological needs, and gratifications.

• Qualitative rating scores to measure program appeal or viewer satisfaction or interest.

• Measure viewing impacts intended by program originators (information gain, reception, and retention of attitudinal statements, discussion of program with others, etc.).

• How viewing affects attitudes and behavior.

## Three Basic Categories

Clearly the first two or three definitions in the list are most interesting to the buyers and sellers of commercial television time. It appears basically then that "qualitative" has three principal meanings in audience measurement:

1. *Quality of audience* is evaluated with regard to buying and consumption patterns and life-style or psychographic factors. These types of measurements are little more than sophisticated demographics describing the audience in terms considered relevant to advertising targets. Syndicated services in this field include Quantiplex, Qualidata, Simmons Market Research Bureau (SMRB), Mediamark Research, Inc. (MRI), Scarborough, PRIZM, VALS, and Nielsen Product Audience Reports (NPAR).

2. *Quality of individual program appeal,* as measured by subjective viewer response on scales from low to high. In effect, the viewer provides a report on each program, and like a child's report card, the format can vary. Services in this category are TVQ, Vox Box, Arbitron/CPB, and Television Audience Assessment (TAA).

3. *Quality of viewing experience* is probed by a greater depth of questioning and more sophisticated analytical treatment of data. Rather than depending solely on respondents' articulation of overall reaction to the program, the effort is directed more at measuring viewing impact—information gain, reception and retention of attitudinal statements, effect of viewing on attitudes and behavior, discussion of program with others, etc. This newer and more challenging area is not represented by any syndicated service at this time, but three extensive pilot efforts have been made: Frank/Greenberg's Segmentation, Television Factor Rating, and Television Audience Assessment, all described in Section III.

## Why Is There No Enthusiasm?

Prior to examining specific approaches and services in the three categories, it is logical to ask why it took so long for this type of rating to develop. Also, why, aside from category 1, which is clearly marketing oriented, is there no more than sporadic interest in qualitative ratings today? There are several reasons why networks, stations, and ad agencies have never been enthusiastic about syndicated qualitative research.

First, quantitative ratings, properly analyzed and interpreted, can yield many answers to questions about quality—at least those dealing with the strength and nature of a program's appeal. It is usually true that high-rated shows also get high marks on various qualitative evaluations. Their audiences can be expected to be more attentive, the shows are more memorable, and commercial recall reflects this.

The extensive historical data bank of meter and diary audience results can be searched for additional answers. The advent of overnight ratings, direct computer access by subscribers, and a proliferation of demographic, ethnic, and geographic data gives the ratings analyst a broad field to play on. Program performance in different time periods under various competitive conditions in diverse markets can show where the program vehicle's true core audience strength lies. The introduction of more sports preemptions, one-time-only features, and short series provides rapidly altered competitive situations that reveal to the shrewd analyst many qualitative aspects of individual program appeal.

The trained researcher has more confidence in findings derived from actual viewing behavior patterns than from many qualitative measurements that rely on verbalizations of people's attitudes and opinions.[2] Agencies are also attuned to buying on established demographic profiles and are often skeptical of qualitative indices that are untested and not necessarily predictive.

Networks, stations, agencies, and producers conduct extensive special qualitative research on individual shows. Pilots are habitually tested by networks before selection and scheduling. This research ranges from simple concept tests to full-scale, in-home exposure by tests run over cable systems, and it can include focus group sessions and test audience exposure in theaters and mobile vans.

Therefore, long before a series is purchased and scheduled the programmer or buyer has a reasonably good idea of where its basic appeal lies and what the key attraction elements are. At the network level, various program and qualitative research efforts account for annual expenditures about equal to those spent on ratings and quantitative analysis. Agencies spend large sums on customized Burke and other tests of commercial efficiency that provide details of audience consumption and life-style patterns.

TV stations, which are primarily concerned with either their overall image in their market or with achieving a highly successful news operation, rely on research consultants such as Frank N. Magid Associates or McHugh and Hoffman to provide qualitative evaluations keyed to the stations' needs as guides to action.

Radio stations have long been active in "call-out research" relative to new music trends, and many program consulting services do considerable audience research. Most recent on the scene is Reymer and Gersin Associates, which seeks to create a radio station's niche by a research technique they call "psychosegmentation."

Clearly there has been plenty of activity in the qualitative field, radio as well as TV. Just as clearly, the picture we see is one of tailor-made studies pinpointed to specific programs or areas. This raises a fundamental question: Can surveys in the third category of qualitative truly be adapted to syndication and become "qualitative ratings." But let us first examine categories 1 and 2, where there have been successful syndicated services for many years.

## II. AUDIENCE QUALITY

Audience quality is most closely linked to conventional syndicated rating services, and several organizations presently have established commercial footholds in the industry, radio as well as television. We first discuss the national services (Simmons and Mediamark), then PRIZM and VALS, followed by the local services.

*Simmons Market Research Bureau* (SMRB) is the oldest and the most widely known of all services dealing with media and markets. The primary purpose of SMRB's Study of Media and Markets is to produce magazine audience measurements using a large national sample of personal interviews simultaneously with product usage data.

Over time, information on TV viewing, radio listening, and newspaper reading has been added to produce comparative data for agency media planning purposes. This information is also used by many broadcast entities for sales development. Simmons' current study has 90 such subscribers—from networks to individual radio stations and cable services.

SMRB does one survey per year in three phases, from August to June. A probability sample of 19,000 households is the base for a random selection of one adult per household. SMRB achieves 75 percent recovery of the predesignated sample.

Phase I includes magazine and newspaper reading and demographics obtained in personal interviews while a leave-behind product-use booklet (750 categories, 3500 brands) is placed.

Phase II takes place about a month later, when the interviewer returns to retrieve the product data. At that time, magazine and newspaper readership are obtained once more (for cumulative purposes) and data on radio listening the previous day are recorded. About 80 percent of the Phase I sample is recontacted, yielding some 15,500 cases.

Phase III involves only broadcast audiences and is conducted simultaneously with the spring and fall ratings sweeps of Arbitron and Nielsen. The spring base is an 11,000 random probability subsample of the original 19,000; the fall base is 9000. These people are interviewed by telephone to (1) obtain the previous day's radio listening (the second such measurement to establish cumes) and (2) recruit them to keep a two-week TV individual diary, which is sent and returned by mail. Returned in-tab TV diary response is 40+ percent; for radio it is 60 percent.

Simmons' "extended cell ascription" method is used to expand data from the returned diaries to the original 19,000 sample. Ascription is a statistical procedure for using probability principles based on data available to ascribe information not obtained. It is widely used in survey work to complete partially filled-out questionnaires or diaries.

However, SMRB uses it on an unprecedented scale in order to get all media data on a common base. This practice has many critics, who accuse Simmons of "making up the numbers." Nevertheless, SMRB is not a broadcast rating service, and users seem to accept the ascription procedures as a reasonable compromise with costs.

Simmons provides a great deal of information in a 42-volume set of reports. National data are broken down on 11 geographic regions (as defined by Nielsen). Local services are discussed here.

*Mediamark Research Inc.* (MRI) was founded in 1979 by two long-time competitors of SMRB—Timothy Joyce and Alain Tessier, formerly top executives of Target Group Index (TGI). Like Simmons, MRI is fundamentally designed as a national survey of magazine audiences, using a "recent-reading" criterion, as opposed to Simmons' "through-the-book" method. MRI also provides broadcast measurements with significant differences from SMRB.

Product-use data collected for 800 categories and the more than 3000 brands reported are accompanied by brand volume as well as product volume. This provides brand share of total volume.

MRI collects data from 20,000 respondents annually, in two five-month surveys of 10,000 each. It claims that "the sample is much more widely dispersed than any other sample used for media/product research. Each year interviews are conducted in 2400 clusters [neighborhoods]."[3]

Half of the sample is allocated to 10 markets, using Arbitron's Area of Dominant Influence (ADI) definition, which makes possible separate major market data (a development covered under the following outline of local services). To provide more efficient magazine and product measurement, the top one-fourth of the areas in income get one-half of the sample, while the bottom one-half receive only one-fourth of the clusters. (A similar procedure is followed by SMRB.)

For broadcast audiences, the MRI design calls for full sample measurement up front "to avoid the vagaries of ascribing data collected from partial samples."[4] Personal interviewers collect recall of yesterday's listening and TV and cable viewing as well as call letters and channel data. The 90-page leave-behind survey booklet requires answers relative to lists of network TV programs and cable activity. MRI updates its questionnaires for each semiannual survey, and fresh data are available each spring and fall on computer tape.

*PRIZM* is not a service, but a geodemographic analysis scheme. Classifying geographic markets by relative affluence, PRIZM uses perhaps the oldest tool in the market research kit. Pioneers during the 1920s used census, utility company, and ABC circulation figures to define counties and metropolitan areas as to crude socioeconomic status or purchasing power potential.

Today, most county units are too populous and heterogeneous to have great marketing significance. Claritas Corp. has attempted to solve the problem by forging a new tool, PRIZM, based on statistically homogeneous ZIP-code market clusters.

PRIZM now employs over 1000 demographic measures from the 1980 U.S. Census for each of the nation's 35,600 residential ZIP code neighborhoods. Analysis of this database ultimately yielded 40 homogeneous groups, called ZIP-market clusters, each with its own distinct neighborhood life-style. This concept assumes that (1) people with similar cultural backgrounds and circumstances will "cluster" and (2) the homogeneous demographic character of a neighborhood is self-perpetuating.

As a result, Claritas maintains that "the demographic measures which accurately describe our place of residence will provide an equally valid statistical mirror of our 'place' in society."[5] PRIZM thus is claimed to be a 40-point life-style segmentation system strong enough to explain, and accurately predict, consumer behavior.

Each of the 40 clusters contains ZIP codes throughout the country where similar people live. Names and one-line descriptions have been assigned with a range from Blueblood Estates to Hardscrabble. The largest categories are Young Suburbia and Blue Chip Blues; others include Levittown USA and Golden Ponds.

For normal media and market analysis, the 40 PRIZM ZIP-market clusters have been composited into 10 cluster groups (three suburban, three urban, two town, two rural), which range from S1 (educated, affluent, elite white families in owner-occupied greenbelt suburbs) to U2 (mixed, middle class, foreign stock, and minorities in dense urban row-house areas) to R2 (mixed unskilled whites, blacks, Spanish, and native Americans in poor rural towns and farms).

Donnelley Cluster Plus is a ZIP-code geodemographic scheme developed by Reuben H. Donnelley Co. It is based on 47 clusters and 10 multigroups. Cluster Plus now appears to exceed PRIZM in popularity. Examples of Donnelley's clusters are: S-01 (top income, well educated, professional, prestige home, children in private schools); S-15 (older urban, few children, white-collar workers, singles); and S-41 (poorly educated, low income, blue-collar families with children, rural South). Donnelley's cluster analysis of ownership of a domestic luxury car shows the S-1 cluster 280 percent above U.S. average, and S-41 at 80 percent below national. Cluster Plus is used by Arbitron Radio and TV in connection with Target/Aid and by Nielsen's NSI. Whereas PRIZM and VALS can be used by either SMRB or MRI, Simmons has exclusive use of Donnelley's Cluster Plus in its field.

VALS (Values and Lifestyles Program) uses a psychographic basis for consumer segmentation. Its premise is that today there is no one homogeneous set of American values and life-styles. Numerous market researchers claim that psychographic segmentation will help advertisers and programmers to "tune in" more closely to people's diverse objectives, personalities, and orientation toward life.

The VALS program, one of the most insightful hierarchies of values and life-styles, was developed by SRI International (formerly Stanford Research Institute). It is being used by Simmons Market Research Bureau and by Mediamark for their media and markets surveys.

VALS segments the national population into nine groups, for which Simmons has provided universe estimates (often lacking in qualitative schemes). They are, from bottom up:

*Need driven* (11 percent), consisting of (1) Survivors (4 percent)—struggling, depressed, distrustful, old, and (2) Sustainers (7 percent)—concerned with security, young, angry but hopeful.

*Outer directed* (69 percent), those who use others as reference, consisting of (1) Belongers (38 percent)—traditional, preservers of status quo, strong group urge; (2) Emulators (10 percent)—youthful, ambitious, emulate the successful; and (3) Achievers (21 percent)—middle-aged, prosperous, comfort-loving, oriented to fame and success.

*Inner directed* (20 percent), paralleling outer directeds but with a personal standard of reference, consisting of (1) I-AM-ME (3 percent—very young, individualistic, impulsive; (2) Experimental (5 percent)—seek direct experience, intense personal relationships; and (3) Societally conscious (12 percent)—socially responsible, mission-oriented, mature, successful, lead simple lives.

*Integrated* (2 percent), meld outer- and inner-directed attitudes into a tolerant self-assurance.

The VALS typology provides copious information about the attitudes, activities, and consumption patterns of these groups as well as relevant media information. Belongers are heavy TV viewers, and the inner-directed individuals are heaviest educational TV watchers.

## Local Market Services

The primary local media-product surveys are highly newspaper-oriented because of print financial support. Nevertheless, they now all provide some measure of television and radio usage by program or station. Most of these studies are confined to the top fifteen markets, but Simmons' 1987 Study of Local Newspaper Ratings covers 56 market areas. Birch Radio is the only broadcast rating service currently providing product use data related to audience measurement.

*Scarborough* is a local market in-depth consumer and media survey organized in 1975 by Harold Israel and Jay Cohen, two former Simmons executives. Syndicated surveys are now conducted in ten major markets on two-year cycles. Local media support is strong in most cases, with practically all newspapers, two or three TV stations, and 8 to 15 radio stations as subscribers.

The quantity of information secured in the product and consumer usage areas is massive because of the retailer questions employed, covering daily, Sunday, and weekly newspapers, TV and radio stations, cable, and selected weekly and monthly magazines. Brand information appears where relevant. The minimum sample size is 2500, with 11,000 for New York. Respondents are randomly selected adults 18 + , only one per household. Scarborough is considered a quality survey but expensive and not likely to expand greatly.

*MRI's Ten Media Market Reports* are essentially a retabulation of Mediamark data for the past two years. They include media and product usage data obtained by personal interviews to secure media information and a 90-page booklet questionnaire to collect product and TV network program viewing, placed by the interviewers and picked up several days later. Market samples vary from 1500 to 4000 for New York.

Mediamark's added broadcast audience information for local markets does not include program audience estimates or ratings. Mediamark's basic components are data on 450 product and consumer activity categories cross-tabbed with individual and household demographics and media measures (local newspapers, local radio stations, radio formats, TV time periods, and local news by station, etc.). Also included are cable and pay cable stations.

Mediamark points to the advantages to buyers and sellers and media planners of having comprehensive data for ten top markets that match with MRI's national study data.

### Simmons Study of Local Newspaper Ratings

First introduced in 1985, this survey effort is now done every other year. The 1987 computer-assisted telephone interviewing (CATI) was conducted from four centrally monitored centers from October 1986 to April 1987. A two-phase procedure is used to produce cumulative audience data. To supply separate reports for 56 market ADIs, approximately 120,000 interviews with 65,000 adult respondents will be employed. The target is an effective sample base of 200 readers for reported newspapers.

The television viewing component is limited to questions relative to local station viewing by day parts. The same national Simmons product data material used by Arbitron's Target Aid will be available to newspaper subscribers.

### Birch Radio Qualitative Product Usage Reports (QPURS)

The Birch Radio service produces special reports that profile audiences by product consumption in addition to limited age/sex demographics. QPURs are produced for total week only 6:00 A.M.–midnight and include up to three demographics per category.

Fifteen qualitative factors are included in both winter and spring surveys. Among them are income, occupation, newspaper readership, soft-drink consumption, fast-food visits, beer consumption, and airline travel. Categories such as department store visits, automobile mileage, and major appliance purchase are reported once a year.

### Former Local Market Services

*Quantiplex* (a John Blair service for local TV) was established in 1980. Based on telephone interviews, Quantiplex supplied a TV market with viewer and consumer (VAC) ratings identifying television viewers and newspaper readers, not just by age and sex, but by what they purchase in specific product and service categories.

VAC defined which programs attract what type of purchasers in what numbers. The survey used the telephone recall technique. Its sample size varied from 1000 to 2000 depending on market size. Quantiplex never achieved the support anticipated in either television or radio (which was entered later) and was permanently disbanded in 1983.

*Qualidata* (Arbitron Radio Service) was introduced in 1980 as a reinterview telephone survey of in-tab diary keepers to obtain consumer profile data that could be related to radio ratings.

Qualidata reported on 15 product usage categories, six socioeconomic divisions, and five readership and media usage classifications.

Telephone reinterviews of diary-keeper households commenced six weeks after the conclusion of the diary survey, running from November into May. With an average response rate of about 70 percent on reinterviews, the sample sizes for individual markets ranged from 1000 to 3000. The radio industry's lack of enthusiasm for Qualidata related to the relatively low (28 percent) response rate (diary 40 percent times 70 percent) and out-of-date data. Qualidata was discontinued as a syndicated service early in 1984.

*Nielsen Product Audience Reports* (NPAR) was introduced in 1983. The Nielsen Station Index spent several years planning and testing the product usage study tied to its NSI local viewers in profile (VIP) reports. The service was directly mainly at usage by TV stations in competition with newspapers. It was designed to provide (1) audiences weighted to the VIP, (2) household and demographic measurement units, (3) locally projected figures with local consumer categories, (4) twice yearly reports, and (5) potential computer access.

The methodology involved use of questionnaires sent to households that had kept and returned diaries in the latest NSI local survey. All household members 12+ had a column to fill out, requiring about 20 minutes per respondent. There were 73 questions, potentially 200 categories. In the full-scale test in the New York DMA in October 1981, based on July 1981 VIP, Nielsen said it achieved an 85 percent return rate for the product-use booklets.

By 1984 Nielsen had been able to introduce NPAR in only eight markets. The service was discontinued in November 1985.

## Summary of Product Use Services

Product data collection done simultaneously with audience data by the same techniques from the same sample could be a plus in data freshness and lack of sample recontact problems. Quantiplex (TV) had this advantage. Mediamark has a single-source booklet for media and product data, but information is accumulated over two years, which introduces a limitation on its utility. Scarborough, although collecting media and market data virtually simultaneously, has the problem of wear-out over a two-year cycle. The limitations of the post audience survey methods—Qualidata and Nielsen Product Audience Ratings (TV)—are that audience and product data were collected for different periods (two to three months apart) and by somewhat different methods, with sample loss especially heavy for Qualidata.

A wide range of data detail characterizes the field. Simmons, Scarborough, and Mediamark, with hundreds of basic product and consumer categories differentiated by brands, are perhaps the most prolific data sources. Services relying on telephone recall for product data (Quantiplex and Qualidata) were more limited in the number of categories provided.

Product usage data require sizable samples to provide bases for detailed breakouts. Only large markets can afford such adequate ratings and often only by combining response data over time. This is a limitation that will restrict expansion of such local services beyond the top 10 or 15 markets.

### Broadcaster Interest Limited

Many broadcasters are getting some experience in how to make product-use analysis pay off, but they are often poorly equipped to do the kind of job for which most major city newspapers are prepared. The main thrust of all the local product services is retail and franchise chain advertising. Broadcasters will have to use this output, not just against their TV and radio competition, but to wean away traditional newspaper dollars from local merchants through shrewd statistical analysis.

Individual stations with the ability to sell with these new data are limited to a few major markets where owned-and-operated network and group-owned stations have the budgets and the research capability to make use of them. The demise of John Blair's Quantiplex, Arbitron's abandonment of the syndicated Qualidata, and Nielsen's surrender on NPAR clearly indicate limited prospects for product-use studies outside of a few major markets. On the other hand, the Birch Radio Service has apparently made a virtue of the inclusion of a limited amount of product data in its local radio rating reports and of computer accessibility of the data.

### Single Source Measurement

The developers of the Audimeter, Robert Elder, the MIT professor whose idea it was, and Arthur C. Nielsen, who refined the basic invention, always had in mind that the meter audience measurement would be accompanied by some measure of product use. Sales effectiveness was their objective. However, Nielsen's efforts were defeated because purchase and usage levels for many products were so limited that sample sizes in Audimeter panel homes were generally inadequate (see Chapter 1).

The idea of a single source for media and product-use data is, of course, one of the attractions of such services as the Simmons Study of Media Markets and the Mediamark Research service. However, these sources, useful for planning, are too slow in delivery and too imprecise in detail to be useful for actual buying and post evaluation. Several attempts to collect limited product-use data in rating surveys have failed, with only Birch Radio producing such data now.

The idea of a single source has persisted, however, and now seems close to reality. In April 1987, ScanAmerica introduced the first single-source people-meter service, in Denver, Colorado, based on a 600-household panel. A national ScanAmerica service of 5000 households is planned for 1988. See Chapter 11 for details of this operation as well as the plans and activities of Nielsen in this area in both the U.S. and Canada.

## III.  QUALITY OF INDIVIDUAL PROGRAM APPEAL

### TVQ

A national mail survey of television viewers, TVQ was established by Henry Brenner's Home Testing Institute in 1958 and is now conducted by Marketing Evaluations. TVQ provides commercial industry decision-makers with (1) awareness measures of national commercial programming and (2) viewers' overall program evaluations for programs they know along a five-point scale from "one of my favorites" to "poor." The TVQ service resulted from surveys conducted by George Gallup for the motion picture industry in the early 1950s. Gallup's studies focused on movie stars, whose pictures were shown to respondents to obtain indices of "enthusiastic quotient" (EQ). Later, NBC experiments with tests of TV performers in Gallup's survey led to the inauguration of TVQ for programs.

Networks and others use the TVQ index primarily to spot new high-scoring programs that have not yet achieved widespread exposure and thus have generated mediocre quantitative ratings. Another important use is to detect declining "liking" scores for old favorites that might still be holding up well in ratings because of viewer habit. Low awareness scores focus attention on programs needing added promotional push to increase exposure.

TVQ is conducted among a nationally representative household mail panel of 1200 households. This sample, selected from a larger national panel of 15,000 households, permits TVQ to send a questionnaire for each household member. About 3500 individual inquiry forms are mailed, and a reminder postcard goes out a week later. Returns are tabulated after about two weeks. In-tab samples consist of approximately 1200 people in 750 to 800 households. Reports are issued seven times per year, more frequently during the October–March period, with only two reports covering April–September.

The information furnished has greatly increased in breadth in recent years. Not only TV series but movies, sports, specials, and other one-time-only shows are included, along with many syndicated productions. Performer Q applies the same measurement technique to performers and is a guide used in casting. This technique has come under attack in California (see Chapter 9), and as a result TVQ has instituted measures to ensure that its samples adequately represent Hispanic population ratios. Cable networks are now listed for evaluation, and respondents are classified as to subscription to basic or pay cable service. Because of the relative size and uneven dispersion of cable households, TVQ scores for cable networks show more variability than others.[6] Theatrical movies are now explored regarding where they are seen: theater, commercial TV, pay TV, tape, or disc. There are obviously many analytical possibilities in such data when received regularly and backed up by a substantial data bank of past attitude scores. TVQ is achieving a higher level of attention from agencies, syndicators, and cable interests, further solidifying its lead in this field.

## Vox Box

This is an electronic response device used by R. D. Percy and Company in Seattle, Washington. (Vox Box was developed by Stanford Research Institute under commission from Percy.) Vox Box is wired to a household's main TV set in 200 homes that agree to provide their evaluations of whatever TV programs they watch. The device consists of two rows of buttons—one for channel selection, the other to record qualitative response using the following button options:

- Excellent.
- Informative.
- Credible.
- Funny.

- Boring.
- Unbelievable.
- Dumb.
- Zap.
- Person—special button to apply response to program personality.


Paralleling the Vox Box activity was a second-by-second accounting from videotaped logs of all programs and commercials aired on the five commercial and one public TV stations in Seattle–Tacoma. The data from the two sources was time linked in one information base to provide highly accurate records of what was on the air, who saw it, how they behaved toward it, and what they thought of it.

The data were published in four sets of standardized reports, two concentrating on advertising research and two evaluating programs. The first group helped advertisers ascertain the percentage of the panel viewers tuned to each commercial, rather than the surrounding program (whether in or between program breaks), competitive share of commercial gross rating points, competitive share of commercial reach and frequency, audience behavior and attitude toward commercials, etc. The program reports showed audience sampling, repeat viewing, audience involvement as to loyalty, stability, and the nature of the audience's response.

The Percy TV Program Performance Guide provided program ratings, reach, loyalty index (a measure of repeat viewing for series), positive response (percentage of all responses defined as "positive"), and a total value factor in which all scores for four weeks are combined.

Percy's Vox Box service, established in 1979, departed sharply from any of the other efforts at qualitative measurement. First, it employed a meter that recorded set usage and also provided an opportunity for viewers to record their responses automatically by voluntarily pushing a button as programs were watched. Second, the precise logging system for local programs provided the opportunity for rating commercials (as distinct from programs). This unique element is one frequently mentioned as a form of needed "qualitative" rating. Percy characterized these measurements as "strictly quantitative," while Vox Box added qualitative indices of audience behavior. In this approach, the qualitative data reflected actual behavior and performance in the panel in normal viewing. Loose verbalizations about programs or commercials were thus avoided. On the other hand, the amount of viewer involvement in button-pushing increased the opportunity for conditioning of respondents.

Limited commercial acceptance led to abandonment of this early Vox Box in favor of a unique peoplemeter system described in Chapter 11.

## Arbitron/CPB

Arbitron's foray into qualitative measurement was sponsored in part by the Corporation for Public Broadcasting (CPB), which was seeking a ratings system molded to serve the interests of noncommercial station programmers. Commercial rating systems were considered inadequate to meet the special mandates and programming objectives of public broadcasting. CPB felt that: "Traditional measures of audience size and demographics tell us little or nothing about the extent to which PTV programs serve and satisfy their viewers."[8]

The first pilot test by Arbitron took place in Boston, where 600 persons kept a one-week qualitative diary in November 1980. David Liroff, broadcast manager of WGBH, said that the results showed clearly that: "the implementation of a qualitative ratings system would substantially increase the program director's ability to evaluate the effectiveness of a station's service by providing detailed audience information not previously available."[9]

Analysis of the Boston pilot results by Arbitron and CPB led to a nationwide study conducted in 20 markets, November 18–24, 1981. A panel of more than 2800 diary keepers was instructed to watch whatever programs they desired and to record in a specially designed personal diary when and for how long they watched each program. Respondents also indicated the degree to which they found each program "entertaining," "informative," "useful," and "different from other programs."

Arbitron developed the four qualitative scales specifically to address public television's mandates of programming excellence, innovation, special interest and minority service, alternative service, and diversity. "The CPB study marks the first time that a major syndicator of audience research has developed a procedure that simultaneously measures viewing behavior and programming evaluations," explained Joseph C. Philport, project manager for the CPB study.[10] The inclusion of qualitative scales did not significantly decrease the survey return rate.

Not surprisingly, commercial television programs fared better on the "entertaining" scale than on the other dimensions. Regularly scheduled network programs identified as the most "entertaining" included "Great Performances," "M*A*S*H," "Odyssey," "Hill Street Blues," "WKRP in Cincinnati," and "Diff'rent Strokes." The most entertaining programs were most likely to have the highest viewing levels.

Public television's "Odyssey," "Great Performances," "Cosmos," and "Sneak Previews" were perceived as the "most different from other television programs." "Hill Street Blues" was the most unique commercial television show.

Eight of the top 10 regularly scheduled "information" programs aired on public television stations, including "Cosmos," "Nova," and "Wall Street Week." Among the programs viewers found exceptionally "useful" were "Nightly Business Report," "Wall Street Week," "Washington Week in Review," "Sneak Previews," and "Over Easy." Again, 8 of the top 10 "useful" regularly scheduled programs were public television shows.

Interest in the Arbitron qualitative survey technique quickly vanished. The CPB Office of Communications Research was eliminated about the time the 20-city survey was released. CPB staff members hoped that individual public TV stations would be interested in keeping the service alive, in some markets at least, but this did not materialize. After custom designing a technique to serve the special needs of public television, Arbitron found that PBS stations did not want or could not use or afford such research. This does not speak well for the future of qualitative ratings in the commercial field.

## III.  QUALITY OF VIEWING EXPERIENCE

The qualitative ratings developed by TVQ is the only ongoing, continuous service, whereas the Arbitron/CPB survey effort stalled after the first nationwide study in 1981 and Percy petered out in Seattle. These three services had one common denominator: All relied on the viewer's subjective evaluation of the program for the qualitative program rating. Various scaling and weighting procedures were employed, but essentially the end result rested on the appeal of the program in the eyes of the beholder as reported by that beholder. Now we move to the third category of qualitative service: the quality of the viewing experience, exploring (1) the viewer's expectations, needs, and attitudes toward the viewing experience in order to determine how and why certain programs are viewed; (2) what characteristics of programs produce high degrees of attention, satisfaction, and loyalty; and (3) the quality of the viewing experience in terms of entertainment, information, and memorability. The viewer's experience and reaction are developed from questionnaires, not from subjective evaluation.

We know, of course, that "listening" and "viewing" can have gradations of attentiveness from rapt to extremely incidental. Probing this phenomenon has been largely left to methodological studies—"listeners" or "viewers" as used in quantitative ratings are defined largely on the judgment of respondents (with some general instructions from the survey organization).

One effort to explore the gradations of listening was a study undertaken by Arbitron (then ARB) to ascertain how the total audience figures were distributed over four categories of radio audience behavior believed to be "most relevant to advertising opportunity": (1) Concentrated Listening (glued to the set, maximum involvement), (2) Listening with Incidental Activity (mentally involved in program, but engaged in routine work or personal chores), (3) Activity with Incidental Listening (primary activity demands greater part of attention), and (4) Incidental Hearing (minimum involvement in program). In 1966 two markets were surveyed by telephone coincidentals (which limited results to in-home listening). About one-sixth of the total fell in the Concentrated Listening group, a slightly smaller proportion than the one-fifth in group 4—Incidental Hearing. Nearly one-half the audience fell in the second group (Listening with Incidental Activity), while Activity with Incidental Listening made up the smallest group (slightly over 10 percent). Peter Langhoff, then ARB president, concluded: "At the moment there appear to be appreciable values in added knowledge which further illuminates the advertising opportunities within the local dimensions of the medium." This type of work was not continued, presumably because there was little industry interest.

A much more comprehensive exploration of the various possible interpretations of listening was produced in Canada by the Bureau of Broadcast Measurement in 1974. BBM, a tripartite (agency, advertiser, broadcaster) industry organization, conducts Canadian audience ratings services for both radio and television. For years, a single diary for both media was employed. This technique came under such increased critical fire that a massive methodological study was mounted to examine diaries and diary keeping in close relation to listening and viewing patterns. After much preliminary work, a three-city study in 1974 produced the following data that finally led to BBM's adoption of separate diaries for radio and TV:

• For radio on a four-part scale listeners distributed as follows: Awareness only, 17 percent; Hearing, 28 percent; Noticing, 17 percent; Paying Attention, 38 percent. The radio-only diary picked up Awareness not reported on the dual diary. This accounted for a 20 percent rise in radio listening levels.

• For TV the four-part scale showed: Awareness, 20 percent; In Room, 7 percent; Noticing, 18 percent, and Paying Attention, 55 percent. The dual diary reported only the two top categories, whereas a TV-only diary brought in the In Room group while Awareness only was not reported for TV as it was for radio.[11]

These studies demonstrate the complexities of unraveling the viewing and listening experience in a manner that might be meaningful to programmers and advertisers. Research conducted by Burke for the Newspaper Advertising Bureau in 1981 showed that unaided recall of the last commercial remembered can be twice as high: (1) for people who choose the program being watched as for those who did not (8 percent versus 4 percent) and (2) for those watching TV exclusively versus those also doing something else (9 percent versus 4 percent).[12] Can these complicated questions be subjected to some form of regular syndicated rating service? Let's look at several efforts in that direction.

## Frank/Greenberg Interest-based Segmentation of TV Audiences

One approach to qualitative ratings was a massive national study of people's leisure interests and needs based on the concept of segmentation used in market studies. Dr. Ronald E. Frank of the Wharton School, University of Pennsylvania, and Dr. Marshall G. Greenberg, senior vice president of National Analysts, a market research firm, developed the approach and carried out pilot studies over three years. The national survey of 2400 people (ages 13 years and over) in TV households was conducted in the fall of 1977 and the results were reported in *The Public's Use of Television* by Frank and Greenberg.[13]

An avowed goal of this project was "to develop a segmentation scheme for the study of how people with different patterns of interests and needs make use of television rather than studying the relationship between demographic variables and viewing behavior." The authors further stated: "We believe that our approach will be useful to a wide range of persons including network chief executive officers, executives in programming and research, executives in program production organizations, program producers and script writers, and those individuals in various public and private interest and regulatory organizations concerned with television as a medium."

Frank and Greenberg measured a broad range of physical, intellectual, and cultural interests using 18 categories containing 139 specific interests and activities. Their goal was to position television viewing as a leisure activity in competition with other leisure-related interests and activities such as athletic activities, community activities, camping, and professional sports.

In order to gain insight into the motivations behind people's interests, the questionnaire was designed to determine what needs the leisure interests and activities satisfied. The need factors were organized into nine categories, and the people interviewed rated the degree of importance of each category.

**NEEDS**

1. Socially stimulating.
2. Status enhancement.
3. Unique/creative accomplishment.
4. Escape from problems.
5. Family ties.
6. Understanding others.
7. Greater self-acceptance.

8. Escape from boredom.
9. Intellectual stimulation and growth.

Questions were also directed at viewing behavior, how TV fits into viewers' daily lives, attention, autonomy in program selection and advance planning, viewing, and attitudes toward public television, etc. Statistical multivariate methods were employed in the analysis. The result was 14 types of people who shared similar leisure interests and activities, such as mechanics and outdoor life, home and community centered, and cosmopolitan self-enrichment. These categories were then examined for their television behavior and preferences.

The end result of this study in terms of credible, usable information is a series of question marks. There is no evidence that the objective of its authors—to provide a useful tool to creators of television programming—was ever achieved in operational terms. Neither commercial nor public broadcast officials have acknowledged its relevance to their decision making.

## TV Factor Ratings

In contrast to the Frank/Greenberg approach, which was underwritten by the John and Mary R. Markle Foundation, Marketing Evaluations secured support from the three commercial networks and CPB to fund its TV Factor Ratings pilot study in 1979. TV Factor Ratings (or Television Qualitative Ratings, as they were known at CPB) were developed by Jack Landis of Marketing Evaluations as a diagnostic tool to determine the sources of viewer satisfaction (or dissatisfaction) with individual TV programs. The method documented the viewer's ability to discriminate among programs based on particular appeal elements.

TV Factor Ratings began in preliminary focus group interviews and analyses of television criticism as a source of 258 descriptions of television programs (delightful, action filled, witty, exciting, boring, predictable, relaxing, etc.). The study profiled 96 commercial and public television programs on these descriptions, using a total national sample of 3000 respondents. A factor analysis employing 33,000 correlations resulted in seven basic dimensions, which accounted for 65 percent of the total variance. The positive and negative of each dimension produced these 14 factors for use in program evaluation:

What the Program Does for the Viewer
   Factor 1—Provides *knowledge and enrichment*
   Factor 2—Provides *diversion and escape*
How the Program Affects the Viewer
   Factor 3—Gives *fun and amusement*
   Factor 4—Builds *tension and excitement*

How the Viewer Feels About the Program
  Factor 5—*positive evaluation*—wants to watch
  Factor 6—*negative evaluation*—not interested
The Program's Type of Appeal
  Factor 7—Acceptable for *kid/family viewing*
  Factor 8—Primarily for *adult entertainment*
The Contents of the Program
  Factor 9—Subject/People are *familiar and realistic*
  Factor 10—Subject/People are *unfamiliar or unusual*
The Viewer Relationship to the Program
  Factor 11—Viewer becomes *emotionally involved*
  Factor 12—Viewer is *interested observer*
Sensory Emphasis of the Program
  Factor 13—Visual stress on *beauty and glamour*
  Factor 14—Aural stress on *wit and clever lines*

Industry interest in TV Factor Ratings as a continuing service two or three times annually was not forthcoming. It never got off the ground, even though it had several practical elements, based on data reduction techniques by Marketing Evaluations.

## Television Audience Assessment, Inc. (TAA)

Based in Cambridge, Massachusetts, Television Audience Assessment, Inc. has, like the Frank and Greenberg survey, been basically funded by the John and Mary R. Markle Foundation. Established in December 1980, TAA describes itself as:

> a nonprofit corporation engaged in the development of a new form of program ratings for cable and broadcast television. This effort is based on the premise that a system of television ratings that takes into account both viewer attitudes and behaviors will (1) stimulate the development of programming more responsive to the diverse needs and interests of today's viewers, and (2) provide industry executives with an important new tool for economic evaluation and decision-making.[14]

Pointing to many technological and programming changes in the communications marketplace, TAA foresees the need for new measurements to meet new diversities of TV service. Initially, research efforts are concentrated on development and validation of two specific indices of program appeal:

- Program appreciation—a viewer's overall enjoyment or liking of a show.
- Program impact—the degree of involvement or stimulation experienced by the viewer.

The utility of these opinion-based ratings was tested with particular attention focused on the relevance of the response measure for advertising decisions related to broadcast and cable media.

In April 1982, a group of leading cable program services and systems operators provided support for a prototype ratings study designed to determine:

- How TV viewers select programs and what differences exist between cable and broadcast.
- Viewer reaction to programs in terms of satisfaction, loyalty, attentiveness, and involvement.
- What program characteristics encourage higher levels of viewer satisfaction or involvement.
- The relationship between viewers' reactions and commercial recall or comprehension.
- Demographic, psychographic, and life-style profiles of programs and networks.
- How unique aspects of cable television affect viewers' relationship to TV programming.

The 1982 pilot study was conducted in two markets with more than 30 channel systems: Kansas City, Missouri, and Hartford/New Britain, Connecticut, with a total prerecruited sample of 3000 cable and broadcast television viewers ages 12 years and over. Random digit dialing and subscriber lists were used. Each test site had at least one strong independent, one PBS outlet, three commercial networks, and a range of cable network and pay-TV services as well as basic cable. The prerecruited sample was drawn from four groups: (1) broadcast only in nonwired areas (2) broadcast only (nonsubscribers) in cabled areas (3) cable subscribers and (4) users of specific cable services: CBS Cable, ESPN, MTV (Music Television) and USA Network.

Specially designed one-day viewing monitors (diaries) were used by respondents to record their watching of 6 P.M.—midnight television programs each day for two weeks. A guide listing all channels and services available was included. All viewing monitors were mailed in or picked up daily. Telephone calls supplemented the Monitor data. The front page of the Monitor included a series of questions measuring on a 1–10 scale: Amount of attention given, "this program touched my feelings," amount learned from program, and degree program is worth remembering. The back page of each sheet asked about specific programs, general patterns of television viewing, other media use, and leisure interests and activities.

Returned Monitors were postmarked and data entered directly to computer by entry clerks using the Computer Assisted Telephone Interview (CATI) system. Exactly 3000 individuals were recruited for participation (56.5 percent) of the eligible households originally contacted). The majority of panelists (52 percent) returned all 14 Monitors, while 76 percent returned 10 or more, yielding 2280 respondents. Monitors were accepted within 48 hours of viewing date (72 hours for Friday and Saturday).

Subgroups of Monitor panelists participated in several telephone interviews on various questions such as what other activities accompanied TV viewing, why the TV set was not on, recall of previous evening commercials, etc. In addition, a random sample of nonpanelists was interviewed by telephone to assess the effect of the Monitor format.

Special efforts were required to get specific cable service users. Relying on screening call estimates of weekly cable network usage proved that they were exaggerated compared to recorded entries.

To recruit 3000 panelists, the staff dialed 13,360 telephone numbers and completed screening interviews with 3454 individuals. Approximately one-quarter of RDD numbers called proved to be not working or nonhousehold. Another 25 percent were ineligible largely due to lack of specific cable services. Noncontacts reached 10 percent, and refusals/language problems came to 14 percent.

## Field Experience

Response rate for the Monitor study can be computed as follows:

|  | All Eligible Households (6608) | Eligible Households Contacted (5308) |
| --- | --- | --- |
| Designated respondents reached | 52.3% | 65.1% |
| Recruitment rate | 86.9 | 86.9 |
| In-tab returns (% of recruited) | 76.0 | 76.0 |
| Net response rate | 34.5 | 43.0 |

TAA suggests that the 19 percent of noncontacts at the screening level was not likely to be biasing because cooperation was refused without knowledge of the study's purpose, a most unconvincing argument for basing response rate on eligible households contacted rather than on all eligible households. Only the 76 percent who returned 10 usable Monitors out of the 14 days were included in the final tabulation; 13 percent returned none, while 11 percent returned less than 10. Around 85 percent of Monitors were received within 48 hours throughout the survey, but there was a decline in response after the initial 6 days.

With respect to media access, the most noteworthy difference was that in both Kansas City and New Britain, the subscribers to more than one premium service showed large differences, with out-of-tab nearly 50 percent above in-tab. TAA's commentary did not touch on this finding, which could be an important one. Do premium pay channel subscribers cooperate less in diary surveys?

Panelists who returned Monitors late (and were in the out-of-tabulation group) reported watching significantly less television than the early returners.[15] Late returners might be less conscientious about recording viewing, a plausible presumption since the screening interview showed no difference between the two groups in viewing.

## Telephone Surveys

The telephone near-coincidental was conducted on two evenings with various panel subgroups from 7:00 to 10:00 P.M. Panelists who said they were watching during the previous hour were asked about their behavior while watching. An overall response rate of 76 percent yielded nearly 800 completed interviews from a sample of 1033 eligible panelists; refusals amounted to only 1 percent. Each night, 100 panelists were interviewed who had not watched television during the preceding hour. A special interview with MTV viewers was administered to 39 respondents.

Day-after recall (DAR) interviews were conducted with panelists between ages 18 and 54 years. To qualify for the interview, a panelist had to have seen one of the specified programs on the previous evening. Only 128 men out of 1024 and 391 of 1071 females qualified. The recall response rate was 78.6 percent of eligible panelists, with females well ahead of males.

Telephone debriefing interviews were conducted during four days shortly after panelists completed the last Monitor. In-tab panelists and out-of-tabs were sampled separately. The final sample achieved of 1238 was made up of 1125 in-tab and 113 out-of-tab panelists (versus the goal of 1000 and 200).

## Panelist Attitudes and Opinions

The effects on viewing behavior of panel participation for two weeks were minimal. The major effect was that panelists reported being more attentive to and critical of programming watched than normal. The Monitor experience may have motivated panelists to use a television guide more frequently than usual, but only 14 percent reported that they planned ahead on programs to watch more than usual. (Other data showed no difference between panelists and nonpanelists on this point.)

The Channel Guide supplied with the Monitor packet was apparently helpful. About one-third of the in-tab group "used it very much," while another 30 percent said they used it "somewhat." The possibility of bias relative to unmeasured behavior is indicated by the finding that about 10 percent of the panelists said they watched at least one program for the first time because of the Guide, while 11.4 percent indicated watching at least one channel more often because the Guide reminded them of it.

TAA's Monitor experience exceeded expectations in quantity and timely returns. Over half of the respondents reported filling out the diary while watching TV, and 90 percent reported completing the daily form the same evening the program appeared. Panelists were not greatly inconvenienced by the daily mailing requirement. Eighty-three percent were either "very willing" or "willing" to take part in another such study. TAA concluded that the "Viewing Monitor has proven to be a viable method of collecting information reflecting the audience's reactions to television programs."[16]

## TAA Reports

The results of the study were released during 1983 in the following four major reports:

*The Audience Rates Television.* This is the principal report in the series, which introduces a new television rating system. The value of qualitative ratings and an analysis of the Program Appeal and Program Impact Indexes is discussed.

*Appeal and Impact: A Program Ratings Book.* Program Appeal and Program Impact ratings for more than 300 broadcast and cable-delivered television programs are provided along with special breakdowns of scores by audience subcategories for age and sex, educational background, and cable access.

*The Multichannel Environment.* A summary of TAA's exploration of the effect access to cable television has on viewers' use of and satisfaction with television.

*Methodology Report.* A full, 200-page technical description of the research design, implementation, and evaluation of the 1982 prototype ratings study.

A *Technical Appendix* gives a brief summary of the Methodology Report, outlining the research design and survey procedures.

## Appraisal

The Television Audience Assessment pilot survey was a well-organized survey in its design, execution, analysis, and presentation of results. TAA and Chilton Research contributed to our understanding of viewer performance in the cable television area. Further results of the TAA and its relevance to cable television are presented in Chapter 6.

The project, originally under Elizabeth J. Roberts, President, plowed much new ground and produced some new approaches to TV audience measurement. The skilled analysis applied to the data provides insights into new dimensions of broadcast and cable television viewing.

TAA's last study, covering daytime viewing, was conducted nationwide in November 1985. Results were released in April 1986. Two executives then in charge, Rolf M. Wulfsberg, President, and Steven A. Holt, Executive Vice President, worked valiantly to create commercial support for a regularly syndicated service based on the findings of the study. Wulfsberg later said, "We had a difficult time convincing people of its commercial relevance."[17] As a result, necessary financing was not forthcoming, and TAA suspended all operations in mid-1986.

Television Audience Assessment had mounted the most professional effort yet to inaugurate a regular qualitative rating service. It is not likely that another will emerge anytime soon.

## IV. SUMMARY

This chapter examined 14 individual "qualitative" ratings efforts. Is there a future for syndicated qualitative ratings? The answer must be, "Don't bet on it."[18] Clearly there is a growing interest in product-use and target customer data. As cable growth squeezes television audiences, both broadcasters and cable operators will look for more definitive rating data (just as people ratings and demographics have replaced the former household base). This trend is further fueled by the brand and product proliferation we see in every field, from cigarettes, breakfast cereals, and pain relievers to blue jeans, lawnmowers, and automobiles. With further market segmentation, why not have more differentiated audience categories to help advertisers hit their target niche on the consumer dartboard?

Anthony J. Adams, research director of Campbell Soup, recently said, in discussing life-style research: "Many product managers are bypassing both life-styles and demographics and moving directly to product usage as the primary targeting device." He believes life-style research has failed to meet its promise, that despite some successes, its users have questions about "discrimination, reliability, validity, and actionability."[19] The single-source services appear to have the best chance to succeed.

When we look at the second two categories discussed, the outlook is murkier. TVQ has earned its spurs over the years and with expansion into cable areas seems a safe bet for the future. Vox Box failed to gain support despite the advantages of a system that provided detailed commercial announcement audience information, a factor often asked for. The onetime expectations that Warner-Amex's two-way QUBE would serve in this area have vanished, as QUBE failed financially. Television Audience Assessment, a major entrant, staked out a broad area covering both quality of program and quality of viewing experience. For several years it had much going for it, not the least of which was security of funding from the Markle Foundation and financial support from major cable interests. Its failure in 1986 to gain commercial support for a continuing syndicated service suggests a bleak future for this form of qualitative measurement.

For such syndicated surveys to be useful, two major hurdles must be overcome. The first is the availability of population figures for newly dimensioned categories, because program nonviewers as well as viewers must be accounted for. The strength of demographics is the availability of an enormous U.S. Census base of data by geography. Services such as PRIZM and Cluster Plus, which build on census figures, can be readily linked to other market and media data. A second and more important requirement is that the media planners at agencies and advertisers use the qualitative service data as an input requirement for buying. Negotiating spot and network buys is a complex and costly operation at the agency level.[20] To simplify the process, the buyers have specific guides for each account. If the qualitative services ratings are slated to be used in buying, the stations and networks will rush to supply them. Otherwise the service's effectiveness in the advertising marketplace is marginal at best, and significant industry support is highly questionable.

## NOTES

1. *Proceedings of the 1980 Technical Conference on Qualitative Television Ratings—Final Report.* Corporation for Public Broadcasting, Washington, D.C., 1980, p. 6.
2. Dr. Paul F. Lazarsfeld, eminent sociologist, was perhaps first to recognize that detailed rating analysis could produce valuable qualitative insights. When Lazarsfeld headed the Princeton Radio Project in 1938, he encouraged the author to pursue such an inquiry, the results of which were published in 1939 by the Office of Radio Research, Princeton University, as "Social Stratification of the Radio Audience." The conclusions appeared in the *Public Opinion Quarterly*, June 1940, under the title, "The ABCD's of Radio Audiences," Vol. 4, No. 2, p. 195. Another distinguished sociologist, Dr. Samuel Stauffer, likewise expressed interest in the potential of ratings data for scholarly analysis.
3. *Focus on the MRI Advantage,* Mediamark Research, Inc., Plan for 1982 Reports, p. 1.
4. Ibid., p. 5.
5. *PRIZM, Geodemographic Market Segmentation and Targeting,* Claritas Corp., 1982, p. 3.
6. Steven Leavitt, president, Marketing Evaluations, telephone interview

with author on July 10, 1984.

7. Roger Percy, president, R. D. Percy, Inc., telephone interview with author on July 10, 1984.

8. *Boston (WGBH) Field Testing of a Qualitative Television Rating System for Public Broadcasting,* Corporation for Public Broadcasting, Office of Communications Research, June 1981, p. 3.

9. Ibid., p. 14.

10. "Qualitative TV Rating Study Shows Viewer Attitudes Toward Programs," Arbitron, *Beyond the Ratings,* May 1982, Vol. 5, No. 5, p.6.

11. "What Do Broadcast Audience Diaries Really Measure?," a presentation to the Advertising Research Foundation Conference, New York, November 11, 1975 by Canadian BBM Bureau of Measurement representatives.

12. *Trends in TV Commercial Recall 1965–1981,* Newspaper Advertising Bureau, New York, 1982.

13. Ronald E. Frank and Marshall G. Greenberg, *The Public's Use of Television: Who Watches What and Why.* Beverly Hills, California: Sage Publications, 1980.

14. *Audience Attitudes and Alternative Program Ratings: A Preliminary Study,* Television Audience Assessment, Inc., Cambridge, Mass., October 1981, inside front cover.

15. *Methodology Report,* Television Audience Assessment, Inc., 1983, p. 38.

16. Ibid., p. 40.

17. *Marketing News,* Jan. 2, 1982, p. 5.

18. The views of two highly respected professionals on this subject are of interest:

> Psychographics is needed only when demographics and socioeconomics do not properly sharpen what we are trying to learn. We have seen that behavior is much better, in many cases, than attitude or description of points of view, because behavior provides an indelible record of what people have done and is not subject to either respondent or researcher bias. [Emanuel H. Demby, "Two Decades Later: Psychographics," *Marketing Review,* American Marketing Association, New York Chapter, May/June 1984, p. 17].

> I don't have a high regard for syndicated segmentation schemes—particularly those based on values and life-styles. I'm against them because they are: too simple; too remote, too rigid; too unreliable . . . my objections to value/life-style measures relate strictly to their syndicated use for segmentation purposes in order to select potential targets. [Sonia Yuspeh, "Slamming Syndicated Data," *Advertising Age,* May 17, 1984, p. m-46].

19. Anthony Adams, "Life Style Research: A Lot of Hype, Very Little Performance," *Marketing News,* May 14, 1982, Section 2, p. 5.

20. Chet Bandes, vice president, Media Research, Doyle, Dane, Bernbach, in "Qualitative Research: Is There a Light at the End of the Tunnel?" *TV/Radio Age,* June 25, 1984, p. 75, remarked, "Analyzing Quantiplex data in conjunction with Arbitron or Nielsen data was fairly cumbersome. It consumed too much time, considering that the buying process is almost always . . . done against a deadline . . . Quantiplex was usually relegated to the position of being a supplemental service."

# 6  Cable Ratings (1979–1987)

Cable television has presented new challenges to the broadcast rating services. Developed originally in the 1940s (and for years known as CATV, Community Antenna Television), cable was strictly an extension of broadcast station coverage. It provided viewers satisfactory station reception in distant or difficult terrain situations by using strategically positioned antenna arrays and amplifiers and coaxial cable lines to carry the pictures to subscribers. The latter were thus able to receive some or additional TV stations with improved picture quality. By the 1960s, however, CATV had become cable. Growing penetration in some major cities such as San Diego and Buffalo, the expansion in number of channels offered to 36, 50 and beyond, and the emergence of Home Box Office and well-financed multiple service operators (MSOs) demonstrated that this was an important new communications medium that went well beyond its CATV beginnings. In 1976, the use of satellites to distribute cable-produced programming nationwide gave HBO, superstation WTBS, and Spanish International Network (SIN) a major upward thrust. This quickly brought in new cable networks led by CBN and USA. Meanwhile, major MSOs were battling each other and local aspirants to capture franchises in every U.S. city with over 100,000 population. This resulted in a phenomenal growth, with 400,000 new subscribers per month being added as 1984 began and industry estimates placing cable penetration at 43 percent of U.S. television households by July 1984.

## I. BASIC CABLE CHARACTERISTICS

In order to understand some of the problems of measuring audiences of cable-oriented programs, one must appreciate the fundamental differences between cable and commercial broadcasting:

160

• Cable is basically a subscriber service, not a 100% advertising-supported medium like broadcast TV. Total cable revenues exceeded $10.5 billion in 1986, of which only $948,000,000 (only 9 percent) came from advertiser expenditures. Doubling and tripling those ad figures will not swing the balance of subscription and ad revenue to anything like the magazine medium's experience (approximately 50/50). This economic fact of life accounts for cable management's priorities. Primary attention must go to increased subscription revenue—by system extension, higher household penetration along routes, better service, reduction of turnover and piracy, more pay tiers, higher revenue per subscriber, etc. The number of subscribers can go down as well as up. Little time or expertise is available for developing ad revenue, even less to concern over viewing numbers and rating services. New 1986 federal legislation giving cable operators freedom to raise rates could tempt franchisees to risk subscriber loss to increase profits.

• Cable, unlike broadcasting, is a capital- and labor-intensive business. The capital costs for a low-power television station serving a radius of 20 miles are about $200,000,[1] compared to an estimate of $60,000,000 for a cable system of 50 channels built to cover 100,000 households on a 50 percent penetration basis in the same area.[2] Capital investment in cable is estimated at $7 billion as of January 1984,[3] and with the accelerating costs attached to cabling such major cities as New York, Chicago, Philadelphia, Washington, Detroit, Baltimore, Cleveland, Minneapolis, and St. Louis, that figure could double by the decade's end. This means heavy debt loads and interest charges when money costs are close to historical highs.

• Cable, with its CATV background, and unlike radio or TV, has been a grass-roots development. It suffers as an advertising and marketing medium from its low penetration of major metropolitan areas. In February 1987, only one out of the top Arbitron Areas of Dominant Influence (ADIs) were credited with better than 50 percent penetration (Pittsburgh), whereas below 40 were New York and Dallas 37, Los Angeles 38, Washington 35, Detroit 36, Chicago 32, Minneapolis 35 and Baltimore 30 percent.

An Arbitron map showing county cable penetration by color code vividly portrays the asymmetrical spatial character of its deployment. The above-50 percent areas are concentrated in a few major regions: (1) the Appalachians from Kentucky north to the Canadian border, (2) Florida and western Georgia, (3) the lower Mississippi Valley, (4) Texas north through Kansas, (5) the Rockies north of Denver, and (6) significant West Coast areas from San Diego to Yakima (with Los Angeles, Fresno, Sacramento, and Portland well below average). The eastern seaboard (except for Connecticut) and most of the Midwest (except for the Peoria/Springfield area) are generally below average with great variability from ADI to ADI and from county to county.

• Cable systems are monopolies franchised by local government units to operate in prescribed limited geographic areas, not licensed by the FCC to operate in a competitive environment. This produces thousands of tiny units operating independent of each other with limited consistency of programming or scheduling across ADI/DMA's, regionally or nationally. Cable networks have no choice of "local affiliation"; if a system operator dislikes contract terms he can scuttle a network's service and the network has no place to go.[5] This monopoly situation affects another factor in syndicated audience measurement: There is only one entity to support local measurement, not a group of local competing TV or radio stations splitting the cost. There are now over 8000 cable systems operating, compared to 1400 TV broadcast stations. About 50 percent of these cable units have fewer than 10,000 subscribers.

• In its formative years cable leaders propounded the philosophy that it must be viewed as a medium akin to magazines, wherein specialized services would attract selective audiences that advertisers would seek and be willing to pay premium prices to reach. The term "narrowcasting" was frequently applied to this concept. Its corollary in audience measurement was that broadcasting's traditional average quarter-hour or average minute ratings were inappropriate. Cable should be evaluated on weekly cumulatives and on qualitative factors, not the traditional CPM of commercial television. A maverick on this point was Ted Turner, who boldly insisted that he was going to beat the networks at their own game. To do so, he encouraged Nielsen to rate superstation WTBS in its NTI report and did likewise with the Cable News Network.

Meanwhile advertiser interest in cable developed, not so much toward qualitative cable audiences as in the direction of cable network audiences as a replacement for rating points lost by commercial networks as a result of the intrusion of cable (especially HBO, which was not commercially available). So the quantitative measure won out, all cable networks went to NTI measurement as soon as they could qualify, and the Cable Advertising Bureau emphasized audience losses suffered by commercial broadcast networks, based on NTI data, and said little about the value of narrowcasting, a term rarely heard at present. One reason for this is that research studies have generally failed to show the substantial qualitative plus that cable exponents once propounded: greater impact and involvement with cable programming. The present desirable economic and demographic aspects of cable households is what we expect with a new medium with a monthly bill attached. This qualitative edge over broadcast TV will tend to diminish if cable penetration reaches the levels of 60 to 70 percent of households passed that many industry experts predict for 1990.

• Cable, in both its media and its measurement dimensions, originally suffered from an absence of accepted population data, especially at local levels. Until 1983 there were a variety of conflicting estimates about even national cable penetration, but the acceptance by both broadcasting and cable networks of Nielsen estimates has removed that obstacle. Some of the problem stems from piracy of the service and from what is called churn: the number of subscribers who cancel and must be replaced. A majority of cable franchises are small systems, operating with limited staffs so that record keeping and reporting on a current basis is an unproductive chore. Some cable systems were unwilling to release information about pay services and tiers.[6] Now both Arbitron and Nielsen supply periodic market penetration estimates (on an ADI and DMA basis respectively) which are based on diary sweep results.

## II. CABLE AUDIENCE MEASUREMENT

Whereas cable operators in the past attempted to position cable as a greatly different medium, superior to broadcast television, subscribers and viewers saw it as simply an extension of television. Going on the cable was much like acquiring an AM-FM receiver when you formerly had only AM: It brought more channels and more choices. (FM once abounded with "narrowcast" classical music stations, but today the program fare of AM and FM is virtually interchangeable.)

Advertisers, too, for the most part, use cable commercial programming much like broadcasting. A primary motive for advertiser use of cable is replacement of audience share lost from commercial TV due to cable erosion.

As a result, it is rational to try to measure cable-originated program audiences alongside broadcast audiences, using the same techniques, samples, etc. This means NTI meters at the national level and Arbitron and Nielsen diaries and meters at the local level. Early on, before the cable networks could qualify for NTI inclusion (because of limited coverage and penetration and low ratings), it became evident that diaries were underreporting cable audiences. Meter and coincidental studies have confirmed the Arbitron and Nielsen deficiencies in this area. (See the Methodological Test section below.)

Another problem in cable audience measurement was the exceedingly uneven penetration levels from county to county and town to town. The lack of uniformity in cable program originations available from one system to another, the lack of accurate program schedules and uncertain channel designations, plus poor system cooperation added administrative problems for the broadcast rating services. There has never been any real financial support from local cable systems for ratings services. In 1987 Paul Kagan estimated that only 22 percent of all U.S. systems representing 71 percent of subscribers were carrying local ads.

In the final analysis, research studies revealed that the failure of diary reporting is probably due to two factors:

1. A lack of a strong identity associated with the various cable networks, and their programs which makes them less memorable than commercial broadcast stations and networks (the problem for years felt by broadcast independents, especially UHF).

2. The remote-control tuning potential frequently associated with cable makes fast switching around from channel to channel much easier. Viewers using this technique (rather than a printed guide, for example) are less likely to know or remember the name of the program source, especially when it is a relatively unidentified new network. Some short tuning spurts during commercials or station breaks are invariably unreported (and this may be when cable network identifiers are missed).

We know that diaries are generally filled out after the fact, rather than concurrently with viewing. Recall omission errors are to be expected and can be tolerated if they are not too great and are random in nature. But we know this is not true, and that poses problems for cable program measurement.[7] Meters are the best answer; coincidentals are also free of the memory factor. Both techniques are expensive, and each has a severe limitation—meters (except peoplemeters) produce no people data; coincidentals produce no cume data (and are limited to certain interviewing hours).

## III. SYNDICATED CABLE MEASUREMENT SERVICES

By far the most meaningful cable rating activity has been produced at the national level, for several reasons. First is cable network interest and financial support from both advertiser-supported and pay cable services. Although cable networks were originally very reluctant to accept any form of broadcast audience measurement, they soon found, especially after WTBS became an NTI subscriber in 1980, that advertiser and agency demands for solid data could not be satisfied in any other way. Second, the Nielsen National Television Index provided cable's highest audience estimates, and, even though the measurement was for the average minute, it overcame the underreporting of cable audiences so prevalent with diaries. Experience in radio and broadcast television would have foretold the leading role of national measurement. In both cases, viable national network services preceded local measurements. Moreover, network services strongly influenced the character and usage patterns of the local measurements, even when different methodologies were applied. We therefore examine the development of network ratings first, followed by the less crystallized local situation.

## Network Cable Rating Services

### Nielsen Pay Cable Report

In December 1978, when cable was in about 18 percent of U.S. TV households, Nielsen announced plans for the first cable report—Pay Cable Report—to be launched in 1979. This report was produced quarterly from 33,000 NSI household diaries to show the national audience within pay cable homes by giving aggregate usage of cable systems—individual broadcast networks, independent stations, public broadcasting stations, superstations, pay cable, and all nonpay, nonbroadcast, cable-originated programming. Data are reported by day part and average day/time period. Audiences for Home Box Office, Showtime, and The Movie Channel are reported separately in the same format.

### Nielsen Individual Cable Network Monthly Pocketpieces

These are not syndicated reports, but are reports prepared to meet the requirements of individual cable network subscribers. The first such report was originated in February 1981 to serve Turner Broadcasting's Superstation WTBS. Cable networks have subscribed as they met the Nielsen minimum number of sample households. As of April 1987 reports were prepared for WTBS, HBO, CNN, CBN, ESPN, USA, Nickelodeon, Nick-at-Nite, Lifetime, the Nashville Network, the Weather Channel, Arts & Entertainment Network, Black Entertainment Television, and Financial News Network, each designed to produce ratings based on the particular cable network population and containing whatever information the network and the sample limitations dictate.

### NTI Cable Status Report

Issued monthly and quarterly, this is primarily a planning report, which reflects viewing within pay cable, basic cable, and noncable households. It provides estimates by day part of broadcast services and cable programming (including cable-originated programs) and is the primary source of industry trend data on aggregate cable audience trends.

### Nielsen Cable Activity Report (NCAR)

This is a special quarterly release that reports on household audiences to all Nielsen metered viewing categories. Ratings, share, and weekly cumulative audiences are reported for specific cable and broadcast networks, for independent TV stations, for total U.S. TV households, and for cable universe and pay cable households. Totals for TV network affiliates and independent stations are shown. It is a one-service comparison of cable and broadcast delivery.

### NTI Monthly National Audience Demographics Report (NAD)

The NTI NAD report provides estimates of national household and persons usage within cable and noncable households. Individual broadcast network program data on a household and person basis are classified according to cable and noncable households.

### Nielsen Cable Audience Profile Report (CAP)

Cable Audience Profile is a local cable audience measurement tool designed specifically to generate average quarter-hour and weekly cumes for 14 advertiser-supported cable networks. Using NSI sweep data, CAP evaluates the performance of the nationally distributed network on a local system or interconnect level by comparing a cable network's local viewership to the national viewing level for the same network. The result of this comparison is expressed as an index. These indices, used in conjunction with national metered cable network ratings, generate approximated local meter ratings for the system or interconnect. Four sweeps per year are reported for all markets and systems with sufficient sample to be reported by Nielsen (617 as of April 1987).

### Pay Cable Satisfaction Report

Developed by Nielsen to serve the concerns of HBO (and other pay cable subscribers), this report is a monthly diary-based survey in which viewer satisfaction is measured (on a five-point scale) along with usage. Satisfaction scores are used by HBO, for example, to produce Total Subscriber Satisfaction (TSS) scores. These are a product of multiplying viewing and satisfaction ratings. As Robert Maxwell, vice president for research at HBO, said: "Our bottom line is installs and disconnects, not ratings . . . consumers use us selectively and we look at such things as Gross Rating Points for multiple showings of movies, Cume, TSS, and Satisfaction. These are indicators of how successful we are at delivering a low disconnect rate and a high install rate. . . ."[9]

### Other Nielsen National Cable Services

Many other NTI reports show audience breakdowns between pay cable, basic cable, and noncable households. In addition, customized reports are prepared to meet specific needs of cable industry components. National cable estimates are released four times a year.

Nielsen annually publishes cable penetration figures on a market-by-market basis, including county estimates. Another important ongoing service is Cable On-Line Data Exchange (CODE), a data base of information on 11,000 headends,[10] including 350 variables for individual cable systems (subscribership, penetration, technical characteristics, programming carried, etc.). CODE is updated periodically to reflect recent developments.

## Local Cable Rating Services

Unlike broadcast television, where local measurement is keyed to 200 + measurement areas defined as ADI (Arbitron) and DMA (Nielsen), cable's 8000 franchise areas represent political rather than marketing areas. The result is a kaleidoscope that defies any systematic measurement.

• The franchise units are generally too small in size and number of subscribers to justify or support syndicated sample surveys. Two antidotes to this problem are (1) "interconnects," whereby several systems in a market area agree to sell availabilities in programming that both carry, thus affording larger audience units, and (2) mergers and swaps among multiple service operators to produce enlarged coverage areas by gaining contiguously owned systems that can be more efficiently managed, programmed, and sold as a larger unit. Although underway, both of these are long-term, not immediate solutions.

• Most (about 78 percent) cable systems serve less than 5000 subscribers; 87 percent less than 10,000.[11] The need for ratings measurement is negligible because there is no national advertiser interest in such small population units and local sales are made on the basis of local experience, not numbers. The competition is probably weekly newspapers, shopping news, and perhaps a local radio station.

• The disparity in channel capacity (12 to 100) between systems makes regularization of program schedules and local promotion difficult. Viewers have problems in reporting channels used, and rating services have problems giving proper credit. Upgrading is helping to solve this problem—by April 1986, 72 percent of systems had a channel capacity of 30 or more.

### Syndicated Local Services

It might be anticipated that ongoing local TV measurements (Arbitron and Nielsen Station Index) would produce cable audience figures. However, as just indicated, there are major barriers to that, and the two services handle this in different ways.

*Arbitron.*  Arbitron supplies local ratings for individual cable networks and superstations based on composite data from all franchises within each ADI. Each network or superstation must show a record of viewing for five minutes or more by a minimum of 20 percent of TV households during a survey week; this information is entered in the day-part summary section of their market reports.

In the November 1986 sweep report, Arbitron included cable audience estimates in 70 of the 214 television rating reports. Superstations were reported in over 200 markets. This is a significant showing considering claims of the Turner Broadcasting Service that diary/meter comparisons indicate that diaries reported only 55 to 58 percent of WTBS usage and 43 percent of viewing of CNN.[12]

*Nielsen NSI.* Nielsen supplies local cable ratings for individual cable networks and superstations within each DMA. Each (network, system, service) must show a record of viewing for at least five minutes by a minimum of 20 percent of TV households during a survey week; this information is entered in the day-part summary section of the *Viewers In Profile* report.

In the February 1987 sweep report, Nielsen included cable audience estimates in *97* of the *209* television market reports.

Nielsen's policy is that "locally originated cable programming would be reported by individual cable system in regular NSI Reports where minimum reporting standards—the same as for a TV station—are met."[13] Nielsen reports that one such programming source met these reporting standards in the February 1987 report. Nielsen provides the following reports:

• The 1987 County/Coverage study reports household audience and share of total viewing to cable-originated and pay cable programming by broad day part in the standard county-by-county format. Cable viewing shares are reported in the Station Summary and DMA Summary of the County/Coverage Study.

• NSI Plus, NSI's on-line computer analysis service, offers the capability of separating cable and noncable viewing and reports audience to cable-originated programming.

• *The NSI Total Activity Report* provides, for each Nielsen DMA, estimates of the amount of viewing for over-the-air affiliates, independents, cable-originated, and pay cable channels as a group. It does not break out channels.

## IV. METHODOLOGICAL STUDIES

In the early 1980s concerns arose in the cable industry about the weaknesses of the diary method of broadcast audience measurement. As evidence mounted that household diaries significantly understated cable-originated programming, several important projects were mounted to test new measurement techniques. The National Cabletelevision Association, Cable Television Advertising Bureau, and leading multiple service operators inaugurated and funded methodological research studies. In addition, Arbitron and Nielsen contributed money, time, and effort to the quest for better diary measurement of audiences to cable-originated programs. The results of three research studies undertaken in 1983—Cable Audience Methodology Study, Arbitron, and Television Audience Assessment—are discussed as follows.

## Cable Audience Methodology Study (CAMS)

CAMS is by far the most ambitious of the technical studies. It began in 1980, when the cable industry sought to clarify the many contradictory claims being made by various research supplies. At that time, an ad hoc committee was organized under National Cable Television Association (NCTA) auspices to explore more accurate measurement methods for cable-subscribing homes. The committee consisted of five cable industry representatives and five agency media research professionals. Gabe Samuels of J. Walter Thompson and William Ryan of Palmer Communications were its cochairmen. In 1981 the committee asked 68 research companies for new approaches to the problem. The committee selected A. C. Nielsen to work with it in designing a comprehensive methodological study.

In the fall of 1981, the newly formed Cabletelevision Advertising Bureau, together with the National Cable Television Association, created the CAB/NCTA Research Standards Committee, under the chairmanship of Jordan Rost, of Warner-Amex Satellite Entertainment Company. This committee, composed of 15 leading cable research and marketing executives, took the ad hoc committee's recommendations, further refined them, and raised the necessary funds to make the study a reality. From this, CAMS was born.

### CAMS Design

This $350,000 project tested six methodologies capable of determining both broadcast and cable viewing for a local franchise area. The six methods tested included two telephone recall and four diary techniques as follows:

1. Twenty-four-hour unaided telephone recall, calling the same person for seven consecutive days. During the first day's call, one randomly selected household member ages 12 years or older was recruited for follow-up calls. Daily calls to the same person used an unaided viewing collection procedure.

2. Twenty-four-hour aided telephone recall—different households were called each day for seven days with one randomly selected person (age 12 + ) interviewed with an aided viewing collection procedure. The fieldworker asked if the respondent watched ESPN, CNN, USA Network, HBO, an independent TV station, a public broadcasting station, WTBS, and/or NBC within the past 24 hours. A supplementary sample of 430 was added to the first day's calls of the unaided telephone recall test call to compare aided and unaided results. (Note: In all telephone recall interviewing, at least five attempts across three day parts were made to contact the randomly selected person. If not contacted within 48 hours of the time period being measured, the person or household was deleted from the sample).

3. Day-part, seven-day household diary—prediary week recruitment by telephone, also letters prediary and with diary, then one household day-part diary for each TV set with printed broadcast and cable channels were used.

4. Day-part, seven-day personal diary—same procedure as in (3) was used but was limited to one diary for one randomly selected individual in each household.

5. Half-hour, seven-day personal diary—one personal diary for randomly selected person in the household providing preprinted space for half-hour entries was used.

6. Standard Nielsen Station Index diary—one closed-end, seven-day, quarter-hour diary (the only quarter-hour test cell in the study) for each TV set was used. (Note: In all diary techniques, at least five attempts across three day parts and two days were made in recruiting household or individual. Besides the initial telephone call, respondent received prediary week letter, diary cover letter, reminder postcards at beginning and end of diary week, and $1 incentive).

With the exception of the NSI standard (quarter-hour) diary, other diaries requested viewing to be indicated by penciling in preprinted ovals for selected time periods to aid tabulation.

CAMS was conducted in June 1982 in two cities—Columbus, Ohio, and San Jose, California—where the cable systems tested (Warner-Amex and Gill Cable, respectively) offered at least 30 channels, with a local origination program channel, at least one text channel, three or more advertising cable networks, one or more pay channels, and three or more important signals. Samples were selected from both subscriber files and listed telephone directories. The two cities were about equally represented, with total sample sizes for test calls varying from 500 to 1500.

The validation tool used was a large-scale telephone coincidental (42,500 calls), with calls grouped so that each quarter hour would be a subsample of the total. Four day parts were measured by coincidentals. In addition, aggregate late-night tuning data for 11:30 P.M. to 8:00 A.M. from the Columbus two-way QUBE system was used as a supplementary validator for the 24-hour diary data and the telephone recall data.

### CAMS Results

Using the coincidental results as its yardstick of reality (even though it was not conducted with all the features attached to the Industry Research Standard coincidental used in many previous methodology studies), the CAMS findings were both eye opening and disappointing for all participants for the following reasons:

• None of the six techniques tested was able to measure audiences to cable-originated programs correctly. The final report said "Cable channels were one of the most difficult categories to measure, almost always being understated."[14]

• The accuracy of the telephone coincidental for producing ratings and share by program category and channel was confirmed by a limited number of comparisons between QUBE and coincidental findings in Columbus.

• The seven-day unaided telephone recall produced the results closest to the coincidental in determining number of persons using television (PUT). Nevertheless, this method overstated the broadcast network share by over 20 percent while understating both basic cable share and pay cable by 40 percent (persons ages 12 + , Monday–Friday 9:00 A.M.–11:00 P.M.).

• The Standard NSI diary, the current measurement technique, produced a low PUT of 15.4, about 20 percent below the coincidental level. On the other hand, broadcast (both network and independent) ratings were not too far below the yardstick numbers,[15] whereas basic and pay cable each lost 50 percent of its rating. The result was that the broadcast network share soared to 65, 23 percent above the coincidental, in contrast to losses of 43 percent and 33 percent respectively for basic and pay cable. The diary technique's response and nonresponse errors obviously dealt reported cable audience a hard blow.

• The personal half-hour diary produced the highest ratings of any of the tested techniques. Overall, it reported PUT 63 percent over the coincidental level but was the closest to the mark for pay cable. An analysis of absolute differences shows this technique furthest from the coincidental for broadcast affiliates and independents.

• The standard NSI diary was the only diary in the study that provided household ratings. It produced household usage levels (HUT) very similar to the coincidental. However, as was true with people ratings, broadcast network shares were overstated, in this case by 24 percent, while combined cable ratings and share were understated by 36 percent. Broadcast independents, as they did in the PUT comparison, came out remarkably close on the two methods.

Table 6-1, developed from the final CAMS report, shows the cost index and cooperation rate achieved for each methodology in the test.

## Assessment of CAMS

The CAMS results were a tremendous disappointment to an industry that had staked a large sum (for a relatively small advertising medium) to get answers to its audience measurement problems. The various alternative methodologies tested proved, with one possible exception,[16] to be inferior to the Nielsen standard household diary in overall accuracy. The fact that none of the tested techniques solved local cable problems meant that the industry had to rely on meters and coincidentals, methodologies which produce average-minute audience ratings, a measurement the cable industry had hoped to avoid. However, the study did confirm three points, to everyone's satisfaction:

1. The standard household diary understates cable-originated program ratings. (Nielsen and others knew this from diary–meter and diary–coincidental comparisons made well before the CAMS study.)

TABLE 6-1
Cost Index and Cooperation Rate for Six Methodologies Tested in CAMS

| Test Methodology[a] | Cost Index[b] | Cooperation Rate[c] |
|---|---|---|
| One-day aided 24-hour telephone recall | 260 | 84.0% |
| Seven-day unaided 24-hour telephone recall | 218 | 59.4% |
| Standard NSI household diary | 135 | 49.7% |
| Half-hour personal scannable diary | 120 | 55.8% |
| Day-part household scannable diary | 109 | 56.0% |
| Day-part personal scannable diary | 100 | 62.8% |

[a]All but the first listed collected seven days of viewing data.

[b]Cost was predicated on sample from subscriber list, 250 cases providing usable data, incentives for mail techniques. One-day recall method required 750 persons to equal other methods in relative accuracy.

[c]Proportion of Gill Cable/QUBE subscribers who were contacted and who provided usable viewing data. Excludes noncontacts and refusals to provide cable subscription data.

2. Coincidentals can accurately measure cable-originated program audiences. (The coincidental–QUBE comparisons, not revealed in the report—at the request of Warner-Amex—are the basis for this CAMS conclusion, again one that was universally accepted based on available meter-coincidental assessments.)

3. Audiences to cable program originations are difficult to measure, and the study showed *how* difficult it was. Nevertheless, it was left to the ratings companies to find a solution. The CAMS committee concluded with the hypothesis that the cable problems stemmed from the relative unfamiliarity with channel numbers on a 30 + system and low-rated cable program fare.[17] That, however, does not explain the situation with pay cable, where HBO had achieved significant audience success with well-known, highly publicized theatrical films. Yet pay cable was generally underrated by as great a degree as basic cable.

The CAMS design had several serious flaws:

• The only meter-type data were from QUBE's Columbus two-way system. This operation is not set up to produce either average-minute or cumulative ratings, and its results were of limited usefulness. Moreover the franchisee, Warner-Amex, sticks to a policy of not making any QUBE data public because it feels bound to subscribers not to.

• There was a lack of comparative data on both an average quarter-hour and a household basis, because the committee wanted to establish new measurements for people on a cumulative basis.

• On the other hand, in seeking to develop new tools for measuring weekly cumulative audiences, the report states: "There is no proven standard by which to validate personal cume data."

• Proposed validation efforts for household cumulatives rested on developing ratios from Nielsen Television Index meters between average quarter-hour and cumulative data for three broadcast and three cable networks. These ratios would be applied to data from telephone coincidentals for each network. After examining the results "It was determined that the data could not be correlated between national rating estimates and the local system estimates provided by CAMS."[18] Rank order analyses were performed to produce correlations of average audience ratings and the corresponding daily cumulative audience for six techniques. The high correlation coefficient persuaded Nielsen that "these methodologies have potential for being used to provide cumulative data for cable channels. However, the cume methodologies must be validated."[19]

The CAMS report closed with the following list of questions and the conclusion that "The cable industry is determined to find answers to these and any other questions that can improve the accuracy of audience measurement:[20]

1. What is the easiest way for a cable viewer to identify and report viewing, channel number, or the name of the service on that channel?
2. What is the effect of different types of converters on the ability to correctly identify the channels being viewed?
3. The half-hour diary is overreporting. Is this a feature of the rostering or the ease of simply checking off boxes in the diary?
4. The telephone recall methods established good PUT levels. What would be the effect of different probes to reconstruct viewing activity?

## Arbitron Two-Way Cable/Cable Diary Test

The Arbitron Ratings Company had conducted a number of tests beginning in 1979 in an effort to find a diary that would overcome the shortcomings of their standard TV household diary in measuring cable-originated program audiences. None of these tests, including experiments with a personal diary (which Arbitron uses successfully in radio), produced any improvements in cable measurement. Focus group research indicated "that cable subscribers were not aware of what services they received. From this we inferred that a viable cable diary would need to specifically 'educate' diary keepers about their cable services, as well as give them general cable instructions."[21]

The Two-Way Cable/Cable Diary Test was designed to answer these questions:

1. Is diary-based measurement appropriate for cable viewing?
2. Can we develop a cable diary to "educate" cable diary keepers and improve their ability to report all set use?
3. Is telephone-aided recall, such as that previously used by Arbitron, appropriate to measure viewing on local cable systems?

Two-way cable measurement was selected as the validation method since by scanning household converters it can provide meterlike average minute data.[22] A big advantage in this design is that the diary and meter data come from *the same households,* thus removing sampling error and permitting significant results from a small sample.

### Method

The following four methods were involved:

1. Two-way cable measurement.
2. Standard diary-based measurement.
3. Special cable-diary measurement, complemented by special cable procedures (letters, phone calls, etc.).
4. Telephone-aided recall measurement.

The special cable diary and procedures began with telephone placement, which identified cable subscribers and system used. Households then received a prelisted cable diary (showing all channels offered by their system) and prelisted noncable diary for each wired and unwired set in the household. The listing contained channel ID/call letters, dial setting, and channel description at the front of the diary. A special "Cable Hotline" was established for subscribers to call with questions about diary keeping, and Arbitron letters and phone calls gave special attention to cable viewing.

Four test markets in the East and South were used. All systems offered over 30 channels with at least one pay service available. Only the South Atlantic system was used in the two-way test.

With the exception of the two-way sample, all research samples were randomly selected from subscriber lists. The single-system two-way sample was part random and part convenience. The initial selection to receive the special two-way converter was randomly selected, but substitution of adjacent locations was permitted. Replacing old one-way equipment with the two-way converter started many months before the actual test (the minimum was three months). At the time of installation, respondents were told that these converters transmitted data to the cable system and might be used by Arbitron for research purposes. Confidentiality was assured and release forms were signed. A total of 170 households comprised this two-way sample.

Possible limitations on the two-way cable validation could emanate from these factors: (1) small size of sample, (2) older than average population with higher ratio of retired, (3) biasing of convenience selection, and (4) conditioning effect on diary and telephone interviews (three to six months after two-way converter installation).

## Test Design

- Use of two-way scan versus standard diary, June 1982.
- Nonscan households received either standard diary or special cable diary, June 1982.
- Test of two-way scan versus telephone-aided recall, October 1982.

## Results

### Standard Diary Versus Two-Way Cable

- Overall viewing from two-way data exceeded diary results by 19 percent (6:00 A.M.–2:00 A.M. day); between 9:00 A.M. and 6:00 P.M. the diary was underreported by 27 percent.
- Basic cable (including superstations) was underreported by 34 percent.
- Pay cable lost 40 percent in average quarter-hour rating.

- Broadcast service estimates for affiliates were fractionally overreported while independents and imported signals were 40 percent underreported in the diary.

### Standard Diary Versus Cable Diary

- Response rate improved 3.6 points for cable diary (from 40.5 percent for standard to 44.1 percent).
- Overall HUT levels rose, with cable diary up by 7 percent.
- Basic cable gained 18 percent in average quarter-hour rating and pay 29 percent in cable diary estimates.
- Cable diary improvements were consistent across day parts.
- Broadcast ratings were virtually unaffected.
- Persons estimates showed the same patterns—slightly higher ratings for basic and pay cable services, with little or no change in broadcast ratings.

*Telephone-aided Recall Versus Two-Way Cable.*   Arbitron found that this test produced "no meaningful comparisons" because two-way data were for a single set and for a household, whereas telephone interview was limited to a single person's recall.

### Arbitron Conclusion

Arbitron reached two conclusions:[23] "Special cable diaries seem to help, but the current information does not indicate much improvement. More testing needs to be done in this area."

Arbitron would not resume use of the aided telephone recall technique. The test survey produced no basis for resuming use of that method, formerly employed in the Arbitron Network Cable Report (ANCR) and its Cable Audience Measurement and Profile (CAMP) studies, which had been suspended in October 1982.

### Assessment

This Arbitron methodological study was a pioneering effort in use of specially placed two-way converters in a sample panel for validation purposes. It produced useful if limited results in terms of testing the standard Arbitron TV household diary. The results show deficiencies in rating cable audiences very similar to those produced by CAMS when Nielsen tested its diary against coincidentals.

The test of a new cable diary with special roster and respondent aids was encouraging in that cable services showed audience gains while broadcast service stayed level with the standard diary. There was enough improvement to hope that the diary may still prove reasonably valid for cable audience measurement. To that end, Arbitron conducted another test in November 1983. They used two diary forms: (1) Arbitron's now-standard "illustrated diary" and (2) a special cable diary along with customized "educational" efforts to motivate respondents to keep accurate diaries. This study is due for release in 1985.

## V. TELEVISION AUDIENCE ASSESSMENT (TAA) STUDY

The details of the pilot survey conducted by TAA in two markets in 1982 were covered in Chapter 5. This survey was financially supported by cable interests who hoped it would produce evidence of a qualitative slant for cable programs—therefore the results are reported here.

### TAA Results

#### Insights Regarding Television Viewing

While Americans are watching more television than ever before, they are also watching more channels. Viewing patterns reflect a new video mobility made possible by remote controls and special format cable programs as indicated in the following TAA highlights:

*Unplanned viewing.* Programs are often selected at the time of viewing. Fewer than half of all programs watched were selected in advance of watching.

*Many dropouts.* Less than two-thirds of the audience for an average hour-long program actually watches it to the end.

*High audience turnover.* On the average, in cable markets, only one-third of the audience for one week's episode returns to watch the next episode of the same series the following week.

*Reduced channel loyalty.* Viewers with cable television switch channels more often than viewers in uncabled areas; viewers with premium-pay services show the greatest mobility.

*Reduced commercial exposure.* Nearly 15 percent of broadcast viewers and nearly 40 percent of cable subscribers report that they "always" or "often" change channels during commercial breaks.

*Increased channel switching.* This is a practice encouraged by new program formats. Two-thirds of Music TV (MTV) viewers report turning to the program service during the commercial break in another program. After a few minutes, about 20 percent stay with MTV but 70 percent return to their original show.

*Viewers leaving the room.* Half the audience leaves the room at least once during the course of a show, and most of these people leave more than once during both program and commercials.

*Numerous distractions.* Forty to 50 percent of the audience is eating dinner, washing dishes, reading, talking on the telephone, or doing something else while the TV is on.

## New Qualitative Ratings

TAA's primary goal in the prototype study was to test the reliability, stability, and utility of its proposed system of qualitative ratings to supplement traditional quantitative ratings data. The system is based on two indexes:

*The Program Appeal Index* measures the overall entertainment value of a television program. It gauges the level of viewers' enjoyment and provides an estimate of whether viewers will plan ahead to watch a program and remain loyal to it over time.

*The Program Impact Index* measures the degree of intellectual and emotional stimulation a program gives its viewers. It relates to how involved or distracted viewers are while watching.

Both indexes, which use a 1–100 scale to assess programs' different effects on their viewers, were tested for television programming and advertising.

## Program Appeal

Program appeal ratings show that Americans enjoy television. On a 1–100 scale, the average Appeal score of over 250 programs rated in the study was 73, and 90 percent of all shows were scored at 50 or above by their viewers. The highest-rated program received an Appeal score of 91, whereas the lowest was 46.

Individual shows can score high or low regardless of their genre; the variation in Appeal scores within each genre is far greater than the differences between genres. A program's Appeal score can vary noticeably among different audience subgroups.

The appeal of series programs is remarkably consistent from one episode to the next, both for first-run network shows and for syndicated "strip" series. This stability is striking in light of the high turnover among viewers of series programs.

High Appeal scores identify which programs people are most likely to plan ahead to view and remain loyal to over time. In the case of ongoing programs, advance planning usually leads to increased viewer loyalty and repeat viewing. Said a TAA report:

> The television industry has an adage: If they watch it, they like it, reflecting the long-held assumption that the bigger the audience, the more appealing the show. In fact, Television Audience Assessment . . . shows: The size of the audience is not a sufficient gauge of a program's appeal. Programs with small audiences can be highly satisfying to those who watch them, and programs with large audiences may rate relatively low on a appeal scale.[25]

## Program Impact

Programs vary more in their emotional and intellectual impact on viewers than in their general appeal. The lowest Impact rating for a program in the prototype ratings study was 14, the highest 86. The Impact ratings given for all shows averaged 44. This wider range indicates that the Impact Index is a more sensitive measure than the Appeal Index. The audience generally finds high-impact programs highly appealing as well. The greater the emotional and intellectual stimulation offered by a show, the more viewers report enjoying the program, while as a rule programs they rate as having low impact, they also rate as having low appeal.

High-impact programs involve their viewers, who tend to give the program their undivided attention. While 44 percent of viewers who rate the program they are watching very low on Impact are doing something distracting while it is on, only 18 percent of those giving a high Impact rating are so distracted. If viewers feel involved in a program, they are more likely to stay in the room during the entire show. For low-impact programs, 46 percent of the audience leaves during the commercials, compared to only 26 percent of viewers who rate the viewed program high on the impact. The TAA report continued:

> These findings suggest that within the basic television audience there exists another, smaller, more realistic and more effective market—the people who are actually present and paying attention. The Program Impact Index provides advertisers and programmers alike with a basis for estimating the size and composition of this second market."[26]

## "The Multichannel Environment"

The TAA report "The Multichannel Environment" contains the findings most relevant to cable. Highlights from the report show that cable subscribers:

• Hold a more positive overall attitude toward television than viewers who had rejected cable subscription.

• Are, on average, younger, larger, and higher-income families and own more TV sets, video cassette recorders (VCRs), and video games than nonsubscribers.

• Have a strong interest in sports and movies, while nonsubscribers lean more heavily toward cultural activities, the arts, social concerns, and news.

• Watch two more channels, on average, than nonsubscribers but less than one-fourth of the channels receivable.

• Give broadcast programming the same scores as viewers without cable.

• Did not find cable programming any more appealing or involving than broadcast programs. Basic and pay cable viewers alike made little distinction between cable and broadcast programming in Appeal scores. In Impact ratings, pay cable viewers actually scored broadcast programming significantly higher on average than cable originations.

• Were not more attentive or more likely to remain in the room throughout programs than panelists with only broadcast TV.

• Watched no more than 30 minutes per week of evening programs offered by advertising-supported basic cable networks. Only two such networks were viewed by more than 10 percent of the available audience during the two weeks studied.

• Watched more sports than nonsubscribers, and multipay subscribers watched most of all. Premium subscribers watched more movies and sports and less news and public affairs than people without pay cable service.

As the TAA sums it up: "In other words, cable is not necessrily associated with higher 'qualitative' program ratings. Variation in viewer response appears to be directly due to the program itself."

*Assessment.*   These findings were a serious blow to the cable industry. The latter had staked much on their claims that cable, with its special programming, would involve viewers and deliver an attentive and premium audience. Cable was now revealed to be what many people had anticipated—an improved delivery system to provide subscribers with a broader selection of program choices; and people watched programs, not channels.

## VI.  WARNER-AMEX QUBE RESEARCH

Researchers concerned with cable have for years been curious about what could be learned about viewing of cable-subscribing homes from the two-way QUBE service of Warner-Amex Cable Communications, Inc. Warner-Amex had released virtually nothing until Dr. Hazel Kahan, vice president of research, gave two revealing presentations to professional groups in 1983. The data presented are not of a methodological nature but does provide new insights into the hetero-geneous nature of viewing in cable-subscribing households.

The first presentation[27] drew on telephone coincidental surveys conducted by Nielsen Home Video Index in sample QUBE households in five markets during June 1983, as well as data from QUBE and other sources. In the five markets (Cincinnati, Columbus, Pittsburgh, Houston, and Dallas), the coincidental showed broadcast getting a prime-time share of 58. Whereas cable programs had no reportable NSI audience, among all TV households they garnered a 49 share on the Nielsen coincidental in QUBE homes. Looking at the situation in individual QUBE systems shows wide variation in shares: from 36 in Columbus (the original home of QUBE) to 56 in Dallas. This variation, said Dr. Kahan, "does not seem to be related to channel capacity as we once thought. Pittsburgh and Dallas each had 80 channels, but cable audience shares were 42 and 53 respectively. Even though we have a QUBE penetration of 70–80 percent in Cincinnnati, QUBE sets are only 29 percent of all TV sets . . . with 73 percent of the viewing going on in prime time on those sets."

Dr. Kahan, citing a Roper survey which reported that the second most-frequent family activity, after eating, is TV watching, concludes: "So families are still watching TV together. That is a very different scenario from the one futurologists have painted of narrowcasting, of television as a personal medium, of people sitting in their own little rooms, each watching their own TV sets."

In her second presentation,[28] Dr. Kahan observed, "Although there is undeniably appeal in the concept of lots of channels, this appeal quickly diminishes . . . and we see the enchantment give way to discomfort as the subscriber understands that *more is not necessarily better . . .*" The subscriber soon finds by flipping around that only a few cable channels actually offer him or her something to watch. Dr. Kahan asserted that her research on limited channel use "will allow us to readjust our thinking, our planning, our programming— for we made false preliminary assumptions about what our subscribers wanted."

Subscribers want more options, and their choice of new programming formats will produce new viewing patterns. The number of viewers per set is considerably higher for cable channels than for broadcast channels, partly because of larger households and partly because people tend to cluster in front of the home's single cable outlet. Adapting to the unfamiliar "megachannel" environment requires time, and the changes in people's usage patterns may somewhat confound researchers.

The Warner-Amex QUBE data show "that 30 channels account for over 95 percent of viewing and that this number of channels reaches 100 percent of our households. The following table shows a consistent picture for three systems":[29]

### Percent Viewing by Number of Channels[a]

| Number of Channels | Percent of Viewing | | |
| --- | --- | --- | --- |
| | System A | System B | System C |
| 5 | 67.4 | 54.1 | 66.4 |
| 10 | 85.3 | 76.1 | 86.1 |
| 15 | 94.4 | 88.8 | 95.0 |
| 20 | 97.8 | 94.4 | 97.1 |
| 25 | 99.2 | 96.8 | 98.5 |
| 30 | 99.9 | 96.1 | 99.9 |

[a]Source: QUBE, 1983.

The pattern is consistent despite the wide range of programmed channels— from 33 to 66. On average, 9 channels are used during the average week, 14 during the month. This, said Dr. Kahan, *"does not tell us that the same nine channels are being used by each household."*

Dr. Kahan's conclusions were that "We need more than four or five channels, we need less than 80 to 108 . . . People recoil from so much choice . . . the number of channels that survive is a function of advertising dollars available *and* a function of the hours people spend watching television."

## VII. SUMMARY

In its search for adequate measurement of audiences to cable-originated programs, the cable television industry has passed several important milestones in recent years.

• Acceptance of broadcast-type measurements (average minute and average quarter hour) by most cable networks; a recognition that cable program audiences are only a share of one total television audience.
• Recognition from the CAMS and Arbitron methodological studies that accurately measuring cable-originated programs will be difficult and that only meters and coincidentals can demonstrably do the job at this time.
• Recognition by both local rating companies that present household TV diaries seriously understate cable program audience size. Arbitron and Nielsen have both tested new diary approaches without any significant success.
• Realization, based on results of studies such as TAA that earlier cable claims about the superior impact of cable programming were largely unsupportable by objective research.
• Until the syndicated local rating services develop more accurate techniques than the present household diary, most local cable program ratings there may well be supplied by custom coincidentals.
• Significant forward steps were taken in reaching better sources for more uniform and reliable universe estimates of cable penetration and households by market area if not by franchise area.
• Realization that "more is not better," that subscribers use only a fraction of cable services programmed, and that 30 to 35 channels account for nearly all viewing regardless of numbers of system channels available.
• Recognition that realistically there is no way that ratings and audience data can be developed at the franchise level. Only a handful of individual systems would have need for or be able to afford such studies. Since each system is a monopoly, there is no syndicate over which to spread costs as in broadcasting— each system would foot the entire bill.

The formation of interconnects, grouping franchises into common market areas which can standardize channel assignments, audience and sales promotion and sales efforts, jointly supported is the way to go (CAB lists over 200 in its 1987 Directory).

The hype of 1981 and 1982 has given way to a realistic appreciation of cable's place in the spectrum of electronic media—alongside broadcast radio and television. Many problems remain, but their solution is more likely now that the industry fully understands what measurements are needed and can be afforded. With earlier misconceptions cleared away, a more realistically targeted approach to cable advertising solutions is possible in the immediate future.

## NOTES

1. William Stiles, executive vice president, Spanish International Network (SIN), operator of several LPTV stations, telephone interview with the author, July 11, 1984.
2. Author's estimate, based on conservative per-subscriber cost of $600.
3. Dennis Leibowitz, of Donaldson, Lufkin & Jenrette, telephone interview with the author, July 11, 1984.
4. "Arbitron Updates U.S. Cable Penetration," press release, February 23, 1984.
5. *The New York Times,* February 21, 1984, reported the intense frustration of several cable networks—Showtime/The Movie Channel, Disney, Playboy, Bravo, and the Nashville Network—which are not carried on Manhattan Cable serving "an area that many industry officials say holds the most desirable cable-television audience in the nation."
6. Ruth J. Betzer, A. C. Nielsen Co., in a letter to the author dated May 17, 1984, enclosing data from Ed Aust, manager of custom surveys, A. C. Nielsen.
7. In Appendix D the biases of recall are delineated in the digest of "Radio Audience Measurement, 1944": older-age programs, longer length programs, and higher-rated programs produce highest recall ratings relative to coincidental measures. The opposites are clearly underrated.
8. Nielsen press release, September 10, 1980.
9. Robert Maxwell, "Pay TV Demands New Research Techniques," remarks before the Radio/TV Research Council, New York, November 28, 1983.
10. A "headend" is the antenna point at which a cable system picks up its programs from broadcast stations and satellites. Some systems (about 20%) have more than one headend because of terrain factors. This means that the cable system can have different programming emanating from each headend. Therefore, Nielsen uses the headend as the unit of record.
11. Cabletelevision Advertising Bureau, tabulations of April 1986.
12. Robert Sieber, vice president for research, Turner Broadcasting System, telephone conversation with the author on April 10, 1984.

13. Roy Anderson, executive vice president, Nielsen Media Services, telephone interview with the author on April 2, 1984.
14. *Cable Audience Methodology Study, 1983*, Cabletelevision Advertising Bureau and National Cable Television Association, p. 55.
15. Average quarter-hour ratings for TV households should be about 5 percent above the average-minute coincidental results.
16. The seven-day unaided telephone recall was marginally better than the NSI diary except for pay cable.
17. "Observations," CAMS report, p. 6.
18. CAMS report, p. 50.
19. Ibid., p. 50.
20. Ibid., p. 59.
21. "Cable: Two-Way Cable/Cable Diary Test, a Summary of Findings, 1983," Arbitron Ratings.
22. This was the first use of two-way cable data as a measurement tool in contrast to the use of telephone coincidentals in the CAMS study. The latter did, however, utilize limited QUBE data in this fashion, but no results were released.
23. "Cable: Two-Way Cable/Cable Diary Test, a Summary of Findings, 1983," Arbitron Ratings.
24. *TAA Methodology Report*, p. 94.
25. "The Audience Rates Television," *TAA Executive Summary*, p. 4.
26. Ibid., p. 5.
27. Hazel Kahan, vice president for research, Warner-Amex Cable Communications, "Means Are Meaningless, or Variance Is the Name of the Game," Cable Television Administration and Marketing Society, San Diego, August 10, 1983.
28. Hazel Kahan, "The Cable Subscriber Speaks: Channels, Choice or Chaos," Advertising Research Foundation, December 15, 1983.
29. Ibid.

# 7

# Using Ratings Data

## I. INTRODUCTION

Just as the human nervous system controls all human functional activity, so do ratings control every functional activity in the broadcast industry.

This chapter discusses many of the different ways in which audience data are used. Nonprofessionals, whose familiarity with rating numbers is largely confined to periodic press accounts of rankings of national commercial networks and programs, are usually surprised to learn what detailed behavioral knowledge audience ratings services provide.

Any discussion of ratings usage must be connected to a fundamental aspect of the broadcast media (radio, TV, cable)—the perishability of electronic communication. Once a program is aired, the audience and the potential commercial time it bears are gone forever, never to be regained. Like the airline seat, empty when the jet takes off, or the tickets still in the box office after Sunday's pro football game, these unsold units are down the drain—there's no chance for revenue recovery by stockpiling or sale pricing at a later date. This aspect of commercial broadcasting creates a situation where marketplace supply-and-demand factors are potent in determining pricing.

Buyers look for the best buy on the basis of criteria established for the product in question using conventional rating parameters. But the ratings by which buyers and programmers alike gauge their activities are only measurements of the past, not the future when the new programs and commercials run. Any given program under consideration is likely to have quite a different audience in November than it did in May (perhaps the last rating available) or in November last year. Changed competition, lead-in, seasonal factors, and long-range trends can all affect the coming November audience. Yet some estimate of the effect of these many factors must be made in order to determine whether the networks' and the advertisers' target objectives are likely to be met. Analysts for seller and buyer alike make estimates but ultimately must come to reasonable agreement for commitments to be made.

Ratings, which are themselves estimates (albeit objective approximations), are now used as a basis for further predictions based on judgmental and subjective procedures. As follows, there are several checks on this process—the postbuy evaluation and the make-good. Nevertheless, in approaching the practical use of ratings, it is important to understand the perishable nature of commercial broadcast time and the necessity for estimating future audience behavior from past ratings. In this complicated activity, what the general public sees—network standings and the rank order of programs on a household basis—has little operational significance despite their value for network prestige and promotion purposes.

To discuss the uses of ratings, we start with the national television network ratings and their use at the network level. This includes a detailed synopsis of the various TV rating services that quantify the many audience aspects of a new network program. Following that we go to local TV ratings and then radio ratings. (Cable rating usage is still in a formative state, as indicated in Chapter 6 and will not be covered here.) In each case, we discuss the broadcasters' usage first because they are primary sponsors of the independent measurement services (defraying about 85 percent of the total cost). Then we look at the station representative firms that conduct the national spot sales function for local stations. Advertising agencies and advertisers are treated next, followed by many other service organizations that facilitate sales—buying services, computer services, etc. Then the use by program producers and syndicators is examined, and finally, applications by those outside the industry: the government, the press, and the public are shown.

## II.  COMMERCIAL TELEVISION NETWORKS

The phone rings on the bedside table in a richly furnished Beverly Hills home. The clock on the table registers 5:05 as a man's arm reaches the phone at the instant the second ring starts. Obviously he has anticipated the call, because he is immediately wide awake and has a pen and preprinted sheet of paper at hand. After a curt "Good morning," he begins furiously writing numbers on the sheet. These are Nielsen rating numbers for the preceding Friday, Saturday, and Sunday nights being read to him by a research department employee in New York. The man in Beverly Hills is the network's program vice president preparing himself for today's possible repercussions from those rating figures. In somewhat different conditions, perhaps, two other network program heads are also getting the numbers at about the same time.

Although the above account is fictional, it is close indeed to reality and not at all exaggerated. Listen to the actual testimony of some who have been there:

"The ratings dominate Mr. Daly's (Robert A. Daly, president of CBS Entertainment) life. They are the first thing he thinks about in the morning, he says, and one of the last things he thinks about at night."[1]

"At the network, every morning a report card comes in on your performance of the day before. . . . The stakes are so high—millions and millions of dollars riding on every show. It's a constant state of tension—high anxiety morning noon and night."[2]

President Thomas Wyman of CBS told a meeting of the New York Society of Security Analysts, "One percentage point differential [in ratings] is more important than the output of all development programs in the next thirty-six months."[3]

The conventional wisdom in 1983 was that each prime-time rating point represents an incremental $50 million in advertising revenue and each daytime point an extra $35 million, and those increments go straight to the bottom line.

If rating points are that important, if they can cause the rise and fall of network heads and other top executives, the ratings are obviously of consuming interest from day to day. In only a few businesses, such as retailing or entertainment or professional sports, are day-to-day performance figures available to management (and in retailing, of course, Macy's doesn't tell Gimbels). The daily Nielsen figures go directly to each network by computer-to-computer delivery early each morning from the rating company's Dunedin, Florida, operations center. These "dailies" are the ratings for prime-time programs broadcast two days previously. In addition, each research department receives the overnight ratings from Nielsen and Arbitron meter services in major markets for the preceding day, also delivered by computer. These two sets of data are processed and copied at top speed because the research departments try to have daily ratings on all executive desks by 9:00 A.M. Occasionally when delays occur, the delivery of 200 reports in the proper pecking order demands an orchestrated effort that would challenge a Toscanini—make sure everyone has the figures before the first phone call about them. William Rubens, NBC vice president for research, states:

> This constant pressure for the "overnights" is partly to satisfy yet another vital need—the psychic need for ratings, that is, the very human need to know how well you are doing. The truth is that for the network executive who is basically concerned with national audiences, the value of the three local overnight ratings reports is limited. . . . As a predictor of the national ratings, delivered just a day later [they are] far from perfect. No matter; the overnights remain must-reading.[4]

In some cases, past trend figures are included in the daily issues while weekly summaries, which may include news, sports, and weekend ratings, are furnished to keep executives abreast of the schedule performance through trend figures provided. So we see here the beginning of a feedback process that starts with crude figures that undergo many refinements throughout the broadcast industry during subsequent weeks and months.

## Rating Streams

The ever-widening stream of rating information that contributes to the large audience data base eventually available to the skilled network analyst can best be visualized by using an example of an imaginary new network program, "Wigwam Waltz." The first thing we learn is that a single initial household rating figure (let's say 15) for "Waltz" is meaningless until we know what time period it was scheduled in, its share, its competition (reruns, regular, and/or special), lead-in, lead-out, previous program in its period, day of week, season of year, etc. We are at first limited to household data from meters, but within 10 days the first demographic breakdowns appear and thousands of new analyses are made possible, while continuous daily meter reports provide important early trends.

If you were the producer of "Wigwam Waltz," you would be like a plainsman waiting for the first spring freshets to enter the dried-out riverbed. The first tiny rivulets are the *"overnights,"* the Nielsen and Arbitron meter figures from a number of major markets that reach networks and others by 9:00 A.M. the next morning covering the previous day from 6 A.M. to 1:00 A.M.[5] Next day, the Nielsen NTI network daily rating (the national Nielsen) is delivered by desk-top terminal. These are now household meter reports followed by demographics a day later and are preliminary in nature. Nielsen's Fast Weekly Households Report (mailed the fifth day following the end of the report week) is the earliest "final" national data available. At about the same time, Arbitron and Nielsen mail their weekly meter audience reports for individual markets to subscribers. These reports supply more complete details on time period and program audience estimates than do the original overnight figures. Four days later, Nielsen (during the first 18 weeks of the season beginning in September) mails the Fast Evening Persons Audiences Reports, which provide the first network persons ratings available (from NAC diary homes). Total persons, 14 age/sex breaks, and other details are provided.

The Nielsen national TV ratings pocketpiece covers a two-week period and is mailed 12 days following the end of the report period. The best-known and longest continuously produced Nielsen ratings report, it would compare in importance to a rise in the plains river to the producer's hip level. The pocketpiece provides the following information:

- Household estimates by individual weeks.
- Person audience estimates for 19 age/sex categories.
- Season-to-date program averages.
- Program type averages.

- Overall TV usage versus previous year.
- TV usage by time periods and day parts.

The arrival of the NTI pocketpiece marks the end of the first cycle of rating estimates. The data flow then becomes more measured. NTI's *Market Section Audiences Report* two weeks later provides data by geography, county size, cable status, and selected demographics including household size, presence of nonadults, and education of head of household. Although issued nine times a year, five of these reports are released for the September-through-December fall season. Thus, "Wigwam Waltz's" performance could well be explored from many angles within a month. Another audience aspect is covered by Nielsen's Program Cumulative Audiences, a report issued five times annually to show the program's cumulative audience reach across four weeks, the average number of telecasts received per household, and a frequency distribution by number of telecasts. "Waltz's" reach and frequency characteristics can then be matched to the requirements of particular advertisers. A brand cumulative audience report provides similar audience information by brands, because so much of television is purchased on numerous commercial exposures spread over several networks and day parts. These come out three times a year (October, February, and July) and present full competitive brand data as well as your own. This data flow brings the river to midriff level.

A data output report comparable to the pocketpiece in importance is the National Audience Demographics report (NAD), which consists of two volumes, revealing the most detailed analysis of television viewing in print. The reports, produced seven times a year (three in the fourth quarter) give a wide variety of television usage data by day parts. Television usage and network program audience by half hours, television usage by lady of the house and working women, for example, gives estimates of total audience ratings for network and other programs. The NAD report provides clients with a multidimensional picture such as women ages 18 to 49 in households with incomes of $30,000 + . The first NAD fall report is mailed in late November, one month after the close of the period covered. A supplement provides costs per thousand viewers data for programs.

The foregoing list is by no means complete—the list of Nielsen reports includes Buying Guides, Tracking Reports, Planners Reports, Cable TV/Status. A two-volume listing of all network feature films and audiences since 1961, is updated three times a year.

### Local Diary Input

Arbitron and Nielsen now provide data from fall local sweeps. These four-week diary reports from some 200+ television markets across the country generally measure the months of November, February, May, and July and are mailed to subscribers three to four weeks later. This information tells the producer and the network airing "Wigwam Waltz" a great deal about its audience delivery in different competitive and regional situations. The producer is now swamped with data and probably needs the professional help of trained research analysts to interpret it. Many special ratings analyses are possible by using computers, either at the network or agency, the rating service or at organizations that make available an endless variety of special tabulations based on published and unpublished data.

With the general picture of ratings output in mind, we can now see how industry elements use the broad data base at hand.

## Network Program Schedules

Developing the annual fall network program schedule is perhaps the most important effort at each network, and ratings plus vast amounts of qualitative research on new programs are used to interlock a night-by-night schedule that will bring in the maximum audience for its shows. These three schedules account for close to 80 percent of all U.S. viewing between 8 and 11 P.M. and eventually produce syndicated series shown in rerun to large audiences for years on TV stations in the United States and around the world. Every one of the nation's TV viewers can be said to have some stake in the programs appearing on network schedules. A major concern at network level is how to break into a bloc of solidly popular evening programs on a competing network. Various counterprogramming strategies based on demographics and qualitative factors are developed, and shows to meet the specifications are sought. Scheduling devices such as hour-long introductions for new half-hour series, special guest stars on the opener, and inaugurating the series against other than the regular competition (reruns, preemptions, etc.) are employed. Demographic data can sometimes point to weaknesses in the competitive lineup and help a lagging network to catch up to its competitors. A high-rated network employs "hammock" positioning for new shows, preceded and followed by solid successes.

The strategies that are involved in molding each network's schedule, when the two competitors' actions are only partially known, require the participation of top management executives. After years in the No. 3 spot, the ABC TV network catapulted to first place in prime-time ratings in 1976, a move that sent shock waves through the industry. A *New York Times* interview with John D. Backe, president of CBS, in January 1979 reported, "His tenure has seen CBS displaced by ABC in the bitter rivalry for prime-time television audiences. It was a stunning comedown, an embarrassment that has fed persistent speculation of dramatic changes at the top of CBS." The No. 1 designation is not only prestigious, Backe said, but also has enormous effect on income and the stock market.[6]

CBS regained its lead but was once more under challenge by ABC in 1983–1984. More recently NBC, for years third-place runner in prime time, has shown a gradual ratings improvement after Fred Silverman was replaced by Grant Tinker as president in 1981. On April 3, 1983, *The Times* reported:

> So far this season, the network's ratings have risen marginally and its demographics—the urban, young, and female audience sought by advertisers—have improved far more, while its rivals have slipped. . . . "We've completely changed the profile of the network in one television season" . . . said Brandon Tartikoff, President of NBC Entertainment.[7]

In the same story Grant Tinker lamented NBC's severe shortage of "building blocks," solid ratings performers around which newer programs can be spotted in the schedule to get maximum exposure and thus win their own fans. By fall 1984 NBC had risen to second place in average prime time ratings, with ABC once again in third position.

Decisions regarding the network schedule are based, of course, on rating predictions, including demographic audience makeup. For new programs on competing networks, only crude estimates are available, while the scheduling network has data from whatever audience testing has been done in advance, some of it quite sophisticated. The network prime-time scheduling takes place over several weeks in April, with much executive shuttling from New York to Hollywood. Those involved are reasonably knowledgeable in interpreting the various rating analyses developed to aid in evolving a strategy. The final schedule, however, is not based solely on ratings. Schedule balance, program diversity, qualitative strength, sales interest, and efforts to start or capitalize on new trends are all part of the decision mix. Such hit programs as "All in the Family" and "Hill Street Blues" were ratings disappointments at first.

The scheduling problem is not confined to prime time—daytime presents its own challenge. And as the new season develops, judgments must be made as to renewal or cancellation or possible reshuffling of shows based on unsuspected data from ratings reports. Similarly, there are tactical questions as to when and where to preempt for one-time-only specials or miniseries. Where will this do you the most good; where will it deliver the biggest blow to your rivals?

Networks have facilities to do their own program duplication studies, an important tool, not only in scheduling but in developing sales packages and in promotion, as we discuss shortly. Audience flow studies, which reveal from Nielsen minute-by-minute data where a show's audience comes from (set off, other stations, etc.) and where it goes when the next program begins, are crucial to constructing a solid nightly audience franchise. When looked at on a demographic basis, these studies can reveal need for schedule shifts to retain specific target audiences such as women ages 18–35. It is even possible to develop data from a household-by-household analysis via computer tape from Nielsen. Networks may do this themselves or contract with an outside service to handle such tabulations, as several do.

## Network Sales

While ratings may not be the sole determinant of program decisions, they come very close to it. The sales departments deal primarily with major advertising agencies representing the country's 100 top advertisers. Ratings and audience estimates and cost per thousand (CPM) data from them are the coinage of the business.

According to David Poltrack,[8] the sale of network television time takes place in three distinct stages: (1) the up-front market where advertisers make full-season commitments soon after fall schedules are announced and which accounts for 70 percent of network expenditure; (2) the scatter market, following the up-front market, which consists of advertisers making quarterly commitments through the year; and (3) the opportunistic market, composed of week-to-week purchases of unsold time.

The up-front prime-time market opens as soon as networks have announced their schedules to affiliates in May and proceeds for about eight weeks of most intense negotiations where commitments of several billion dollars are made. The procedure involves the major national advertisers and their agencies, who first submit a plan request to each network. This request specifies budget by quarter, the demographics on which to base the buy, and special requirements. The network responds with detailed program schedules, quarterly audience projections, and estimated CPMs for total households and target demographics.

The network's offer is almost never accepted at once but serves as the basis for spirited negotiations as to programs to be included, cost per thousand, audience guarantees, etc. Both buyer and seller have made their estimates of the anticipated rating performance of the shows involved, but these figures are not revealed because the buyer generally refuses to accept network estimates until it seems necessary, but then he may get the guarantee. Poltrack states: "The net result of these buyer-seller strategies is that negotiations focus on program mix and number of announcements included in the package, as opposed to the final price of the plan, which stays fixed."[9] The two parties then come to terms, and the plan is put on hold to provide the agency negotiator a stated time (up to several weeks for large buys) to get management and client approval before finalizing the order.

A vital element in this up-front agreement is the network's guarantee to meet a certain minimum audience level that will yield the advertiser the cost per thousand demanded for households or target demographic groups such as women ages 18–35. Should the planned schedule of announcements not attain the required rating level, the adjustment is made, not in monetary refunds but in kind, by the network's furnishing "make-good" announcements in programs acceptable to the agency that will raise the total gross rating points and the net reach and frequency of the schedule to a satisfactory level. On the other hand, the network gains nothing when aggregate ratings exceed the estimates: It's strictly a bonus for the advertiser and a feather in the agency's cap.

Once the fall ratings start to trickle in during mid-September, all concerned are watching for the hits and the flops. Network salespeople must juggle disappointed customers with the needs of short-term scatter and opportunistic advertisers. Announcement prices move up and down to reflect program rating performance and the strength of advertiser demand. Scatter-plan buyers may get bargains or pay premiums relative to the up-front customers. The biweekly Nielsen pocketpiece becomes the umpire calling the shots between seller and buyer.[10]

As the season lengthens, the network rating standings are affected by many factors, some anticipated, others not. Preemptions of the regular schedule for special events, sports events such as the World Series and the Olympics, political conventions, and various miniseries all have extensive ratings impact on competitive network audiences. By December, major moves generally occur—failing series are replaced and schedules are reshuffled in efforts to obtain higher ratings by improving audience flow and counterprogram elements. Adjustments and make-goods for up-front clients who are hurt by show failures and fall below their guarantee target become a major sales preoccupation.

Sports and special events such as political conventions and inauguration ceremonies have their own special requirements for rating analysis. Such sports events as the Superbowl, World Series, and Olympics produce large audiences and command high prices because of such delivery, and their audience characteristics, which tend toward a heavier young and male makeup than average network programming (plus the publicity and attention value involved). The Superbowl has finally generated the "million-dollar minute." CBS sold 30-second commercials for $480,000 each for the 1984 game, and ABC reports selling minutes at the $1 million level for 1985 (a discounted price which may go higher). ABC priced "Winds of War" commercials at $350,000, while CBS sold 30 seconds at $450,000 each for the two-and-a-half-hour finale of "M*A*S*H." Average per minute ratings for these three events were: "Winds of War," 38.6; final "M*A*S*H," 60.2; and Superbowl XVII, 48.6, yielding cost per thousand households of $10.90, $9.00 and $11.90, respectively. ABC priced 30-second commercials for Superbowl 1988 as high as $675,000 each.

## Network Research Departments

The primary mechanisms by which ratings are received, analyzed, and disseminated throughout network organizations are the research departments. These departments, staffed with from 40 to 60 professionals, are involved in a wide range of audience, market, opinion, and social research. Syndicated audience measurement does, however, take about half the budget, and much of the remainder goes to various forms of program testing and qualitative probing. The research department is responsible for providing detailed analysis of the ratings and for interpreting the significant developments and trends to management, programming (news included) and sales. A department representative participates in program scheduling, decision making, and developing network plans and strategy.

The research department heads negotiate contracts for network rating and also local market rating services, which are valuable in station relations as well as some analytical work. Print readership services such as Simmons and Media Mark are also used in their efforts to find marketing pluses for sales purposes. The research department efforts are further refined and targeted by sales and market development groups within network sales departments.

Research departments are eternally trying to improve the quality, reliability, and usefulness of ratings data. They do this by keeping pressure on Nielsen for improvements, by exploring possible new services such as the AGB peoplemeter, and by active participation in such industry groups as the Electronic Media Rating Council and the Committee on National Television Audience Measurement (CONTAM), the Committee on Local Television and Radio Audience Measurement (COLTRAM), and the Advertising Research Foundation.

## Station Relations

The network-affiliate relationship is a close one because each contributes to the other's business prosperity. Affiliates particularly depend on the audience success of their network's program schedule for their own commercial results. A strong network rating performance in prime time and daytime benefits these stations in several ways: (1) greater station compensation from the network, which becomes more sold out (the station collects on announcement minutes sold) (2) higher rates made possible for commercial positions it can sell in and around network shows and (3) overall audience buildup and flow, which benefits all ratings of its local and other nonnetwork programming. Therefore, affiliated station executives keep a sharp eye on network rating trends.

A major concern of affiliates is that their network put its best programming foot forward during the local market sweeps by Arbitron and Nielsen (see Television Stations later in the chapter.) The networks help affiliates by scheduling during each four-week measured period some choice movie titles and high-visibility special programs while avoiding low-audience-appeal documentaries. Top guest stars turn up on regular series while story lines reach for suspenseful highlights. This form of program hyping is accompanied by unusual promotional activity also, a product of network and affiliate collaboration. This type of activity is of no direct benefit to the network, except by presenting a chance for a well-publicized rating event, because the network is measured daily and the effect of hyping is quickly and easily discerned by network buyers. On the other hand, spot buyers have little choice but to use the ratings as published, except where they may make some subjective corrections. (See Chapter 8 for a fuller discussion of this topic.)

The strength of a national network is not due entirely to its program popularity. The network's particular aggregation of local stations in some 200 markets across the country plays a role in its success. The stations in any individual market are rarely equal in physical plant and coverage, management, local programming (especially news), promotion, etc. Although their overall rating position is influenced strongly by network programming, standout local stations often contribute audience muscle to their network too. The local market ratings indicate which stations these are, also what weaknesses a particular network may have in each market. Switches of network affiliates occur only infrequently because they mean uprooting relationships of many years' standing. Nevertheless, they do occur, usually when a network has a strong ratings story that can be translated into added revenue for the station. The ABC network, once a poor third in station coverage factors, has pulled up in recent years by using its rating surge to woo popular affiliates from NBC and CBS.

Another aspect of ratings use in affiliate relations involves station clearance procedures. Affiliates frequently assert their independence by scheduling some other programming in a network time period. The network then tries for at least a repeat of its displaced show at an acceptable time. In an effort to recapture live clearance time, the station is constantly reminded what damage the preemption does to itself and/or the network by using data from local rating reports.

## Publicity and Promotion

Ratings play a prominent role in each network's publicity and advertising to the general public and to the trade press. The demand for and use of ratings data increase year by year as the viewing public becomes more aware of audience ratings. Americans are likely to be impressed with a program's or network's audience leadership, even though it may not correspond to their personal viewing. Nielsen limits its public release of data to top 15 prime-time and daytime programs as shown in biweekly pocketpieces. Most other ratings releases are generated by the network research and press relations to develop credible stories for the press.

Audience promotion has the objective of drawing viewers to the network's program schedule. New programs must win "triers," who it is hoped will find something they like in the first sampling and become habitual viewers. One-time-only and special series require intensive audience promotion efforts because (1) they are generally costly and require audience levels above normal to be successful and (2) to achieve a successful rating level they must break normal weekly viewing patterns and capture followers of other network series.

Although various print media and other promotional devices may be used, a major form of audience promotion is the "audience promo" announcement tucked into various network shows during the weeks before the broadcast. Determining where to place these promos for maximum effect is a problem for the rating analyst—matching the estimated demographic profile of the promoted show with comparable shows now in the lineup. It doesn't take much study to know that a football broadcast is a good place to promote a basketball matchup, but what kind of viewers will respond to a Holocaust series and where do we reach them in our present schedule? A searching and detailed rating analysis will turn up the answers that guide the scheduling of Holocaust promos. Now that radio is widely used to promote TV audiences, using radio rating demographic reports is essential for maximum efficiency in reaching the target audience.

## Financial Planning

Network financial planners involved with profit and loss estimates, future budgets, cash flow, and capital outlays make extensive use of forward rating projections. This is especially true in the mid 1980s when the future impact of such new technologies as cable, home video cassettes, direct broadcasting service (DBS), and video text services could offer competition to commercial network shares and audience levels. The network share erosion has already been significant in prime time, but much of the loss has been to other broadcasters (independents, public broadcasting stations, and superstations), while increases in overall usage and in population help to enlarge the total pie. Where this will lead network audiences and the revenue streams they generate in the 1985–1990 period is of great significance for all television networks, especially when major program commitments must be made more than a year ahead.

Current rating standings and trends and their probable effect on a network's revenue and profit for the fiscal year are of course assiduously monitored and evaluated from month to month. To help fourth-quarter results, for example, a network's pricing formula might be altered more speedily than usual to maximize revenue from poor ratings performers. Budgets and outlays for replacement and new pilots and series must be kept in line with anticipated success or failure of present offerings.

## Other Network Uses

In dealing with Washington agencies—the FCC, FTC, and the various congressional committees and subcommittees that formulate and enforce government policy affecting the networks—ratings and audience data are often produced to support an industry position. Viewing public choices and patterns are pertinent to many issues under discussion, and there is some degree of interest in what the audience measurements show. The FCC uses Arbitron's Area of Dominant Influence (ADI) data for ranking TV markets in some of its rules applications.

## III.  PUBLIC BROADCASTING SERVICE

The above account of ratings usage is keyed to the three national commercial networks—ABC, CBS, and NBC. The PBS service differs in several significant ways from its more popular brethren: It does not sell advertising exposures, PBS stations frequently run a program several times during a week, and its programs are not always broadcast on a unified live schedule cleared by the affiliates.[11] Rating services concentrate on measuring commercially sponsored programs. Nielsen NTI does not report sustaining or nonsponsored shows on commercial networks, and local services have often lumped local educational and public service stations in an "all others" category. PBS has, therefore, had to arrange for special ratings data from Nielsen to provide its management, producers, and local stations with necessary audience data. The ratings, including all the usual demographic breakdowns, are secured 10 weeks out of the year. This helps PBS in its scheduling; in dealing with stations on financing, carriage, and promotion problems; and in its ceaseless efforts to induce corporations to fund some of its output.

Nielsen cable reports based on compositing the local NSI services on a national basis do show PBS ratings and share and, as of 1983, both local services were providing local audience data for public broadcasting stations as well. NTI data shows a slow but steady increase in the net weekly cumulative audience of PBS to 50 percent of all TV households in 1983.

## IV.  TELEVISION STATIONS

In contrast to network TV, television stations face a situation in which two highly competitive services (Arbitron and Nielsen NSI) vie for subscribers, in which the weekly viewer household diary is the preeminent measurement tool, and in which the important ratings are generated in four "sweeps" per year.

Since advertising agencies usually subscribe to only one local rating service and the two competitors split that market about 50–50, all TV stations find it necessary to subscribe to two services that measure their market at the same time, using virtually identical diary methodology. Sample size and report format may vary slightly, but basically Arbitron and Nielsen are duplicates in the eyes of the trade. The principal differences are generally in service features: computer tapes, special reports, delivery speed, and in some situations contract terms such as price and length. Report total in-tab household sample sizes vary from 200 to 1600. Most market reports involve 400–600 diaries with little difference between services.

The expansion of local meter services changes some of the rules of the game. Household ratings (on a sample of 300–500) are delivered the next day every day. Demographics are available from larger samples at least for all sweep periods and in the larger markets for 6 to 10 four-week periods. By early 1985, local market meter services will be provided by both services in top markets comprising about one-third of U.S. TV households.

Inasmuch as the ratings companies require station subscribers to move from diaries to meters at costs approximating 250 percent higher (the diary ratings are no longer computed except for demographic data, because the household estimate now comes from the meter), there has been strong resistance to meter service from local broadcasters in markets below the top five, where most major stations have subscribed to both services.

Independents, which usually gain audience share with meters in comparison to diaries, are the strongest station supporters. Affiliates are unenthusiastic, and they command the major share of subscriber revenue for the raters. The economic impact of meters on stations and services may force a trend toward a single local service, but only time can answer that. Arbitron, the aggressive meter advocate, insists that local stations can afford two meter services, while Nielsen's strategy has been to move where it is reasonably assured of local support from network affiliates. Nielsen's moves to match Arbitron have been stimulated by agency interest in meters. Nielsen could not afford to give Arbitron a significant lead in markets metered.

## Coverage

By covering every U.S. county in their syndicated diary surveys, the ratings companies collect large enough samples over time to produce county-by-county coverage studies that define where each station has reportable audiences. These studies define broad market areas identified with metropolitan areas or cities. Arbitron calls these Areas of Dominant Influence (ADI); Nielsen, Designated Market Areas (DMA). The areas essentially delimit by county the area in which viewers tune primarily to stations located in a given metropolitan area. By eliminating overlap, this procedure produces 200+ nonduplicated market areas that are mutually exclusive and additive. Because of today's dominance of television in national advertising and marketing, the ADIs and DMAs have been adopted for many corporate marketing and control functions and are widely used as the basis for the geographic distribution of advertising expenditures for radio, newspapers, and other media. Each station in the market thus has two ways to benefit in geographic extension of coverage—larger audience potential for programming and, to the extent it can contribute, a broader-based, larger ADI/DMA.

Rating services annually rank ADI/DMA markets, and this can be significant for stations in markets close to breakpoints used in allocating spot budgets—top 10, 25, 50, or 100. For example, in Arbitron's 1983–1984 list, Houston replaced Cleveland as No. 10, and Greensboro–Winston Salem–High Point went to No. 50 at the expense of Wilkes Barre–Scranton. Of course, population trends were at work here too, but the net result was that certain markets (and their stations) benefited by automatic inclusion in certain "buy lists" while others suffered.

When analyzed in detail, including subcounty geographic units down in some cases to zip code combinations, coverage studies show stations where they should aim special audience promotion efforts or where new station physical facilities may be advisable to overcome weak performance. After action is taken, subsequent coverage studies enable management to assess results.

## Programming

Except for major markets measured daily by meters and a small number of other top markets that get six to eight diary reports a year, the "sweeps" reports represent the only syndicated measurement for the 200 + U.S. television markets. Each network is therefore under some pressure from its affiliates to put its best foot forward during the sweeps, because that translates into higher ratings on which they can price and sell. The networks themselves and most of their owned stations have little to gain (because they get daily meter reports), but the need to keep affiliates happy is of great importance. Thus, during the sweeps rating periods the network movie packages will carry some of the best in the inventory and anticipated high-audience special programs and miniseries appear.

Ratings use by TV stations follows the network pattern, to a degree. A major split, however, separates affiliates (which have limited local time to program) and independents (which program an entire schedule). In recent years, rating analyses to aid programming decisions have become more widespread, especially in major markets where meter or frequent diary services exist. Some individual stations such as superstations WTBS and WGN also find NTI, with its U.S. TV household base, a valuable tool, even though they may get their own ratings keyed to their respective coverage patterns (not on the national basis of the three networks).

Independent stations have been strong supporters of meter services, because they get higher ratings than through diary reports (which understate the shares of independents) and because they can use more frequent data to guide their many programming decisions. The many group-owned stations have the benefit of centralized research and employ ratings analysis for programming and negotiation for syndicated productions.

Aside from news and a limited amount of other locally originated programming, the available time of both affiliates and independents is filled with syndicated product purchased from producers or marketing syndicators. Much of this is motion picture packages and so-called off-network programming—successful network series that have accumulated impressive rating performances as well as significant inventories of episodes. Their network rating record is readily available (even for the individual market in which the interested station is located), so station and program management can have considerable confidence in the audience data on which their decisions are based. In the case of movies or syndicated series lacking network exposure, ratings from other comparable markets serve as a good basis for estimating audience potential. Rating services publish periodic reports that show network and syndicated ratings of all such programs in every U.S. market. Arbitron offers an on-line computer system called TAPP (Total Audience Profile for Programs), which enables users to develop rating information for specific syndicated programs under various competitive conditions. In the rare case of the newly produced show, the station staff must make its own estimates much as networks do for new up-front series.

The growing use of minicomputers and the expansion of computer service organizations bring stations new opportunities for rating analysis not previously possible within time and cost constraints. Nielsen, for example, offers the Cassandra computer service, which generates selected data (including up to twelve demographics) for a target program in all markets in which the syndicated show appears.

## Sales

Station sales to national advertisers are largely in the hands of the station's national spot representative firm. The station's sales force concentrates on local and regional advertisers and their agencies. Ratings' sophistication at the local level has increased enormously in the past decade as market and media research and computerized data have become widespread and television has grown as a local medium.

The availability of station ratings data on tape and in computer banks such as Arbitron's AID (Arbitron Information on Demand) and NSI's Nielsen Plus provides stations opportunity to offer advertisers announcement packages in a group of programs to meet the particular audience target needs. The station can analyze "what happens if" certain unproductive spots are replaced. The sales force, aided by perhaps one or two research people, carries out the task at the local level. But the greatest source of revenue for most stations is national advertisers.

The Television Bureau of Advertising developed (through Interactive Market Systems Inc.) a software module called Maximizing Media Performance (MMP), which enables stations to use calculators and printers to estimate net reach and frequency and cost per thousand for TV, radio, and newspapers or any combination for various proposed schedules. Local department stores and agencies are also users—over 500 installations were in use in mid 1983.

In the major markets served by local meter installations (11 by mid 1984), ratings analysis for local sales increases as a result of the continuous availability of daily and weekly ratings. Daily tracking of programs goes to salespeople, weekly averages go to key customers. Minicomputer runs to check audience delivery for client packages help spot problems and opportunities.

## V.  TV STATION REPRESENTATIVES

Every television station is represented in major buying centers (e.g., New York, Chicago, Los Angeles, San Francisco, Dallas) by a national spot sales representative to sell its announcements to national advertisers (through their agencies). These "spot reps" are extremely well equipped with ratings-wise and computer-competent research and sales staffs. They respond speedily to any agency request for "availabilities," in which the parameters for a given "buy" in terms of gross ratings points, reach, and frequency are spelled out. This starts a small negotiation, during which the rep may try to improve the original submission by working with the client station, using various computer-run formulations. All involved recognize that they can only work with the past data without much estimating and projecting, as was true with up-front network selling. However, given the time and economic constraints there is no alternative.

Station representatives also advise their client stations on program moves as a result of rating evaluations of schedules and the tracking of syndicated features in comparable markets. Their greater research resources (subscription to NTI, for example) and experience in many markets make their contribution a vital one.

A computer service such as Mini-Pak converts all ratings report data to computer tapes, which their spot rep clients can then use to make specific demographic breakdowns not actually appearing in the printed report. Computations of audience estimates for various day parts (not necessarily as defined by the rating service) and availability combinations to achieve advertiser target goals are therefore possible with great speed on computers installed by the rep firm.

Major TV rep firms have pioneered in computer programs and other analytic rating aids to assist their stations and buyers. For example, Katz Communications in 1983 introduced the KATZ-Rule, a form of plastic slide rule. The effective Reach/Frequency Planner was designed to help select the desired frequency by adjusting reach level and Gross Rating Points (GRP) level as specified by the client. In four months over 3000 KATZ-Rules were distributed.

## VI.  RADIO

Radio today is vastly different from what it was 20 years ago. It is as unlike television as an advertising vehicle as it is a communications medium. Major differences stem from the great disparity in number of commercial stations and in the physical area served by those stations. And, of course, the aural medium relies heavily on recorded music, talk, and news as basic staples of programming, with individual stations dedicated to particular narrow formats such as album rock, country, top 40 hits, news, or classical music. Table 7-1 gives an idea of the relative position of the two media.

Whereas TV programming and selling are based on individual programs, radio revolves around individual stations whose format draws listeners in certain categories. Compared to television, radio rates are very low and permit advertisers to achieve heavier frequency and substantial reach also by properly scattering commercials over stations and day parts.

In measurement, television is still basically a household medium (with persons data somewhat secondary), whereas radio audience is measured and reported solely on a basis of individual diaries or interviews with no household listening data at all. Whereas all television reporting is confined to home-set viewing, radio attempts to measure personal listening wherever it takes place—at home, at work, in the car, in a restaurant or other public place, at play (beach, picnic), or walking. Because radio measures a people universe (and there are 2.75 times more people than households), radio ratings would naturally be lower than TV

TABLE 7-1
Key Comparative Data
Television Versus Radio

|  | *Television* | *Radio* |
|---|---|---|
| Number of U.S. commercial stations on air[a] | 896 | 8,359 |
| Sales in millions (1983) | | |
| Network | $  6,985 | $    305 |
| National spot | 4,820 | 1,015 |
| Local | 4,285 | 3,910 |
| Total | $16,090 | $  5,230 |
| Average number of stations reported by Arbitron—top 10 markets | 10.5 | 33.7 |
| Average of Arbitron average quarter-hour audiences, total station area, top 10 markets, top 3 stations in rating rank, All Persons 12 + | 302,500[b] | 74,300[c] |
| Average total daily usage all persons 12 + | 4 hr 12 min[d] | 3 hr 9 min[e] |

[a]As of June 30, 1984, according to *Broadcasting* magazine, July 23, 1984, p. 111.
[b]Arbitron TV Fall 1983, sign on–sign off.
[c]Arbitron Radio Summer 1983, 6A.M.–midnight.
[d]Nielsen NTI, 1982–1983 (November, February, May, July).
[e]RADAR, 1983–1984.

household ratings. In fact, radio station comparisons within a market are universally based on share figures. Of course, ratings must be employed to get projected audience figures and cost per thousand data. Because of the number of stations per market, many radio rating comparisons are made on a rank order basis. Station audiences for various demographic groups and day parts are ranked to make time buying and selling easier. Agencies often select stations on the basis of their share rank in the market for a target demographic group.

## Radio Networks

For decades, network radio consisted of four interconnected networks—ABC, CBS, Mutual, and NBC. This all began to change when ABC, borrowing from radio's local experience, in 1968 dramatically substituted four different format networks for its one "all things to all people" operation. The four were ABC Contemporary, ABC Entertainment, ABC-FM, and ABC Information. Later two other networks—ABC Rock Network and ABC Direction Network— were added. Thereafter, two independent black networks emerged and RKO came in with two more radio networks in the late 1970s. Eventually NBC added the Source, a separate youth-oriented network, and CBS created the Radio/Radio Network.

As of early 1984, 15 interconnected radio networks were in operation, and the medium was thriving. In addition, a new type of noninterconnected quasi-network has come onto the scene. Sponsored by national spot rep firms, these "networks" are nothing more than large packages of stations in markets across the country that the rep firm sells at unit prices low enough to compete with interconnected networks. There is no unified program schedule or consistent day-in-day-out identification attached to such noninterconnecteds. In 1984 eight of these groupings were operating.

Another type of radio network includes those offering long periods of programming daily such as Satellite Music, Star Station and Star Dust, Bonneville, and Music Country Network and featured programs by the United Stations and others.

### RADAR Network Measurements

The lone true network rating service is RADAR, which was discussed in Chapter 2. This service confines its audience data to interconnected networks, and as of early 1984 all 15 of these were users. RADAR reports are issued twice annually, spring and fall, based on a compilation of 48 weeks of interviewing data.

The reports provide the following basic national audience estimates by age, sex, and day parts for each subscribing on-line network:

1. Potential audience data—compilations based on network's complete station lineup regardless of what programming is carried. Supplementing this is a radio usage report by day part by demographics.

2. Audience data for cleared networks related to network commercials carried, whether within network programs or elsewhere on a playback basis.

3. Audience data for networks based only on network commercial carriage within cleared network program.

In addition to the hard-copy reports, Statistical Research Inc., the research organization that conducts RADAR surveys, makes available computer tapes for much data and supplies computer accessibility for special probes and analyses that networks may want for programming or sales purposes. RADAR on Line (ROL) is a flexible subscriber service that helps networks develop rotation and scatter plans with estimates of reach and frequency, GRP level, etc. So-called build-up analyses are possible to answer "what happens if" certain additions or substitutions are made.

### Arbitron Radio Network Report

Measurement of audiences to nonwired networks as well as to interconnected networks is provided annually by Arbitron Radio. These estimates are based on samples of about 250,000 diaries covering all U.S. counties. The sample is accrued by supplementing the returns from Arbitron's local market radio sweep in the spring each year (257 radio markets in 1983) with additional diaries placed in counties not sampled in that survey. The interconnected networks view the Arbitron data as being of little value because they show only potential, not actual, audience that takes station clearances into account. Moreover, the data are presented only once a year, and there is no way to update network data as affiliates are added or switched as is done with RADAR.

### Other Radio Network Uses

The sale of radio network audience exposure is conducted somewhat like spot sales, since few of the seasonal program elements and uncertainties of network TV are a factor. Radio network CPM's for demographic groups are among the lowest of all electronic media, probably because of the abundance of availabilities.

Radio networks do not have the same degree of internal management usage of ratings as do their television counterparts. Program schedules are keyed more to gaining station clearances. Audience trends in taste are derived from what happens in local ratings in the competition between stations broadcasting a variety of formats. Special programs (concerts and other live musical events) and sports are areas in which ratings information can be useful in acquisition and promotion.

## Radio Stations

Local radio ratings are essentially an Arbitron exclusive. This company dominates the field, and a number of aspirant competitors have found it impossible to overcome Arbitron's hold (see Chapter 2 for details). For several years the

Birch service has been attempting to gain acceptance, and it seems now perhaps to have gained a foothold as a supplementary service. Arbitron's personal diary provides the more reliable weekly cumes, which are used widely. Birch's weekly cumulative data is crude and this new service is still not used in major agencies for buying decisions. It does, however, provide more frequent tracking than Arbitron.

The Arbitron service now produces quarterly reports based on diary sampling spread over 12 weeks. Over 250 radio market reports are issued; many, however, only for the spring sweep, which encompasses the entire list. The fall sweep covers the vast majority of markets but reports for winter and summer quarters measure only 11 and 23, respectively. Arbitron's radio diaries for individuals are placed in telephone households (listed and nonlisted). Sample sizes vary from 4500 to 500 in tab, with around 1000 for mid sized major markets.

Radio stations and their rep firms use just about all the analytical devices previously described for television. Computerization of Arbitron data provides on-line AID (Arbitron Information on Demand). Target Aid is another addition, which combines Arbitron audience data with two other dimensions—Donnelley's Cluster Plus (geodemographic life-style clusters) and Simmons' product service and brand purchaser profiles. Target Aid thus enables agencies to reach their target audience through the broadcast medium, either radio or television. An example is a local agency that normally splits the budget of an exclusive clothing store 40/60 between Station A and Station B. Station A, using Target Aid, demonstrates that although its audience is smaller than Station B's, it is concentrated in the most affluent zip codes, whereas B's audience is generated mainly in average blue- and white-collar homes in less affluent sections.

Reach and frequency analyses have played a major role in keeping radio a viable medium. A leader in this field since 1964 has been Group W Radio Sales. In 1968 they introduced radio's new math, which provided a new tool for estimating the reach and frequency of any schedule of announcements on any radio station in any market. A year later a new math calculator simplified computations, and over 30,000 were distributed to broadcasters, agencies, and advertisers. Beginning in 1970, computer programs were developed to plan campaigns on multiple stations in the market. Finally, in 1978 Group W introduced Numath 80, which utilized Arbitron data from tapes to yield a wide variety of day-to-day uses such as station ranking by day parts and exclusive cume reports.

Arbitron's ethnic procedures now are confined to Differential Survey Treatment (DST), which involves special follow-up interviews and money incentives to insure cooperation from black and Hispanic listeners in markets where these groups appear in significant numbers. Special ethnic reports are issued for nearly a score of major markets to provide major age/sex groups for a dozen day parts. Customized Qualidata reports, based on specific product use obtained by telephone interviews following up diary-keepers, combined with normal geodemographic breakouts can be a powerful sales tool.

## Radio Station Representatives

Radio station representative firms operate much the same as those in television, but differ from their TV counterparts in several significant respects. Their lists of stations are much longer, and they may represent more than one station in a market. Most sales involve packages of commercials developed to reach prescribed reach, frequency and gross impression goals. Program-specific commercial positions are not a factor except in news, sports, and special programs such as live rock or jazz concerts. In these cases, ratings estimates from past performances must be made. Another difference is that all major radio representative firms sell "off-line" networks (packages of stations from their represented list) at group rates competitive with those of interconnected networks (and well below the rates charged for individual spot purchase). This practice creates some friction between reps and stations, who see something akin to a conflict of interest involved. Radio representatives defend it as better for the station than losing the advertiser to a competitive on-line network affiliate. Off-line networks use Arbitron's annual spring Network Audience Estimates as their rating base.

A significant service is provided by Radio Information Center, which uses a computer to develop a comprehensive analysis of Arbitron reports such as AM-FM listening trends, trends by station format and day parts, reach and frequency by day parts, etc. Every U.S. radio station is covered, and data by syndicators and networks are produced in hundred-page reports.

## Other Radio Rating Uses

Other types of radio ratings users are program syndicators and record companies, which are closely tied to the aural medium and are vitally interested in audience trends. Among users are program consultants, who not only utilize ratings analyses extensively, but also conduct a substantial amount of original survey research to help stations find the unique niche in the marketplace that will bring success in ratings and profits.

## VII.   ADVERTISING AGENCIES

As representative of the advertiser, the agency has primary responsibiity for developing the advertising plan and for the buying decisions in implementing the media aspect of the plan (unless a TV buying service is involved). The importance of network television in terms of cost and budget for the top 100 national advertisers[12] is such that this activity is often carried out by a small separate group of specialists, who plan, negotiate, and monitor the network purchases. They are responsible for the agency's forecasts of TV network program rating performance and for gaining the necessary agency and client approvals for the deals negotiated. They furnish all agency executives with buying guides forecasting the anticipated cost per thousand for various demographics to assist budget planning. Advertisers and their agencies (major advertisers usually have several agencies handling different product lines) make their plans based on product needs and budget provided. Once an allocation of dollars by media has been set, the agency develops detailed plans for television network and spot usage keyed to the product's marketing plan. The agencies are now ready to enter the network buying arena, where they have three general options: (1) enter the up-front market, which for prime time begins after the network affiliate meetings in May, (2) wait eight weeks and go into the scatter market, or (3) hold off for the in-season opportunistic market.

In addition to planning and buying, the agency has a third responsibility, in which final TV ratings are the yardstick. This is known as the postbuy analysis. It serves the agency and the advertisers by showing how close to the original target objectives (gross audience, net reach, frequency, etc., relative to households or specific demographic groups) the actual performance was. In the case of network, this stewardship report is rendered to the advertiser monthly or quarterly and serves two purposes: (2) it shows the client how well the agency did its job of selecting announcement positions in the up-front negotiations and (2) it gives the agency the basis on which to approach the network for audience deficiency announcements (so-called make-goods) at no extra cost to bring the cost per thousand of audience level close to the projected goal. Although this form of adjustment is not necessarily a written guarantee, it is standard practice to the extent that a network can execute it. A disastrous season could make it impossible to meet all such claims, but if the agency's buys have been across all television networks they may have pluses there to offset rating deficiencies on the unsuccessful competitor. The postbuy analysis protects both the advertiser and the agency—the show business risks fall on the broadcaster.

An important aspect of strategic media planning in recent years has been near universal acceptance of the "effective frequency" concept. Simply put, this doctrine maintains that reaching a prospect once is not enough to achieve any significant advertising purpose.[13] This means that in calculating the total effective cumulative audience of an announcement schedule, people or households reached once (or twice) are eliminated. The present consensus, based on a number of studies, indicates that the effective threshold is three exposures, so those in the once or twice category are discarded in estimating effective reach. At the same time, efforts are made in planning a schedule to minimize high-frequency exposures (above 10, for example) as being wasteful. With rating details in computer banks, it is relatively easy to develop frequency distribution analyses that will guide action in this area as the season develops.

One simple example involved a client whose needs were to obtain maximum reach among women ages 25–34 with a total of 200 gross rating points and an effective frequency of three. The computer runs supplied by the spot rep showed that a normal scatter plan using 30-second announcements spread vertically by time segment on three stations and horizontally across the week produced a good reach of 75 percent but average frequency of 2.6 times. Other combinations were tried to raise the frequency, but always with a loss in reach. Two good combinations involved cutting vertical dispersion. With fewer day parts the reach went to 64 percent and frequency to 3.1. When commercials were stripped in the same programs dispersed throughout the week, reach went to 66 percent and frequency to 3.1. Bringing frequency to 4.5 reduced reach to 45 percent.

One buying strategy used is the "roadblock"—purchasing commercial positions on all three networks during the same quarter hour. This ensures that whatever happens to the share distribution of the respective programs, you have a 100 percent opportunity to reach all network viewers at that time.

There are many agency media activities at a major shop, with a large corps of researchers, planners, and buyers who handle spot television and radio. On the other hand, it is often said that agency media departments don't have the time or manpower to adequately use all the data available. Here's what a former senior vice president/media director reports about what one agency did to try to solve this problem:[14]

Rather than allow media research to become a specialized practice removed from the planning process, we need to reintegrate the research and planning functions to cope with the communication choices and make our media plans effective. . . .

. . . the best use of media research is right on the planning line . . . we train our media researchers and planners in each other's areas . . .

Integrating planning and research in our media department gives our clients our best shot. Rather than make the media function an assembly line process with a number of people each making a small contribution, we have turned to the type of [team] production situation [where] we get better media plans—plans built with individual involvement and group dynamics; . . .

The plans, of course, are only as good as the planning tools. And that's what media research is—a planning *tool*.

We all know that syndicated audience information reports the audience of the medium, not the advertising . . . when we buy space or time, we're buying opportunities to be seen: a potential audience. . . .

At FCB, we've . . . come up with a two-stage media weighting process . . . the probable audience [and] . . . the influenced audience.

Our process decreases the syndicated audience numbers. We think these are closer to what really happens to advertising, and we believe that our system produces the most cost-effective plans for our clients' budgets.

Agencies use a variety of outside computer-based data systems such as Donovan, Telmar, IMS, and Mediacomp to analyze ratings reports. Time sharing (combined with use of in-house mainframes) is widespread. Using microcomputers for media analysis and planning is widespread among major agencies, in most cases supplemented by Telmar's Micronet or IMS's Microsystems. These small computers (Apples, IBM PCs, etc.) save money and perform analyses not practical or cost effective on a time-sharing basis. Nevertheless, in the final analysis, the planner or the buyer must make the decisions or the decision rules that turn the ratings data into actionable form.

## VIII.  BUYING SERVICES

A relatively new element in the sale of broadcast audiences is the time buying service. This emerged in the early 1970s when the advertising agency business was going through one of its periodic changes.

Whereas the preceding decade had seen the major agencies becoming marketing-communications companies with emphasis on size and diversity of services (market research, direct mail, public relations, etc.), a new strain of small boutique agencies now emerged with the goal of concentrating on creative ideas, copy, and art. This new breed was largely headed by successful creative stars, formerly with top agencies, who fashioned lean organizations creating ads that would match the genius of Bill Bernbach or Leo Burnett. These men generally knew little about media, research, and marketing but were eager to accept outside help in those areas rather than try to build and administer such services internally. Another factor was the growth of spot television and the fact that agencies found it a high-cost, manpower-intensive medium to buy. The caliber of the professional buying declined as younger, less experienced people were brought in and delegation was expanded.

A few top-flight media buyers recognized the problem and began organizing their own media buying services. These companies are small but staffed with highly skilled analysts and experienced professionals. They work directly for the advertiser and deal directly with broadcast networks and stations. Highly sophisticated computer bases are involved, and personal contact with station management enables the buying service to obtain an advertiser's TV schedule at a lower cost per thousand than the conventional agency-spot rep route.

Detailed ratings analysis is one of the principal aids in achieving greater efficiency in their buys. Greater attention is paid to the specific period, program, and commercial position being offered. Computer analyses may reveal, for example, that a local news program may consistently get higher ratings at the program's beginning or on Monday; the buyer seeks those positions in order to give his client an edge. One buying service claims to guarantee audience delivery as projected and (since, unlike networks or stations, it cannot make good in kind) refund to the client in cash if the purchase fails to deliver cost-per-thousand goals.

## IX.  ADVERTISERS

It is estimated that in 1983 U.S. advertisers spent $16 billion for television advertising, $5.2 billion for radio and $400 million for cable commercials, a total of $22 billion. This vast outlay provides the enormous muscle that gives the electronic media their viability and vitality. In the final analysis, from a commercial standpoint the advertiser has the most to lose if the ratings used in guiding his advertising use of the media are inaccurate or misleading. Recall from Chapter 1 that advertisers inaugurated the first rating service—the Cooperative Analysis of Broadcasting—without any financial support from either agencies or broadcasters. Agencies quickly came in, however, and when they did, advertisers tended to drop out as subscribers and leave the principal financial support in their hands. Then, several years later, networks were accepted as subscribers, and the financial baton passed to them. Nevertheless, during the life of the CAB, from 1930 to 1945, advertisers maintained strong control over the service.

Today there is only modest advertiser interest in the conduct of ratings services. Why is this true? For the most part, because advertisers are content to accept the existing ratings as a reasonable guide to electronic media purchases. The results of numerous validation studies, the existence of the Electronic Media Rating Council[15] as an independent monitoring agency, the integrity of such rating measurement firms as A. C. Nielsen Company and Arbitron, and the relatively high quality of broadcast measurement data versus print give the advertisers confidence and faith in the numbers used. The final guarantor for the advertiser is the agency. Major advertisers are clients of top agencies staffed with highly skilled and experienced media research specialists. The agency is held responsible for the quality and accuracy of the measurement used and for apprising the advertiser of rating weaknesses and the adjustments often made to make estimates more applicable to the client's problems and objectives.

As a result of the close advertiser–agency relationship on ratings, we find a relatively small number of advertiser firms actually subscribing to ratings services themselves. Most rely on their agencies for ratings data and the various analyses required for planning, budgeting, and postbuy evaluation. There are only 40 NTI subscribers, including such major companies as Procter & Gamble, General Motors, and Gillette, but also Apple Computer and the U.S. Army Recruiting Service. Local TV market ratings are of great interest to national advertisers who operate with local franchises—automobiles, fast-food chains, and bottlers—while such retail chains as Sears, J. C. Penney, and K Mart are of course interested in specific local markets.

### National Advertisers

Whether interested enough in week-by-week ratings to be a Nielsen subscriber or willing to accept reports from agencies periodically, every national advertiser must utilize audience data in planning advertising strategy brand by brand.

Appropriations and budget allocations hinge on reach and frequency targets considered necessary to protect or improve brand share or to penetrate new markets or launch new products. The agency's proposals require sophisticated evaluation by the client's own advertising department, and staffs are retained for such work. In most cases, once agreed on, the plan is left largely for the agency to implement. It is only in the case of up-front major network purchases or reactions to program failure and rescheduling or to unsuspected competitive moves that the advertiser becomes once again an active participant in decision making.

The leading advertiser users of television maintain larger staffs and retain more control over the implementation of advertising plans. In a number of instances, they use "house" agencies[16] to handle this function. In other instances, the advertising department does the buying, especially of network time. In more traditional setups among the leaders, the media section plays an active role in both network and spot media buying decisions made by agencies. In one large company, for example, the Nielsen NTI pocketpiece goes to several dozen media managers and supervisors, program supervisors, advertising managers, and advertising research analysts. These advertising departments do not receive daily ratings; they rely on agencies for analyses requiring computer output.

One major advertiser reports that they are getting more reliable data faster and in a more flexible format than in the past. Compared to the 1960s, ratings are playing a greater role in advertisers' decision making because they plan changes more frequently and agency spot analyses are more precise and detailed. There is increasing involvement by management in media planning and evaluation. The complexity of today's media picture has brought about more sharing of responsibilities with their agencies.

The postbuy evaluation procedure is significant for the advertiser, providing an independent measurement of how well the plan is being implemented by the agency. Are their "buys" producing anticipated goals as to households and persons (in specific demographic categories and frequencies reached)? If not, what action has the agency already taken or does it propose, to redress the situation? On the other hand, if the agency's performance is superior (well above targets in reach and frequency), it raises questions as to "overkill." Shouldn't the budget have been less or better distributed among other brands? Here's where the advertiser's muscle shows. The program rating "report card," which the network executive faces every day, has now become an agency report card. Kept from month to month or quarter to quarter, depending on advertiser needs, it can be a major determinant in client satisfaction with agency media buying performance.

## Local Advertisers

In local markets, the big spenders such as fast-food restaurants, banks, department stores, supermarkets, and auto and appliance dealers are likely to be ratings clients. The wide range of local advertiser users ensures that there will be a variety of use patterns determined by the field and the policies of franchisers. Co-op advertising support from national chains and many manufacturers is a potent force in local ad expenditure, and ratings data can document how effective these expenditures are. A major use of local ratings reports is to keep a sharp eye on what the competition is doing—Coke wants to know about Pepsi; Chevrolet, Ford and Plymouth want to know about the Japanese; and McDonald's, Burger King, and Wendy's all want to know about each other. Comparisons with your own strategy and buys and significant changes in advertising volume, demographic appeal, day parts, or stations used can signal changes in competitors' policies.

An interesting advertiser ratings use is found in New York City, where six major banks support an extremely effective joint analysis of Arbitron local TV ratings in that market. This cooperative effort results in the 40-page quarterly Competitive Bank Advertising Report, which provides detailed data for the TV (and print) activities of seven commercial banks, six savings institutions, and six brokerage houses. Starting with total television household rating points and dollars expended for each bank, various analyses of rating points and dollars are provided for each institution by 11 service categories such as checking accounts, certificates of deposit, Individual Retirement Accounts, and automatic teller machines, for each month. There are also monthly analyses of commercials by number and length, showing rating points for total TV households, total adults, and adults ages 18–49. Individual banks go further by interpreting ratings figures on a CPM basis by time period, TV station, and more detailed demographic breakouts of gross rating points.

At the local level, agencies and advertisers work more closely together on a day-to-day basis. Local market and competitive factors, aside from media and ratings, can be of greater importance. Interpreting and countering moves of competitors and following trends of availabilities on local programs is easier for both agency and advertiser. The expertise and manpower for detailed rating analysis is severely limited. In recent years, however, with the growth of computerization of ratings and availability of more frequent (including dailies in major markets) surveys, local advertisers are gaining in skillful use of ratings.

## X.  PROGRAM PRODUCERS AND SYNDICATORS

Hollywood movie and program producers and independent syndication firms that market series and film packages (many of which have had network exposure) are significant users of network and local market rating reports. Where network first-run experience is involved, the producer's concern is with the show's performance and the prospect of a continued run over the network. The opportunity for profitable off-network and foreign syndication increases dramatically when a network series has completed several years in prime time.[17] Generally speaking, these accumulated network episodes are run on local stations on a strip basis—the same time five days a week. Therefore, a minimum of 100 episodes is generally necessary to achieve a viable package. During 1983 and 1984 there was increasing use of old network series on advertiser-supported cable networks (e.g., such favorites as "Wagon Train," Groucho Marx, "Dragnet," and "Lassie").

The producer of a new series works closely with the network's program staff to strengthen the show's appeal and ratings. Shifts in script and cast emphasis can sometimes save a faltering property. In the case of a sagging series, special "stunts" that are promotable and attention getting can help arrest ratings anemia. Guest-star appearances and dramatic script changes can be worked into the show as devices to halt a ratings decline. Close attention to demographic viewing differences in a time period can suggest what future the series may have. Strength among such prime commercial targets as working women, men ages 18–34, or adults ages 25–50 may indicate potentials not evident from gross household ratings and share.

Producers of theatrical motion pictures, who may gain handsome profits from residual sales to television networks and stations, watch ratings of features on the networks (including pay cable) to assess how to package pictures for later station syndication.

Success at the box office is no guarantee of comparable audience attraction, whereas some theatrical "also rans" turn out to be "sleepers" insofar as video audience performance is concerned. Now that the first exposure on home TV screens is often via pay cable channels, the ratings of these showings can better indicate what a film's audience appeal may be on commercial TV. In the case of the burgeoning field of made-for-television and made-for-cable feature pictures, network and local audience performance is crucial for sales. Syndicators of series and packages of films are alert to the ratings achieved in their first local market exposure. It can affect pricing policy for subsequent market sales. Local rating success is well documented and advertised in trade publications and promotion to buttress firms' negotiating position in other markets.

Syndicators of specialized program fare, such as game shows, children's cartoons, sports features, or live talk shows such as Donahue and Merv Griffin must watch ratings closely, both for signs of audience erosion and for every possible selling point that could gain additional station outlets and assist their client stations in sales of commercials to national and local advertisers.

Lee Rich, president of Lorimar Productions, producer of "The Waltons," "Eight Is Enough," and "Dallas," is an outstanding example of the businessman–creative producer who is credited with poring "over ratings reports (back copies of which he keeps at his fingertips) with the intensity of a time salesman or a network executive . . . he sees himself at a distinct advantage over his competitors" because of a background in advertising agencies.[18]

In addition to Hollywood entertainment producers, the NTI service serves other firms and associations that have a stake in television programming. Among subscribers are Goodson-Todman, game-show specialists; Madison Square Garden and the National Basketball Association in the sports field; cable networks such as Warner-Amex Satellite Entertainment, HBO, and the Weather Channel, and the Televison Bureau of Advertising.

## XI.  FINANCIAL INSTITUTIONS

No one understands the relationship of ratings to the "bottom line" better than the financial community involved with the broadcast field. Investment bankers and commercial lenders know that profits flow from audience and that high ratings are the best security they can have for loans and underwriting offers. The volatility of ratings requires that money merchants maintain a close watch over trends.

Major Wall Street firms are staffed with analysts who are quite proficient at forecasting revenue streams and earnings of network companies and broadcast station groups (Cox, Capital Cities, Metromedia, etc.) from the ratings performance of the networks and/or stations they own. Management representatives appear regularly before group meetings of security analysts, where they predict ratings and earnings for future quarters and face probing questions from researchers relative to audience, rates, programming, and sales.

These financial evaluators are not often subscribers to ratings. They pick up much of their information from major users such as networks and from the vast flow of ratings data published in the trade press.

## XII.  TRADE AND PUBLIC PRESS

The trade press, and particularly *Variety,* the bible of show business, became interested in ratings in the early 1930s, shortly after radio's Cooperative Analysis of Broadcasting began. *Variety* had a long tradition of publishing estimates of weekly box-office gross for the Broadway theater and for Hollywood movies. Naturally, they were greatly interested in any audience numbers they could obtain for this new entertainment medium. The CAB made no release of its program ratings, and the reports were closely controlled. Nevertheless the agencies, which at that time produced virtually all prime-time commercial programming, were not above releasing figures favorable to their productions. Gradually more and more of the CAB results reached *Variety* and some other trade journals such as *Billboard.*

Walter Winchell and Ed Sullivan, the two most widely read columnists of the day, began referring to ratings figures for various personalities and shows, so that the general public became vaguely aware of ratings' existence. When coincidental calling was at a peak during the early 1940s, many people were interviewed, so that public knowledge spread. C. E. Hooper, early in his operation, began issuing for each prime-time report a list of 15 top-rated shows. Radio columnists found these of interest and began publishing them. Network personalities and comedians used them as a butt for jokes, and cartoonists had a field day joshing the ratings makers. On the other hand, Hooper was hailed in a leading national magazine article as "The Biggest Man in Radio"[19] and in June 1948 appeared as a bona fide celebrity in white tie and tails on the first telecast of "We the People," hosted by Danny Seymour (later president of J. Walter Thompson).

But ratings themselves came into their own in the public press when Jack Gould, then radio/TV editor of *The New York Times,* began to feature data from each Nielsen TV pocketpiece in the late 1950s as soon as it was published. Nielsen, who had originally released no ratings to other than subscribers, saw the benefit of Hooper's action and had already adopted the top-15 release pattern. Now, however, much more complete release was being made, with networks and agencies cooperating with Gould. Ratings had reached a new level of visibility and respectability; henceforth they were quoted (and misquoted) by the press everywhere—not only program ratings and trends, but competitive network standings (the result of intensive network rating promotion in the consumer press as well as trade journals).

Today there are few household TV ratings for major programs which do not reach the press, not from Nielsen but from subscribers, primarily the networks. Of course, not all are newsworthy, nor are the detailed demographics of much interest except to some of the trade publications. Local market sweeps ratings are published, and certain trade journals release many detailed market standings and trends.

Ratings companies publish a stream of summary reports on an annual or semiannual basis, Nielsen being especially active in this area with many excellent analyses of major national trends in viewing, in program typologies, in top-ranking national sports, movies, and other event (one time only) programming.

*TV Guide,* the widely circulated weekly magazine, devotes considerable space to ratings trends of shows and networks, presumably because readers find it interesting. No viewer has to go far to find out how his or her favorite show rates locally or nationally or whether a bemoaned cancellation was tied to a waning rating performance.


## XIII.   COMPETING MEDIA


During the past two decades the print media—newspapers and magazines—have seen their share of the national advertising pie shrink with the emergence of television. TV now accounts for 25%, compared to 21% 20 years ago.

Obviously, these two competitors are looking for any chink, any weakness in the electronic audience position in which to make a competitive thrust. The more refined broadcast ratings become in regard to demographic breakdowns, the greater the opportunity for such efforts. Therefore, major publications give considerable attention to ratings trends for whatever competitive sustenance they can provide. For example, in 1983 the loss of several percentage points in network share (due to local TV and cable audience gains) encouraged substantial anti-network promotional efforts by the Magazine Audience Bureau as well as by individual publications. At the same time, agency and other savants feed these hopes for diminished network audiences by forecasts for 1990 that predict further significent network losses.

## XIV.   GOVERNMENT AGENCIES AND OTHERS

The ratings services do not accept subscriptions from federal government agencies because that would make all their data available to anyone on a public-access basis. They do, however, provide such specific information as agencies such as the FCC, the FTC, or congressional staffs may request. The FCC uses the Arbitron ADI ranking of markets in certain procedures.

Among subscribers to NTI ratings are such organizations as the American Society of Composers, Authors and Publishers (ASCAP), the U.S. Chamber of Commerce, and the Major League Baseball Promotion Corporation.

## XV.   SUMMARY

Ratings come in many shapes and sizes to fit the needs of a wide range of users—from average minute per program to annual average per network. The gamut includes average quarter-hour, day-part, daily, weekly, and monthly cumulatives and shares; demographics of sex, age, and race; geographics from national and census region to unduplicated market areas and zip code areas; with delivery speed in terms of hours, days, and weeks and user computer access to practically any special analysis needed. If, as the futurists state, we are entering an age to be dominated by information production and use, we can certainly point to electronic media ratings as being in the vanguard of that development. From the network president whose career and job stability are intimately tied to ratings, to the average viewer who wants to know only the chances that his or her favorite shows will remain on the air, the ratings play a role in every aspect of TV and radio broadcasting. Decision making by programmers, advertisers, and their agencies depends on the vast flow of accurate audience estimates presented in timely and useful formats by the most thorough and speedy feedback system ever developed for a nationwide field of activity.

## NOTES

1. Robert Lindsey, "The Man Who Plots CBS's Climb Back to the Top," *The New York Times,* January 27, 1980.
2. Edwin T. Vane, ABC vice president in several top program positions 1966–1979, *Broadcasting,* August 11, 1980.
3. *TV Digest,* Vol. 21, No. 9, March 2, 1981, p. 7.
4. William S. Rubens, "A Guide to TV Ratings," *Journal of Advertising Research,* Vol. 18, No. 1, February 1978. Since 1978 the number of local metered markets has expanded, but their predictability of national ratings is still rated poor.
5. Markets so served as of September 1984 are New York, Los Angeles, Chicago, San Francisco, Philadelphia, Detroit, Boston, Dallas, and Washington—all by Arbitron and Nielsen; Arbitron alone provides service in Miami and Houston, but Nielsen is planning to add those cities in early 1985 plus Denver in November 1985.
6. Edwin McDowell, "CBS Strives to Retain TV Lead," *The New York Times,* January 11, 1979. Backe resigned from CBS on May 9, 1980.
7. *The New York Times,* April 3, 1983.
8. David F. Poltrack, *Television Marketing; Network, Local, Cable* (New York: McGraw-Hill, 1983), p. 95.
9. Ibid, p. 99.
10. It is said of umpires that they classify themselves in three groups: the objectives, who claim they call balls and strikes exactly as thrown; the subjectives, who call them the way they see them; and the existentialists, who maintain that the pitch is only what they call it. No one has recorded into which category Nielsen falls.
11. The Public Broadcasting System operates on a "common carriage" basis for four nights a week (Sunday–Wednesday) beginning at 8:00 P.M.
12. Advertising expenditure for network TV is estimated at close to $7 billion for 1983, with 100 leaders accounting for 77 percent; they contribute about 45 percent of the $5 billion spot TV total.
13. Krugman, Herbert, "Why Three Exposures May Be Enough," *Journal of Advertising Research,* No. 6, 1972, p. 11.
14. Madeline Nagel, senior vice president–media director, Foote, Cone & Belding, New York, "Media Diversity Challenges Today's Ad Agencies," *Advertising Age,* August 18, 1980.
15. Formerly the Broadcast Rating Council (1962–1982).

16. House agencies are agencies owned by the advertiser and dedicated to serving the interests of that advertiser exclusively.
17. Viacom Enterprises claims that the 197 "I Love Lucy" episodes that ran on CBS from 1951 to 1957 still command a weekly audience of 1.8 million. In 1983 it aired in 57 U.S. markets covering 50 percent of U.S. TV households. *Advertising Age,* Feb. 6, 1984, p. 35.
18. "Lee Rich and Lorimar: On a Roll," *Broadcasting,* May 5, 1980, p. 48. In mid 1983 Rich returned to the agency business on a limited basis when Lorimar acquired Kenyon & Eckhardt, a sizable national agency.
19. Collie Small, "The Biggest Man in Radio," *Saturday Evening Post,* November 22, 1947. In Esquire two months later, John Keating in "Mr. Hooper Counts Ears" called Hooper "the most powerful voice in radio . . . "

# 8

## Ratings: Servant or Master?

### I. INTRODUCTION

We have seen by now that ratings are indeed a feedback mechanism to the industry the same way that the human nervous system is to the human body. Advertisers started the first rating system in 1930 to assure themselves of the audience delivery of programs they sponsored. Until that time they were "flying blind," fed a maze of claims, faced with uncertainties. When did people listen? By the day? By the hour? What did they listen to? How many and what stations were received? Only an organized measurement of audience could provide answers. Without such answers, the broadcast media could never move ahead to today's prosperity. The Cooperative Analysis of Broadcasting (CAB) in 1930 established the essential feedback mechanism required to engender advertiser confidence.

Once established, the ratings system provided important decison-making data for advertisers' use of network radio because at that time commercial prime-time programming was largely in their hands. Networks sold time, not programs, and had little control over their own schedules.[1] Advertising agencies, with assistance from talent agencies and some independent consultants, produced the programs in which the sponsor placed the commercials.

With the growth of television, a much more expensive medium, few advertisers could any longer sponsor weekly hours or half-hours but went to alternate-week sponsorship. As that too became unaffordable, the networks gradually took over the programming responsibility, and advertisers bought one-minute (later 30-second) commercial positions. This arrangement made it possible for advertisers to spread their advertising over more programs, networks, and time periods, a move made productive because nonduplicated cumulative ratings figures could be supplied by Nielsen Audimeters. With the networks in charge of their own schedule, no longer could a George Washington Hill (of American Tobacco fame) or a Firestone family dictate program fare for the nation.

As networks became more in control, they sought more ratings feedback because audience size determined the sale (and the price) of the commercial positions that had to be sold to support the entire structure. The inevitable changes in public taste could be more closely monitored, while ratings use assisted networks in developing audience flow patterns of similar demographic groups and in counterprogramming against strong competition. The net result was the rapid growth of television as the most powerful communications and advertising medium we have seen.

Critics of broadcasting (professional and amateur), as well as our society's elitists, have few kind words for what is broadcast. But generally their most venomous remarks are reserved for broadcast ratings and their so-called tyrannical influence on programming. According to David Halberstam, William S. Paley of CBS created "the modern structure of broadcasting, with its brutal ratings system and its unparalleled profits."[2] Halberstam fails to say in what respect the ratings system is "brutal." Would Halberstam characterize the newspapers' Audit Bureau of Circulation, whose figures are also used by advertisers in decision making, in the same way? Many daily newspapers and dozens of magazines have died because of poor circulation figures. Nor can one ignore the fact that publishers are as keenly concerned that their books appear in *The New York Times* best seller list[3] as any network or advertiser is in the latest top 10.

The sports world is attuned to the effect of individual star performances on team success on the field and at the gate, all measured by statistical data. Moreover, college football and basketball teams are ranked by sportswriters to provide a weekly top 10 list. These are only a few of the parallel examples that may be drawn in related fields of communications, entertainment, and sports.

Insofar as the record of major newspaper failures is concerned,[4] would such an end have come if their editors had had a daily or weekly rating report card on readership of individual stories versus their competition? Effective mass communication requires an efficient feedback system. With it, the medium can meet the needs and interests of its audience. Trial and error is possible because mistakes can be detected quickly. New entertainment and information forms can evolve under systematic oversight of audience response. Without feedback, a medium cannot efficiently serve its audience and sooner or later will fail.

The ratings system looms large in the minds of intellectuals as the black-hatted culprit who wipes quality programming off the air. Clearly, many overall criticisms of the television medium are laid at the door of ratings. Some disparagements of ratings are based on misunderstandings of their nature and function. It is more likely, however, that much of such criticism is really finding fault with the television medium and with the tastes of the American mass audience it serves. Whereas once the targets for the literary elite were the Hollywood "dream merchants," then radio programs' "pandering to the masses," it is now commercial television's "vast wasteland" that debases our culture. Beyond that, it is no doubt a dislike of advertising and a distrust of the competitive market economy that finances the media.

A major problem is that television as a medium, as a business, lives in a goldfish bowl. It is on stage for public viewing 18 to 24 hours daily, seven days a week, 52 weeks a year. Adults (18 and over) watch TV over four hours on an average day. *TV Guide,* with a weekly circulation of 17 million, and every Sunday newspaper, plus most dailies, carry complete program schedules, plus reviews, news, and summaries of ratings reports, including the top 15 shows. Television programming is a major topic of daily conversation in and away from home. When corporate management changes take place, *The New York Times* generally reports them in the business section; when network changes occur they receive front-page news treatment.

Americans are "hung up" on statistics, so the idea of Nielsen ratings intrigues them. At the same time, their lack of sophistication about statistical sampling raises serious doubts in their minds about how good the ratings are. Pseudointellectual types find it impossible to believe that "tripe like 'Beverly Hillbillies' or 'Dukes of Hazzard'" could indeed have been America's number one show. They never watched them, nor did they know anyone who had.

They would probably be just as surprised to learn that in January 1982, "The current best-selling book on campus, according to the *Chronicle of Higher Education,* was *Garfield Bigger Than Life,* a volume of cartoons about a corpulent housecat." The next 5 of the top 10 were made up of other cartoon anthologies, plus two solution books for Rubik's Cube. Harlequin paperbacks were very popular also. A spokesperson for the *Chronicle* says, "Pretty disgusting, isn't it. . . . Every once in a while I get mad and write an article about it, but things keep sliding down further."[5]

From the time we got our first report card at school, and Brownie points in Cub Scouts performance, measurement of some type became part of life. The number and precision of the measurements increase as one enters the world of academic and sports competition. High school grade-point averages and SAT scores determine what colleges one can enter, just as college grade levels determine who makes the dean's list or edits the law review. The athlete's "stats" in football or basketball determine his chance for a scholarship or for success in the drafts and free agent market. Accountability and readiness for promotion in most fields are judged in terms of performance according to established criteria—meeting quotas or budgets, increasing sales or profits, decreasing expenses or labor problems, improving corporate image or stock price.[6]

Advertisers, who initiated broadcast ratings in 1930, did so because based on their then limited use, they realized the potential advertising power of radio.

They were unwilling, however, to commit increased budgets to the new electronic medium unless they had some tangible measure of the unseen audience they reached by this miraculous medium. That's where ratings started, and that's where they will remain as long as radio, television, and cable are commercial media. Joel Swerdlow is correct when he says, "The key to any real change in the rating system lies with the advertisers. Only they among the players have the incentive to find something better. . . ."[7]

Twenty billion dollars is quite an incentive. That's the total gross amount spent by all advertisers on electronic media in 1983. Narrowing it down to expenditures by national advertisers only on television—network and spot—the total becomes $12 billion. Major spenders are some of America's blue-chip corporations: Procter & Gamble ($577 million), General Foods ($303 million), American Home Products ($197 million), General Mills ($201 million), General Motors ($191 million), PepsiCo ($163 million), AT&T ($161 million).[8] Why are these well-run, highly regarded business organizations apparently satisfied with the current ratings system? After all, this money is spent to develop more sales—the lifeblood of any corporation. If they were being misled or short-changed, would not someone hear about it? Would hundreds of corporate managements and boards of directors sit still for budgets allocated on faulty data?

There are several very good reasons, which, if the industry's critics would listen, they might understand. The advertiser's confidence in ratings starts with his knowledge of surveys and market research. He knows that the ratings figures are estimates, but he also knows that the errors that may accompany an individual figure tend to even out when many programs and spots are purchased. The advertiser also, from the enormous amount of independent survey work conducted on share of market, marketing new products, copy themes, tests of commercials, etc., has available a vast amount of detailed data that enables him to confirm the ratings reports.

## II.  RADIO RATINGS—RARELY MENTIONED

Americans spend almost as much time daily listening to the radio as they do watching television. Our radio system is pervasive indeed, with 9000 AM and FM stations and at present a total of 15 interconnected national radio networks operating.

The use and importance of ratings are considerable, especially in network and major market operations, sales, and programming. They have the same effect on station income and value and on management security and bonuses that we noted in television. If ratings are so evil for television, why are they not also vilified in respect to radio?

Critics might reply that radio is an unimportant, secondary medium, that the proliferation of outlets assures a certain diversity of program fare. But the fact remains that ratings—average quarter-hour, weekly cumes, and share figures on a persons basis—are a "medium of exchange" between buyer and seller, station owner and management, program manager and program packager or consultant, just as in TV.

TV's critics spend a great deal of time criticizing ratings and the networks over the jockeying of schedules in response to rating weaknesses. They fail to realize, however, that these maneuvers by professionals help to give the television medium the vitality that has brought it to the peak position it now occupies as a communications medium. Audience pleasing, audience serving, audience building—those are the basic objectives of a mass medium. The big rating numbers make all else possible—worldwide news organizations, coverage of national events, $2 billion sports contracts, etc.

An important element in coping with change is to have a feedback system. Otherwise, how is management to know that the old ways of doing things no longer meet public needs? The God-given gift of creative genius is not enough in today's world. With cable, VCR's, home computers, direct broadcast satellites, teletext, and videotex threatening the status quo, broadcast management more than ever is dependent on measurement of public behavior.

## III.   WHAT'S WRONG WITH RATINGS?

There is widespread recognition of the positive factors that ratings bring to the mass media of radio and television—the help provided communications companies to serve their public and the aid given advertisers in using the media effectively and supporting its ever-rising program costs with increased advertising appropriations.

Criticism of the ratings system may not be heard so frequently or so loudly at present, but the distrust is still there in many quarters. It is not confined to intellectuals and academics but is present among many who are active on the creative side—program producers for TV or radio. The latter may accept the industry's audience measurement standards because they have no choice if they want to work and compete. However, they will not hide their true feelings when a pet project dies because of ratings anemia.

An examination of the national criticisms of broadcast ratings shows them to fall into four broad categories defined as follows and discussed individually:

1. *Ratings are not accurate.* The samples are too small, viewers and listeners give biased or partial answers, interviewers are untrustworthy, cooperation rates are too low, different services give different answers, ethnic groups are poorly represented.

2. *Ratings are biased.* Networks and stations "hype" during ratings weeks by scheduling special programming, top movie attractions and guest stars, by

extraordinary promotional and publicity efforts. Rigging by people on the outside or inside is possible.

3. *Ratings are misleading.* Even if accurate, ratings are limited to quantitative audience measurement. They say nothing about the viewer/listener reaction to the program, how well liked it was, what effect it created, or whether or not exposure of individual commercials took place.

4. *Ratings are misused.* Network and station programmers are tyrannized by the ratings; they lead to the lowest common denominator in programs; quality programming is rejected or canceled. They stifle creativity, distort news programming, overemphasize "the bottom line."

## Rating Accuracy

Questions about the accuracy of broadcast ratings invariably start with sample size. How can a sample of 1200 (or 1700, the size employed since the fall of 1983) Nielsen households reflect accurately the viewing patterns of 84 million U.S. television households?

There are many proofs that such a relatively small sample is adequate: statistical, comparative, and inferential. Appendix D reviews several thorough investigations of the question—one by a congressionally sponsored study involving a blue-ribbon committee of the American Statistical Association; the other by the Committee on National Television Audience Measurement, an industry group set up initially to conduct research to answer questions by the Harris Committee Congressional hearings of 1962.

Little notice seems given to the relatively small samples used continuously by government agencies in estimating key economic activity: the Consumer Price Index, wholesale price changes, unemployment levels, etc. The salient word is "estimates," which is what all ratings are. The size of the statistical error in various rating estimates can be computed so that some notion of the reliability of any given estimate can be expressed in a range. An NTI rating of 10, for example, has an approximate range from 8 to 12 (on a 95 percent certainty basis). It is incumbent on the user to understand the sample error limitations attached to ratings figures and to comprehend the notion that they are merely approximations—in many cases rough ones, at that.

Aside from purely statistical evaluation of sample size, we have the confirmation supplied by compositing local ratings from Nielsen and Arbitron national sweeps, which are compiled from over 1.5 million completed diaries annually. The statistical correlation between such composite diary ratings and the Nielsen NTI figures, when based on 1200 households, is extremely high. Similarly, at the local level the correlation of the two diary service results confirms the use of household samples as small as 300 cases as the base for smaller market ratings. At these levels, of course, sampling error becomes much larger. The rule of thumb is that to cut sample error by half requires that sample size be quadrupled. Thus we could conclude that the sample error for the 300-base market is twice that for a four times greater 1200 household sample. Note that this comparison incorporates the principle that statistical error in ratings is not affected by the size of the market surveyed. To achieve the error range of a national 1200 sample requires a sample of 1200 in the smallest measured market.

In addition to the national–local comparisons, television ratings have been subjected to the unprecedented series of methodological studies described in Appendix D. The CONTAM group of studies of meter results during the 1960s and 1970s, the New York and COLTRAM studies of the late 1970s devoted to local meter and/or diary measurement, the ARMS radio project of 1962–1963, and the CAMS cable viewing research of 1982 have all validated (generally by use of telephone coincidental comparisons) the degree to which meters and diaries accurately measure broadcast audience. (CAMS and Arbitron studies, reported in Chapter 6, showed that 1982 type television household diaries were deficient in estimating cable-originated and pay-cable programming.) No technique is perfect, but the fact that there are several in use ensures us against being misled by the weaknesses of any one—weaknesses of which we are aware from the comparisons and methodological research.

Added to the more formal methodological projects just referred to are the hundreds of market and advertising research surveys conducted by other than ratings companies. Some of these are large in scale and sample size (Simmons, Mediamark, and Burke), whereas others are products of individual advertisers and agencies carried out by telephone or by personal interviewing in shopping centers or in cable test markets. If these studies did not substantially confirm NTI results year after year, Nielsen and the networks would certainly know about it.

### Response Cooperation Rates

Research professionals are always concerned about the degree to which a designated sample (hopefully picked on a probability basis) is actually achieved. Lack of cooperation or response by chosen sample members leads to the suspicion that nonrespondents may not be represented by respondents, creating a possibly serious nonresponse error or bias. Cooperation rates vary greatly, depending on methodology—RADAR achieves over 70 percent, Nielsen NTI around 60 percent and the diary services approximately 50 percent of the initially designated sample (after elimination of business institutions, vacant homes, non-TV, etc.). All services make a determined effort to maintain the highest possible levels by persistent recruitment, incentives, and multiple communication (telephone and mail follow-ups) during the survey. Nevertheless, the best that can be hoped for in the nonresponse problem is that it not get worse.

The effect of nonresponse can be determined only by use of a yardstick of reality that achieves a high cooperation rate and can yield a rating that includes those who will normally not cooperate in meter and diary surveys. The methodology surveys reviewed in Appendix D have enabled the industry to examine what bias, if any, the nonresponse problem produces. As anticipated, responders in general view slightly more television and somewhat differently than nonresponders. Nevertheless, these differences, when merged into the total ratings picture, are so small as to have little practical effect on ratings estimates and projections. This relationship is, however, one that should be verified periodically for various demographic, geographic, and ethnic groups.

### Ethnic Group Measurement

A special problem is presented by the ethnic groups (black and Hispanic) for two reasons: low cooperation rates and significant viewing/listening differences from whites. The poor response by these groups is the result of suspicion and illiteracy. Most blacks and Hispanics are found in the lower socioeconomic groups where protection of privacy is of great importance. The incidence of nonlisted telephones is nearly as high among these disadvantaged as it is among the famous and wealthy in the upper socioeconomic strata. They want to feel safe from bill collectors or the authorities who may be checking their welfare or citizenship status. Strangers asking questions are frightening and avoided as possible arms of the government establishment. On top of this concern is the literacy and language problem, especially where diaries are involved. Understanding and following instructions for daily entries can be very difficult.

A second important factor in ethnic measurement is the existence of a considerable amount of programming designed especially for that audience. This is especially true in radio, where black-oriented and Spanish-language stations are found in virtually every U.S. major market. In television, specialized Hispanic stations are found in over 20 markets today—in several there are two Spanish-language TV outlets. Obviously, if Hispanics are underrepresented in a diary sample, ratings for the Spanish stations will be understated. Similarly, black-oriented stations may suffer in radio ratings reports.

Over the years, ratings services have used two techniques to cope with these problems: Weighting and special field procedures to raise cooperation. The serious black nonresponse problem exists in major cities where that group is concentrated in certain geographic areas. One solution involved describing these areas as discrete sampling units to be separately weighted in the composite for the area. Weighting diaries returned from black households up to the estimated proportion of black households in the market was another device.

Although it removed some of the bias, weighting alone was not a satisfactory solution, because returns came from an unrepresentative subsample of the ethnic population. What was needed were efforts to develop better returns—in number and representativeness—from ethnic households. In 1970 Arbitron initiated separate special procedures for blacks and Hispanics for both radio and television. In certain markets with concentrated black audiences, daily telephone calls were made by interviewers to record the listening/viewing of the preceding 24 hours. For Hispanics, the technique was placement of Spanish-language diaries by personal interview using Spanish-speaking field workers. In 1982 and 1983 Arbitron Television and Radio replaced these procedures with its Differential Survey Treatment (DST), a procedure involving greater monetary incentives to induce blacks and Hispanics to keep and return diaries.

Nielsen introduced Spanish-language diaries in its local diary service in 1971 but otherwise relied on market segmentation and weighting to handle the ethnic problem until 1980. Then Nielsen introduced a procedure whereby Hispanic and black households received special letters, additional incentives, and midweek interview calls to boost return rates.

Ethnic problems are serious, but the steady progress made by services to handle them assure these viewers that they are represented in all of today's ratings.

## Different Services Give Different Results

Sampling error alone would account for different ratings if two surveys were conducted side by side in the same area, by the same company for the identical period. Of course, the differences would fall within the statistical ranges attributable to the sample size (See Appendix D, Study 8). Nonresponse may vary widely from one survey to another. Ratings developed by different methods, often for different periods and areas, are bound to differ. Reasons for differences, in addition to sample size and nonresponse, include the following:[9]

1. *Definitional differences.*[10] Are definitions of audience and viewing identical?
   a. Total audience rating versus average quarter hour versus average minute audience versus some form of cumulative audience.
   b. Program audience (including delayed telecasts) versus time-period audience versus station audience.
   c. Tuning versus viewing versus presence in room.
   d. Viewing only at home versus all viewing (including away from home.)
   e. Time periods, total day (what hours included?), one week, or multiple weeks averaged.
   f. Audience composition, for example, households, persons, persons by age/sex group.

2. *Measurement period differences.* Date of measurement can affect estimates in many ways:
   a. Actual dates covered can create variance.
   b. Seasonal differences in viewing habits.
   c. Daylight versus Standard Time (affects both TV schedules and living habits).
   d. Reruns versus originals (may not affect all stations or all time periods equally).
   e. Unusual weather, natural disasters, world events.

   f.  Changes in competitive programming.
   g.  Guest stars or unusual promotion, sports, miniseries.
3.  *Universe differences*
   a.  All households versus all phone households versus listed phone households.
   b.  Persons: in total (including institutional), in households only, age and/ or sex categories, with or without visitors included.
   c.  Geography.

4.  *Sample frame differences* The sample frame is a list—or a method of generating a list—from which the sample is drawn. Ideally such a list includes all members of the universe or population to be surveyed and a way of identifying each member. In practice, sampling frames usually consist of census data, maps, address lists, directories, telephone numbers, etc. Frames may differ in coverage (some members of the universe may be excluded) and age (the length of time between creating the frame and drawing the sample).

5.  *Differences due to response errors.* The two types of response error are those relating to the measurement of activity per se, and those relating to the proper identification of the person or household reported on. Respondent data are obtained in a number of ways, such as the meter, diary, recall, and coincidental. The use of questionnaires, diaries, and interviewers may result in respondent or interviewer error, or both, inappropriate questionnaire or diary design, misunderstanding or inaccurate completion of diary or questionnaire.

6.  *Differences due to data processing procedures.* Procedures used in processing data affect the audience estimates.
   a.  Standards for accepting or rejecting viewing information from the sample.
   b.  Checking, coding, and editing procedures.
   c.  Accuracy of program name or network lineup information.
   d.  Accuracy of information about cable TV facilities and carriages, the cable TV universe, superstations, translators, etc.
   e.  Ascription procedures to cope with incomplete data, such as viewing data for persons but not age/sex data, household program viewing data without audience composition.

7.  *Differences in computation procedures.* Are the procedures used to derive the reported audience estimates from the data obtained from the sample units (i.e., households, persons, etc.) the same? Computation procedures may include weighting and other statistical adjustments such as ratio estimates or stratification. If statistical adjustments are used, the accuracy of the weights and/or controls can affect the audience estimates.

Any combination of differences in one or more of the above factors—for Survey X versus Survey Y—may rationally and sensibly explain differences in the final results.

## Ratings Are Biased

This complaint category questions ratings as being subject to artificial stimulants in the form of "hyping"—the scheduling of unusually strong programming and promotion for rating periods and the possibility of "rigging" by outsiders or insiders.

### Hyping

During sweep weeks of the TV local market surveys, TV networks frequently schedule special programming, just as their affiliates launch provocative news series. Both put on their stronger movies and advertising and on-air promotions are stepped up. Each network attempts to give its affiliates the best chance for a strong local rating result (the direct importance to the network is marginal—its customers look at national ratings available for 365 days a year—but for months the stations must sell on results from the latest book). Industry critics assert that this practice distorts ratings by beclouding the true standing of the regular weekly network schedule around which national advertisers' spots appear.

In radio, where programming is relatively fixed within a station's format, the hyping options are more limited. Special guest appearances by record stars or other personalities, contests with large prizes such as cars, cash, and vacation trips, and reminders over the air regarding filling in diaries are among those used. Newspaper, TV, and billboard ads exhort listener attention. One must believe that much of this special fury is ineffectual in part because such efforts could cancel each other out. Nevertheless, the concern over hyping is real—buyers and stations alike would like to see it controlled or halted.

Philosophically, it is human nature to "put your best foot forward" when you know you are being measured, inspected, or examined—the student cramming for a final, the used car seller tuning it to a T, the Army post commander putting on the eyewash for the general's visit, the corporation treasurer "dressing up" the balance sheet for the annual report all have one thing in common—making things look better than they really are day in and day out. This is generally understood, and where professionals are concerned the results are somewhat discounted. There is no practical way that such behavior can effectively be abolished.

What then can be done about hyping? One alternative occasionally proposed is "secret rating weeks," unknown to broadcasters. Because of the extent of advance preparations and activities, the knowledge of survey dates would be impossible to limit. The situation would be compounded if some stations learned the dates and others didn't.

There are several antidotes, varying from 100 percent riddance of incentive to weak protective measures:

1. The ultimate is using round-the-clock daily results on full view. Buyers are not required to make any guesses or allowances predicated on ratings possibly distorted by hyping.

2. Lacking daily ratings, spread the rating periods over as many weeks as possible. In 1982, Arbitron Radio began shifting 4-week sweeps to 12 weeks, thus making it more difficult for special stations efforts to be maintained throughout a rating period. Station resistance has prevented numerous efforts to bring about such an improvement in local TV measurement. Objections are keyed to concern that costs might go up (they would, slightly) even though sample size would not be altered, that rating results would be delayed, that weekly data now possible with 4-week samples would be lost in 12-week reports. A major effort to overcome hyping indigenous to sweeps was launched by the ARF Television Audience Measurement Committee in 1976. A proposal to redistribute the diaries used in sweeps to provide a 4-week "buyer report" earlier than the normal November sweep followed by three quarterly reports was not welcomed by the industry or ratings services. Fundamentally, most television stations do not want additional weeks rated—they generally opposed the services' July rating books (desired by agencies) and are resisting local meter service in several major markets. Stations seriously question their own and agency's ability to digest, analyze, and capitalize on the vast sea of numbers presented daily and weekly, and they are not happy that buyers will have new data with which to bargain on rates.

3. Use Nielsen NTI national data to alert buyers to the rating effects of sweeps-weeks network hyping efforts. This had been done by establishing a norm of 100 percent for each prime-time half hour for each network for each night based on rating levels of weeks preceding the local rating period and then indexing the sweep rating period relative to the norm. Thus, if ABC shows a high index for 8:00 P.M. Sunday night for the sweep period compared to the norm, agency analysts can discount ratings for the ABC affiliates accordingly when using local reports. This technique, also developed by the ARF Television Audience Measurement Committee in 1976,[11] was employed to produce sweep-weeks Network Share Index Reports from 1976 to 1979. It was discontinued because a survey of agency recipients concluded that it was not being used. No alternative proposals were forthcoming.

4. Disclose unusual contests and prizes and on-the-air promotion activity of individual stations in ratings books. This is basically confined to radio stations where hyping activity is most prevalent. It depends largely on competitive station advice about such activity (which is then confirmed with the station in question). There is no strong evidence that radio time buyers pay much attention to it, because it is difficult to assess the effect of such activity levels.

5. Government intercession has been urged, and in the past both the FCC and the FTC gave some attention to the hyping problem. However, such interest has faded in recent years and is unlikely to resurface in an era of deregulation.

All in all, the industry appears to live with hyping without too much concern. It is a normal competitive manifestation, and ratings deemed to be affected are questioned and discounted. The waves of extraordinary TV programming and promotion no doubt help the medium attract more viewers.

### Rigging

Whereas hyping is directed at increasing audiences during rating periods so that ratings will be affected, rigging aims to boost ratings by manipulating the survey itself. There are no doubt many ways that could be conceived to do this, and a number have been tried. However, unlike the incentive for fraud and embezzlement where money is concerned, ratings are a secondary medium of exchange—they have a monetary value only for the program producer or the broadcaster. The knave with a scheme gets no payoff unless a third party can be persuaded to pay for the rating manipulation. The likelihood of enlisting either program producers or broadcast personnel is small indeed—this involves risks for them far greater than any possible benefit. Nevertheless, there have been one major effort and many smaller attempts to fraudulently push up ratings.

The major effort was masterminded and implemented by no less than a former congressional staff investigator, Rex Sparger. Sparger had been deeply involved in the investigations of rating services conducted as part of Representative Oren Harris's committee ratings probe of 1961–1963. (See Chapter 9 for details.) Sparger then concentrated on detailing weaknesses of the Nielsen Audimeter service and consequently developed enough knowledge on which to base his plot.

Sparger somehow acquired the names of some Nielsen service men and either trailed them as they made service calls on sample homes or stole files of names left in service men's unlocked cars. In any event Sparger acquired the identity of 58 NTI households in Ohio and Pennsylvania. He approached Charles Lowe, executive producer of a forthcoming special entitled "An Evening with Carol Channing," scheduled for CBS-TV 8:30–9:30 P.M., February 18, 1966. Lowe, Channing's husband, apparently agreed to send questionnaires to each of the 58 homes designed to influence them to watch the show. Each questionnaire, calling for watching the entire program, was accompanied by $3.00, and an additional $5.00 was promised for completion and return.

Nielsen's security precautions triggered the scheme quickly, and the 58 homes were omitted from the NTI sample for that evening. Nielsen moved rapidly by filing a $15 million lawsuit against Sparger in Oklahoma City on March 24, 1966. The following day Sparger told the Oklahoma City *Times* that he had rigged ratings on four network shows and had more than the 58 names Nielsen mentioned. He was doing this to collect material for a book, which he later said would be titled "How to Rig the Ratings for Fun and Profit."

Nielson won the day in court on September 2, 1966, when Sparger signed a consent order "virtually conceding charges he illegally attempted to distort Nielsen ratings of the Carol Channing Show last February."[12] In return Nielsen dropped its claim for punitive damages. Sparger acknowledged that he attempted the illegal action "for purposes of obtaining financial enrichment," that Nielsen's security system was adequate to detect attempted rigging, and that other attempts did not work because Sparger had incorrect names. Sparger was given 10 days to deliver to Nielsen all records and documents relative to the Nielsen organization and was enjoined from writing or publishing books or articles referring directly or indirectly to Nielsen without referring them to Ernst & Ernst, certified public accountants, for review of "false or libelous" statements about Nielsen or its business.

In contrast to the Sparger plot, other rigging efforts have been small indeed. Whereas Sparger exploited a producer, most efforts are directed to broadcasting personnel—either managers or on-the-air personalities who often publicly expose their concern over their own ratings. One effort in this direction was taken in Memphis by a post office employee, who identified incoming Arbitron radio diaries by the envelopes, opened the mail, and surreptitiously peddled them to a friendly local station disc jockey. In another case, someone in a sample diary household attempted to sell an individual or several diaries to some local on-the-air personality. Station personnel accidentally included in diary surveys have been known to "load up" the diary for their station. Radio tends to be more vulnerable to such manipulation because people often listen to a single station for hours at a time and false claims are not easily detectable.

Because of the lack of payoff incentive, rigging of ratings has not been a serious problem. One troublesome practice has been special announcements sometimes made exhorting a station's audience to be sure to fill out and mail a diary during a sweeps week. This could prove biasing by selectively increasing the response rate for that station's audience. Another ploy is for the station to conduct its own survey during a rating week, offering large prizes and publicizing them over the air. There is danger that diary-respondent listeners to that station could believe that they might be eligible for prizes. This might artificially increase listening and response rate for that station, consequently biasing the measurement.

Strong forces against rigging include the integrity of the broadcasting estab-lishment and the universal policy that no network or station personnel participate in rating surveys, often under threat of dismissal if they do. Arbitron provides subscribing stations with large red-and-black bulletin board posters to advise and warn employees about engaging in any such activity.

## Conditioning

Researchers trained in the natural sciences are often incredulous that meas-urement of people's behavior is carried out with the knowledge and cooperation of the measured person or households. This is so alien to the rigorous steps taken to ensure the utmost in objectivity and control of natural science experi-ments that these skeptics find it difficult to accept the many forms of social science research in which the possibility of conditioning is present. This is a legitimate reservation and one that is always present in audience measurement where interviews, diary cooperation, and meter placement are involved.

In broadcast audience surveys, this conditioning could take several forms: Panel members might unconsciously change their viewing or listening behavior, or they might consciously try to affect the ratings by claiming more viewing or listening to certain programs and stations that are their favorites. The rigid standards applicable to clinical research are simply not possible in measuring mass media audiences, whether the subject is television or radio or readership of newspapers or magazines. The best we can do is validate the procedures used by more accurate techniques. The coincidental telephone survey, which asks only for a report on viewing or listening at the time the phone rang, is the least likely to incorporate such conditioning. That is one reason why coincidental surveys are used as the yardstick of truth in methodological surveys.

## Ratings Are Misleading

This criticism attacks ratings for not doing things they never attempted—generate qualitative data such as viewers' attitude toward and involvement in programming or their exposure to or attention to commercials or their use of product categories advertised on each program. Unfortunately, the term "ratings" implies that there is some judgmental process involved, whereas in fact broadcast ratings are essentially quantitative, "counting the house" statistics, which measure only set or people behavior.

In saying this, it should be recognized, as pointed out in Chapter 5, that many qualitative attributes can be developed from the detailed breakdowns of audience data. Geographics, age and sex, household economic status, educational level, and employment are all factors that can be developed for any program's audience. Other services provide liking scores, commercial recall, and product use characteristics by network program. The ratings user, with today's access to computer tapes and data banks where much of these details are recorded for quick analysis, has an enormous resource of qualitative information.

Experience shows that Nielsen and other ratings services can reveal audience shifts to "quality" shows such as "60 Minutes," "Hill Street Blues," "Roots," and "Shogun." To change the ratings, it is not necessary to revise the rating technique; what must change is the taste of the audience, which will then accept changed programming. The expansion of news in the past three years is an example of this phenomenon. A qualitative system that emphasized subjective factors and suppressed quantitative audience numbers would serve only to weaken television's economic base, which rests on its broad reach and heavy frequency characteristics. Audience size must remain the foundation of a successful measurement system for broadcasting.

A determined effort by Television Audience Assessment to launch a new syndicated qualitative rating service will test the industry's interest in such data. A description of this company's pilot studies was discussed in Chapter 5. TAA sees its place as a national supplement to Nielsen NTI quantitative ratings, providing networks, advertisers, agencies, and producers with measures related to program appeal, program effect, and commercial effectiveness. Initial industry reaction has been mixed, but further studies in 1984 will provide an answer as to the future viability of this proposed service.

## Ratings Are Misused

Here we deal with "ratings tyranny." Ratings, it is charged, so dominate the decision making of networks, stations, and program suppliers that they lead to the cancellation of quality programs and result in programs appealing to the lowest common denominator. It is said that ratings distort news judgment and lead to the scheduling of lurid and sensational news stories and investigative reporting. Such allegations obviously have a factual basis. Ratings are the lingua franca of broadcasting, and little is to be gained by arguing otherwise. As commercial advertising media, with no subscription income (except for PBS stations), the financial health of each broadcasting enterprise must be ensured to maintain the many program services that may not be self-sufficient.

A major misperception in making ratings the scapegoat is the failure to understand that they are only the end result, not the cause. Ratings cancel no programs, sell no spots, revise no schedules, negotiate no make-goods—ratings *users* do. The same can be said for sales and profit figures produced by accountants. They too are a managerial tool to guide decisions directed to maintaining a healthy, profitable enterprise.

The Carnegie Commission on the Future of Public Broadcasting in its report "A Public Trust" quotes Gary Steiner:[13]

> At the end of a concert at Carnegie Hall, Walter Damrosch asked Rachmaninoff what sublime thoughts had passed through his head as he stared out into the audience during the playing of his concerto. "I was counting the house," said Rachmaninoff. The principal test of public broadcasting's accountability to the community is whether anybody is listening or watching.

We saw in Chapter 7 that PBS is a regular subscriber to and user of national and local ratings reports. The BBC had its own rating service for many years. Ratings services operate in scores of countries around the world, from Switzerland to Hong Kong. Many of these broadcasting systems are government operated and/or non-commercial. Broadcasters have to make a greater effort to "count the house" than the concert artist, theater manager, or ball-club owner because of the intangible character of the audience.

The intellectual and cultural level of our society is not what our elitist critics wish it to be. The average American looks to TV primarily for light entertainment, something to take the pressure off, help him or her relax and forget the day's problems. The commercial networks and independent stations (programming similar fare but with greater emphasis on movies and sports) have continued to garner close to 90 percent of all television viewing, despite the "higher-quality" program offerings of public television stations and the variety of cable television originations. With live opera, symphony, and ballet performances, National Geographic specials, the McNeil-Lehrer News Hour, and the best of BBC drama in its schedule, PBS was able to capture only an average audience share of 3 percent in the spring of 1984. Two cable networks, dedicated to supplying subscribers with "quality programs," folded after less than a year's operation. Can Nielsen or network executives be held accountable for the failure of the public to select such programs?

What about people in the television establishment itself? Here we find distrust of ratings greatest among the creative people, who often believe it is an unfair and faulty form of report card.

No one has better analyzed the conflict between program creation and broadcast research than Paul Klein, whose credentials to do so are impeccable.[14] Klein contends:[15]

> . . . probably in no area of research other than television is the criterion variable fed back to you so quickly—usually within weeks, maybe even days. TV ratings might well be the fastest dependent variable in research history.

> Why is the rating so important to us? Why do we hold our breath every day when we come to work? Because our pricing, our scheduling, our budgeting, our jobs all are dependent on our ability to predict this number with reasonable accuracy. If we miss in our forecast, it costs us money—either "lost opportunity" money through underpricing, or "makegood" money through overpricing. In both cases these are real dollars. . . .

> The creative people sometimes feel they should have the right to a "quality" program regardless of the ratings. They resent the fact that they are forced to accept audience popularity as part of the standard by which they are to be judged. . . .

> The creative person's concern that "research corrupts" means in part that "research tries to channel me into playing the numbers game. I want to remain true to the standards of my art." Ultimately, of course, there is no option. We are, all of us, in the communications business—and the business of business is making money. . .

> One factor that is often omitted in discussions of research is that the fact that we *have* the research doesn't mean we have to *use* it—we can choose to ignore it. To have information about viewer attitudes towards a program is not in and of itself a threat to creative integrity. It is the potential of pressure to "do something about it" that is the underlying concern. But that is not *research* pressure (though it may be management pressure, expressed or implied).

One can easily see that Klein is following the stern admonition of Samuel Johnson: "Sir, no man but a blockhead ever wrote except for money."

Perhaps William S. Paley, longtime CBS chairman and the dean of network programmers, expressed the dilemma best. In early 1980 at age 79 he was having overnight audience ratings phoned to him at home every morning because of the close CBS–ABC rating race. He explained, "I don't think people always understand that television is a mass medium. I care about quality, but I also care about the bottom line."[16]

The pressure for high ratings is alleged to result in local news organizations seeking sensational and lurid topics, especially during sweeps weeks. This is when series on abortion, teen pregnancy, incest, rape, child abuse, and so on are unveiled, it is charged. The accusations are not baseless, but the dimensions of the practice and the extent of its influence on ratings are overblown. Local news ratings and revenue are critical for stations. They can't risk losing any share to competitors during a rating period and therefore present promotable features for the early or late news shows. Journalistic practices and ethics are probably not much different in television than in newspapers. Some take the sensational route, others focus on investigative reporting of local politics and education, suspected chicanery by elected officials, or upcoming city budget crunches. As discussed above, the incentive for such shenanigans would quickly wither if the sweeps weeks were replaced by 52-week surveying.

The print field is not without its exponents of large audience numbers. *Newsweek* has had six top editors and seven presidents in the past 12 years. *Time* magazine, commenting on the January 1984 editor change, states:[17] "One major reason for the frequent turnover, according to company executives," is owner Katherine Graham's "dissatisfaction with the pace of *Newsweek's* efforts to catch up with *Time*." The 1982–1983 comparisons showed *Time* widening its lead in both circulation and ad revenue—the "ratings" that count in the magazine business.

The president and chief executive officer of *U.S. News & World Report,* James H. McIlhenny, frankly says, "In the ancient marketplace promoters provided minstrels and jugglers for entertainment to attract people to the market. We provide news, *People* provides gossip, and *Playboy* magazine provides lust to attract people . . . our advertisers come to our market not so much because we sell them but because we deliver a known market of buyers."[18]

The charge that ratings encourage imitation (and by implication discourage "truly creative" efforts) is frequently heard. For example, Eric Barnouw says, "Many executives say their personal preferences would move them in other directions but that their duty is to mass preferences as evidenced by quantifiable trends. Such evidence—as in Nielsen ratings—inevitably encourages imitation of current successes."[19] True enough, but is imitation of current successes a legacy attributable to broadcast ratings alone?

In discussing the phenomenal success of Rupert Murdoch as a multinational publisher, Tom O'Hanlon[20] comments, "Murdoch will give a job to anyone who can make a sales chart move," and quotes Murdoch's view that ". . . the problem with U.S. journalism is that they simply don't know how to compete." O'Hanlon, explaining Murdoch's Fleet Street background, writes:

> . . . at a time when many U.S. newspapers are dying and the public is turning to the tube, the British daily press continues to get bought and read. If the American press struggles to advance social justice and to achieve something called responsibility, the British press struggles to be bright and inventive and to be involved with what actually interests ordinary men and women.

Robert Dahlin, a long-time observer of the book field, in discussing publishers' successes and failures, states: "We should remember that nobility of publishing is anchored, however loosely, in the bottom line." In reporting the phenomenal and unexpected success of *In Search of Excellence: Lessons from America's Best Run Companies* by Thomas J. Peters and Robert H. Waterman, Dahlin says: "Now similar books are scheduled from a variety of publishers."[21] A smash hit musical on Broadway is invariably followed by many others (*Chorus Line, Forty-second Street, On Your Toes, Evita,* for example). Hollywood imitative cycles are legendary, ranging from space drama to horror films to single parents to spy pictures. The astonishing success of the Cabbage Patch Kids brought almost instant imitators. Magazine successes featuring female nudity, health and exercise, personal finance, travel, and home computers quickly experienced numerous imitators. Is it somehow more legitimate to imitate on the basis of dollar or unit sales, box-office attendance, or circulation than for higher ratings, which are the prime broadcasting audience gauge?

## IV.  VIEWING PUBLIC'S INTEREST

In the final analysis, the fundamental question to be answered is, "Do ratings serve the viewing public's interest?" The first answer is that, so far as can be ascertained, no one has proposed an alternative feedback system. A mass medium requires mass audience for success. Broadcast management needs audience response data for programming, selling, promotion, and many other purposes; advertisers who invest more than $20 billion annually in television, radio, and cable must have vast amounts of detailed audience data, which their agencies analyze, evaluate, and act on in an accountable manner; creative program producing and syndicating organizations need data on audience size and changes in public tastes as indicated by trends in program popularity. Ancillary data, qualitative or otherwise, may be useful, but there is no substitute for a basic quantitative "head count." That's true for every commercial publication, play, movie, professional sport, or concert feature. It seems even to be accepted in radio—

it is only in the television medium that critics condemn audience counts as evil instruments.

A root cause of this criticism is the elite's dislike of much television program fare. The intelligentsia would appear to be quite willing to deprive the blue- and white-collar workers of their beer and pretzels if they themselves could have wine and cheese instead. That is the road to disaster for the television medium, as well as for those viewers who would find their favorite programs scratched for entertainment and information they have voted against time and time again. Does this meet what the FCC requires of its licensees—that they operate in the public interest, convenience, and necessity?

Television is an intrusive medium. It is difficult to view it at all without being exposed to programs (or program elements) one may not like. It's not as easy to scan and skip as one does in reading a newspaper or magazine. The all-pervasive power of television as the quintessential mass medium does not encourage the program of highly specialized interest. Perhaps the newer video forms—cable, video cassettes, teletext, and videotex—will be better suited to the narrowcasting mode.

As already stated, ratings are actually a form of taskmaster. That report card, delivered every day to network executives (and to station managers in major markets) represents facts that will not go away. The show that doesn't measure up, that indicates serious audience weakness, must eventually be jettisoned, even though the executives involved in that decision personally like it. Otherwise, a diminished lead-in will damage the audience level of following programs, and that entire evening's schedule is jeopardized. This is the essence of the free competitive broadcasting system.

Faltering program series may be canceled quickly, moved to what may be a less competitive spot, or removed temporarily for further work or for a more favorable environment. Schedules constantly shift, and probes for adversarial weaknesses are made by specials and miniseries.

Whatever the nature of the aspersions cast on ratings, they must be doing something right in guiding television to the position it holds in our society. A December 1982 nationwide Roper Organization survey[22] shows that, when questioned about the kind of job television stations and other local institutions are doing, the scorecard shows the following:

|  | *Excellent or Good (%)* | *Fair or Poor (%)* |
|---|---|---|
| *Television Stations* | *70%* | *27%* |
| *Churches* | *69* | *19* |
| *Police* | *65* | *31* |
| *Newspapers* | *59* | *36* |
| *Schools* | *50* | *37* |
| *Local Government* | *39* | *53* |

In the same survey, television was chosen by 65 percent of respondents as the source of "most of your news about what's going on in the world today"; newspapers were named by 44 percent, radio 18 percent.

Another national poll, this one on leisure time in May 1982,[23] showed television as the most popular leisure activity, with 72 percent saying they watched television every day or almost every day. Respondents estimated that they have an average of 4½ hours of leisure time a day and that they spend about 2 hours 50 minutes (63 percent of the total) watching television. Ratings surveys show that these recall estimates are understatements—Nielsen data for a comparable period showed that the average TV household tunes to television about 6½ hours a day and the average person age 12 + watches about 4 hours daily.[24]

The *TV Guide* circulation of 17 million, the record sale of 20 million TV sets in the United States in 1983 (consistently outpaced in 1984) and the burgeoning sales of home video cassette recorders, which are principally used to record and play back commercial television programs, are tangible testaments to the American public's favorable reaction to and involvement in the output of television and cable.

Every time a network makes a substitution, it is testing a new program that it has reason to believe could do better than its predecessor. The audience gains by constantly getting new choices of programs from the three networks.

William Rubens, NBC vice president for research, recently said:[25]

Let me remind you that we want to present popular entertainment and news to as many people as possible. As far as we know, we reflect society's values, and I think there is more evidence that the media are socialized by the audience than that the audience is socialized by the media. In other words, you viewers out there have much more effect on us than we have on you.

A keen and objective student of mass media, Dr. W. Russell Newman, co-director, Research Program on Communications Policy, Massachusetts Institute of Technology, believes that:[26]

A . . . mechanism of media influence seems to be a pattern of cultural homogenization . . . emphasizing common elements of audience appeal and incorporating cultural strands into the mainstream. . . . The American public is not held hostage by the technology of television. The rating system makes the networks very responsive to changing audience tastes and interest. . . . The elements of adventure, humor, violence, sex and politics have been consistently predominant in the primordial myths, nineteenth-century novels and modern media fare (perhaps in roughly equal proportion).

Dr. Newman concludes: "Those who feel the media stifle and constrain diversity might pause to consider to what extent the media have and will continue to reflect the strong commonalities of human interests and concerns."

*Time* magazine in an editorial comment[27] following a deep scrutiny of the jury system in 1982, wrote: "TIME observes that trial by jury realizes an essential democratic ideal; that a citizen's security is best protected not by any institutional or intellectual elite, but by the common sense of his fellow citizens . . ." In a meaningful way, ratings are also an expression of democracy in action—viewers and listeners have free choice of a wide variety of free entertainment, news, and information. No other medium anywhere in the world can match the variety and quality of the total output of the programs that weather our ratings system to reach the American public.

## NOTES

1. The initial break in the tradition that the advertiser owned the time period came in 1954, when NBC forced the Firestone Tire and Rubber Company, sponsor of the "Firestone Hour," a semiclassical music program on NBC at 8:30 P.M. Monday evenings since September 1949, to relinquish its time period. The program's ratings were always abysmally low, and as TV competition heated up NBC decided that Firestone must move to a new time period on Sunday afternoon. Sylvester (Pat) Weaver, president of NBC Television, took the proposal (with ratings analyses) to the Firestone family in Akron because Mrs. Harvey Firestone, widow of the founder, had a personal interest in the program. The NBC move was rejected (one Firestone family member remarked that "everyone is playing polo on Sunday afternoon"), and Firestone moved to ABC, where it occupied its 8:30 Monday time period for three years.

2. David Halberstam, *The Powers That Be* (New York: Alfred A. Knopf, Inc., 1979), p. 39.

3. Based on computer-based sales figures from 160 bookstores in every region of the U.S.

4. Since January 1976 daily newspapers have suspended operations in Chicago, Philadelphia (2), Boston, Washington, Cleveland (2), Buffalo, Hartford (2), Oklahoma City, and Memphis. Scores of newspapers have disappeared through suspension and mergers in other cities.

5. *The Wall Street Journal*, February 3, 1982, p. 1.

6. There's an old saying in Washington: "Until you can count the problem you can't solve it."

7. Joel Swerdlow, "The Ratings Game," *Washington Journalism Review*, Washington, D.C., October 1979. The odd part about this comment is that neither Swerdlow nor any of the scores of other professional critics of ratings ever seem to discuss their concerns with advertisers.

8. Television advertising expenditures for 1983 as estimated by the Television Bureau of Advertising, based on data from *Broadcast Advertiser Reports*.

9. This comparative assessment has been adapted from an undated publication of A. C. Nielsen Media Research entitled "Comparative Audience Estimates from Different Sources."

10. See Appendix A for further details of definitions and basic rating arithmetic.

11. This ARF committee was chaired by Ms. Jackie Da Costa, Ted Bates vice president, who vigorously pursued solutions to the hyping problem.

12. *Broadcasting,* September 5, 1966.

13. Gary Steiner, *The Creative Organization* (Chicago: University of Chicago Press, 1965), p. 207, cited in *A Public Trust: The Report of the Carnegie Commission on the Future of Public Broadcasting* (New York: Bantam Books, Inc., 1979).

14. Klein served in top audience research and programming posts at NBC after marketing experience in the ad agency field. Following creative experience with his own independent production company, he became president of the Playboy cable network.

15. Paul L. Klein, *"TV Program Creation and Broadcast Research:* Conflict or Harmony?", New York Chapter/AMA Conference, Waldorf Astoria Hotel, April 13, 1981.

16. Tony Schwartz, "An Intimate Talk with William Paley," *New York Times Magazine,* December 28, 1980.

17. "Newsweek's Outsider Bows Out," *Time,* January 16, 1984.

18. *Marketing News,* October 29, 1982, p. 12.

19. Eric Barnouw, *The Sponsor* (New York: Oxford University Press, 1978), p. 113.

20. Tom O'Hanlon, "What Does This Man Want?", *Forbes,* January 20, 1984.

21. Robert Dahlin, "Commentary on the Unpredictability of Readers," *The Christian Science Monitor,* November 4, 1983.

22. *Trends in Attitudes Toward Television and Other Media: A Twenty-four Year Review,* report by the Roper Organization, Inc. Television Information Office, New York.

23. "Where Does the Time Go? The United Media Enterprises Report on Leisure in America," Research and Forecasts, Scripps-Howard, New York.

24. Aside from respondent memory weakness, the differences here may be accounted for by viewing while performing nonleisure activities—eating, cooking, sewing, ironing, cleaning—and by out-of-home viewing.

25. William S. Rubens, "The Role of Media on Democratic Policy," presentation to the National Decisions Program Seminar, Political Science Department, University of Pennsylvania, October 1983.

26. W. Russell Newman, "Communications Technology and Cultural Diversity," paper presented at American Sociological Association annual meeting, San Francisco, California, September 1982.

27. *Time* magazine advertisement in *Advertising Age,* April 1982, p. 39.

# 9

## Government Intervention

### I. INTRODUCTION

Industry discontent with local syndicated rating services grew during the mid 1950s. It stemmed from a deep-seated skepticism about the techniques used and, in some cases, the integrity of rating companies. Television and radio station owners felt that the advancing importance and use of ratings, which in effect put a value on their broadcast properties, was counter to their interests. Furthermore, the rating results differed so much from one service to another that some investigation was warranted.

Stanley Breyer, manager of radio station KJBS, San Francisco, ran a full-page advertisement in the July 3, 1950 issue of *Broadcasting-Telecasting* to highlight the troublesome problem. He proposed a test to determine whether either Hooper or Pulse were measuring radio audiences accurately.[1] Breyer's initiative brought about the organization of a Special Test Survey Committee by the National Association of Broadcasters. This committee's specifications for a comprehensive study, estimated to cost $140,000, produced no results.

The Advertising Research Foundation (ARF), meanwhile, found strong interest by advertisers and agencies in methodological research into various ratings techniques. In July 1952 the ARF Committee began its deliberations, the only tangible result of which was publication in 1954 of *Recommended Standards for Radio and Television Audience Size Measurements*. The most significant recommendations from the ARF Radio-TV Committee, chaired by Dr. Lawrence Deckinger, Director of Research at Biow-Bern-Toigo, were that set tuning should be the basic measurement and that anyone in the room with a set on be counted in the audience. The committee's design of test specifications met the same dismal fate as the earlier NAB proposal.

242

With the failure of the NAB and the ARF to produce any action toward a true investigation, broadcasters finally sought relief from receptive members of Congress. Senator A. N. "Mike" Monroney, chairman of the Senate Interstate and Commerce Committee, who in 1956 was conducting hearings regarding several aspects of television, took an interest in such an investigation because of the number of inquiries and complaints received about rating services. At Monroney's request, Senator Warren G. Magnuson, chairman of a subcommittee on communications, initiated action with a letter to ratings services dated March 27, 1957, inquiring into their techniques and procedures. One student of the field states: "This letter stands as a most important document as it represents the first specific government effort to pry into the matter of ratings, their derivation and application."[2]

After considerable staff review of replies, the Magnuson committee (with Kenneth Cox as counsel) held a one-day hearing on June 26, 1958, at which Arthur C. Nielsen, Sr., James Seiler (ARB), Edward Hynes (Trendex), Sydney Roslow (Pulse), Allan Jay (Videodex), and Albert Sindlinger appeared. The session was largely devoted to descriptions and defenses by each company representative of its particular technique and practices—an educational briefing for the senators.

The Monroney–Magnuson hearing did not satisfy the critics: It tended to sharpen the adversarial positions of government and ratings companies. In December, 1958, a detailed questionnaire was sent to advertising agencies in anticipation of further hearings, but those never materialized. But the quiz show scandal of 1958–1959 focused more attention on the role of the ratings.

Robert W. Lishman, chief counsel for the subcommittee that investigated the rigged quiz shows, reported that every producer who testified said that a rigging was needed "to command a large audience and therefore a high rating."[3] In November 1958, Monroney commented: "Without a doubt the struggle for rating supremacy led to the rigging of the TV quiz programs." He believed that ratings were "inadequate" rather than inaccurate or rigged.

The FCC, which had been carrying out a lengthy investigation of network practices, responded to congressional concerns by enlarging its study to include "the policies, practices, mechanics, and surveillance pursued and carried out by networks, station licensees, and others in connection with programming."[4] During the next five years, the FCC conducted sporadic hearings that dealt primarily with program and sales practices but included scrutiny of the role played by ratings. Philip D. Jursek concluded from his study:

> These hearings clearly divided the opinion on broadcast audience measurement into two camps: (1) the proponents, almost always members of the broadcasting and advertising community, who said that ratings were not only justified, but were needed to provide a viable program service which would be responsive to the dictates of the popular taste; (2) the critics, who argued that ratings were inaccurate, evil, and responsible for the depths to which programming had sunk.[5]

The Federal Trade Commission (FTC) began an investigation of rating service practices in April 1960. Little information about its purpose or scope reached the broadcast industry until the signing of consent decrees by Nielsen, ARB, and Pulse in December 1962. Actually, it was a thorough, detailed look at methodologies, involving extensive field inquiries to check the actions versus the claims of the three major rating companies.

## II. THE HARRIS COMMITTEE 1960—1966

In 1960, Representative Oren D. Harris of Arkansas, chairman of the House Committee on Interstate and Foreign Commerce and of that committee's Special Subcommittee on Investigations, turned his attention to broadcast ratings. Harris had headed subcommittees which had produced widely publicized actions. Sherman Adams was dismissed as chief of staff to President Dwight D. Eisenhower, Columbia University Professor Charles Van Doren was cited for rigging answers to "Twenty-One," a popular quiz show, and a number of record company executives were found to have enriched radio disc jockeys with "payola" for favorable treatment. Many in broadcasting looked forward to another round of screaming headlines in the afternoon newspapers.

Chairman Harris, however, proved to be a careful investigator who did his homework. In March 1960, he wrote to Dr. Morris Hansen, president of the American Statistical Association, asking that Hansen establish a committee "to examine into and evaluate the statistical methods used by the principal rating services in determining the 'rating' ascribed to television and radio programs." Hansen acceded to the request (the work and outcome of the Madow Committee is covered in Appendix D, which synthesizes the report submitted in 1961).

The Harris committee employed two special investigators to augment the normal counsel staff, and many searching interviews about ratings methodologies, practices, and uses were conducted among survey companies, networks, stations, advertising agencies, and the like. Thus, between the Madow report and their own painstaking investigatory activities, the subcommittee and Chairman Harris were well prepared for the public hearings, which opened March 5, 1963. When the hearings ended on September 23, 1964, after 30 days of actual testimony and cross examination, an exhaustive record of 1714 pages had been compiled. Most of the committee's time had been devoted to witnesses from the rating services, with special emphasis on the Nielsen Television Index. Industry witnesses represented networks and advertising agencies.

The subcommittee's 22-page final report dated January 13, 1966,[6] pointed out that the hearings were divided into three phases: (1) "Making a reasonably complete and accurate record of practices and procedures followed in connection with the preparation and uses of broadcast ratings," including examination into "numerous alleged malpractices and abuses . . . " (2) "Several industry groups and the FCC presented programs aimed at coping with several of the problems developed by the subcommittee during phase 1," and (3) "presentation of progress reports on industry programs detailed in phase 2." Additional reports and conferences with industry groups took place to ensure the appropriate implementation of the programs presented to the subcommittee. The report's introduction clearly propounded the views of chairman Harris:

Rightly or wrongly, sponsors react to the audience rating systems. Millions of dollars turn on the rating levels. The immediate and long-range future of all types of programs—news reports, mysteries, comedies, westerns, etc.—are controlled by the ratings which each show receives. If this rating system is to continue we must make certain that the rating received is the rating achieved—no more, and no less.

If public reaction is an appropriate measure, then the public reaction should be free from any tampering or adjustment for private purposes. If public surveys are to be used to determine where, when, and what will be broadcast, we must assure that such surveys are not misused.

The broadcasting industry as a whole shares this responsibility. Fortunately, a number of responsible business interests are aware of this and share the view that the reliability of audience measurement techniques and the proper use of audience measurement results constitute an important aspect of broadcasting in the public interest.

The first half of the report detailed broadcast industry accomplishments in setting up the Broadcast Rating Council to accredit and audit syndicated rating services. Another section covered the research programs mounted by the broadcasting industry to tackle the questions raised and the need for improving methodologies as a result of the Madow report and the committee hearings.[7]

Under the heading of "Law Enforcement," the subcommittee described its conception of the responsibility of the Federal Communications Commission and the Federal Trade Commission relative to ratings and their use: "The two agencies have recognized that they have a joint responsibility in these areas which requires proper coordination. On June 13, 1963, these two agencies issued separate coordinated policy statements regarding their respective responsibilities. . . ." The FCC statement stressed that broadcasters must act responsibly in using ratings, must take reasonable precautions to ensure validity, and must refrain from quoting portions of surveys out of context leaving false and misleading impressions. The FCC stresed that "ordinarily it intends to refer complaints dealing with the questionable use of ratings to the FTC," but any FTC orders on the subject would be taken into account "in determining whether a licensee is operating in the public interest."

The FTC stated that it would take vigorous action against any broadcaster whose claims based on surveys are "false and deceptive." The FTC statement referred to the three orders entered into by the commission in December 1962 against three major rating services—A. C. Nielsen, Pulse, and CEIR, Inc. (parent company of American Research Bureau)—ordering them "to cease and desist from misrepresenting the accuracy and reliability of their measurements, data and reports." These orders are still in effect. According to former FTC Chairman Paul Rand Dixon, the purpose of the orders "is to require the rating services to publish sufficiently detailed explanations of their respective methodologies so as to permit purchasers of audience measurements prepared by these services to assay the value of the measurements."

On July 8, 1965, the FTC issued guidelines to be followed by broadcasters and others in making claims based on survey results in order to avoid possible violations of the Federal Trade Commission Act. The guidelines require that audience claims be "truthful and not deceptive." The practice of "hyping" is defined as "activities calculated to distort or inflate" survey data "by conducting a special contest, or otherwise varying his usual programming or instituting unusual advertising or other promotional efforts, designed to increase audiences only during the survey period." Other admonitions related to (1) unfairly basing claims "on results achieved only during certain periods of the broadcast day or on a survey of only a segment of the total potential audience"; (2) because audience data are statistical estimates and "inherently imperfect," claims should be qualified by "a disclosure that any figures cited or quoted are estimates only and are based on estimates, and are not accurate to any precise mathematical degree unless based upon a true probability sample"; (3) claims should not be based on survey reports that do not reflect current conditions because "the passage of time has made the data outdated, or because a later survey report . . . has been published."[8]

## Harris Committee Recommendations

The 1966 Summary and Recommendations of the Harris committee report makes these points:[9]

1. The federal government must be concerned with the reliability of ratings because shoddy measurements and improper ratings use can impact broadcaster ability "to achieve high quality commercial broadcasting in the public interest."

2. Effective enforcement of laws with regard to unfair and deceptive practices and improper use of ratings is the responsibility of the FCC and FTC, the two agencies that should coordinate their law enforcement efforts to achieve "proper practices with regard to ratings."

3. "The enactment, at this time at least, of legislation providing for government regulation of broadcast audience measurement activities is not advisable." Effective industry regulation is the best answer.

4. Such industry regulation will depend on the broadcast industry assisted to some extent by advertisers and other users of ratings. The rating services may

accept such industry action "as a necessary evil" but they are not likely to undertake a program of self-regulation on their own.

5. Information coordination relative to ratings complaints must be achieved between industry groups such as the Broadcast Rating Council and the FCC and FTC.

6. Industry regulation, to be effective, requires continuing exercise of oversight by appropriate congressional committees.

7. Development of new and improved rating techniques depends on the support primarily of broadcasters and other ratings users, but hopefully also by the rating services themselves.

8. Support by the federal government should be provided for research relative to sampling techniques and statistical measures.

9. "Broadcasters, in order to perform in the public interest, must become more sophisticated with regard to the rating tools which they employ."

10. "Improvements in the broadcast rating picture which have been made in the last 3 years have been due primarily, if not entirely, to the investigations and proceedings conducted by this subcommittee. If these efforts have improved not only ratings but, indirectly at least, have resulted in making broadcasters more responsible in the conduct of their licensed activities, the time and effort spent by the subcommittee have been well worth while."

The Harris hearings produced a number of constructive results. A number of examples of shortcomings, unprofessional practices, shoddy workmanship, and lack of adequate controls were disclosed. The broadcast industry mobilized immediatley to take corrective action.

## III.   THE ELECTRONIC MEDIA RATING COUNCIL
## (FORMERLY BROADCAST RATING COUNCIL)

The Harris committee hearings induced the industry to initiate a joint program of action to remedy obvious deficiencies and to probe further the areas of possible methodological weaknesses that were revealed. While the hearings were still underway in the spring of 1963, the industry program was developed by the Research Committee of the National Association of Broadcasters (NAB) under the chairmanship of Don McGannon, president of Westinghouse Broadcasting Co. On May 23, 1963, the proposal outlined to the committee by Roy Collins, NAB president, and McGannon called for two major efforts: (1) the establishment of a Broadcast Rating Council to organize a system to accredit and audit each rating service to prepare specific standards and to ensure that ratings met these standards, said what they did, and did what they said they were going to do; (2) methodological research to answer questions raised at the hearings and elsewhere and to develop improvements in the techniques of audience measurement.

The methodological research was to operate simultaneously in four areas: network television, local television, network radio, and local radio (a number of these studies are summarized in Appendix D).

The Broadcast Rating Council began operating in 1964. Actually, much preliminary work had been conducted by the NAB Research Committee prior to that, so under its executive director, Dr. Kenneth Baker, the BRC moved rapidly to implement its chartered responsibilities: (1) "to secure for the broadcasting industry and related users audience measurement services that are valid, reliable, effective, and viable; (2) to evolve and determine minimum criteria and standards for broadcast audience measurement services; (3) to establish and administer a system of accreditation for broadcast audience measurement services; (4) to provide and administer an audit system designed to insure users that broadcast audience measurements are conducted in conformance with the criteria, standards and procedures developed."

The original Broadcast Rating Council was broadened in scope in 1982 to represent cable and other electronic media. In June 1982, the council was renamed the Electronic Media Rating Council, but its activities, under Executive Director John A. Dimling, are substantially the same as those of the BRC.

## Accreditation

Rating Council accreditation relies on voluntary compliance and cooperation of the individual rating services. All syndicated broadcast, cable, and other electronic media audience measurement services are invited to apply for Council accreditation. To be accredited, services must agree to:

1. Supply complete information to the Rating Council.
2. Comply substantially with Rating Council minimum standards.
3. Conduct their service as they represent to subscribers and the Rating Council.
4. Submit to audits by the Council.
5. Pay the cost of these audits.

After completion of these steps and approval by the Council's board of directors, the rating service is entitled to use the Rating Council "double check" symbol on all accredited reports. Accreditation may be withdrawn at any time if any of the above criteria are not met.

## Minimum Standards

The Minimum Standards of the Rating Council, which ratings services are expected to meet to merit continued accreditation, involve such items as:

Ethical and operational standards—governing the quality and integrity of the entire activity.

Disclosure standards—specifying the detailed information about a rating service which must be made available to users, as well as the form in which the information should be made available.

To supplement the minimum standards, the Rating Council has worked with other industry groups (e.g., NAB, Television Bureau of Advertising, Radio Advertising Bureau, Station Representatives Association, Cabletelevision Advertising Bureau, and Advertising Research Foundation) to develop Recommended Technical Standards which amplify and interpret the basic minimum standards.

Audit reports are used by the Council to evaluate services' qualifications for continued accreditation, as well as to recommend procedural improvements, but are not publicly released. An illustrative Rating Council Audit Report is available, however, to depict the scope and detail of the audits.

Reports summarizing audit findings are supplied to the Rating Council and reviewed by a board committee. The executive director may then make suggestions or recommendations to the service for corrective action or improvement of procedures. In the event of material departures from the above criteria, the executive director then has the responsibility to recommend to the Council suspension or revocation of a service's accreditation.

## Costs

Audit fees, which are paid by rating services but borne ultimately by subscribers, have totaled nearly $4 million since 1964. In addition to these fees, each rating service provides Council auditors with staff and computer time and on-premise working facilities on a virtually continuous basis. Total annual costs for the Rating Council's current monitoring, including Council administration, approximate $500,000.

Two major CPA firms—Ernst & Whinney and Touche Ross & Co.—presently conduct audits for the Council. The nature and timing of their inspections is determined by the Rating Council and the auditors.

Over the past 10 years, well over 700 individual city ratings surveys have been scrutinized by Rating Council auditors. In a single year, about 6000 man-hours of time of professional auditors, computer system specialists, and statistical experts are expended in the Rating Council's careful step-by-step examination.

## Results

Among significant developments that bear the stamp of the Rating Council's monitoring are the following:

• Field interviewing is more accurate, records are more carefully maintained, and contacts between home office, supervisors, and interviewers are more frequent than in pre-Rating Council days.

• Security procedures in the field and in processing centers have been strengthened. Opportunities for tampering with research results (either by outsiders or insiders) have been virtually eliminated.

• Descriptive material accompanying rating reports has been expanded greatly, providing subscribers with a clearer picture of the methodology and limitations of the service (with additional detail furnished in annual supplements).

• Sample error estimates have been improved in accuracy and made more accessible to users.

Even more important, rating services acknowledge that the greatest value of Rating Council audit activity is its beneficial psychological effect on rating service performance. Knowledge that their work may be independently reviewed by CPA auditors is a powerful spur to quality work by all field and home office personnel.

## Services Accredited

These syndicated rating services carried full accreditation by the Electronic Media Rating Council, as of August 1984:

Arbitron Ratings Company
    Television Market Reports
    Radio Market Reports
    Television Meter Market Reports
A. C. Nielsen Co.
    Nielsen Station Index (NSI)
    Meter Market Service (MM)
    Nielsen Television Index (NTI)
    National Audience Composition (NAC)
Statistical Research, Inc.
    RADAR (Radio's All Dimension Audience Research).

The Electronic Media Rating Council does not accredit research organizations or companies. The Rating Council's accreditation and monitoring activities are limited to the specific syndicated rating services named and do not in any way involve other surveys or special reports that may be produced by these same companies.

## Mediation Procedures

Working with broadcast trade associations and rating services, the Rating Council conducts a cooperative plan to mediate complaints that arise between a station and a rating service that may not have been resolved through normal relations between the station and service.

Under this procedure, when efforts to resolve a complaint through normal channels have not been successful, the parties to the complaint may participate in an informal, nonbinding mediation process. A mediation panel of industry professionals is appointed, based on nominations from the appropriate industry trade associations and input from the rating service. This panel then considers the complaint in an informal, off-the-record, nonadversary proceeding, after which the panel makes a recommendation to the parties involved in the complaint. EMRC membership, as of October, 1984, comprised:

National Association of Broadcasters
American Broadcasting Company
Cabletelevision Advertising Bureau
Capital Cities Communications, Inc.
CBS Broadcast Group
Cox Communications, Inc.
McGavren Guild Radio, Inc.
Metromedia, Inc.
National Broadcasting Company
National Radio Broadcasters Association
Radio Advertising Bureau
RKO Radio Networks, Inc.
Standard Communications, Inc.
Station Representatives Association
Storer Communications, Inc.
Television Bureau of Advertising
Westinghouse Broadcasting and Cable, Inc.

These organizations are represented on the EMRC's board of directors (with the NAB supplying four members). In addition, two liaison observers, each from the American Association of Advertising Agencies and the Association of National Advertisers, attend board meetings. Advertiser and agency representatives also participate in many of the Rating Council's various working committees.

## IV.   WHO SHOULD CONDUCT RATINGS SERVICES?

The early experience with ratings services in the United States (in which the nonprofit Cooperative Analysis of Broadcasting gave way to Hooperatings, a strictly entrepreneurial private enterprise), did not entirely dispose of efforts to try other approaches. Elsewhere in the world, broadcast audience measurement was for the most part not in private hands, and from time to time explorational efforts with the objective of developing an industry-controlled service have been initiated in this country. To address this question systematically, let's examine the major four alternatives: (1) private, completely independent firms, which has been the U.S. way, (2) conduct of the service by a private firm under contract to an industry bureau or board, (3) establishment of a nonprofit cooperative organization participated in by broadcasters, advertisers, and agencies on any one of a variety of bases, and (4) government agency measurement.

## Private Independent Competitive Firms

Here, the ratings company advances its particular technique for industry approval, markets it to potential users, puts up the necessary capital, takes the risks involved, and hopes for a free-enterprise profit commensurate with those risks. User input is important if the service is to succeed, but final decisions are in the hands of the survey organization.

There are many advantages here that have stood the test of time. First is the independence of the research firms—they can be objective and the ratings will be more credible and more valuable because they are. Of course, since broadcaster/subscribers pay about 85 percent of the total bill, it can be said that they swing more weight. Nevertheless, the advertising buyers, by their use of particular services, have a very powerful voice. A second advantage is the ability to make quick decisions. In a dynamic field such as broadcasting, that is important. A third plus is the presence (actual or potential) of commercial competition, which tends to induce the private company to improve its market position. Opposing this position is the belief that today the amount of capital needed to bring a new service to success is too large and the risk too great. Nevertheless, we see in 1984 new challengers to the Nielsen NTI and the Arbitron Local Market Radio Services. Commercial services can fold—and have done so—if they lack capital or marketing sophistication or don't satisfy industry needs: witness Hooperatings, Sindlinger, Pulse, RAM, Burke, and TRAC 7.

The emergence of the Electronic Media Rating Council to audit the work of rating services by using CPA firms has done much to quiet the qualms that existed about private ratings companies before the congressional hearings.

## Private Firms Under Contract to Industry Group

In many countries of Europe, in Australia, and elsewhere in the world, ratings services have been set up by an industry board or bureau, with cooperation from broadcasters and advertiser interests. The usual pattern is for the group to adopt a particular methodology (either after some pilot tests or based on competitive submissions from research firms), establish standards and specifications, and ask private survey concerns to enter bids for a multiyear contract. Participants in the group represent virtually all possible users, and since there is not likely to be any effective competitor, the group contract ensures the survey firm that they will have practically 100 percent of the participants as subscribers. Thus the ratings company takes little risk (other than setting up an organization) and doesn't have to worry about competition until the next bidding round some years hence.

Renewal is by no means automatic because invitations for competitive proposals go to many potential applicants. In the last British experience involving a five-year contract, the Broadcasters Audience Research Board sent invitations to bid to about 140 companies, some 40 of which requested detailed specifications. There were 4 companies in serious contention at decision time, a process that consumed close to a year's time on the part of participants.

One major advantage in this system is that the survey organization, freed from the costs of marketing its service, can concentrate on service and on technological improvement that may help it get a contract renewal. Cost to subscribers could be less because of the lack of significant marketing costs and because the monopoly pattern means that every prospect must become a subscriber and help share the expense.

Disadvantages would be that, without competition, incentive for improvement is relaxed, and we would probably find the controlling board slow in reaching major decisions because of the diverse economic interests of participants. The only recent attempt in this country failed utterly because the original sponsoring group, the Radio Advertising Bureau, did not truly represent the industry and because they were attempting to mount a service, TRAC-7, in competition with an entrenched commercial service, Arbitron Radio (see Chapter 2).

## Establishing a Nonprofit Cooperative Organization of Major Users

A possible model for this is the Audit Bureau of Circulation, a nonprofit, tripartite, self-regulatory, voluntary organization established in 1914 and supported by the entire print media and advertising industry. It employs its own specially trained auditors and an administrative staff totaling 175 people for planning and controlling audits and printing and distributing reports of newspaper and magazine audited circulation figures. The ABC board is composed of elected representatives of all membership elements—national and regional advertisers (11), agencies (7), daily and weekly newspapers (8), and three categories of magazines (6). The ABC dues structure reflects a common pattern for such organizations. Advertisers pay a modest annual fee (under $100); agencies pay up to $1000, and publications are billed at higher rates for membership plus the cost of the circulation audits. ABC has been very successful because of its long institutional history and because the audit function (like that of EMRC) tends to be essentially noncontroversial. Policy changes come slowly and require long discussion before revisions are made.

In broadcasting, the Canadian Bureau of Broadcast Measurement (BBM) has, among its members, a large proportion of the leading broadcasters, agencies, and advertisers of Canada. The bureau has its own research staff and conducts television and radio diary ratings surveys on a regular schedule throughout Canada. Its only competition is a Nielsen television diary service covering a limited number of Canadian markets.

A major problem with such organizational setups is how the power and the costs will be distributed between opposing broadcaster and customer interests. The experience of the U.S. Cooperative Analysis of Broadcasting is instructive. It was originally run and paid for exclusively by advertisers; as soon as agencies were admitted as subscribers, most advertisers dropped out because they could get their figures from their subscribing agency. Later, when networks were admitted, at a large and rapidly accelerated fee, they soon found themselves footing the major share of cost. That gave them economic control, so that when the survival of CAB was at stake they swung the ax, even though a majority of advertiser and agency members wanted to continue. Without the network income, the CAB was dead.

A different experience was that of the Broadcast Measurement Bureau (BMB), established by broadcasters in 1945 to conduct radio station coverage surveys on a nationwide basis, using a mail ballot form. A private research firm that had done much of the test work was engaged to do a study that was well supported by broadcaster subscriptions. Based on the seeming success of this survey, a second one was launched in 1948, only to strike out because many stations didn't like the results of the first study or liked them so much they didn't want a new survey to rock the boat. As a result, the BMB failed and NAB had to put up $100,000 to see survey reports finished for subscribers.

These experiences explain why it is difficult to achieve a successful cooperative effort in this country with its heterogeneous and independent business operators whose instincts are to put their economic interests first. Long-range commitments to a newly established cooperative organization would come only under extremely urgent conditions. In 1978, the Television Bureau of Advertising had a major survey conducted among advertisers, agencies, and stations by Booz Allen & Hamilton to determine if there would be support for an industry-sponsored local market TV survey. The result was a resounding "No."

## Government Operation or Control

Government operation of survey services to measure audiences of government-run monopoly broadcasting is not unknown. Most famous, perhaps, was the British Broadcasting Corporation's[10] daily personal interview recall survey of a sample of 2500 people in the United Kingdom, which operated for many years until it was abandoned when the BBC joined commercial broadcasters in supporting the Broadcasters Audience Research Board in 1981 (see Chapter 3).

The only serious proposal in the United States for government control of ratings came in December 1959 from two academicians appearing before the

Federal Communications Commission. Professor Ithiel de Sola Pool of the Massachusetts Institute of Technology argued that the government should finance and oversee all ratings, surveys, and research in radio and TV. "Research should become a major function of the FCC," said Pool, and proposed possibly farming out the conduct of ratings to foundations with budgets "in the millions." His view was supported by Percy Tannenbaum, University of Virginia professor of economics, who asserted that ratings should not be in the hands of private individuals because the profit motive can affect results.[11]

These proposals were a product of the period of rating confusion that preceded the FTC investigations resulting in the consent decrees of December 1962, the release of the Madow report of the American Statistical Association, and the outcome of the Harris committee hearings in 1963. No one took them to be anything but academic "brainstorming"—certainly the FCC made no moves in that direction, and no proposal was forthcoming as to how commercial services could be silenced or bypassed; how broadcasters, agencies, and advertisers could be required to use the government figures; and what the subscription fees would be, if any.

In this country, the major role of government in the ratings field has already been played effectively. The Federal Trade Commission restraint orders of December 1962 are still in effect for the two major competitors. By requiring certain disclosures and limiting service claims, they introduced a well-needed discipline in the quantitative syndicated ratings field. EMRC standards and audits have, through voluntary support by accredited services, established a healthy industry mechanism of continuous oversight of private rating operations. This organization and the methodological studies of the 1960s and 1970s were outcomes of the Harris committee hearings and the American Statistical Association Madow Committee report, both of which called for more basic testing of ratings methods.

During the 1970s, the FCC periodically expressed interest in or concern about ratings and their use. Hyping was frowned on, and stations whose personnel were involved in unethical practices were sometimes called to account. About 1980, however, the FCC backed away from this type of inquiry and in effect turned the entire scrutiny of ratings practices over to the FTC. In recent years, with the prevailing climate of deregulation, this has not been an active area of federal government involvement.

A new form of government intervention, however, appeared in January 1984 when California state senator Art Torres of Los Angeles introduced a bill aimed at banning use of TVQ survey results in casting decisions (see Chapter 5). The bill would force TVQ to correct its sampling to properly represent all population elements (especially Hispanics and blacks) and to present on its roster of performers to be rated a larger and more representative (ethnically) list. The bill had support from the Screen Actors Guild and the NAACP, while it was vigorously opposed by television networks, motion picture producers, and the Council of American Survey Research Organizations (CASRO).

The original draft of the proposed legislation was so broad that it encompassed all ratings and other research companies.[12] After hearings were conducted, a modified bill passed the Senate, but it was defeated in Assembly committee in July 1984. This legislative act would have made it unlawful (1) to use a survey in preemployment screening of entertainers "unless the surveys provide a bona fide sample of the employee pool and audience characteristics." Entertainers would have the right to "be included in any survey used for preemployment screening or hiring upon his or her written request."[13]

As a result, TVQ accelerated action to revise its sample to reflect more accurately the ethnic segments of our population.[14] Note that this is the first instance of threatened governmental intervention with respect to a syndicated qualitative measurement. If such services gain wider use and influence in program decisions, it is not unlikely that governmental agencies or industry groups such as EMRC will become involved in the area in the future.

It seems clear enough that no one—government, industry, producers, artists, or the public—really sees any merit in government involvement in the syndicated ratings field. The potential for intervention seems enough to assure continued and effective industry discipline.

## NOTES

1. Lawrence Meyers, Jr., *An examination of television audience measurement methods and an application of sequential analysis to the telephone interview method,* doctoral dissertation, Syracuse University, New York, June 1956, p. 44.
2. Philip D. Jursek, *An analysis of broadcast audience measurement: Recent government investigation and methodology research, with an assessment of the current state of the art,* doctoral dissertation, Graduate Division, Wayne State University, Detroit, 1970, p. 34.
3. Harold Mehling, *The Great Time-Killer* (Cleveland: World Publishing Co., 1962), p. 240.
4. Federal Communications Commission, Order No. 59-1136, November 1959.
5. Jursek, p. 47.
6. *Broadcast Ratings,* Report of the Committee on Interstate and Foreign Commerce, Special Subcommittee on Investigations, U.S. Government Printing Office, Washington, D.C., 1966.
7. This includes the work of the Committee on National Television Audience Measurement (CONTAM) in its first three studies, and the NAB-ARB All-Radio Methodology Study (ARMS), both described in Appendix D.
8. Jursek, p. 12.
9. Ibid., p. 31.

10. Strictly speaking, the BBC is a separate quasi-governmental organization, but for many years it operated as a monopoly in radio and television. Its interviewers introduced themselves as being "from the BBC."
11. *Broadcasting,* December 14, 1959, p. 16.
12. "Actors Fighting TVQ Influence," *Television Digest,* April 16, 1984.
13. "California Senate Sends TVQ Bill on to Assembly," *Daily Variety,* June 15, 1984.
14. Steven Leavitt, president of marketing evalutions (which conducts TVQ service), in a telephone interview with the author, July 20, 1984.

# 10 What We Have Learned: 1930–1987

Over 50 years of ratings history provide some significant insights into this constantly changing, ever-growing measurement field. As the ratings sphere faces its third major challenge with the emergence of the new video media—cable originations, home video cassette recorders, teletext—some of the lessons of the past merit attention.

The first 20 years produced three significant findings, which have been confirmed in this country during the past three decades:

1. Broadcast ratings should be furnished by private, independent entrepreneurs, not by industry-controlled groups or cooperatives.

2. Ratings, to be of maximum service to users, must be projectable, that is convertible from percentages to numbers of households or persons on a realistic (if not totally defensible) statistical base.

3. Inevitably the media pay the major part of the tab for ratings (80 to 90 percent), but advertising agencies, which must accept the figures for media planning, buying, and evaluation, play a crucial role in determining which services will be successful.

## I. WHY PRIVATE INDEPENDENT SERVICES ARE NEEDED

The Cooperative Analysis of Broadcasting (after the Association of National Advertisers took over from Crossley in 1933) was a powerful establishment group, with no competition, when C. E. Hooper began competing in 1934. A. W. Lehman, formerly a key staffer for the ANA, was executive director of the CAB. Its board of governors, for many years headed by D. P. Smelser of Procter

258

& Gamble, also contained such research pioneers as George Gallup of Young & Rubicam and L. D. H. Weld of McCann Erickson. But Hooper's technique was superior, recognized as such by networks and agencies, and the CAB faded. Meanwhile, Nielsen appeared with his panel meter service, which promised an impressive array of new data on a projectable base (when the whole country was sampled).

Thus the CAB had two prime competitors, Hooper on one side and Nielsen on the other. When the trade press and industry spoke of "The Battle of the Ratings" then, they referred to the CAB–Hooper–Nielsen conflict (not, as today, to the three-way network fray; NBC then was clearly dominant on everyone's rating charts). Had Crossley been able to make his own decisions, he would first have given the networks subscriber status and some voice in the direction of the service, and then could have been expected to push for national projectable figures and local reports. At any rate, he would undoubtedly have made a closer race of it. The CAB finally adopted Hooper's technique—the telephone coincidental—and did it none too well. The radio networks supported the CAB by progressively higher subscription assessments each year, even while subscribing to and using to an even greater degree the less expensive and more accurate Hooperatings. The networks were reluctant to offend ANA members, who controlled the organization, by not "going along." But in the end, the networks, by threatening to withdraw their major financial contributions, prevailed in killing the Cooperative Analysis of Broadcasting.

We now have competitive services in local TV (Arbitron and Nielsen), local radio (Arbitron and Birch), and network television (Nielsen and AGB). The benefits of competitive services have been seen in more attention to technology, better service, and restraint on prices.

Over the years, there have been many attempts by broadcaster organizations to respond to their station members' unhappiness with commercial ratings services by developing an industry-financed and -governed service. The NAB, the RAB, and the TVB have all tried. When rating services elsewhere in the world use group organizations to do this job, why does the United States not follow suit? There are four major reasons:

1. *Legal.* Antitrust considerations, not often mentioned, are a real factor in the United States, with its strict laws on the subject. When the CAB was organized, it was a pioneering service: No one else was in or contemplating going into the field. Therefore, collaboration by advertisers was not questioned; no private enterprise was threatened. Today, commercial services are operating in every broadcast field, so an industry-financed and -sponsored service would be open to restraint of trade challenges from ongoing services and from prospective new entrants.

2. *Financial.* Starting a radio or television rating service today involves far more resources than was the case with Hooper, Seiler, and Roslow. (A possible exception could be measurement in the new fields of cable originations and VCR's.) The recent experience in radio of Audits & Surveys (TRAC 7), Burke,

and RAM clearly point to multimillion dollar capital requirements to sustain losses until a viable level of agency acceptance and medium support is achieved in a competitive environment. (Chapter 2 shows that Birch, by building on Mediastat, may prove an exception). Few buyers or sellers are willing to encourage new services with subscriptions while they are neither very useful nor widely accepted; it's difficult to hold an industry combine together for such financing. In the CAB experience, the bulk of the initial advertiser members dropped out when they could get the numbers from their agency. When the networks were accepted as members, they were soon assessed a major share of the costs. But ultimately their financial control proved decisive with the demise of the CAB, even though a majority of subscribers favored its continuance.

Industry experience with Broadcast Measurement Bureau, the NAB-sponsored coverage service which operated from 1945 to 1948, is also instructive. After years of development the second BMB survey was a financial failure and had to be bailed out by $100,000 from the NAB treasury.

3. *Managerial.* "I would have been more surprised if a committee had done it," was the response of William Kettering, research vice president of General Motors, when his wife exulted over Charles Lindbergh's achievement in flying solo across the Atlantic in 1927. Just as the CAB board found it difficult to cope with Hooper's competitive thrusts, so have other industry nonprofit research groups found themselves unable to produce crucial decisions. When many diverse interests, points of view, and professional egos and reputations are at stake, decisive action is a scarce commodity. Competent corporate managerial executives, backed by bright staff people, in close touch with their clients and their needs, have a major advantage over the group effort in meeting the challenges of a rapidly changing field.

4. *Acceptability.* The CAB was an advertiser cooperative, and the original survey reports were limited to advertisers (and, two years later, agencies). No competitive service existed, so there was no problem of acceptance by these radio buyers and users. Compare that situation with one where the new service is sponsored and financed by the medium in competition with an independent service. Ad agency media and research people, and other advertising executives as well, will cast a suspicious eye on audience measurement from such a source, especially if it produces larger audience figures than existing surveys.

An example of an unacceptable broadcaster effort to control ratings measurement occurred in the early 1950s when television was in its infancy. Many pioneer TV stations were owned by major newspapers, which had also been early leaders in radio broadcasting. These publishers were never happy with the average-minute type of ratings produced by Hooper and Nielsen especially when they compared the results with the more generalized ABC circulation figures that newspapers use for selling. A major group of papers, determined to see that television was not committed to "overmeasurement" by radio-type ratings, launched a pilot project to develop a circulation measurement system for TV under NAB coordination. The Alfred Politz organization conducted a study using a meter for validation of a telephone recall circulation (cumulative) measure. The results were unclear and not promising; meanwhile, agencies and advertisers had clearly demonstrated their interest in average quarter-hour ratings as a far sharper tool for buying and evaluating the video medium while yielding comparability with radio. Why have a different measure? It was tough enough to compare broadcast and print as it was.

A Nielsen or an Arbitron, with whatever methodological limitations a given service may have, is at least an impartial umpire and accepted by buyers as such.

RADAR, the radio network service produced by Statistical Research, Inc. is an exception. Started by four radio networks after both Nielsen and Sindlinger abandoned the network ratings field, it addressed a wide-open need and faced no challengers. A cooperative effort of four parties managed to put out a high-quality, highly accepted radio service by careful development, top-flight implementation and patient educational effort with buyers.

## II.  NEED FOR PROJECTABLE RATINGS

Rating and share index figures fall far short of satisfying the basic needs of buyers and sellers of broadcast advertising. Cost per thousand (CPM), reach (total cumulative audience), and frequency (number of commercials delivered per schedule or time period) are intrinsic elements of every broadcast advertising deal. Whether the unit is households, children ages 6 to 11, men ages 18 to 49, or working women, the numbers have to be in total population terms (projected from percentages). This means that basic rating services (network or local) must produce reasonably valid projectable numbers, not just ratings. Unprojectable ratings can be of limited use to station management for tracking trends and evaluating programming and format changes. However, they do not substitute for projectable numbers in buying and selling.

## III.  THE MEDIA WILL PAY THE BILLS

Rating service costs today are paid for largely by the media, and this is unlikely to change. The agency payment is primarily to ensure that it receives all reports on time and has access to computerized data and special analysis features. An agency not subscribing could gain limited access to the reports through a station or network subscriber, but without computer access it would be hampered in analytical aspects, postbuy evaluation, etc. It is in the interest of the subscribing station salespeople that the agency customer be a subscriber—then their sales proposals are readily accepted. Therefore, most TV stations subscribe to both

Arbitron and Nielsen so they can be prepared to use whatever service the agency uses. Agency subscriptions generally split about 50-50 between the two services. No amount of broadcaster fulmination on the subject of cost sharing is likely to alter this situation. Agencies and advertisers consider ratings part of the medium's expense of doing business.

## IV.    THE TELEVISION ERA: 1950–1984

Whereas the ratings drama of the first two decades revolved around the out-in-the-open struggle for survival and leadership among three individuals, each advocating a particular technique, the next 33 years revealed many changes. Which of the existing services would survive the emergence of television and which would come out on top in TV? Would new names and firms such as Seiler's ARB, Roslow's Pulse, and Hynes and Rogers' Trendex carry the day, or could Nielsen and Hooper's company advance to new high ground in the ratings world? But now it was a more complex situation. Radio was still strong for nearly a decade (TV revenues first passed radio's in 1954 and doubled the older medium's take in 1958). Local measurement for both radio and TV became a more important prize as national spot grew rapidly, just as Hooper had predicted.

Many of the more fascinating scenes in the drama were played out not on the public stage but in directors' meetings and executive suites of the services. As they strove to cope with the dual media problem, ARB, Hooper, and Pulse all had one or more management changes, with ownership turnovers as well. Techniques were no longer related to a particular service: Nielsen began using diaries, Arbitron launched several different local meter services, and C. E. Hooper Inc. used diaries in early TV days just as Nielsen used Hooper coincidentals for share figures for about nine months in 1950.

Out of the interplay of these services and the media and audience trends in which they were involved came a number of critical new elements that contributed to ratings improvement and success:

1. "People" ratings became significant in addition to or in lieu of household figures; there was greatly increased emphasis on "demographics."

2. One-week and four-week cumulative rating data were used to produce reach and frequency measurements.

3. Adding nonlisted households improved the quality of telephone samples.

4. Special procedures were developed to enhance response and representativeness of ethnic audiences.

5. Weeks of measurement by nonmeter services were added to avoid bias of atypical rating periods and potential for hyping and to provide users with more frequent, fresh data.

6. Computers were extensively used for data processing, calculation, printing reports, and supplying special analyses; report delivery was speeded up.

7. Successful and viable "instantaneous" meter measurement services were developed—close to the ultimate in delivery speed.

8. Unduplicated markets known as ADIs (Arbitron) and DMAs (Nielsen) were developed and used for all media and much market planning and budgeting.

9. Rating service operations were opened up to permit inspection and study of diaries by station subscribers and their representatives.

10. There was a growing understanding that "all ratings are estimates" and subject to both sampling and nonsampling errors. Rating services provided improved standard error estimates and more easily understood and usable disclosures to users.

11. Congressional hearings stimulated the inauguration of industry methodological research groups and the Broadcast Rating Council (now the Electronic Media Rating Council) to accredit and monitor services.

12. Syndicated qualitative ratings have made some progress in areas such as program and talent appraisal, product use, and geodemographic segmentation.

13. Cable television has introduced new and vexing problems in measuring viewing behavior.

14. Remote-control and VCR playback usage have created advertiser concern about lowered commercial exposure.

The following discussion amplifies the significance of these developments:

*People-based Ratings.* An important new element in post-TV radio measurement was the move to the people base in contrast to the conventional household base. Early experiments (1945–1948) with individual measurement were not followed up, but the in-home competition of television and the increasing out-of-home opportunities presented by automobile radios and portable AM-FM sets made a people basis essential for radio. Thus Sindlinger in 1962 and RADAR and Arbitron in 1967 made the individual the unit of radio audience measurement. Hooper and Pulse, still basically sampling households, suffered as a result. The demand for more refined demographic details has created an explosion in the number of columns of data appearing in all ratings books for both television and radio.

While radio went in the direction of people, television embraced the meter household measurement more firmly than ever (supplemented later by diaries to provide demographic data). After an earlier abortive effort, Arbitron entered the local meter field in competition with Nielsen in New York and Los Angeles in 1976. By 1985, 11 major markets would be served by local meter services installed by both companies. At present there is strong interest in a people meter technique for measuring television to meet the broadened demand for more accurate TV demographics compatible with household meter findings. The entry of Britain's AGB into the U.S. ratings scene has stimulated accelerated activity by Nielsen and Arbitron to develop and test people meters. Early research tests indicate that the meter may be the most accurate tool for measuring cable network and local audiences at the household level.

*Cumulative Data.* The arrival of the successful Nielsen Radio Index in the late 1940s provided the rating analysts with their first potential for using cumulative (unduplicated) data. Weekly cumulatives for five-day-a-week programs became possible, as did advertiser cumulatives for multiple-show sponsors. Nielsen (using a unified sample[1]) could provide cumulative four-week reach figures. The ARB TV diaries provided the basis for many of the same weekly cumulative measures. At first these measurements were developed only by special (and somewhat slow and costly) tabulations. As demand increased, however, all services began providing these "cumes" (cumulative figures) along with increased demographics, in published reports. The cumes became especially significant in radio as proliferating station competition and declining average quarter-hour ratings changed the whole nature of the medium. Most listeners now dialed station formats rather than programs, and saturation campaigns directed to specific target audiences became the rule. Whereas radio ratings services of the 1930s and 1940s provided average-minute or average quarter-hour ratings, the addition of cumulative ratings contributed two new dimensions: reach and frequency (the second a by-product of average quarter-hour and cumulative ratings). As we saw in Chapter 8, these dimensions subsequently became the talismans of the media.

*Adding Nonlisted Telephone Households to Samples.* Over the early years, telephone directories had been the traditional sample frame for television and radio diary studies, as well as for the coincidental services. In the mid-1960s concern grew over evidence of a mounting number of nonlisted telephones (voluntarily unlisted subscribers plus outdatedness of current directories). This segment of telephone households was rising to what became in some large cities more than 40 percent of total metropolitan area subscribers. Random-digit dialing (RDD), using computer-generated numbers (Chapter 4), was a procedure used to bring the nonlisted households into the sample. Studies showed that unlisted households tended to use television and radio somewhat more than their listed counterparts. Although the overall differences were not of serious concern, there were indications that program and station differences could be more significant.

In 1972 the RADAR study, the first conducted by Statistical Research, Inc., used RDD. RDD was also used by SRI in several industry methodological surveys. The NSI TV diary service introduced the Nielsen version of RDD, known as Total Telephone Frame (TTF), in 14 markets in the fall of 1976 and rapidly expanded this feature so that by October 1980 it was in use in all U.S. counties. Arbitron's inauguration of what it calls the Expanded Sample Frame (ESF) also began in 1976. Arbitron uses this sampling procedure in all ADI areas for TV and in radio metropolitan areas.

Unquestionably, random-digit dialing samples are technically superior in representativeness to listed-only samples.

*Ethnic Audience Measurement.* Corollary to the efforts to bring nonlisted telephone households into rating samples (a move in part prompted by concern for better sampling of blacks and Hispanics, who are underrepresented in directories) were specific moves to increase return rates from urban ethnic homes. Cooperation from such homes was generally poor because of literacy and language problems and the tendency for those population elements to be suspicious of surveys in general. (As previously mentioned, a principal reason for the change of name from American Research Bureau to Arbitron was to avoid any suggestion of government bureaucracy.)

Arbitron instituted Spanish-language diaries in 1965 and two years later made a major move by introducing telephone retrieval (of listening and viewing data) in high-density Hispanic areas.[2] These measures, albeit subject to some methodological questions, succeeded in raising black and Hispanic response to levels equal to or above Arbitron norms for nonethnic sample households. Arbitron now uses its Differential Survey Treatment (DST) for ethnic concentrations.

Nielsen first moved, in 1967, to separate socioeconomic sampling units for hard-core poverty (and normally ethnic) concentrations. Shortly thereafter, Spanish-language diaries and interviewers were introduced. In 1978, Nielsen abandoned the socioeconomic control areas and instituted increased incentives and midweek call-backs and succeeded in bringing ethnic response up to nonethnic levels.

The moves to ensure adequate ethnic sample representation have been reasonably successful. The result is that, especially in radio, where Spanish-language and so-called black format stations are widespread, these stations rank high in many markets.

*Added Weeks of Measurement; Development of Four-week Sweeps.* Although meters provided continuous measurement, no other service did so until Sindlinger's network radio service in 1962. ARB's original local TV service measured one week per month, as had Hooper's successful coincidental radio services. When Nielsen started the NSI local service in 1955 for both radio and television in 32 markets, surveys were 8 weeks long. This was to provide a more average picture, particularly in a period when advertisers often employed TV program sponsorship on an alternate-week basis. By 1957, 4-week reports were also issued to speed delivery. In 1959 ARB initiated the sweep principle, in which all surveyed markets were covered during a simultaneous 4-week period. Nielsen adopted this practice in 1961. While major markets are surveyed more frequently, the two, three, or four annual sweeps furnish the bulk of the computerized data used for agency planning, buying, and evaluation.

Arbitron Radio moved to a 12-week spread of sample as a substitute for 4-week surveys in all markets, beginning in January 1982. All proposed new radio services in recent years have promised continuous daily interviewing. Efforts by some agency and broadcaster interests to extend television sweeps from 4 weeks to 13 have met with substantial station resistance because of concern over increased cost and loss of weekly data resulting from sample inadequacy.

*Expansion of Computerization.* In a business beset with serious "number crunching" problems, as data demands intensified, the ratings industry welcomed the growing magnitude of computer power. Arthur Nielsen first recognized computer potential at the close of World War II. In 1949, he contracted with the inventors of the first commercial computer, UNIVAC, for delivery of computer number one. This was never received because of UNIVAC corporate problems, but Nielsen installed an IBM in 1954. Arbitron's first computer was introduced in 1959. From then on, they and other ratings firms moved up from one computer generation to the next, and today all are extremely well equipped to handle regular production and special requests on very fast schedules. Consequently, delivery schedules for diary services improved steadily while accuracy gained as well.

More impressive is the degree to which users now receive all report data on tape and can access rating service computers for special analysis data. The utility of ratings data has therefore increased manyfold in the past two decades as computers created improved speed and flexibility. Now that many users (agencies, station reps, networks, groups) have their own computers, direct computer-to-computer access is frequently possible.

*Successful Instantaneous Services.* The coincidental telephone survey had provided overnight ratings on special order since the Hooper radio days. Trendex picked this up for television in 1950, and for over 20 years special overnights were used regularly by networks during the early fall season for new programs, or for schedule changes or special events. During political conventions these ratings were obtained on a quarter-hour basis within an hour of the time period rated. These coincidentals also provided audience composition and who-selected-the-program data not available from meters.

In 1946, Arthur Nielsen demonstrated to network and advertising executives a small-scale model of an instantaneous on-line radio Audimeter system. Twenty-four homes in the New York area were hooked up to Nielsen's office by telephone line, and a panel of lights recorded which sets were on and what station was tuned in. This was more a stunt than a proposed new service, but it demonstrated the vision of its creator and established a goal for the future.

In July 1948, Sindlinger began installation of his RADOX instantaneous measurement system in Philadelphia. The RADOX sample grew to 642 households but was never commercially successful, and it was discontinued in 1950. The next instantaneous meter was introduced in New York by the American Research Bureau in 1957. Known as Arbitron (a name later to become the company name of ARB), this meter service folded in 1971. In 1959, meanwhile, Nielsen started a New York instantaneous service, which expanded to additional top markets in 1970. Full conversion of NTI to overnight (48 hour) ratings delivery via client terminal took place in 1973. In 1976, Arbitron reentered the meter field with local services in New York and Los Angeles and then expanded to other major markets in 1982–1983. Thus Arbitron pulled ahead of Nielsen in this area, 11 to 9 by the close of 1984 (but with Nielsen due to draw even by mid 1985).

With computer printouts available in 24 hours on a year-round daily basis for individual markets and 48 hours for national television ratings, new highs in delivery speed have been achieved. No longer is there a need for networks to order overnight coincidentals because the Nielsen report is six weeks down the road. In 1974, NTI made home-by-home sample data available on magnetic tape for client purchase.

*Development of ADIs and DMAs.* The need for unduplicated station market areas was recognized by NBC in the 1950s when it released television market estimates on such a basis. The concept was lost sight of for a period, but the American Research Bureau saw the need for such a system when TV markets across the country began to jostle each other. Thus, in 1956, ARB's Area of Dominant Influence (ADI) was born. NSI, which had instituted exclusive NSI areas in 1955, now matched its competitor with a Nielsen counterpart, Designated Market Area (DMA). In each case, counties were assigned to markets based on fixed standards of viewing performance.

ADIs and DMAs were additive (with no duplication problems) and could easily be computed for lineups of network or spot stations used by advertisers, as could audience projections from these market units. Very quickly, ADIs and DMAs (which were often identical and seldom varied by more than one or two small outlying counties) became basic market and media units of measurement for sales quotas, advertising appropriations, and other marketing distributions. The FCC adopted ADI market ranking as a basis for certain regulatory guidelines. Radio and newspaper audience data are published on this geographic unit. Television's prime marketing role for national advertisers was confirmed by industry acceptance and use of ADIs and DMAs.

*Opening Diaries for Inspection.* The most significant local market rating services are Arbitron and Nielsen Station Index (NSI) for television and Arbitron for radio. Their subscribers are hundreds of local TV and radio stations across America. Most station managers (and their program and sales managers) are untrained in statistics or research. They are uniformly wary of the ratings services, which have such a towering impact on the fortunes of their stations and their careers. For years these broadcasters did not understand why their station lost ground to a competitor or what might be done about it. One move toward such understanding was the bold decision by American Research Bureau to let subscribers come to its operations center and inspect (and make informal tabulations of) diaries from the station's market survey. ARB inaugurated this system in 1964; by 1981 it had grown to a point where viewing offices were set up at

Laurel, Maryland, where 45 stations a week could be scheduled to review diaries. Nielsen also instituted a similar system. Such disclosures have engendered greater understanding of the data collection aspect of rating services, as well as providing stations a detailed look at viewing and listening patterns. Station management often call on professional audience analysts to aid them in these inspections.

*All Ratings Are Estimates; Improved Standard Error Estimates.* The entire question of reliability of audience estimates has become better understood, but much education on the subject is still needed. Under the aegis of the Broadcast Rating Council and its successor, the Electronic Media Rating Council, all rating services have performed major studies to calculate more accurately the standard of all estimates they produce. Along with this has come improved presentation of standard error data in ratings reports, so that users can more readily judge the reliability of figures presented.

Unfortunately, few users of audience ratings and estimates are alert to or appreciate the value of the error figures in selecting numbers for decision purposes. Nevertheless, the services have done their job, and users who ignore the implied warnings involved do so at their own risk. There is no magic sample size that will insure error-free audience estimates, nor do any two figures in a rating report have the same relative error. The chances vary from one comparison to another. We are still a long way from the day when the rating report subscriber will use it with a full comprehension of its many limitations and the fact that "all ratings are estimates."

*Government and Industry Concern; Electronic Media Rating Council.* Government concern with ratings surfaced with a brief set of hearings before the Committee on Interstate and Foreign Commerce of the U.S. Senate in June 1958. But that was only a preview to a more extensive investigation by a Special Subcommittee of Investigations of the House of Representatives Committee on Interstate and Foreign Commerce, 1960–1966. This probe included a report by the American Statistical Association, intensive investigatory work by subcommittee staff members, and appearances by the top officials of all operating radio and television services.

The findings of the Harris committee (Representative Oren Harris of Arkansas was chairman) were not shocking, but they revealed certain sloppiness and unprofessional practices. Two marginal services consequently went out of business, and a number of revisions in policy were made by all (Nielsen, for example, added the Mountain Time Zone to its NTI sample and agreed to a mandatory five-year sample turnover).

A major result of the hearings was the formation of the Broadcast Rating Council (BRC) as an industry self-regulating body to accredit and audit independent rating services. Paralleling the BRC, the NAB agreed to establish independent industry committees to explore methodological problems and help advance the science of audience measurement (these became CONTAM[3] and COLTRAM). These committees conducted a series of methodological studies to assess the accuracy of the major rating tools in use today: the diary and the meter.

A number of other industry- and rating service-sponsored committees have been organized in the past decade. They have all had two general purposes: To strengthen communication and understanding between rating services and customers, and to improve the quality and utility of audience estimates.

*Syndicated Qualitative Ratings Services.* There has been slow progress in this complex area. Where extensive product use data are available (Simmons Market Research Bureau, Media Mark, and Scarborough, for example), it is being used to a greater degree. Geodemographic segmentation (PRIZM and Donnelley Plus) has caught on in spots. The old standby in opinion ratings for programs and talent, TVQ, seems well supported and used. The recent California legislative attempts aimed at controlling its use seem testimony enough to its operational value. On the other hand, several syndicated product use surveys (Quantiplex and Qualidata) have failed, partly because of limited lists of products and services covered.

The jury is still out on the ability of advertising agencies to coordinate qualitative ratings data with quantitative measurements in spot-buying activity. In the case of network planning and buying, such data will surely be more utilized. Services such as Television Audience Assessment and Roger Percy's Vox Box promise advertisers and agencies some measure of commercial exposure and/or impact. Whether the interest expressed in such research is strong enough to support such services is an unanswered question.

*Cable Television's Measurement Problems.* Cable television, by introducing dozens of new channels of service to the home screen, has complicated the syndicated researcher's life. The Cable Audience Methodology Study (CAMS), conducted in 1983, showed (1) how much standard household diaries undermeasure viewing of cable-originated programming, both basic and pay, and (2) that no experimental techniques devised by A. C. Nielsen or the committee of cable and agency researchers was any improvement.

Several factors are undoubtedly at the root of this problem. Cable networks are relatively new; their channel numbers have not been ingrained in people's minds; their programs often attract transient, not consistent, viewing and furthermore are generally low rated and perhaps not terribly memorable. The automatic push-button dialer associated with cable converters encourages frequent channel switches. In total, these factors present a problem for any technique depending on memory. The net result is that meters and telephone coincidentals are considered the only reasonably accurate tools for measuring cable audiences in mid 1985.

Both Arbitron and Nielsen are experimenting with revised household diary types, but reports of significant progress are lacking. Only time and tests will say if the goal can be reached.

*Remote Control and VCR Playback Problems.* Not only has the introduction of remote-control devices, accelerated by the advent of cable, brought measurement problems; it has created advertiser concern over commercial exposure. The quick channel shift to avoid an obtrusive commercial is now much easier—

so easy, in fact, that it's called "zapping." If not switched out, sound volume can be reduced. Where VCR time-shift recordings are played, the tape can be "fast-forwarded" through the commercial (or it can be edited out).

Advertisers and agencies sense a loss of commercial exposure and effectiveness as these devices and their concomitant use for zapping commercials increase. This sentiment could foster demand for a syndicated qualitative service which may provide measurement of commercial audience exposure.

In Chapter 11 we discuss the future, with emphasis on the measurement problems that may be created by new technologies.

## NOTES

1. A unified sample is a subsample of the total panel of Audimeter households that contributed acceptable in-tab records for each of the four weeks measured.
2. Made possible by removal of legal prohibitions on asking race questions in the initial interview. Such questions had been proscribed because they might lead to charges of "racism."
3. CONTAM: Committee on Network Television Audience Measurement. COLTRAM: Committee on Local Television and Radio Audience Measurement.

# 11 A Look to the Future

"The future is where we will spend the rest of our lives," was the way General David Sarnoff, longtime head of RCA, used to emphasize the need to look ahead, even when the view is a hazy one.[1] Today we hear much about "the New Electronic Media, the "Information Society," "New Technologies," or "Video-tech," and certainly these new arrivals will have some effect on audience measurement in the future. This is a broad area indeed, and in order to approach it for our purposes some definitions and parameters are essential. How far ahead are we looking? What specific technologies should be considered? And finally, as the new mass communication field evolves, what new system will be required? How will audience delivery be measured?

The time frame will be limited to 1990, the end of this decade. Experience dictates that five to six years is the maximum period for which there is any likelihood that forecasts will be even marginally correct. Moreover, the electronic media in 1984 are in one of their most dynamic transition periods. As Don Menschel, president of MCA Television, remarked, "In this business you come to expect what you least expect."[2] So whatever the forecasts may be for 1990, watch out for surprises.

A further consideration is that rather than focus on technology and processes (hardware), our look is directed toward content and services to the consumer (software). This means primary consideration of program and economic aspects rather than the physical aspect of newer services.

The future look is directed at three major categories of video service: (1) the present broadcast spectrum and systems, (2) existing nonbroadcast technologies in which we have experience—one-way cable and VCRs, and (3) the truly new technologies such as two-way cable, DBS, electronic publishing (Teletext and Viewtex), and home computers, which are now jockeying for position. The

271

major audience measurement developments are certain to focus on the first two categories during the next five years, but attention must also be given to the possible needs of newer technologies, if and when they get past the first lap of the course.

The following sections list and briefly define the alphabetic melange of technologies that the industry faces. The gamut of "improved" ways to reach the public's TV set with a particular entertainment or information service is a wide one indeed. Our overview starts with services existing as of January 1984.

## I.   PRESENT BROADCAST SERVICES

### TV Broadcast Service

The major technological changes here is the introduction of perhaps thousands of low power television (LPTV) stations capable of serving a 15- to 20-mile radius as booster satellites for nearby full-service TV stations plus limited local originations in some cases. It will take time to discern just what effect such LPTV stations will have. Commercial broadcasters do not seem too concerned that LPTVs will be effective audience builders, whereas cable franchise operators see them as more of a threat for local ad dollars.

Qualitative audio improvement could come from adding stereo sound to TV broadcasts. The FCC in March 1984 approved a multichannel TV sound (MTS) system using amplitude modulation of sound subcarriers. The first subcarrier can be used only for stereo sound. Industry consensus is that the Broadcast Television Systems Committee (BTSC) stereo system developed by Zenith-dbx and recommended by BTSC of the Electronic Industry Association will be adopted virtually 100 percent. TV manufacturers and broadcasters both are enthusiastic about the consumer appeal of stereo and of another capability possible with multichannel sound—foreign-language audio translations, of great interest to stations with large Hispanic audience potential. The latter use may develop most quickly because it requires less investment by broadcaster and set owner. Stereo demands new studios and transmitters by the broadcasters and adaptors or new sets by viewers. This reequipment process will begin immediately and should be well along by 1990.

Accompanying the improvement in TV sound systems will be a "quantum leap" in picture quality. Enhanced or high-quality TV (HQTV) on the present 525-line TV system is a high-priority project for all major set makers. "View among many TV set engineers and product planners is that first significant enhancements in pictures could come within two years, as digital framestore technology comes down to consumer cost levels."[3] Doubling the number of lines in the picture, removal of "noise" elements, virtual elimination of cross-color effects, eradication of line flicker and ghosts are among flaws to be overcome in the digital storage chips.

Obviously every technology that uses the home television set as a display device stands to benefit from these developments. However, these improvements in sound and picture will be largely applicable to TV as an entertainment medium rather than as an information source. Standard commercial television stations and networks, which will continue to dominate the audience universe in 1990, will be the major beneficiaries of these enhancements. They offer alluring new challenges for the creators of advertisers' commercials.

## Subscription Television (STV)

Subscription television broadcasts over existing broadcast stations (usually UHF) for limited periods each day, using an encoded (scrambled) version of normal signals so that only subscribers with a decoder can receive the service—either feature motion pictures or major sports events. STV services, supplying only a single pay program option, were no match for cable with its multiplicity of channel choices. STV is diappearing as superior, newer technologies (cable, multichannel multipoint distribution service—MMDS—and direct broadcasting satellites) take over.

## Multipoint Distribution Service (MDS)

Multipoint distribution systems use omnidirectional line-of-sight microwave signals to deliver a single pay TV service to subscribers. MDS is actually a common carrier service, which traditionally leases channels to pay-movie entrepreneurs who obtain subscribers in apartment buildings, hotels, etc., which are served via a common rooftop special receiver and decoder. Like STV, MDS, offering a single channel, is outclassed by either the services offered by cable or the emergence of the newer multichannel MDS.

## II. PRESENT WIRED SERVICES

### One-Way Cable

Cable's spotty growth, discussed in Chapter 5, still has problems ahead, especially in major cities where construction has been slow to start. For example, in New York, after 10 years, cable penetration in Manhattan was little better than 50 percent of potential. Construction in the four outer boroughs of New York has just begun and will take until 1992 or 1993 to complete at a cost of close to $2 billion. Billions more are needed to complete cabling in Chicago, Philadelphia, Detroit, Baltimore, Washington, Cleveland, St. Louis, and Minneapolis-St. Paul. Again it will be after 1990 before all this construction is finished. Low inner-city penetration rates, construction cost overruns, and high-expense underground and apartment wiring made these cities less attractive. Multiple service operators and venture capitalists shied away from most of them. Slow progress is anticipated because local entities often lack financial resources, management know-how, or marketing skills. In New York, corruption and political kickbacks have brought progress to a standstill in Brooklyn and the Bronx in 1987. Until these major markets are penetrated cable will remain a disadvantaged advertising medium by not being able to deliver truly national audiences.

*The New York Times* summarized the 1984 cable situation as follows: "All across the country, cable operators are struggling to bolster their earnings—or pare their losses—by shrugging off many of the onerous requirements of franchise agreements that were signed in more hopeful times a few years ago."[4] Drew Lewis, chairman of Warner-Amex Cable Communications, is quoted as telling Dallas officials, "We just promised too much and now we find that to break even, we can't live up to those promises."

In a March 1984 request to the City of Pittsburgh for approval to sell the Warner-Amex franchised system, Lewis said Warner-Amex "simply cannot continue to operate in the face of such significant operating losses and such bleak prospects."

The original number of cable networks diminished due to failures and mergers, but there have been new additions such as the Nashville Network and Disney. Industry leaders see a further shakeout ahead, which would leave perhaps six or eight advertising-supported entertainment networks plus a sports and a news network and several premium-pay or pay-per-event networks by the end of the decade.

Cable's future growth as an ad medium will be to some extent determined by whether or not existing premium-pay TV services such as HBO, Showtime, Cinemax, and the Movie Channel become advertising vehicles. The present economics seem against it, but experience in the magazine field suggests it may be merely a matter of time: *Reader's Digest,* after 22 years, changed its policy in 1955 with no detriment to circulation growth. *Changing Times* had a similar experience. Research studies indicate that such advertising would meet a minimum of objection if it were discreetly positioned in order not to interrupt feature pictures and particularly if some reduction in subscriber rate were involved. Subscribers in some cases already get advertising on premium-pay tiers because franchisers package advertising-supported networks that way. The distinction between basic and pay cable is thus evaporating.[6]

Considering the early dominance of cable audience delivery by pay cable (HBO especially), its acceptance of advertising would overnight propel cable into a new circulation level as an ad medium. At last, advertisers could get direct access to the audience lost from commercial broadcast network TV due to pay cable. Until that happens, the growth in cable network ad revenue will probably be modest.

Cable advertising networks are finally showing some ability to produce or acquire programs that will win audiences against TV and pay networks and independents (including superstations). Nielsen data show that for the first three months of 1987, cable originations (excluding pay service and superstations) accounted for 13 percent of the total weekly minutes viewing in all cable TV households on a 24-hour basis.

At the community franchise level, systems are just gearing up for the opportunities to bring TV advertising power to local merchants. Interconnects of numerous local franchisers to produce market units attractive to national advertisers represent a viable approach, but to be effective they require uniformity in networks carried, effective audience and sales promotion, and standardization of channel positions for these networks. A Paul Kagan Associates survey estimated that in 1986, 15.5 million homes or 40% of all subscribers were served by interconnects (ICS) and that these ICS accounted for $75 million in gross billings. The substantial volume of billings needed to justify regular local market syndicated ratings will develop slowly. In contrast to broadcasting, where a number of stations jointly support measurement reports, a lone cable franchisee must foot the total rating bill, except where viable interconnects operate.

Cable growth, estimated at 400,000 new subscribers per month at the beginning of 1984, has dropped to around 200,000 monthly. A realistic projection for 1990 is 54 percent cable penetration, a six-point increase over February–March 1987. Assuming 93 million TV households, the cable universe then would become 50 million TV households.

## Satellite Master Antenna Television (SMATV)

Not particularly new, but growing in importance in major cities, SMATV systems are installed on apartment complexes. They enable a master antenna distribution system to furnish pay services while avoiding local franchising requirements, as long as city streets are not crossed. A receiving dish atop the building picks up satellite signals so that several pay services can be added to the local broadcast channels already distributed by the existing system. Installation costs are a fraction of what would be required for cable.

SMATVs are inexpensive and efficient, and once established, they substantially foreclose cable's opportunity to serve those households. SMATV efforts to protect their turf from cable system competition, however, have failed in the courts. In most cases economics limit SMATV to apartment buildings with more than 200 units. Cable operators view SMATV as a serious barrier to urban subscriber penetration, especially in major cities such as New York, Chicago, and Philadelphia, where cable will generally arrive after SMATV service is established.

## III. PRESENT RECORDER SERVICES

### Video Cassette Recorders (VCRs)

Rivaling cable as a significant force in home entertainment is the video cassette recorder. Conservatively estimated to be in eight million homes as of January, 1984, this video device has been phenomenally successful. It will continue to outpace cable growth during the remainder of this decade. Even should its uptrend not continue to parallel that of color TV, we can look for close to 60 percent penetration of TV households by 1990, well ahead of the anticipated cable level.[9] Thus, by the beginning of the last decade of the century, more than half of all television households will have either cable or a VCR (in most cases, both; surveys show a large overlap between the two).

VCRs, of course, serve their owners in several ways:

1. Immediate time shift—a desired program is taped while the owner is watching other programs live or is out or otherwise occupied. The recording is played back at a time convenient to the viewer, usually within a week. The tape is then erased and reused.

2. Recording for retention—outstanding programs may be recorded, either while being viewed live or in absentia, and retained for future use and reuse as part of a videotape "library."

3. Tapes prerecorded by others—motion pictures, music and special interest videos, or tapes made by friends—can be replayed. Motion picture tapes can be either purchased or rented.

4. Home video photography tapes—portable video cameras (camcorders) enable viewers to make electronic "home movies" and play them over the TV set via the tape recorder.

Time-shifting was originally the prime motivation for VCR ownership. Taped movies were scarce and expensive, and cameras were cumbersome and very costly. During the early 1980s, that changed, first with the introduction of rentals of feature film tapes, then a rapid rise in the number of attractive movies available paralleling a rising tide of locally convenient video shops in operation. Then came "club plans," which greatly reduced rental fees (to the $1–$2 range), and sales prices for some features dropped from $69.95 to $39.95, thus broadening the market. Then came the potential of the music video, a 13- to 15-minute tape featuring a young rock star in a dazzling production of a popular tune, dramatized by Michael Jackson's fantastic success. Jane Fonda's exercise series became a smash hit, and scores of other health, sports, and "do-it-yourself" cassettes appeared.

In the camera field, many companies are marketing new, lighter, more sensitive camcorders, and many more improvements are just ahead in this field. Costs have dropped materially, and sales soared.

Despite the enhanced attractiveness of these newer uses, time shifting continues to be the major use of VCRs, enlarged in scope now by the availability of more varied offerings, especially full-length theatrical movies without commercials, brought to the home by pay cable.

## Videodiscs

Videodisc players were first introduced nationally to the consumer market in 1980, but two different, incompatible versions experienced slow growth. The videodisc machine is strictly for playback of prerecorded material and thus lacks the recording, time shifting, and camera uses of the VCR. Its virtues are lower cost for the machine and the higher technical quality of the discs. Discs are simple to use, and users buy far more prerecorded material than those with VCRs.

When RCA, the major promoter of the video disc, withdrew from the field in April 1984, it spelled the end of this device as a home instrument. The surging sales curve of VCRs swamped the single use disc.[10] The future growth of discs will be in the business and educational fields, where random access features are important.

## IV.  NEW TECHNOLOGIES

Up to this point, discussion has focused on known services that have been on the market long enough to have been tested by the consumer. Now we look at some of the newer technologies. These have had little or no public exposure— if so, the type of service provided has not truly tested their viability. First we will look at MMDS, then DBS, followed by Teletext, then two-way cable and videotex linked together. No account of the future can overlook the role and impact that may be created by electronic home communications from home computers and the telephone system, so those are treated as well, even though they are not normally thought of as "future technologies."

## Multichannel Multipoint Distribution Service (MMDS)

MMDS was created by the FCC in mid 1983 when it took unused spectra from instructional television fixed services (ITFS) to create two blocks of four channels in each market for commercial pay TV programming. There were now 10 channels available for MDS programming in each market, but a single operator would be licensed for only 5. On the other hand, additional channel space can be leased from ITFS operators, creating more MDS channels, perhaps up to 8.

This FCC move to inaugurate "wireless cable" created something akin to the Oklahoma land rush—cable operators, broadcasters, satellite broadcasters, MDS licensees, telephone companies, and many others flooded the commission with nearly 17,000 applications by December 1983[11] with individual companies applying for over 100 licenses nationwide. At least six telephone companies, from Pacific Northwest Bell to New Jersey Bell, are in the contest for licenses, some without specific plans for use. To meet the deluge, the FCC decided to grant licenses by lottery.

A prime attraction of MMDS is its cost. A facility to cover a small local area is estimated at $400,000, compared to $10 million for cable wiring. Microband Corporation estimated it could build MMDS facilities in each of the top 50 markets within two years for a total cost of only $35 million.[12] Another plus for MMDS is lack of local franchise fees and much bureaucratic regulation and red tape. Moreover, four to eight additional channels of service may be sufficient to satisfy the vast majority of viewers who would otherwise be cable prospects, especially in urban areas where availability of standard broadcast reception is no problem.

The cable industry, represented by Thomas E. Wheeler, president of the National Cable Television Association, considers the emergence of MMDS and DBS the industry's most important issue. "No doubt about it . . . we're afraid of these unregulated and deregulated competitors. If they beat us to some of the major cities, the cable industry could be stopped dead in its tracks."[13] Wheeler will have little to fear from DBS in the next few years, but MMDS is going to be launched in a number of major markets in 1984 and 1985—markets such as New York, Washington, and Milwaukee not yet cabled.

## Direct Broadcast Service (DBS)

The vision of a synchronous-orbit satellite 23,000 miles in space serving home viewers directly was science fiction only a few years ago. By mid-1984 there are estimated to be between 700,000 and one million homes in the United States receiving cable network signals on backyard dishes. By employing 6- to 8-foot dishes, at a cost of well over a thousand dollars each, remote viewers on farms and ranches can receive HBO, Showtime, and other cable networks from present C-Band satellites, with no program charges. The term for this group is TVRO (TV Receive Only). It is one of the forms of "piracy" that HBO, Showtime, and other pay-cable networks hope to overcome with scrambling devices in 1985. These pay-cable operators expect to sign up TVRO users as subscribers so they can get the scrambled picture via decoder.

In addition to TVRO users who use C-Band signals from present satellites, and the true high-power DBS Ku-band service scheduled to commence in 1986, there is a third category, known as early-entry DBS systems. These operate at medium power (20 to 40 watts) and require 3½- to 6-foot receiving dishes. Satellites equipped to generate such signals are now operating, and several entrepreneurs have sought to get a 2-year jump on the field by launching quasi-DBS services now.

The Skyband service of international publisher Rupert Murdoch, due for launching with five-channel nationwide quasi-DBS in the spring of 1984, was abandoned in January 1984, with $75 million in startup losses.

United Satellite Communications, Inc. (USCI), another entrant, offered service early in 1984 in six states, based on five transponders on a Canadian satellite, leased for $1 million per month. USCI promoted a $995 sales plan giving subscribers the dish plus a year of programming.

USCI, despite early backing from Prudential Life Insurance Company, to obtain further financial help in mid-1984 sought a merger with Satellite Television Corporation, the Comsat subsidiary. Merger talks broke down, however, when Comsat decided to cease DBS efforts. The fate of USCI's existing operation (with its 10,000 to 20,000 subscribers) seems dismal.

The dishes used in the present TVRO service are large, heavy, and expensive because the C-Band satellite signal is weak (only 9 watts). True DBS, originally intended to debut in 1986, involves use of Ku-band transmission with 230 watts of power. The stronger signal means that household receiving dishes can be reduced to the 2-foot level and thus be mounted on rooftops. The original group of eight DBS companies authorized by the FCC in 1982 was reduced to three when Comsat announced in December 1984 that it was not going to pursue its application. CBS, RCA, and Western Union had dropped out earlier in 1984, and the FCC had eliminated another applicant. The most aggressive entrant had been Satellite Television Corp. (STV), a subsidiary of Comsat, so that company's decision to halt its efforts was a blow to DBS from which it may not recover.

Observers see the USCI-Prudential experience, added to the defections by RCA, CBS, Western Union, and Comsat, as chilling Wall Street financial support for further DBS ventures. The total cost of equipping and launching a Ku-band service covering the entire country is estimated at well over $500 million. When added to the many unanswered programming, technical, and marketing questions about DBS, it seems unlikely that we will see any Ku-band DBS service in place before the decade ends.

## Teletext

Teletext (in contrast to two-way videotex, discussed shortly) is a one-way type of information service receivable on home TV sets. It consists of a cataloglike series of "pages" of information that can be accessed by hand-held keypads. Information offered consists of news, sports results, stock market quotations, weather, entertainment listings, traffic data, airline schedules, shopping data, etc. Listings such as those now found in the phone directory yellow pages or newspaper classified ads are also possible. The latter competitive prospect has stimulated keener interest in Teletext on the part of telephone companies and newspapers than of broadcasters or cable operators.

Three possible page characteristics are predicted on the standard used: (1) the simple alphanumeric form, which presents only words, numbers, and symbols;

(2) the World Standard (used in Great Britain), which provides rough color graphics in alphamosaic form; and (3) the North American Broadcast Television Standard (NABTS), employing alphageometric pictures of much higher definition than the World Standard. The advantage of the World system is the availability of relatively inexpensive decoders; NABTS decoders are still very expensive, and bringing costs down has been difficult.

Teletext pages can reach the household set in three ways: (1) by use of vertical blanking intervals (VBIs) in present TV transmissions; (2) via a cable channel; and (3) by a separate telephone line connection. Field experiments have tested all three. In the broadcast version, about 100 to 200 different pages of information can be transmitted. In some cases, these are rolled onto the screen consecutively until the viewer stops the picture at the page wanted. The NABTS, which was pilot tested on CBS and NBC blanking intervals, allows the viewer to turn up the page number desired with a 2- to 10-second wait. The limited amount of time and attention that it can command (U.S. tests have shown it to be about 15 minutes) militates against its effectiveness as an advertising medium except for marketers with highly specific audience requirements. Because home decoders have been expensive, tests of viewer response have been limited. Both NBC and CBS discontinued their pilot operations when manufacturers seemed unable to bring receiver prices down.

Cable channels provide more bandwidth than VBIs, and therefore it is possible to provide 500 pages of information per second. The one major test of cable Teletext, by Time, Inc., was canceled as economically unpromising. However, Group W cable began testing a high-capacity, high-speed Teletext service in its Buena Vista, California, system in July 1984. Up to 5000 pages of information were supplied. Known as Request, the service offered home shopping through Comp-U-Card and charged a fee.[14]

Teletext by telephone connection is also possible. However, in the case of both cable and telephone connections, the major operational focus has been on videotex, with its much greater potential via the two-way call-up facility and better-quality graphics.

Teletext must still be proven, and the lack of economical home decoders will seriously delay the full-scale market testing needed. Its effect on total TV audience numbers by 1990 will be minimal.

## Two-Way Cable and Videotex

These two "new technologies" are linked here because of the alternative relationship expected to develop in the second half of the 1980s. They have common features: There is two-way viewer interaction rather than the traditional passive watching; they provide information-based rather than entertainment-driven programming; they will be basically subscriber supported, not advertiser sponsored;

and they can produce an accurate record of usage (users will pay for services on the basis of minutes accessed).[15]

Two-way cable experience has been largely limited to Warner-Amex's QUBE, first introduced in Columbus, Ohio, in 1974. After securing franchises in such cities as Dallas, Houston, Pittsburgh, and Milwaukee with promises of installing this two-way facility, Warner-Amex in 1983 began to backtrack. Drew Lewis, its president, in applying to Milwaukee for cancellation of the franchise commitment to supply QUBE service, said its limited use in other cities proved it to be uneconomical and not worth the capital expense involved in studios, equipment, and cable lines. Franchise cutbacks in number of channels and services rather than extension into two-way activity will be the rule for several years at least. One-way cable plus telephone use for command purposes is more likely to prove viable.

Major videotex interest in the U.S. has involved newspapers and local telephone companies in small-scale operations. Two multiple newspaper owners, Knight-Ridder and Los Angeles Times-Mirror Company, had originally been most active, the first in the Miami-Ft. Lauderdale area and the latter in California. By the mid-1980s both had abandoned their pilot projects. In Great Britain, Prestel has operated for a number of years but has not made a major place for itself in the mass communication field. If successful, videotex will prove to be a target marketing medium akin to cataloguing and direct selling rather than to be a true mass medium.

A potentially powerful entrant in videotex is the Twintex project, jointly backed by IBM and Sears. CBS, the third original partner, dropped out in 1986. The present partners still plan major videotex developments during the late 1980s. It appears that telephone lines will provide the home connection and that introduction may be on a market-by-market basis.

It seems unlikely that we will see a resurgence of interest in two-way cable because an upstream circuit lacks the switching facilities of the telephone system. Videotext, with a marriage of home computers (with their own monitor screens) and telephone connections (which can access unlimited data banks) will undoubtedly steal the show.

## Home Computers

Videotex is making its major growth using telephone equipment and lines and home computers as the interactive mechanism. Comp-U-Card Interactive, the nation's leading electronic merchandising service, with over a million subscribers paying for a telephone-based home shopping service, computerized its constantly updated data base of 100,000 pieces of information on products and prices in 1979. Its Comp-U-Store users with home computers can directly access this data bank.[16] Following on the heels of the highly successful introduction of banking machines, electronic home banking experiments using telephone service are taking place in many areas of the country. In New York, for example, both Chemical Bank and Citibank introduced home banking systems, which use computers to provide over the home telephone line such services as bill paying, fund transfers, and up-to-the-minute account information. Progress has been slow because home installation of personal computers has failed to reach expectations. Office use, where PCs are widespread, is now being tried. Many had expected home banking to be received as enthusiastically as banking machines. This seems not to have occurred, perhaps because technology has yet to deliver cash electronically.

Home computers, along with telephone lines, are going to be growing factors in bringing videotex and other interactive services into the home. A new generation of computer-wise young adults will be using computers as easily as the last generation adapted to employing hand calculators. The interrelationships between two-way cable, telephone lines, and home computers will determine the future of all three to a major degree. By decade's end, various experiments now in progress or planned will result in a clearer view of the ultimate shape of projected interactive services. Many serious questions about costs, subscriber versus advertiser revenue potential, and the nature of services that will be actually used by the public will be answered so that commercial development may proceed in the 1990s.

## V. TELEPHONE COMPANY INVOLVEMENT

Telephone service, as we have seen, is being used for many tests of teletext, videotex, home shopping, and home banking. This stems from the interest of local telephone companies in these services, an interest greatly intensified since the breakup of AT&T. Telephone companies have also been active in other directions on the cable front. Bell Atlantic companies are aggressively pursuing opportunities to perform system cabling and technical maintenance for franchisers in Washington, Baltimore, and Philadelphia. The Chesapeake and Potomac subsidiary, after legal clearance, has contracted to construct the cable wiring system for the District of Columbia franchiser. In several other cases, including Cleveland and Detroit, franchisers with limited capital resources welcome the chance to let a pro do the wiring and lease the lines on an economical basis.

In Palo Alto, California, in October 1983, Pacific Telephone proposed a hybrid coaxial and fiber-optic, 422-mile telecommunications system to serve the city and surrounding communities. Pacific Telephone proposed leasing 80 of 112 channels to the cities served, enabling them to manage their own cable systems by sublease of channels to competing service providers. Here we have the telephone company providing the entire physical plant using the latest technology—fiber optics—and shouldering the capital costs. The initial proposal was rejected by the city, but an alternative is under study.

Is this the wave of the future for cable? Why do we need two lines into every cable-subscribing household, one for cable, one for telephone service? Isn't it economic to have the entire wired plant, including home connections, installed by a company that has equipment, trained manpower, trucks, and emergency procedures known for unparalleled efficiency and service? The cable system has expanded rapidly, but in the coming years we may see more soul searching as capital costs for modernizing systems mount and franchises expire.

Another possible merger of telephone and cable interests appeared in March 1984 when AT&T Communications of New York warned the state Public Utilities Commission that high access charges by New York Telephone would force it to explore the possibilities of using cable for bypassing local phone exchanges.

Whatever the outcome of such proposals in the near term, they indicate the direction of thinking by telephone companies around the nation. These have been extremely active in videotex experiments (using the AT&T Sceptre terminal) and clearly have, through their switching system, a resource not available to cable operators for two-way cable. Therefore two-way cable may become cable one way (downstream) and telephone, the other (upstream).

## VI.   THE FUTURE OF PRESENT AND NEW SERVICES

The emergence of new techniques to provide users more flexibility in tuning, larger choices of programs, and the ability to use TV for many nonentertainment purposes is going to prove mind boggling to all but a small segment of the television audience. We know from diffusion theory, as well as from experience with LP records, FM radio, color TV, cable and VCRs, how many years it takes for the public to accept and enthusiastically embrace new devices, techniques, and procedures. The more sophisticated these become, the greater will be consumer resistance. People's budgets, both of time and money, are not open ended. Moreover, without exception, the hardware in new technologies always outpaces software by several years. Prospects have nothing to lose by waiting, knowing that even with hardware prices coming down, designs will be perfected, operation will be simplified; meanwhile the uses and program offerings will improve, and they will be better able to assess the service's benefits to them.

Few forecasters seem to appreciate these considerations, nor the fact that the various new technologies have an impact on each other. There is an inevitable tendency to overpredict the growth rate for new technologies and underestimate growth for those on the steep upslope of the growth curve. Cable is close to the deceleration stage now, while VCRs are at full thrust. Most of the other technologies (except as they may substitute for cable in small pockets and outlying areas) are not likely to have the impact hoped for by their promoters prior to the 1990s.

The foregoing analysis of the outlook through the 1980s for present and new home services has not dealt in a significant way with programming—the essential element for the success of any of them. Larry Taishoff, president and publisher of *Broadcasting,* summarized his reaction to the new technologies thus:

> . . . two conclusions come into focus. One is that the public is media-neutral; it doesn't care which delivery system forwards its programming. The second is that there are turning out to be far fewer programming sources than had been generally anticipated. Thus it is clear that the future's TV competition will involve a rapidly enlarging universe of media outlets competing for a slowly enlarging universe of popular programming."[17]

Other major ingredients are the impact of politics and economics on future developments. Commenting on this, Professor Anthony Oettinger, chairman of the Harvard Program on Information Resources Policy, says: "Transmission and switching facilities are a social infrastructure, like roads and electrical-power facilities. Many of the new competitive arenas depend on this infrastructure. The prices of transmission and switching services—long-haul, short-haul or local—affect *every* business and *everyone's* life style."

*Harvard Magazine* added: "Access to the wired society's wires will determine a lot about who decides to offer what quality of which communications services to what markets where."[18]

Will the new technologies be able to create new service and convenience for the user? Or will they fail as did home facsimile in the 1950s because an existing service (in the case of facsimile it was the daily newspaper) is more economical, convenient, and complete? Arthur Nielsen, Jr. pointed out: "While new technologies make change possible, they cannot bring it about themselves. Deep-seated socioeconomic factors will in the final analysis be the major determinants."[19]

The preceding overview enables us to identify cable and video cassettes as the significant new home electronic forces in the late 1980s. Cable substitutes—SMATV, MMDS, and DBS—will grow in enclaves and areas not reached by cable. Teletext serves a narrow field of interest and will be limited in growth. The greatest potential will be some combination of two-way cable, videotex, home computers, and telephone line switching which delivers a multi-faceted home interaction service at a reasonable cost. VCRs supply several new opportunities to viewers to control their program content; interaction with the system will provide others.

## VII.   THE FUTURE OF AUDIENCE MEASUREMENT

The previous description of the changes to be anticipated in electronic mass communication makes one realize the challenges that face those who hope to refine the system to enable it to function properly. Forgetting technology and focusing on services in terms of viewer interest, it is apparent that it is cable and VCRs that command the most attention. A third and perhaps more significant area that will be a target of industry attention in the next three years is testing the "people meter" to replace the TV household diary to measure audience demographics. Since the people meter is primarily designed for broadcast and cable audience measurement, our first attention is focused on this development.

## PEOPLEMETERS

### Introduction

The most far-reaching development in the rating field in more than three decades has been the rapid emergence of the peoplemeter as the preeminent measurement system for network television. By the fall of 1987 the Nielsen Television Index, which has served as the sole national measurement service since its inception in 1950, will be out of operation. In its place will be two competing services, Nielsen and AGB, both using peoplemeters to measure audiences in national panels of 2000 households each.

The peoplemeter is a device by which viewers record their presence in the television audience by pushing buttons on a small keypad. Thus audience composition data are automatically recorded simultaneously with household set usage. This feature replaces the ancillary parallel diary panel (National Audience Composition) that over the years Nielsen has been using to supply its demographic data.

In addition to AGB and Nielsen, two other research companies have entered the peoplemeter competitive fray—ScanAmerica and R.D. Percy Inc. ScanAmerica (a joint venture of Arbitron and Time Inc.'s SAMI/Burke) is inaugurating a local Denver service in May 1987 and a national measurement by the 1988–1989 TV season. Percy is projecting a local New York report in summer 1987, with expansion to other markets later.

The essential elements of each of these four services are delineated below. Following the descriptive material, the research and business practice implications of peoplemeters are discussed.

### AGB Television Research

The U.S. pioneer peoplemeter service proposal was made by a British firm, AGB Research PLC, in October 1983. Based on its experience with fixed push-button peoplemeters in Ireland, West Germany, and the Philippines, AGB's remote peoplemeters were completely installed in the company's United Kingdom measurement panel during 1984.

AGB's initial proposal to the American broadcast industry offered a national sample of 5000 metered households (13,000 to 18,000 individuals) at half the cost of the Nielsen Television Index (1700 households and 865 diary homes for its audience composition data). An extensive one-market test was part of the proposal.

AGB acquired an interest in Information and Analysis Inc., a media research firm which had been established by Norman Hecht in 1980. Hecht became president of AGB Television Research Inc., the U.S. operating company. In October 1985 Hecht resigned, and Stephan Buck, a director of AGB Research PLC, became CEO of the U.S. subsidiary, with Joseph Philport installed as president.

### AGB Boston Test

AGB's proposal for an extensive test (six months or more) of the operation of its meter in 400 households attracted widespread industry support. Thirty-seven supporters (networks, agencies, cable groups, and others) contributed $850,000 toward a test in Boston. This sponsor group served as an advisory panel for the Boston test, which began in February 1985 and ran for 14 months. For validation purposes, the panel was divided into set-meter and peoplemeter segments. Comparisons with results from Nielsen household meters and diary sources as well as the local Arbitron diary service were possible.

Unfortunately, AGB did not issue a report of any description on the tests. Evaluation was left to the individual sponsors, and this was spotty and uncoordinated. Some supporters were impressed enough to become subscribers to the AGB national service; others remained unconvinced that AGB had answered all pertinent questions or that its national service would prove superior to the Nielsen competitive service, now prepared to meet AGB head to head in fall 1987.

### AGB Peoplemeter Features

AGB equipment consists of a set monitor and a small keypad. The monitor records both set usage and people data. It contains a lighted display that shows the assigned number of each member of the household or guest who has punched in as present in the television audience. The monitor lights flash at 10-minute intervals to prompt viewers to make changes, where necessary, in which individuals are watching. The keypad is connected to the monitor by remote control, which uses either infrared or ultrasonic signals to avoid interference with TV set remote controls. Separate monitoring instruments are used for cable converters and VCRs. None of these require hard wiring (soldering) to the monitored device; they operate with sensing devices placed to extract necessary electronic information. All units operate on normal household electric circuits or telephone lines; no dedicated lines need be installed or rented. The system is capable of handling up to eight family members and eight guest viewers.

AGB states that it can measure up to 16 sets and 16 VCRs. As an operational matter, it does not attempt to measure sets of less than six inches; nor can it measure portable sets when used with battery power. AGB claims a "breakthrough" in its use of a "fingerprinting" sensory device (smaller than a cigarette package) that can be attached to the back of a VCR. It automatically records date, time, and channel of any VCR recording. When the tape is replayed, it is possible to (1) measure the program's audience and (2) determine which program commercials may have been zapped (deleted in recording) or zipped (fast-forwarded) in playback. AGB collects data on a 15-second basis.

### AGB Plans and Prospects

AGB's planned national roll-out schedules a completed 2000 household sample by September 1987, to be increased to 5000 by September 1988. Each of these samples will really be a subsample of a much larger probability enumeration sample of the U.S.—10,000 in 1987 and 50,000 in 1988. The larger samples will (1) furnish estimates of multiset homes, cable subscribers and VCR penetration and (2) be the source of replacement households. Every U.S. television market will be sampled. Complete sample household turnover will take place in three years.

Support for AGB has been modest; many are still trying to make the hard choice: Should they subscribe to AGB in addition to Nielsen, in lieu of Nielsen, or stick with Nielsen. AGB subscribers as of April 1, 1987, were CBS, BBDO, NWAyer, Ted Bates, Grey Advertising, Scali/McCabe, Young & Rubicam, Leo Burnett, DMB&B, MTV Network, Orbis Communications, and two syndicators.

### Nielsen Media Research

The Nielsen Television Index was inaugurated in September 1950 with a sample of 300 households. However, it was not until July 1960, when the sample reached 1100, that NTI began reporting profitable ratings based on total U.S. TV households. In 1954 Nielsen added its National Audience Composition (NAC) service to supply people viewing data from a parallel sample panel of households. In 1983, when Nielsen raised the NTI sample from 1200 to 1700 households to accommodate cable network needs, it failed to enlarge the woefully small NAC sample, which remained at 865 for any weekly report (actually about 625 in tab).

Industry discontent with the size of the NAC sample, plus dwindling regard for the accuracy of diary results in an era of growing cable, independent TV, and VCR penetration, opened the way for a competitor, AGB, in 1983. Nielsen began experimenting with peoplemeters in 1974 and had pilot-tested several versions in Tampa. Nevertheless, despite industry concern over the accuracy of NAC demographic data, no effort was mounted to introduce such meters until AGB announced its plans in 1983. Nilesen quickly responded by commencing installation of a peoplemeter sample; 300 households were operating in October 1985, and 1000 were hooked up by January 1987. Monthly reports on peoplemeter program ratings were inaugurated in January 1986.

### Nielsen Peoplemeter Features

A Nielsen microprocessor-based device, called Homeunit, controls the measurement system installed in a metered household. The Homeunit is really a family of data collection devices. The specific device used is determined by cost, ease of installation, and the video equipment of each household. Nielsen maintains that a variety of data collection is needed to measure all tuners with the desired accuracy.

The device used in the majority of sample homes, the local oscillator attachment (LOA), is installed by inserting an insulated probe into the tuner. A second device is used in most other households, especially those with cable converters and VCRs.

Other more sophisticated and expensive connections are employed by Nielsen where cable converters are designed "to prevent subscribers from stealing pay services," or in homes that utilize a variety of technically complex interconnected video equipment (such as a VCR that can be switched to play on either of two TVs in separate rooms).

In addition to the eight-button keypad, Nielsen supplies a keyboard that is placed on or near the set. It contains the lights used to display the currently registered audience status and to prompt for input when the set is activated or the channel changed.

Initial visitor data, including age and sex, must be entered on this set-top box. Thereafter, a visitor may use the remote control during a particular viewing session. Nielsen is alone in providing two keyboards for each set metered in all households.

Nielsen's set meters have, since 1978, measured record/play of VCRs as well as channel tuned during recording. They have credited VCR recording as television usage. Separate reports now show the VCR-created increment, but no record so far can be made of playback.

A new fingerprinting VCR system is planned by Nielsen for installation in the 1987–1988 season. This will provide playback credit for all home-recorded sources. Acquired tapes will not be identified unless tapes are identified by the supplier with the Nielsen code.

Whereas all peoplemeter keypads use infrared, ultrasonic, or wireless for their connection to the set tuning unit, connections from the tuner to the main control unit (from which data are read out daily) vary. Nielsen uses hard wiring to assure blacking out spurious impulses or noise (which it claims can emanate from FM transmissions and other noise sources).

Nielsen now uses established telephone lines for daily readouts of stored information. For nontelephone households and party lines, a dedicated line is installed. Time is kept accurate to one second by checks made during daily data collection calls, generally made between 3:00 and 8:00 a.m. Eastern Time. Certain reprogramming of household control units is possible by phone calls from collection controls.

The Nielsen system collects data on a 30-second basis. These data are transformed into average-minute viewing records by central computers.

Nielsen equipment generates a prompt command (a) when the set is turned on, or (b) when the channel is changed. The prompt consists of all lights, including the OK and individual lights, flashing on the front and the top of the set-top box. These flash until a button is pushed. If, when the set is on, any person button is pushed or when a channel switch takes place or an OK button is pushed (signifying no change in audience), the audience is registered with no flashing light. Nielsen, after experimenting with regular-interval prompting, decided that it violated psychological principles by "punishing" cooperators unnecessarily. If no button is pushed, all buttons flash as a prompt.

Nielsen acknowledges that child peoplemeter ratings are definitely lower (by 127 on Saturday morning) and different from NTI/NAC ratings. They point to the lack of an accurate independent measure by which to verify either diary or peoplemeter results for children. Nevertheless, recognizing that conscientious button-pushing by young kids seems to be a problem, Nielsen has taken the following steps toward remedial action:

• Periodic special incentives for children.
• Making every effort to instruct all nonadults in accurate peoplemeter use.
• Instructing parents to assume responsibility for children's correct usage and assist the very young by button-pushing.
• Engaging an expert consultant in child psychology and motivation.
• Producing a videotape to assure that specific instructions to children are uniformly delivered. Field reps will carry VCR playback devices to cover non-VCR homes.
• Monitoring tuning without viewing (especially during first two weeks) in homes with nonadults for follow-up coaching where necessary.

### Nielsen Plans and Prospects

Nielsen orginally planned to substitute peoplemeter results for the NAC service as the source of demographic NTI data in September 1986. Early results, however, showed disparities and problems that troubled many subscribers, especially the TV networks. The networks persuaded Nielsen (in part by additional payments) to continue NAC another year while further analyses of the peoplemeter sample and results could be completed. When it came time for making definite fall 1987 plans, Nielsen was faced with two alternatives: (1) use peoplemeter data strictly for demographics as a replacement for NAC diaries and retain the NTI household sample intact (the so-called "conformed" solution); or (2) scrap the existing NTI sample and adopt the "integrated" mode with both household and demographic data based on the single peoplemeter sample.

Nielsen clients split on which course they preferred. The broadcast and cable networks as well as independent stations were unhappy with the differences in household usage levels and demographics between the NTI service and the peoplemeter findings based on a sample of 1000, which Nielsen claimed was nationally representative. On the other hand, a majority of major agencies believed that the advantages of a single meter source for household and demographic data outweighed the evidence that the peoplemeter sample was understating TV audiences. There was a significant cost advantage for Nielsen in adopting the integrated approach, as well as a competitive factor when it would be facing direct competition from AGB with just such a sample in the fall.

In January 1987, Nielsen announced its decision to go the integrated route with a 2000 peoplemeter sample replacing the venerable NTI-NAC service as of September 1987. Nielsen backed its decision with statements that its tests had "shown that households accept the Nielsen People Meters" and that even though cooperation rates were slightly below those for the household meters, it was convinced that it could "count on response rates at, or above, 50 percent."[20] The test showed that people *do* push the buttons and that the level of tuning without viewing is "relatively low."

Nielsen will expand its peoplemeter sample to at least 4000 households by September 1988. (A larger sample could result from Nielsen's efforts to launch local peoplemeter services in New York and Los Angeles by that date.) Full electronic measurement of VCR playback will be implemented by fall 1988 for network and syndicated programs. In the interim, Nielsen will use an ascription method in which the demographic characteristics of peoplemeter-measured audiences will be attributed to VCR recorded household ratings. The purpose is to overcome understatement of persons estimated when household VCR recording takes place and is recorded in HUT but people information is available on the live audience. VCR contributions to NTI household ratings in the fourth quarter of 1986 (which Nielsen finds correlates very highly with parallel peoplemeter contributions) amount to .3 rating points for major affected areas—All Monday–Friday Daytime programs (with 4.5 percent increment), Daytime Dramas (5.8 percent increment), Regular Prime Time (2.1 percent) and Prime Time Specials (1.7 percent). Gains due to VCRs were negligible in other program areas.

### Nielsen Competitive Maneuvers

Like a shrewd sailing race skipper, Nielsen, having covered AGB with an integrated 2000 peoplemeter household service in fall 1987, next maneuvers to take the wind out of the sails of two more recent competitors. ScanAmerica, as we shall see later, plans to provide a "single source" national service to 5000 households in 1988. Single source denotes a service in which household product purchase data come from the same panel as television-viewing (or other media audience) data.

Nielsen's response to ScanAmerica has been to develop and pilot test in Chicago and in Canada a scanning device more sophisticated than the Scan-America wand. The Nielsen scanner would be used either at home or on shopping trips to stores, where product packages would be scanned as they were taken from the shelf and placed in the shopping cart. The device provides for entry of store code, price, and any coupon used in the purchase.

The Marketing Research Division of Nielsen plans a national panel installation of 15,000 households by 1988 if this device or a similar one proves effective in current tests. Merging this service with the peoplemeter sample is contingent upon their Canadian experience, where Nielsen has won a contract with the Bureau of Broadcast Measurement (BBM) to supply the industry-sponsored national peoplemeter service. Nielsen Canada is experimenting with a single-source panel in Toronto, and if successful it will be expanded Canada-wide. A similar move in the U.S. is anticipated if Canadian and Chicago tests are favorable.

While attempting to outmaneuver AGB and ScanAmerica, Nielsen has not neglected to glance over its shoulder at the late starter Roger Percy, whose sails are looming on the horizon. Percy's passive heat sensor for verifying the number of peoplemeter button-pushers has a strong attraction, if it works. Nielsen is actively testing this and other passive techniques.

At the ARF Annual Conference in March 1987, John A. Dailey, Senior Vice President of Nielsen Media Research, said: "Nielsen is committed to incorporating a passive element in our measurement system." Several sonar and infrared techniques have been developed and field-tested, and a large pilot test in 1987 is projected. Nielsen, in order to get network contracts, agreed in late 1987 to reduce its minimum turnover of homes from five years to two.

### ScanAmerica

Arbitron is Nielsen's arch competitor in the local measurement field, including metered markets, where as of May 1987 Arbitron had 13 markets metered, compared to 14 for Nielsen. Arbitron over the years has made clear that its ultimate aim is to field a national meter service in competition with Nielsen. The advent of peoplemeters was the opportune opening for such an entry.

Arbitron began testing peoplemeters in 1983, but its real opportunity arose when it acquired a 40 percent interest in Burke Research in October 1984. Burke had secured U.S. rights to an advanced peoplemeter system they developed jointly with a Canadian market research firm, PEAC. A U.S. corporation, ScanAmerica, was launched simultaneously by Arbitron-Burke with William McKenna, a Burke executive who spearheaded the system's development, installed as President. Later SAMI (a Time, Inc. subsidiary) acquired 100 percent of Burke in May 1986, with ScanAmerica then operated as a joint venture between SAMI-Burke and Arbitron.

In August 1987 Arbitron acquired the remaining 50 percent of ScanAmerica from SAMI/Burke. William McKenna, inventor and founding President of ScanAmerica, resigned. SAMI/Burke agreed to "remain involved." Arbitron announced that plans for ScanAmerica national service by September 1988 were canceled in order to reevaluate recent marketplace developments. In October Control Data Corporation announced the acquisition of SAMI/Burke from Time

Inc. This marketing research company, providing warehouse and retail scanner product tracking, custom research, test market and decision support services, provides a complement to CDC's Arbitron Ratings Company.

In October 1981, Joseph Philport became President of AGB Research upon the resignation of Norman Hecht. Michael J. Pochner became President and CEO in June 1987. Shortly thereafter, in August, Philport resigned to join Nielsen. A number of experienced managers were added to strengthen AGB's operations and service.

### ScanAmerica Peoplemeter Features

The ScanAmerica device possesses several features that differentiate it from the more "look-alike" competitors previously described. Briefly, these are:

1. Use of a pretuner that substitutes for the TV set or VCR tuner. This avoids time-consuming probes or connections, especially for cable and VCRs, thus simplifying installation. It also assures accurate identification of all set tuning.

2. On-screen prompt messages that remind viewers to punch in when set is turned on and ask panelists to change whenever the audience changes. Should a half hour pass with no response change, the prompt again appears on the screen. The upper left quadrant of the TV picture is used to flash instructions whenever the set is turned on or a change of channel takes place. Any people data first entered is carried back to the time the set was turned on provided it is within eight minutes. Otherwise the set tuning is adjusted to the first peoplemeter entry. These procedures assure an integrated base for HUT and demographic ratings, avoiding ascription.

3. A product scanning wand to be used to record the Universal Product Codes (UPCs) of all household package goods purchased as they are unpacked after shopping.

The first two elements are designed to limit the amount of unidentified tuning or listening. The product wand, which records its data along with the viewing audience component, can produce the long-sought single-source service. Compositing program viewing data with product and brand purchases will enable advertisers to close many of the gaps between today's media exposure and action at the checkout counter. The advertiser will look at a universe of product and brand users (the target audience) and how they view television.

ScanAmerica's household installation consists of three units. The central Data Collector unit, measuring $12 \times 10 \times 5$ inches, contains (a) the pretuner, (b) a minicomputer for data storage, and (c) a clock device. The two other units are the keypad, which provides 17 buttons identified by color, name, symbol for household members, and several additional buttons; and the product scanner wand. Recording visitor viewing is somewhat complex. When the visitor button is pressed, the screen displays a vertical array of nine age categories, with two column headings—Male and Female. Using a cursor on the keypad, the visitor designates his or her category. Each visitor must complete this to be recorded.

ScanAmerica's unique on-screen prompt system is central to its claim that panel members will be instructed to push buttons in a proper and timely fashion. ScanAmerica aims for a completely unified household and peoplemeter sample, with no household data accepted without accompanying people data. By requiring positive people identification each half hour, edit assumptions are sharply reduced. VCR playback people audience will be measured in the national service.

Sampling fieldwork and operations for ScanAmerica will be performed by Arbitron from its Laurel, Maryland, operations center. Arbitron's stratified sampling plans used in installing local household meter panels will be utilized, with some adjustments to provide the national sample.

### ScanAmerica's Plans and Prospects

Springing as it does from Arbitron, a locally oriented service, it is not surprising that ScanAmerica has opted to inaugurate a local service before going national. The Denver ADI was selected for the initial field test of the ScanAmerica system. This ran from November 1985 to December 1986 in 200 households. From this test, a quantity of data on panel performance, viewing patterns, and product purchase profiles have been developed. In April 1987 ScanAmerica completed installation of a 600-household sample in the 44 County Denver ADI stretching from Nebraska to Wyoming and turned on the first commercial syndicated peoplemeter service with the sweep period beginning April 29, 1987.

ScanAmerica's plans to install a national sample of 5000 were put on hold in 1987.

### Roger D. Percy, Inc.

Roger D. Percy's early experience in attempting to launch a unique rating service, known as Vox Box, is outlined in Chapter 5 (page 144). In 1986 Percy announced a peoplemeter service different from that of the three major players—in addition to button-pushing for individual viewers, it added (1) a passive heat-sensor device that recorded the number of people in view of the set; and (2) an on-screen prompt message whenever the passive and push-button counts were at variance. Percy also carries forward his original Vox Box feature of emphasizing commercial audience in his reports. This is achieved by highly accurate timing of viewing and commercial contact so that the two can be matched to produce commercial audience by brand and by demographics.

### Percy Plans and Prospects

The Percy strategy is to limit the service (at least in the foreseeable future) to three major markets: New York, Chicago, and Los Angeles. Large samples would be employed, and installation of 1200-panel households in the New York ADI-DMA began early in 1987. Service start-up has been postponed several times. Some early data may be available before that date. Roger Percy is convinced that advertisers will be the key to his success because of its emphasis on commercial audiences. He has concentrated marketing efforts on the advertiser community, with secondary attention to agencies and broadcasters. On the other hand, the intense interest of networks in Percy's heat-sensor passive measurement device has brought in tentative New York subscriptions from NBC and CBS. In mid-1987 a series of tests were mounted to test the efficacy of the heat measurements as well as the prompt system, using cameras in seven homes.

### Peoplemeter Strengths and Weaknesses

Much of the push toward peoplemeters can be attributed to two factors: (1) a deep-seated desire by the industry to see the Nielsen monopoly broken by the entrance of competitor AGB; and (2) widespread dissatisfaction with the diary demographic measurement, especially the rickety Nielsen NAC service. Competition could bring better service, lower costs, and needed innovations, it was believed. Events seem to bear out this proposition—in three years Nielsen has moved faster and in more directions than had been the case for decades.

*Strengths.*   On top of the aforementioned factors, the peoplemeter has other advantages, such as:

• Continuous demographic measurement, in contrast to periodic weeks of diary-keeping. This means that all programs are covered so that one-time-only specials and miniseries are fully reported (as well as their effect on competitive shows). Four-week or longer cumulative ratings provide reach and frequency data that previously could only be estimated.

• Household and people data from a single sample without the statistical adjustments formerly necessary to marry meter and diary data.

• Speedier delivery of demographic data, which has in most cases assumed greater significance than household ratings.

• Live-time meter recording by viewers rather than after-the-fact recall so often used with diaries.

*Weaknesses.*   The name peoplemeter implies more than it delivers. Unlike the passive set (or so-called "household") meter, which is out of sight and out of mind, requiring no effort or activity by the panel member, the peoplemeter is constantly visible and demands great precision in use to be effective. It has been called an "electronic diary," a more descriptive term, with "people pushing buttons instead of pencils." Let's run down some of the weaknesses of peoplemeters as seen by critics:

• The push-button mechanism is a stern taskmaster. The right buttons must be pushed at the right time or an irrevocably incorrect record is registered. Diary entries, often made after the program, could be changed, especially when recall by several family members was involved. (Admittedly, some of this recall may have been faulty.)

• Button-pushing could prove tiresome and may be less accurately performed (especially by young people, it appears). Attrition in cooperation could be serious over time.

• The button-pushing task has already been demonstrated to affect sample cooperation rates. A lower proportion of the originally designated sample will accept these devices than was the case with the passive set meter. Moreover, voluntary dropouts are greater. There is evidence that such sample problems are not random but could create bias (blue-collar class drops out faster than others, for example).

• The likelihood of conditioning cannot be overlooked. Week-in week-out button-pushing could affect how and what people watch. It is a far more demanding task than keeping a weekly diary periodically.

• There is evidence of a lower sensitivity in audience composition change from program to program than reported by diaries. Does this mean that the mechanized system is better or just different in its own biased way, as the diary may be?

• The peoplemeter's physical presence in a family's home completely violates the security rules that have hitherto applied to household participation in meter and diary studies. Neighbors, friends, relatives, casual visitors will all be aware of sample households. The door is opened to many possible nefarious schemes to rig or hype individual ratings.

Satisfactory answers to many questions raised about peoplemeters have not yet been fully provided. A growing number of skeptics and critics would like to see more sound evidence that peoplemeters will produce a real advance in rating accuracy. The rush to get national services on stream has left little incentive, time, or money for integrated methodological studies designed to answer research questions.

## THE SRI/CONTAM COINCIDENTAL STUDIES

### Introduction

The Committee on National Television Audience Measurement (CONTAM) has functioned as a methodological group for over 20 years. Its membership comprises the three major television networks with an observer from the National Association of Broadcasters. The A. C. Nielsen Co. joined with CONTAM in 1986 in sponsoring high-quality coincidental studies for both daytime and prime time to serve as an independent yardstick of reality in evaluating peoplemeters versus the prevailing NTI-NAC methodology. CONTAM invited observers from the Electronic Media Research Council, the Cable Advertising Bureau, the American Association of Advertising Agencies, and the Association of National Advertisers. The daytime telephone studies were conducted in May 1986; the prime-time study was in the fall, from October 28 to December 11.

Statistical Research, Inc. was commissioned to do the studies, and its procedures generally followed those described as the Industry Sponsored Research (ISR) coincidental in Chapter 4 using random digit dialing.

### SRI-CONTAM Results

*Prime-Time Survey.*   The prime-time survey covered 8:00–10:00 P.M. Tuesday–Saturday with separate results for individual half hours and by days of the week.

The following results are based on reports delivered by SRI to CONTAM in April 1987 for Prime Time and in May 1986 for Weekday Daytime. The Homes Using Television standard (HUT) is the measure SRI calls HUT III, which is based on two dialing attempts of 8 + rings as well as follow calls on nonanswers to ascertain TV ownership.

*Prime-Time Comparison—HUT Levels.*   Peoplemeter (PM) and NTI levels are significantly above the yardstick SRI/CONTAM figure of 59.1.

| | | Difference | |
| --- | --- | --- | --- |
| *SRI/CONTAM* | *HUT* | *Actual* | *Relative* |
| SRI/CONTAM | 59.1 | — | — |
| PM | 62.5 | +3.4 | +5.1% |
| NTI | 63.2 | +4.1 | +6.9% |

The greatest differences occur between 9:00 and 9:30 P.M. and on Tuesday night. In both cases they are about 7 percentage points.

*Viewers per Tuned Household (VPTH).*   Comparisons of the number of viewers 2 + per household shows a complete reverse from HUT levels. Here we find:

| | | Difference | |
| --- | --- | --- | --- |
| | | *Actual* | *Relative* |
| SRI/CONTAM | 1.94 | — | — |
| PM | 1.80 | −.14 | −7.8% |
| NAC | 1.76 | −.18 | −9.3% |

Both differences are significant at the 95 percent confidence level. However, individual day or half-hour differences are generally not significant.

In the case of the SRI/PM comparison, the differences are accounted for by four demographic categories: male and female 18–34, teens 12–17, and children 6–11. Minimal differences occur in the five other categories.

In the SRI/NAC comparison the same four categories plus children 2–6 are the laggards behind the yardstick.

### Estimates of Total Viewers

Because television advertisers are basically interested in audience numbers to determine reach, frequency, and CPMs, perhaps the most meaningful figures from a practical standpoint are estimates of the numerical number of viewers (a product of HUT × VPTH × number of TV Households). SRI shows these comparisons of estimated viewers (including the combination of NTI and peoplemeter whenever the latter replaces NAC diaries for demographic data). A figure of 100,000 viewers is assumed to be reported by SRI/CONTAM, which then becomes an index of 100.

|              | *Viewers* | *Index* |
|--------------|-----------|---------|
| SRI/CONTAM   | 100,000   | 100     |
| Peoplemeters | 98,300    | 86      |
| NTI/NAC      | 97,200    | 83      |
| NTI/PM       | 99,900    | 88      |

A tabulation of the 10 demographic categories (including total persons 2 + ) to determine which of the above three are best or worst relative to our SRI standard shows:

|             | *Best* | *Worst* |
|-------------|--------|---------|
| Peoplemeter | 3      | 3       |
| NTI/NAC     | 3      | 5       |
| NTI/PM      | 4      | 2       |

In many instances the margin of superiority is close indeed. The consistent tendency is for children, young teens, and adults (18–34) to be underreported, indicating a lack of cooperation on their part with both diaries and peoplemeters.

A second survey of program shares for selected prime time periods was also conducted simultaneously. Its HUT levels and demographic viewer data showed close correspondence to those achieved in the basic usage studies—a comforting corroboration of the standard.

## Daytime Survey

The SRI/CONTAM Daytime Survey was conducted in May 1986, covering Monday–Friday 10:00 A.M.–4:30 P.M.

### HUT Level Comparison

Using SRI/CONTAM as the base, the overall comparison showed NTI 10 percent above, while the peoplemeter panel was 4 percent below that standard.

|             | *HUT* *10–4:30* | *Difference* | |
|-------------|-----------------|--------------|-------------|
|             |                 | *Actual*     | *Relative*  |
| SRI/CONTAM  | 24.1            | —            | —           |
| NTI         | 26.6            | + 2.5        | + 10.4%     |
| Peoplemeter | 23.2            | − 1.0        | − 4.0%      |

Individual half-hour figures show these differences to be reasonably consistent with a few exceptions here and there.

### Viewers per Tuned Household (VPTH)

The number of average daytime VPTHs produced by NAC exactly matched the SRI/CONTAM level, whereas Nielsen peoplemeters showed a significantly lower level.

| | VPTH | Difference | |
| | | Actual | Relative |
| --- | --- | --- | --- |
| SRI/CONTAM | 1.30 | — | — |
| NAC | 1.30 | .0 | .0 |
| PM | 1.22 | −0.9* | −6.9* |

*Based on reported SRI/CONTAM figure of 1.31.

The .09 difference is significant at the 95 percent confidence level. In four demographic categories (especially children and teens) PM shows the widest spreads; in three categories NAC and PM are tied. NAC's most overstated numbers appear among women 35–49 and 50+.

### Projected Viewers, Persons 2+

Here we find the combination of slightly lower HUTs and significantly lower VPTHs for peoplemeter create sharp differences.

| | Viewers 2+ (000) | Difference | |
| | | Actual | Relative |
| --- | --- | --- | --- |
| SRI/CONTAM | 27,100 | — | — |
| NTI/NAC | 29,700 | +2,600 | + 9.6 |
| Peoplemeter | 24,300 | −2,800 | − 10.3 |
| NTI/PM | 27,000 | − 100 | − 0.4 |

The peoplemeter weakness is most pronounced among children and teens. Women 18+ are the principal daytime target category, and the comparison for this key viewer group is:

| | Viewers (000) | Difference | |
| | | Actual | Relative |
| --- | --- | --- | --- |
| SRI/CONTAM | 14,490 | — | — |
| NTI/NAC | 16,910 | +2,420 | +16.7% |
| Peoplemeter | 13,750 | − 740 | − 5.7% |
| NTI/PM | 15,760 | +1,270 | + 8.4 |

The peoplemeter short count is whittled in half for women viewers. Nevertheless, the difference it produces relative to current NTI/NAC estimates is substantial (3,160,000 women viewers, or 18.7 percent). Peoplemeter employment will undoubtedly create sales pain for television broadcasters.

## Summary of SRI/CONTAM Results

It is a difficult task to crystallize the findings of the SRI/CONTAM studies. In attempting to do so, it must be kept in mind that they do not cover all time periods—early morning (pre-10:00 A.M.), early fringe (5:00-8:00 P.M.), late night (after 10:00 P.M.), Saturday and Sunday were not surveyed. Another limitation is the size of the Nielsen peoplemeter sample panel (about 650 when the daytime survey was fielded; around 1000 when the prime-time survey was conducted). We also have seen little at the program rating level by which to judge peoplemeters. Sample size limitations have precluded any publishable data on cable viewing levels from Nielsen peoplemeters.

Accepting the SRI/CONTAM coincidental as the best measure of reality, the principal conclusions relative to NTI/NAC and Nielsen peoplemeters are that:

* In prime time the peoplemeter seems to be marginally better.
* In daytime the peoplemeter's 7 percent deficiency in viewers per tuned household and 4 percent deficiency in HUT levels create serious questions about how conscientiously the push buttons are used by children and teens. Nevertheless, even narrowing the daytime comparison to women 18+ produces a 6 percent undercount.
* NTI/NAC is from 7 to 10 percent high on most measures (the exception being daytime VPTH, where it matches the standard).
* For those who believe "two wrongs can make a right," the use of the NTI/PM conformed combination (with PMs supplying lower demographic figures than NAC diaries) brings the best estimates of total viewers in both prime time and daytime.

## Other Comparative Results

At the 1987 Advertising Research Foundation Annual Conference, John A. Dimling, Senior Vice President, Nielsen Media Research, presented these comparisons of peoplemeter and NTI/NAC results:

* In prime time, the number of women watching television is slightly lower—about 4 percent—in the peoplemeter. Men are about the same—although if January data had been included, men would be slightly higher on the Nielsen peoplemeter. Children and teen numbers are generally higher —10 to 15 percent.
* For late-night television, the adult numbers are generally higher in the peoplemeter—up to 15 percent higher—with children and teens substantially higher—but they are not of interest to advertisers in late night.

• Saturday morning is the day part in which the difference between people-meter and NTI for a key demographic group is most pronounced—the people-meter puts the figure for the child audience about 12 percent lower than NTI.
• One of the networks reports that the differences between NTI and Nielsen peoplemeter HUT are statistically significant at the 95% confidence level for both prime time and daytime.

## Peoplemeter Future

With the commercial introduction of peoplemeters, the industry is witnessing in 1987 the most startling change in television audience measurement to take place in over three decades. No one can fully foresee the consequences of this radical change. The jury is still out on whether or not these new push-button devices will in the long run prove superior to the old system. Not only relative accuracy levels, but such questions as participant conditioning and rapidity of panel turn-over with possibly resulting biases can only be answered over time.

The commitment of all industry elements has come so quickly and been based on such limited validation that many ratings users will accept the new services with skepticism. The SRI/CONTAM studies reveal serious undercounts in peo-plemeter results for young viewers (under 18). Strong efforts to correct this situation are in order. More extensive research is required to guide improvement in the new methodology.

The entry of ScanAmerica and Nielsen's serious experimentation in single source measurement could eventually result in whole new strategies for using the television medium. Interest in more passive devices such as that introduced by R. D. Percy could foster further technological advances. Nielsen in mid-1987 displayed serious interest in single-source measurement by acquiring National Product Diary and attempting (but unsuccessfully) to merge with Information Resources. A single-source service in three major test markets was announced for Fall 1988. All one can say now is that come 1990 we expect the television medium to look and be evaluated in ways far different than we have known to date.

## Definition of Households Using Televison (HUT)

The bedrock base for most rating measuring is Households Using Television (and its corollary, Persons Using Television, or PUT). When TV games first appeared in the 1970s the Broadcast Rating Council (now EMRC) developed an industry consensus that excluded from HUT computations TV usage for games, security services, and VCR or videodisc usage other than time shift of home-recorded broadcast programs.

A similar consensus must now be developed to deal with those new services that may emerge in the immediate future, especially the two-way and other interactive possibilities such as home shopping or home banking. Provided that our preceding analysis of the new technologies holds up, we will find this a relatively simple task. If videotex develops primarily around the home computer linked to a telephone line, we see that this is clearly not television as we have known it but an entirely new information system. The use of the television tube for pictures or graphics would not change that situation. It would not be included in the Households Using Television universe. Two-way systems, by their nature, can accumulate audience usage data. Teletext, using vertical blanking intervals of broadcast signals and the home screen for display, poses the most prickly problem of definition as well as measurement.

## One-Way Cable Audience Measurement

Meanwhile, the rating services struggle to make the diary a better measurement instrument, especially for cable viewing. Its serious understatement of viewership of cable-originated programs makes TV household diary results largely unacceptable at this time. Both Arbitron and Nielsen are trying to devise diary improvements that will meet the problem. No significant success has yet been reported, and there are skeptics about future progress.

Several major hurdles must be faced. The cable networks lack an established identity comparable to network affiliates, and they lack the structured schedules and audience appeal of national broadcast networks. More effective promotion and higher rated cable programs will overcome much of the problem (as they have for independent TV stations in recent years), but that takes time. More serious is the manner in which people tend to watch cable programs. The technology that is making the biggest audience impact is not orbiting satellites or two-way shopping services but the hand-held remote control device.

Once set control moves from the face of the set to the separate control panel or keypad, the viewer has a newfound switching convenience at his or her fingertips. Added to the new program options presented by cable, the viewer can now quickly skip from channel to channel. When commercials or dull spots appear, the viewer goes to CNN for news or MTV for a few musical minutes, or ESPN for sports results. Movie and sports buffs have learned how to watch two features at once by agile and shrewd switching back and forth. Such viewing behavior, especially associated with younger audience elements, may make for less accurate diary keeping. It makes advertisers nervous because diary entries are made in a set diary, which may not be handy at the armchair where the tuner is manipulated. And even if it were, the erratic tuning would be difficult to record.

Perhaps the people meter will handle this problem better than the diary. Its usage in other countries has not presented the multichannel scope of U.S. cable homes. The 1984–1985 tests should clarify this. On the other hand, meters are expensive and unlikely to be viable in most markets. The economy, efficiency, and flexibility of the diary is hard to match, so we can expect determined efforts to devise one that works moderately well for cable program audience measurement without adversely affecting the accuracy of broadcast audience numbers.

## VCR Audience Measurement

While cable has been in the forefront of measurement problems, the usage of VCRs, the other new and rapidly growing service, has had minimal attention. There are several reasons: limited VCR use compared to cable, and apparent acceptance by industry users of the protocol that a broadcast program recorded by VCR is a program viewed. Since present-day meters cannot register VCR playback use, the initial off-the-air clocking is the only record made. Diary treatment is similar and has advantages and disadvantages. It is simple and forecloses many problems involved in measuring replay. It automatically excludes any credit for playing purchased, rented, or borrowed prerecorded material, in keeping with the accepted convention relative to nonbroadcast use of the TV set.[21]

VCR time shifting tremendously complicates measurement by unhinging the program from the broadcast time period (which in the past was the only time it could be seen). Now TV has something similar to magazines' pass-along audience (and those who have struggled in that area know how confounding that has been). The author in 1977 asked such questions as:[22]

- What kind of audience composition is credited to a program recorded when no one is at home?
- What credit should be given when replays occur weeks later?
- What about two replays? Three?
- Should PUTs have different rules than HUTs?

Because VCR growth lagged behind cable, little serious attention has been given these questions. With video cassette sales burgeoning during the rest of the 1980s, with VCR penetration passing that of cable by 1990, and with time-shift usage increasing because of smaller, simpler machines, the industry, especially advertisers and agencies, willl demand answers.

VCRs are a new and novel threat to the established order, so all industry elements are treating them gingerly. Is it good or bad that some users edit out commercials when tapes are recorded? One advertiser opinion abhors such editing while another considers it the ultimate in thorough commercial exposure (compared to that of the average uninvolved viewer). More threatening to commercial exposure is the VCR's fast-forward button, which enables the viewer to zip through commercials at five times the normal rate (in some cases with the screen going to black in the process). Recording and reporting such behavior is a challenge to both meters and diaries.


## STV, SMATV, MDS, MMDS, and DBS

These services have several common characteristics affecting viewer usage and measurement:

- They use directional (line-of-sight) broadcast signals (except for STV, which uses standard TV broadcast signals).
- They use coded or scrambled signals to limit programs to subscribers.
- They are pay services requiring monthly subscription (plus pay per view in some cases).
- They are readily adaptable to present-day measurement techniques (including meters and diaries).

These services will flourish only as either auxiliary to cable or as a substitute for cable. Subscription television (STV) and MDS, which supply only a single additional channel, will gradually lose out. Satellite Master Antenna Television (SMATV) will compete more directly with cable. Multichannel Multipoint Distribution Service (MMDS) and Direct Broadcast Satellites (DBS) will offer from five to eight channels to supplement normal broadcast stations. MMDS could substitute for cable in urban areas, while DBS is more likely to grow in sparsely settled, uncabled sections but could also be a factor in uncabled cities.

None of these services pose any more difficult problems than cable audience measurement. The problems may be far smaller because of the limited number of channels and the likelihood that programming schedules would be more structured and more widely promoted than cable. A February–March 1987 national survey indicated that in combination they accounted for 3 percent of all U.S. television households.[23]

## Two-Way (Interactive) Cable

True two-way cable has so many possible permutations that its measurement must be looked at on two levels: (1) its effect on HUT and (2) service usage. Where cable presents home shopping, banking, education for credit, security services, and access to data banks through home terminals or computers, these represent nontelevision uses such as the video games and purchased tapes or discs, which are excluded from Households Using Television (HUT). Further-more, these uses: (1) are not uses in which advertising is likely to be placed (other than for the specific store or bank involved), and (2) can be specifically measured by the two-way technology for the benefit of the individual users. The effect on and participation by rating services would therefore be negligible. The industry might want a gross measure of time devoted to such interactive viewing, but that can be ascertained fairly readily from computer records.

## Teletext

Measuring broadcast teletext (using vertical blanking intervals) will require spe-cial elements in present-day meters. These elements could produce time devoted to teletext without reference to the pages accessed. Special meters capable of measuring page exposure have been developed for use in limited experiments, but they are quite expensive.

In teletext via telephone line or cable connection, the time measurement becomes slightly simpler, but page exposure can still be difficult. In the case of any of the three possible delivery systems, diary measurement of time spent may be possible, but may require special diaries for page measurement. Such meas-urements are not expected to develop in this decade, because home and advertiser acceptance of teletext is due for slow growth.

## Videotex and Home Computers

The two-way form of "electronic publishing" with data bank accessibility should not be too difficult to measure in terms of hours of usage with either meters or diaries. Specific data accessed could perhaps be measured at the computer on a total basis, thus precluding need for any sample survey data. This is especially pertinent if there is industry consensus in exclusion of videotex usage from HUT.

Home computer usage of TV terminals for display and of two-way cable links for data access or down-loading software are additional examples of services and usages not directly relevant to broadcast advertising measurement procedures.

## Two Roles of Home Electronic Service

As technology brings the TV set into closer companionship with the home computer or the computerized data bank, it seems most important that, as far as possible, a clear distinction be made between the two roles then assumed.

One is the original passive role of the viewer as an element in a mass audience for entertainment and information; the other as an active participant in two-way interaction—whether requesting data, banking, shopping, or utilizing a home computer keyboard as a means of communicating outside the home. It seems likely, however, that homes will tie the personal computer to the interactive telephone link and use its display monitor for informational purposes. The computer-information system will be in a room where homework, home banking, investment and budget calculations, household ordering, etc. will take place. This information unit will be separate from the home entertainment center built around the television receiver with its ancillary cable and VCR connections.

## Qualitative Ratings

To meet the demand of product use and target customer data (discussed in Chapter 4), Simmons Market Research Bureau and Media Mark Research have increased the data and analyses that provide media planners with product and brand usage for network and syndicated TV programs. More widespread use of these services may be expected. Geodemographic evaluations possible from services such as PRIZM and Donnelley Cluster Plus will also be more frequently used. On the other hand, the demise of Quantiplex and Nielsen's Product Audience Report and Television Audience Assessment demonstrate industry reluctance to find syndicated surveys in this area.

Syndicated qualitative research relative to viewer reaction to programs now again consists solely of the long-term industry standard—the TVQ service. It has enriched its "liking score" output with further refinements and has widely extended its scope. Qualitative measures of viewer reactions apparently are deemed either not appropriate to the specific advertising programs they encounter or not cost effective. Television Audience Assessment had more going for it than any previous effort. With its failure in 1986, the future for such syndicated qualitative ratings looks grim.

## The Industry's Assessment of Needs

A Needs Definition Conference, sponsored by the Electronic Media Rating Council, was held in January 1984. Executives representing broadcasters, cable companies, advertisers, agencies, and audience measurement services participated. The summary report of the conference and a follow-up survey[23] revealed the principal future needs as follows:

1. Expanded measurement of individual viewing (people ratings), finer demographic breaks—cable, income, geographic, life-style.

2. Increases in sample size to strengthen reliability of subsamples involved in (1).
3. Development of ratings for commercial exposure and commercial impact.
4. Expanded television ratings to provide total TV set use, out-of-home viewing, VCR recording and playback, remote-control use, continuous ratings (not just quarter-hour units).
5. Development of direct line access to raw ratings data to enable users to create customized ratings analyses (longer term need).

There were, of course, significant differences in the priorities assigned by the diverse interest groups involved (e.g., measuring commercial exposure and commercial impact was of high value to advertisers and agencies, whereas flexible geographic divisions was important to cable and broadcaster participants). The EMRC scheduled follow-up conferences with more technical industry groups in an effort to focus research attention to the consensus results of the January conference. These showed that the greatest interest lies in the potential of peoplemeters and the need for measuring exposure to commercials on a household and individual basis.

## VIII. SUMMARY

In the foregoing overview of where mass electronic media are headed during the remainder of the 1980s and the possible effects of audience measurement practices and methodologies, many problems have been identified. Nevertheless, the almost frightening array of possibilities becomes manageable when the services are grouped by viewer benefits rather than by electronic technologies. Broadcasting and cable have had their primary success as entertainment media, secondarily as purveyors of information (principally news and news-related features). Audiences have been relatively passive recipients, limited in immediate response to on–off switching and dial twisting/button punching.

Two-way services, whether by cable or telephone line, are generally information oriented. This means that small, special audiences can be counted by the system's computer. This separate feedback audience should not be included in the normal households or persons television figures. Excluding these nonadvertising, nonentertainment elements along with current exclusions (video games, purchased/rented video cassettes, electronic home movies, and videodiscs) will keep the measurement of conventional television on the yardstick the industry knows and expects. Trends and year-to-year comparisons would consequently be preserved.

For audience measurement purposes, most major problems have been anticipated. The primary concerns have already arrived: how to cope with measuring cable (except by meters) and VCR time-shift usage. Concomitant with those questions are the measurement implications of frequent remote-control switching and consequent avoidance of commercials (known as zapping), especially among cable subscribers, and the fast-forwarding or editing out of commercials in VCR households.

Can diary weaknesses be overcome by peoplemeters? This question can only be answered when currently planned national services produce actual results in the 1987–1988 broadcast season. Even this test alone cannot answer questions about conditioning and panel wearout with peoplemeters. Additional time will be required. Even a positive answer would leave much of the nation without the benefit of the meter solution, so local TV ratings services have to press forward in quest of improved diary accuracy relative to cable originations. We can expect a serious search for viable means to achieve passive measurement systems to replace or supplement push-button peoplemeters.

Over the years the methods and the accuracy of ratings systems have frequently been challenged. However, the integrity, objectivity, and fairness of the people delivering the audience numbers have rarely been questioned. This is the legacy of Crossley, Hooper, Nielsen, Roslow, and Seiler. These pioneers set ethical and professional standards that have been carried on by their successors. May we see the imprint of their principles on those services that may emerge to measure electronic media audiences in the future.

## NOTES

1. Few people were as successful as David Sarnoff not only in foreseeing the future but in making it happen. Some examples are his 1915 vision of mass radio audiences receiving music, news events, and sports results over a "Radio Music Box," his founding of NBC to provide quality radio service, his foresight in 1929 in backing Vladimir Zworykin to successfully pursue electronic television, his determination to launch commercial television at the New York World's Fair in 1939, and his indefatigable pioneering and $200 million commitment to compatible electronic color (now used in 90 percent of U.S. households) in the face of vicious competitive attacks.
2. "IRTS Brings Big Names Together," *Broadcasting,* February 6, 1984, p. 52, a report on the twelfth annual faculty/industry and college conference of the International Radio and Television Society.
3. "Enhancement—Next TV Set Revolution," *Television Digest,* March 19, 1984, p. 11.
4. Sandra Salmans, "Cable Operators Take a Bruising," *The New York Times,* March 4, 1984, Section 3, p. 1.
5. "TCI Buys Pittsburgh System," *Television Digest,* March 26, 1984, p. 6.

6. The implication that there is any cable service but pay cable will disappear along with that artificial distinction.

7. Cabletelevision Advertising Bureau, New York.

8. Hugh M. Beville, Jr., "VCR Penetration: Will It Surpass Cable by 1990?" *Television/Radio Age*, July 9, 1984, p. 27.

9. Ibid., p. 110.

10. *Advertising Age* (April 9, 1984) characterized the RCA move as "a hammerblow" to the entire videodisc market.

11. Jill McNiece, "Cable Ops Place Bets on Multichannel MDS," *Multichannel News*, December 12, 1983, p. 40.

12. Watson S. (Jay) James, "The New Electronic Media: An Overview," *Journal of Advertising Research*, August/September 1983.

13. Bernie Whalen, "Cable's Home Pentration Rate Keeps Rising, But New Competitors Could Fragment Market," *Marketing News*, November 25, 1983.

14. "Group W Schedules Trial for Teletext," *Advertising Age*, July 9, 1984, p. 3.

15. "The International Telecommunications Union has agreed that the word *videotex* should be used for electronic systems that use a modified television set to display computer-based information." David H. Weaver, *Videotex Journalism* (Hillsdale, N.J.: Lawrence Erlbaum Associates 1983), p. 5.

16. Udayan Gupta, "COMP-U-CARD Has Head Start in Electronic Merchandising," *Electronic Media*, March 21, 1984, p. 13.

17. "The Name of the Game," *Broadcasting*, February 13, 1984, p. 67.

18. "The Wired World of Anthony Oettinger," *Harvard Magazine*, May–June, 1982, p. 36.

19. Arthur C. Nielsen Jr., in an address to the World Congress of International Advertising Associations, Rio de Janeiro, Brazil, May 21, 1982.

20. Dimling, John A., Senior Vice President, Nielsen Media Research, "Managing the Transition to People Meters: Dealing with Change." Address to the ARF 33rd Annual Conference, New York Hilton, March 4, 1987.

21. ". . . only cable originations . . . should be included in broadcast ratings and HUT levels . . . home usage of video games, electronic cameras, purchased discs and tapes should not be included. Of course these uses may warrant measurement, possibly by ratings services. . . . But my concern is to make sure . . . that nontelevision activities will not become an element in HUT and affect station shares." Hugh M. Beville Jr., executive director, Broadcast Rating Council, in *How Will Home Cassette Players Affect Ratings?* Radio and Television Research Council, November 14, 1977, p. 7.

22. Ibid., p. 16.

23. *Electronic Media Ratings—The Next Ten Years,* Summary Report on the Electronic Media Ratings Council Needs Definition Conference, New York, May 1984.
24. Statistic Research Inc. Memorandum dated April 15, 1987 to sponsors of CONTAM Television Ownership Survey, February–March 1987.

# Appendix A
# Ratings Basics:
# Terms, Calculations, and
# Relationships

This appendix is provided for those who are unfamiliar with basic ratings terminology and arithmetic. Remember that ratings come from sample surveys and that *all ratings are estimates*.

## I.  WHAT ARE RATINGS?

Expressed in Television Terms:[1]

1. A *rating* is the estimated percent of all television households, or of all people within a demographic group, in the survey area sample who view a specific program or station.

$$\text{Rating } (\%) = \frac{\text{Households, viewers, or listeners}}{\text{Sample universe total}}$$

2. *HUT* (Households Using Television) is the percent of all television households in the area surveyed with one or more sets in use. It is the sum of all program ratings for each time period.[2]

3. *Share* is the percent of Households Using Television (HUT) tuned to a particular program or station for a specific time period.

---

[1]TV examples are used for simplicity. Radio ratings' nomenclature and definitions are similar except that they are based on measurement of people listening—the household base is not employed in radio except for sampling purposes.

[2]This assumes a household is viewing only one program. Where two or more programs are viewed simultaneously on multiple sets, the sum of ratings will exceed HUT because the household is only tallied once. In such cases, the sum of shares for the period exceeds 100 percent.

If you know any two of these figures, you can derive the third. It's conventional to ignore all percent/decimal references, although these are implied. Let's assume a rating of 18 and a HUT of 60 and work an example:

$$\text{Share} = \frac{\text{Rating}}{\text{HUT}} \qquad (\frac{18}{60} = 30)$$

$$\text{Rating} = \text{Share} \times \text{HUT} \quad (30 \times 60 = 18)$$

$$\text{HUT} = \frac{\text{Rating}}{\text{Share}} \qquad (\frac{18}{30} = 60)$$

## II. DEMOGRAPHICS—PEOPLE RATINGS

Similar computations are applied to obtain People Using Television (PUT) and Persons Using Radio (PUR) ratings, with people universe[3] data as the base used.

Whereas household ratings are the basic foundation of much of television audience measurement, the importance of demographics has grown. Radio does not use household ratings at all. Ratings for 15 to 20 age/sex categories are customarily provided, and much product targeting is keyed to these data. Any of the dimensions described in this appendix can be calculated for such categories as men aged 18–34 or women aged 50 and over.

## III. RATINGS PROJECTIONS

As percentages, ratings have limited utility. They can provide program and time period comparisons, but a more important need is a translation into estimated *numbers* of viewers or listeners.

Multiplying the base number of TV households (the population) by the rating yields the number of "households delivered." The January 1984 national population is estimated at 83,800,000 U.S. television households. A program with a 20 NTI rating reaches 20 percent of these, or 16,700,000 households. Similarly, projections of individual market and demographic estimates can be made by using appropriate universe data.

## IV. DEFINITIONS OF AUDIENCE; TYPES OF RATINGS; SHARE OF AUDIENCE

The rating during the average minute of programming is called the average audience. Meter-generated and coincidental telephone survey ratings are reported as average audience ratings. (The meter's continuous household record, however, makes it possible to develop many other types of ratings; the coincidental does not.) This is the most widely used measure in national network activities.

---

[3]The terms "universe" and "population" are interchangeable. Both refer to the total number of units to which the rating will be applied to develop audience members (households, total adults, 18 and over, total working women, etc.)

## Total Audience

The number of households that tune, view, or listen to a program for five (or six) minutes or more during its duration. This measure is used primarily to report audiences for long-form or multiepisode programs. It is useful for advertisers only in the case of the rare exclusive-sponsor event.

## Average Quarter Hour

This is primarily a product of diary surveys, where tabulations are produced on a quarter-hour basis with five minutes as the mininum recorded receiving or listening required for qualification in a given quarter hour. Diaries are ruled to permit respondents to report on a quarter-hour basis, so quarter hours become the basic unit of audience, in contrast to minutes in the case of meters and telephone coincidentals. The average quarter-hour figure for a day part or station or program package is thus the basis for local TV and radio evaluations. The equation for calculating the average quarter-hour rating for demographic groups is:

$$\text{Average quarter hour rating } (\%) = \frac{\text{Average quarter hour persons}}{\text{Population estimate}}$$

## Share of Audience

Share uses the total HUT or PUT for a specific time period (quarter or half hour, day part, or week) as the 100 percent base and shows the ratio (percentage) of that audience going to each contributing program or station:

Share is a relatively stable figure, not highly subject to seasonal, weather, or other factors that influence ratings. Therefore, share is a good measure of program trends and provides a rough comparison of program popularity of shows in different time periods.

Even though share is the best quantitative measure of popularity provided by ratings surveys, it does not measure inherent program strength because each program operates in a different competitive climate. To eliminate such variables, additional (nonrating) research is needed. In radio, station share figures are generally used for overall comparative purposes. Television ratings are often quoted in trade journals with share also shown; thus "Hill Street Blues" 15.7/26 means a rating of 15.7 and a share of 26 percent of all viewing homes between 10 and 11 P.M. Thursday, the time of broadcast.

## Gross Rating Points (GRPs)

GRPs represent the sum of all rating points achieved (or sought) in a given market area for a particular time span. But most advertisers want more detail. GRPs tell nothing about the number of different people (or households) exposed (reach) or how many times each of these people is exposed (frequency). A schedule delivering 30,000 projected gross impressions could be reaching 30,000 people one time each or 10,000 different people three times each. This leads to cumulative ratings, the basis for reach and frequency analysis.

## Cumulative (Cume) Ratings; Reach and Frequency

Cumulative ratings report the number of different households or persons who tune to a particular program or station or combination of either over a specified time period. Cume ratings provide measures of net unduplicated audience for various combinations: daily and weekly for programs and stations, weekly and four weekly for commercial exposure on several stations, etc. To obtain cume ratings, the viewing or listening records (meter or diary) are examined, and any duplication is eliminated to produce a net rating figure of one or more exposures. The following diagram illustrates this principle:

An advertiser buys a 30-second commercial on four different programs, each on a different station, with these rating results:

The advertiser has purchased 32 gross rating points. However, he needs to know the unduplicated reach, that is, the net audience reached one or more times. Rating analysis, by successfully eliminating duplication of Program B, C, and D viewers who have watched Program A, produces the unduplicated (or cume) audience of 20, shown as follows:

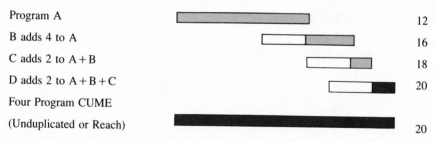

Since all duplication has been eliminated by this analysis we have a net reach (cume) figure from which to compute average frequency of exposure:

$$\text{Frequency} = \frac{\text{GRP}}{\text{Cume}} = \frac{32}{20} = 1.6$$

The average viewer has been exposed to 1.6 of the advertiser's commercials.

In radio, cume concepts have greater significance than they do in television. Cume combinations of different stations with diverse program formats make significant contributions to advertisers' radio reach. Radio cumes estimated by random duplication formulae have proven acceptable for estimating purposes.

## V.  COST TERMS AND RELATIONSHIPS

### Gross Impressions (GIs)

This is the counterpart of gross rating points in audience terms. Total gross impressions for an advertiser's schedule is the sum of the average audience (households or persons) for all commercial placements.

### Cost per Thousand (CPM)

The cost of delivering 1000 gross impressions.

$$CPM = \frac{\text{Cost of schedule}}{GI} \times 1000$$

This can apply to any demographic category as well as households.

### Cost per Rating Point (CPP)

The cost of each rating point for a specific schedule.

$$CPP = \frac{\text{Cost of Schedule}}{\text{GRPs}} \quad \text{or} \quad \frac{\text{Cost per Spot}}{\text{Average Rating}}$$

## VI.  OTHER FREQUENTLY USED MEASURES

### Time Spent Viewing (Listening)

An estimate of the amount of time the average person (household) spends viewing or listening during a specified time period.

$$\text{Average time spent viewing (listening) per person or household} = \frac{\text{Average audience}}{\text{Cumulative (unduplicated) audience}}$$

### Turnover Factor

The ratio of a cumulative audience over several periods of time (e.g., four weeks) to the average audience per period of time (e.g., per week). Turnover indicates the relative frequency with which a program's or station's audience changes over time. The higher the ratio, the greater the turnover.

### Audience Flow Analysis

In program schedule building, the size and nature of the audience to the preceding program (as well as competitive factors) is crucial to the rating success of each individual program. Various types of demographic rating analyses can show where different audience segments are in the period preceding the potential placement position. The objective is to hold the *lead-in* audience and build on it by drawing from competing stations or networks at the time break.

## SOURCES

*A Pocket Full of Information*, Arbitron Television, New York, April 1980.

*Standard Definitions of Broadcast Research Terms*, by Dr. Gerald J. Glasser, National Association of Broadcasters, Washington, D.C., 1970. This is the authority, covering 200 terms and concepts.

*Terms to Keep You on the Right Road*, Arbitron Radio, New York, November 1981.

*Understanding Broadcast Ratings*, Broadcast (now Electronic Media) Rating Council, New York, 1981.

Poltrack, David F. *Television Marketing: Network/Local/Cable*. New York: McGraw-Hill, 1983. Excellent treatment of basic ratings arithmetic appears in Chapter 2.

# Appendix B
# Offices and Services of Principal Syndicated Ratings Companies Operating on a National Basis

**AGB Television Research**
New York:
  540 Madison Avenue
  New York, NY 10022
**Services**
  National television audience measurement service utilizing peoplemeter technology. Provides many services. Data available 365 days a year. Reports contain comprehensive demographic data.
*Broadcast Network Reports*
  Network overnight ratings available on-line. Printed network weekly and monthly reports. Printed weekly, monthly, and quarterly trend reports.
*Cable Reports*
  Cable overnight ratings available on-line. Printed syndicated and customized cable reports.
*National Syndication Reports*
  Weekly on-line transmittal reports for subscribing syndicators. Printed weekly and monthly reports.
  Special customized analyses over any extended period of time relating to cumulative audiences, program loyalty, reach and frequency, audience flow, VCR playback, etc.

**Arbitron Ratings Company** (A Control Data Company)
  New York:
  Metropolitan Towers
  142 West 57th Street
  New York, NY 10019
*Regional Offices:*
Chicago:
  1807 Tribune Tower
  Chicago, IL 60611
Atlanta:
  300 Embassy Row
  Atlanta, GA 30328
Los Angeles:
  5670 Wilshire Boulevard
  Los Angeles, CA 90036
San Francisco:
  One Maritime Plaza
  San Francisco, CA 94111
Dallas:
  14801 Quorum Drive
  Dallas, TX 75240

Washington:
   The Arbitron Building
   Laurel, MD 20707
ScanAmerica:
   541 North Fairbanks Court
   Chicago, IL 60611

### Television Services

*Arbitron Television Market Reports* (accredited by Electronic Media Rating Council). Four-week diary reports, four sweeps annually plus additional months in selected top markets.

*Peoplemeter Services.* ScanAmerica, a syndicated research service currently in operation in Denver, uses a peoplemeter to electronically track television viewing of individuals and a portable UPC scanner to record product purchases by the household, the basis for single-source measurement.

*Meter Services* (accredited by Electronic Media Rating Council). Meters furnish daily and weekly household audience estimates in thirteen major markets. The *Television Market Reports* for these markets provide demographics based on integrated meter and diary data seven times a year.

*Computer Tapes.* A variety of detailed current, analytical, and trend data is available to subscribers on specialized computer tapes.

*Arbitron Information on Demand* (AID). A computerized data base enables clients to develop audience estimates on customized day parts, program packages, demographics, survey areas, etc. Target Aid provides viewing data by life-style and product usage by employing Donnelley Cluster Plus geodemographic segmentation and Simmons Market Research Bureau product and brand usage data.

*TV Maximi$er.* A comprehensive software research and analysis package for television stations using Arbitron Television estimates to create custom presentations.

*County Coverage Reports.* Provide station circulation, cable penetration, and fringe area details.

*Commercial Monitoring.* BAR (Broadcast Advertiser Reports), a commercial monitoring service, provides reports of competitive expenditure information and syndicated monitoring of network and spot broadcast advertising for television, radio, and cable networks.

### Radio Services

*Arbitron Radio Market Reports* (accredited by Electronic Media Rating Council). Each report provides person listening estimates for the average of 12 weeks interviewing. Over 250 markets are covered up to four times a year, principally once (spring) or twice (spring and fall).

*Arbitrends.* Delivers to a client's microcomputer rolling averages for three recent survey months or for standard quarterly report. Various format options available.

*Computer Tapes, AID,* and *Target AID.* Same services available as for television.

*Arbitron Radio Nationwide Network Report.* Listening audience for interconnected and noninterconnected national networks based on Arbitron diary results, once a year.

*FasTraq.* Applications software system for radio stations based on data from the Arbitron Radio Market Reports, combining easy-to-read graphics and Arbitron ratings for a given market.

*County Coverage Reports.* Documents radio listening on county-by-county and station-by-station basis, once a year.

### Radio and Television

*Broadcast Negotiator.* A personal computer workstation for advertisers and agencies using a personal computer to eliminate hand calculations and paper work. Provides graphic displays, reports, and printouts.

**Birch Radio Inc.**
Birch Research Corporation
  12350 NW 39th Street
  Coral Springs, FL 33065
Birch Radio Research
  44 Sylvan Avenue
  Englewood Cliffs, NJ 07632
*Regional Offices:*
Atlanta:
  2110 Powers Ferry Road
  Atlanta, GA 30339
Illinois:
  5105 Tollview Drive
  Rolling Meadows, IL 60008
Dallas:
  14800 Quorum Drive
  Dallas, TX 75240
California:
  18425 Burbank Boulevard
  Tarzana, CA 91356
*Radio Services*
  Birch Radio Quarterly Summary Reports
  Birch Radio Monthly Trend Reports
  Birch Radio Qualitative/Product Usage Reports
  Birch Radio Standard Market Reports
  Birch Radio Condensed Market Reports
  Birch Radio Capsule Market Reports
  BirchPlus, a microcomputerized system of ratings retrieval and analysis through inter-
    action with data base.
  *Trend America,* a summary of six-month trends in all monthly markets.

**A. C. Nielsen** (A Dun & Bradstreet Company)
Nielsen Media Research
Nielsen Plaza
Northbrook, IL 60062
*Regional Offices:*
New York:
  1299 Avenue of the Americas
Atlanta:
  301 Perimeter Center North
  Atlanta, GA 30346
Chicago:
  410 North Michigan Avenue
  Chicago, IL 60611
Texas:
  333 West Campbell Road
  Richardson, TX 75080
Menlo Park:
  70 Willow Road
  Menlo Park, CA 94025

Los Angeles:
> 6255 Sunset Boulevard
> Los Angeles, CA 90028

San Francisco:
> 423 Washington Street
> San Francisco, CA 94111

**Nielsen Television Index** (NTI) (accredited by Electronic Media Rating Council). National rating service for television and cable networks; provides many services.

The formats include *Overnights,* which is a tabular report offering households and persons audience data; a *Grid* report, arraying audience data in a comparative network program environment for one or seven days; *Persons Share Trends,* showing current week and prior week shares; and a *Ranking Report,* giving a one-week ranking of all broadcast network programs for that week.

Overnights are offered four ways:

*Total Network Programs,* which gives statistics per program on all network programs for selected day part.

*Programs by Half-Hour, Network Only* for selected day parts.

*Programs by Half-Hour, Network Plus Other Viewing Sources* for prime-time day part.

*HUT/PUT By Half-Hour,* Households Using Television (HUT) and Persons Using Television (PUT).

Additionally, Dailies Plus offers 38 building-block demographics that clients can combine to yield over 380 target audiences for immediate analysis.

Clients can view their reports directly on their personal computer screen, print them, or enter them into DOS or DIF files. The latter enables users to input Dailies Plus data into a format usable with other software applications such as Lotus or dBase III. The overnights are also available on tape, as well as via a computer-to-computer transmission.

*Brand Cumulative Audiences* (BCA). Provides estimates of the cumulative audience and frequency of reach by individual brands, plus commercial costs and cost per thousand (CPM). Three four-week periods are reported per year.

*National Audience Demographics* (NAD). Produced eight times a year in two volumes, the series provides comprehensive demographic data, with working women and lady of the house receiving special breakouts.

*Cost per Thousand and Tracking Reports.* These cover both households and persons.

**Nielsen Station Index** (NSI) (accredited by Electronic Media Rating Council).

*Viewers in Profile* (VIP). TV market reports based on weekly diaries issued four times annually for most markets.

*Metered Market Service* (accredited by Electronic Media Rating Council). Daily and weekly reports in 11 markets by 1985. Monthly VIP reports for these reflect combination of diary and meter survey results. Numerous additional reports on syndicated and network programs and county coverage are published.

*Nielsen Product Audience Report.* Product use data for 200 categories matched with previous TV diary viewing records. Available in limited number of major markets done on an annual basis.

*Cassandra.* A computer software system that provides most frequently required data tailored to client specifications.

*NSI Plus.* Provides assess to the flexibility of special studies of target audiences, zip code characteristics, viewer tracking, flow analyses, etc.

**Home Video Index**

*Pay Cable Report.* Audiences to major pay cable services in comparison with network affiliates, independents, etc. Issued four times annually.

*Cable Network and Superstation Reports.* WTBS, CBN, HBO, CNN, USA, and ESPN are provided network-style rating reports based on their respective universes on schedules tailored to the network's needs.

**Statistical Research, Inc.**

111 Prospect Street

Westfield, NJ   07090

RADAR (Radio's All Dimension Audience Research) (accredited by Electronic Media Rating Council). Audience estimates provide national measurement of radio usage and radio network program and commercial audiences. RADAR data are presented in three volumes, twice annually. *Volume 1, Radio Usage*, provides estimated audiences of all AM and FM radio stations in total and for several segments of radio usage and of the population. *Volumes 2 and 3* provide estimates of network audiences to all commercials (including commercials within and outside of programs), and network audiences to commercials within programs (excluding commercials outside of programs), respectively. For each of these two volumes there are two parts: a report with projections for individual programs/commercials, and a report with projections and ratings for day parts.

*RADAR On-Line* (ROL). Provides instantaneous analysis of total radio usage and network audiences via computer terminals in client offices that are connected by telephone lines to SRI computers. Network audience tabulations include individual week and multiweek reach and frequency and optimization plans.

# Appendix C
# Audience Measurement
# Highlights
# U.S. Total Population

TABLE C-1
Average Time Spent per Day

|  | TV Usage[a] | Radio Usage[b] |
|---|---|---|
| All persons 21 and over | 4 hr 15 min | 2 hr 57 min |
| Men 18 and over | 3 hr 57 min | 3 hr 1 min |
| Women 18 and over | 4 hr 53 min | 3 hr 0 min |
| Teens 12 to 17 | 3 hr 29 min | 2 hr 32 min |

*Source:* (a) A. C. Nielsen, NTI. Average of November 1985, February, May, July 1986.
(b) RADAR (SRI), 1986.

TABLE C-2
Annual Trend in Time Spent Viewing per Day per Television
Household
September–August Broadcast Year

| 1959–1960 | 5 hr 4 min |
|---|---|
| 1964–1965 | 5 hr 31 min |
| 1969–1970 | 5 hr 54 min |
| 1974–1975 | 6 hr 12 min |
| 1979–1980 | 6 hr 34 min |
| 1982–1983 | 6 hr 55 min |
| 1983–1984 | 7 hr 8 min |
| 1984–1985 | 7 hr 7 min |
| 1985–1986 | 7 hr 10 min |

*Source*: A. C. Nielsen, NTI. 48-week average excluding unusual days.

TABLE C–3
Hours of TV Usage per Week by Household Characteristics
November 1986

| | | |
|---|---|---|
| *Household Size* | | |
| | 1 | 41 hr 4 min |
| | 2 | 47 hr 35 min |
| | 3 + | 61 hr 54 min |
| *Presence of Nonadults* | | |
| | Adults only | 47 hr 50 min |
| | With nonadults | 59 hr 33 min |
| *Household Income* | | |
| | Under $15,000 | 54 hr 48 min |
| | $20,000 + | 51 hr 41 min |
| | $30,000 + | 51 hr 34 min |
| | $40,000 + | 51 hr 31 min |
| *Cable Status* | | |
| | Pay subscriber | 59 hr 43 min |
| | Basic subscriber | 55 hr 25 min |
| | No cable | 47 hr 49 min |

*Source*: A. C. Nielsen, NTI.

TABLE C–4
Stations Receivable per Household (in percent of All TV Households)

| | 5 *or More* | 9 *or More* | 15 *or More* |
|---|---|---|---|
| 1964 | 59 | 8 | — |
| 1972 | 83 | 31 | — |
| 1983 | 95 | 61 | 18 |
| 1984 | 96 | 64 | 18 |
| 1985 | 96 | 68 | 21 |
| 1986 | 97 | 71 | 22 |
| 1986 Channels Receivable | 97 | 85 | 53 |

*Source*: Nielsen Report on Television

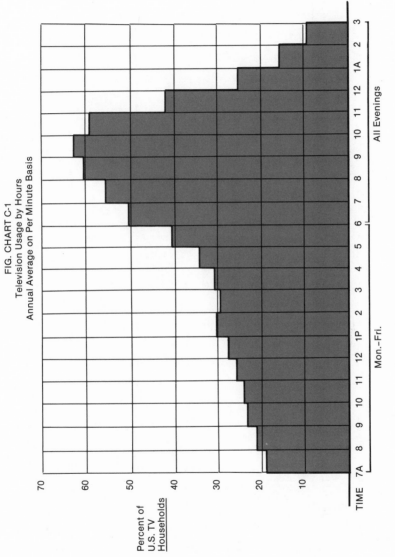

FIG. CHART C-1
Television Usage by Hours
Annual Average on Per Minute Basis

NY Time except NYT + 3 Hrs in Pacific Territory
Source: Nielsen Television Index, September 1984–August 1985

## TABLE C-5
### National versus Local Ratings: Top NTI Prime Time Programs Compared to Local Market Ratings November 1985

| National Rank and Rating | | Local Market Rank and Rating | | | | | |
|---|---|---|---|---|---|---|---|
| | | New York | Chicago | Los Angeles | Philadelphia | Detroit | San Francisco |
| 1. "Bill Cosby Show" | 31.4 | 1–31.7 | 1–33.3 | 1–31.1 | 1–34.3 | 1–36.7 | 2–31.5 |
| 2. "North and South," part 6 (s) | 29.4 | × | 6–27.4 | × | 3–30.9 | 2–36.2 | × |
| 3. "Family Ties" | 29.2 | 2–29.8 | 2–32.6 | 2–27.9 | 2–33.0 | 3–34.6 | 5–26.5 |
| 4. "North and South" part 3 (s) | 28.0 | 8–23.5 | 7–27.2 | 5–23.8 | 5–30.7 | 4–31.1 | 10–21.5 |
| 5. "Murder She Wrote" | 26.1 | 5–26.1 | × | 3–25.6 | × | × | 3–28.2 |
| 8. "60 Minutes" | 25.0 | × | × | 4–25.5 | × | × | 4–27.9 |
| 10. "Dynasty" | 22.9 | 7–24.2 | 3–27.6 | × | 7–28.8 | 8–28.6 | 6–22.6 |
| 12. "Cheers" | 22.6 | 3–27.0 | 4–27.5 | 6–23.6 | 8–27.9 | × | 7–22.3 |

× indicates program ranked below top 10 in the market.
(s) Special (not regularly scheduled)
Source: 1986 Nielsen Report on Television, p. 16.

TABLE C–6
Nielsen Television Index: Top Three Prime Time Programs,
February 1970–1986

| Year | Program | Average Audience Percent | Share |
|------|---------|--------------------------|-------|
| 1970 | "Chrysler-Bob Hope Show"(s) | 35.7 | 50 |
| | Born Free (s) | 34.2 | 53 |
| | "Ringling Brothers Circus" (s) | 31.1 | 45 |
| 1971 | Ben Hur (s) | 37.1 | 56 |
| | "Marcus Welby, M.D." | 33.6 | 60 |
| | "Movie of the Week" | 31.1 | 46 |
| 1972 | "All in the Family" | 38.3 | 59 |
| | "Flip Wilson Show" | 30.6 | 45 |
| | "Marcus Welby, M.D." | 30.3 | 53 |
| 1973 | "All in the Family" | 34.9 | 54 |
| | The Ten Commandments (s) | 33.2 | 54 |
| | "The NBC Sunday Mystery Movie" | 32.3 | 46 |
| 1974 | "All in the Family" | 34.3 | 53 |
| | "The Waltons" | 33.3 | 49 |
| | "The Autobiography of Miss Jane Pittman" (s) | 30.8 | 47 |
| 1975 | "All in the Family" | 33.2 | 54 |
| | "Sanford and Son" | 32.5 | 55 |
| | "Police Woman" | 32.2 | 57 |
| 1976 | "All in the Family" | 31.6 | 45 |
| | "Laverne and Shirley" | 31.5 | 46 |
| | "Six Million Dollar Man" (s) | 30.9 | 45 |
| 1977 | "Roots" (s) | 51.5 | 71 |
| | "Roots" (s) | 45.9 | 66 |
| | "Roots" (s) | 45.7 | 71 |
| 1978 | "CBS Sports Special Broadcast" (s) | 34.4 | 51 |
| | "Laverne and Shirley" | 34.0 | 49 |
| | "Happy Days" | 33.9 | 50 |
| 1979 | Rocky (s) | 37.1 | 53 |
| | "Mork and Mindy" | 34.0 | 51 |
| | "Three's Company" | 33.0 | 49 |
| 1980 | "Dallas" | 29.9 | 47 |
| | "Dukes of Hazzard" | 29.1 | 44 |
| | "Winter Olympics" Sat. 8:00 P.M. (s) | 28.9 | 47 |
| 1981 | "Dallas" | 33.2 | 53 |
| | "60 Minutes" | 29.5 | 44 |
| | Hooper (s) | 29.2 | 41 |
| 1982 | "60 Minutes" | 29.8 | 45 |
| | "Dallas" | 28.7 | 46 |
| | "ABC Monday Night Movie" | 26.9 | 39 |

TABLE C-6
(Continued)

| Year | Program | Average Audience Percent | Share |
|------|---------|:---:|:---:|
| 1983 | "Super Bowl XVII" (s) | 48.6 | 69 |
|      | "Winds of War," part VII (s) | 41.0 | 56 |
|      | "Winds of War," Part II (s) | 40.2 | 54 |
| 1984 | "Dallas" | 26.5 | 41 |
|      | "60 Minutes" | 26.1 | 39 |
|      | "Dynasty" | 25.4 | 38 |
| 1985 | "Bill Cosby Show" | 26.7 | 39 |
|      | "American Music Awards" (s) | 25.8 | 37 |
|      | "Dallas" | 25.5 | 39 |
| 1986 | "Bill Cosby Show" | 36.2 | 52 |
|      | "Family Ties" | 31.4 | 45 |
|      | "Cosby Show Special" (s) | 27.6 | 40 |

(s) Special (not regularly scheduled)
Does not include ratings for noncommercial programs such as Presidential candidate debates. For example, the first Reagan/Mondale debate of October 7, 1984, on all three commercial networks aggregated an average audience rating of 43.5, or 38,500,000 households per minute. A total of 50,200,000 households viewed 6 minutes or more of the broadcast.
*Source*: A. C. Nielsen, NTI

TABLE C–7
Cost per Thousand for National TV Networks
(Regularly Scheduled Programs)

| Cost per 30-Second Commercial Prime Time | Dollar Cost | CPT Households |
|------|:---:|:---:|
| Average 1985–1986 Season | $ 99,000 | $7.83 |
| February 1986 | | |
| Average | $ 93,700 | $6.49 |
| "Bill Cosby Show" | $236,100 | $7.59 |
| "Family Ties" | $193,100 | $7.16 |
| *Cost per 30-Second Commercial Persons, February 1986* | | |
| "Bill Cosby Show" | Women $8.41 | Men $12.47 |
| "Family Ties" | Women $8.05 | Men $11.84 |

*Source*: Nielsen NAC Cost Supplement, February 1986

TABLE C–8

Top 25 Programs: July 1960–January 1987, Average Audience Estimates

| Rank | Program Name | Date | Network | Minutes Duration | Average Audience Percent | Share | Average Audience Thousands |
|---|---|---|---|---|---|---|---|
| 1. | "M*A*S*H Special" | 2/28/83 | CBS | 150 | 60.2 | 77 | 50,150 |
| 2. | "Dallas" | 11/21/80 | CBS | 60 | 53.3 | 76 | 41,470 |
| 3. | "Roots," part VIII | 1/30/77 | ABC | 115 | 51.1 | 71 | 36,380 |
| 4. | "Super Bowl XVI" | 1/24/82 | CBS | 213 | 49.1 | 73 | 40,020 |
| 5. | "Super Bowl XVII" | 1/30/83 | NBC | 204 | 48.6 | 69 | 40,480 |
| 6. | "Super Bowl XX" | 1/26/86 | NBC | 231 | 48.3 | 70 | 41,490 |
| 7. | "Gone with the Wind," part 1 | 11/ 7/76 | NBC | 179 | 47.4 | 65 | 33,960 |
| 8. | "Gone with the Wind," part 2 | 11/ 8/76 | NBC | 119 | 47.4 | 64 | 33,750 |
| 9. | "Super Bowl XII" | 1/15/78 | CBS | 218 | 47.2 | 67 | 34,410 |
| 10. | "Super Bowl XIII" | 1/21/79 | NBC | 230 | 47.1 | 74 | 35,090 |
| 11. | "Bob Hope Christmas Show" | 1/15/70 | NBC | 90 | 46.6 | 64 | 27,260 |
| 12. | "Superbowl XIX" | 1/20/85 | ABC | 218 | 46.4 | 63 | 39,390 |
| 13. | "Super Bowl XVIII" | 1/22/84 | CBS | 218 | 46.4 | 71 | 38,800 |
| 14. | "Super Bowl XIV" | 1/20/80 | CBS | 178 | 46.3 | 67 | 35,330 |
| 15. | "ABC Theater" ("The Day After") | 11/20/83 | ABC | 144 | 46.0 | 62 | 38,550 |
| 16. | "Roots," part VI | 1/28/77 | ABC | 120 | 45.9 | 66 | 32,680 |
| 17. | "The Fugitive" | 8/29/67 | ABC | 60 | 45.9 | 72 | 25,700 |
| 18. | "Super Bowl XXI" | 1/25/87 | CBS | 206 | 45.8 | 66 | 40,030 |
| 19. | "Roots," part V | 1/27/77 | ABC | 60 | 45.7 | 71 | 32,540 |
| 20. | "Ed Sullivan" | 2/ 9/64 | CBS | 60 | 45.3 | 60 | 23,240 |
| 21. | "Bob Hope Christmas Show" | 1/14/71 | NBC | 90 | 45.0 | 61 | 27,050 |
| 22. | "Roots," part III | 1/25/77 | ABC | 60 | 44.8 | 68 | 31,900 |
| 23. | "Super Bowl XI" | 1/ 9/77 | NBC | 204 | 44.4 | 73 | 31,610 |
| 24. | "Super Bowl XV" | 1/25/81 | NBC | 220 | 44.4 | 63 | 34,540 |
| 25. | "Super Bowl VI" | 1/16/72 | CBS | 170 | 44.2 | 74 | 27,450 |

TABLE C–9
Trend in National TV Network Prime Time Audiences
February Each Year 1970–1986[a]

| Year | U.S. TV Households (millions) | Percent Households Using TV | Average Audience All Program[b] | | Three Network Share Percent |
|------|------|------|------|------|------|
| | | | Percent | Millions | |
| 1970 | 58.5 | 63.7 | 19.5 | 11.4 | 92 |
| 1971 | 60.1 | 65.0 | 20.0 | 12.0 | 92 |
| 1972 | 62.1 | 63.4 | 20.6 | 12.8 | 97 |
| 1973 | 64.8 | 63.3 | 19.5 | 12.6 | 92 |
| 1974 | 66.2 | 63.7 | 20.2 | 13.4 | 95 |
| 1975 | 68.5 | 63.0 | 19.7 | 13.5 | 94 |
| 1976 | 69.6 | 63.4 | 19.7 | 13.7 | 93 |
| 1977 | 71.2 | 64.4 | 20.1 | 14.3 | 94 |
| 1978 | 72.9 | 64.0 | 20.1 | 14.7 | 94 |
| 1979 | 74.5 | 64.3 | 20.0 | 15.0 | 93 |
| 1980 | 76.3 | 65.6 | 20.0 | 15.3 | 91 |
| 1981 | 77.8 | 65.5 | 18.9 | 14.7 | 87 |
| 1982 | 81.5 | 63.9 | 17.6 | 14.3 | 83 |
| 1983 | 83.3 | 66.8 | 18.3 | 15.2 | 82 |
| 1984 | 83.8 | 65.2 | 17.3 | 14.5 | 80 |
| 1985 | 84.9 | 65.9 | 17.1 | 14.5 | 78 |
| 1986 | 85.9 | 65.4 | 16.8 | 14.5 | 77 |

[a]Prime time includes 8–11 P.M. Monday–Saturday; 7–11 P.M. Sunday.
[b]Includes regular and special programs.
*Source*: Nielsen NTI/NAC.

Table C–10
Weekly Radio Usage by Day Part Persons 12 +, Monday–Sunday
Spring/Fall 1986

| | |
|------|------|
| 6 A.M.–10 A.M. | 5 hr 23 min |
| 10 A.M.–3 P.M. | 6 hr 24 min |
| 3 P.M.–7 P.M. | 4 hr 25 min |
| 7 P.M.–midnight | 3 hr 03 min |
| 6 A.M.–midnight | 19 hr 15 min |
| Total 24 hours | 20 hr 39 min |

*Source*: Developed from RADAR 34 data, Statistical Research, Inc.

Local time

TOTAL PERSONS
12+ (000)

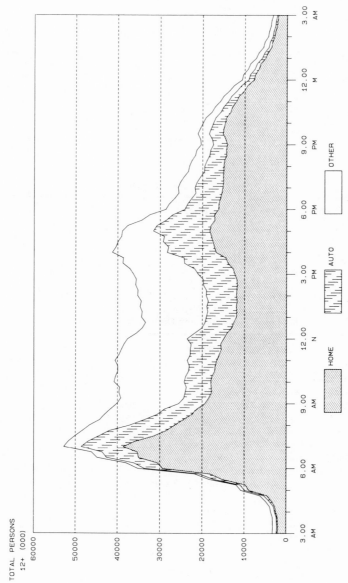

**Fig. C-2** Location of radio audiences of all AM and FM stations by quarter hour—Monday through Friday, Fall, Spring/Fall 1986.
*Source:* Statistical Research Inc., RADAR 34.

TABLE C-11
Weekly Radio Usage by Age and Sex Persons 12+
Monday–Sunday, 6 A.M.–Midnight
Spring/Fall 1986

|  | Total Radio | FM Share |
|---|---|---|
| Total adult men | 19 hr 28 min | 71% |
| Men 18–34 | 19 hr 33 min | 86 |
| Men 35–49 | 16 hr 15 min | 67 |
| Men 50 + | 16 hr 15 min | 48 |
| Total adult women | 19 hr 42 min | 70 |
| Women 18–34 | 20 hr 32 min | 87 |
| Women 35–49 | 19 hr 55 min | 73 |
| Women 50+ | 18 hr 40 min | 48 |
| All teens 12–17 | 16 hr 29 min | 93 |
| All persons 12 + | 19 hr 15 min | 72 |

*Source*: Developed from RADAR 34 data, Statistical Research, Inc.

TABLE C-12
Seasonal Radio Listening Patterns by Day Parts, 1985
Total Persons 12+
Indices of Total Average Quarter-hour Data

|  | Winter | Spring | Summer | Fall |
|---|---|---|---|---|
| All Days 6 A.M.–Mid. | 100 | 102 | 100 | 97 |
| Mon.–Fri. 6 A.M.–10 A.M. | 103 | 102 | 94 | 101 |
| Mon.–Fri. 10 A.M.–3 P.M. | 99 | 100 | 105 | 96 |
| Mon.–Fri. 3 P.M.–7 P.M. | 101 | 102 | 99 | 98 |
| Mon.–Fri. 7 P.M.–12 Mid. | 95 | 103 | 107 | 95 |
| Mon.–Fri. 1 A.M.–5 A.M. | 98 | 101 | 103 | 98 |
| Sat.–Sun. 6 A.M.–12 Mid. | 101 | 103 | 100 | 96 |

*Source*: Arbitron study of 14 markets surveyed four times (winter, spring, summer, and fall) in 1985.

TABLE C-13
Black listening versus total audience: hours spent per week

|  | Blacks | Total |
|---|---|---|
| All persons 12+ | 30 | 25 |
| Men 18–34 | 31 | 27 |
| Women 18–34 | 31 | 24 |
| Men 50–64 | 30 | 24 |
| Women 50–64 | 31 | 27 |

Source: Radio Today, 1984 edition, Arbitron Ratings Co. based on special diary sample of 10 metropolitan areas.

TABLE C–14
Cable Viewing Data: Share of Total Television Audience
(Monday–Sunday, 12 hours)
October 1985–September 1986

|  | In Cable Subscriber Households | In Total TV Households |
|---|---|---|
| Ad-supported cable (network and local) | 15) | 8) |
| Superstations | 9)  34 | 6)  19 |
| Pay cable services | 10) | 5) |
| Network affiliates | 56 | 66 |
| (Network programming) | (34) | (43) |
| Independents | 15 | 15 |
| PBS | 3 | 3 |
| Total weekly household viewing | 55  hours | 50  hours |

Sum of shares exceeds 100% because of simultaneous usage of multisets.
Source: A. C. Nielsen data developed by Cabletelevision Advertising Bureau.

TABLE C–15
Trend in Cable Program Shares in Cable Households
May 1980–1986

|  | 1980 | 1981 | 1982 | 1983 | 1984 | 1985 | 1986 |
|---|---|---|---|---|---|---|---|
| Ad-supported cable (network and local) | 3.1 | 4.6 | 6.8 | 10.8 | 13.5 | 14.0 | 16.3 |
| Pay cable | 4.8 | 6.5 | 13.2 | 10.3 | 11.6 | 11.2 | 8.8 |
| Superstations | NA | NA | NA | 8.1 | 9.2 | 9.3 | 8.8 |
| Total cable | — | — | — | 29.2 | 34.3 | 34.5 | 33.9 |

*Source:* A. C. Nielsen data developed by Cabletelevision Advertising Bureau.

TABLE C–16
Cable Shares of Total Household Viewing by Day Parts
October 1985–September 1986

|  | Ad-supported | Pay Cable | Total |
|---|---|---|---|
| Daytime (10:00 A.M.–4:30 P.M.) | 24 | 6 | 30 |
| Early fringe (4:30 P.M.–7:30 P.M.) | 23 | 5 | 28 |
| Prime time (8:00 P.M.–11:00 P.M.) | 19 | 10 | 29 |
| Late fringe (11:00 P.M.–1:00 A.M.) | 20 | 16 | 36 |
| Weekend (1:00 P.M.–7:00 P.M.) | 30 | 10 | 40 |
| Total Day (24 hours) | 24 | 10 | 34 |

*Source*: A. C. Nielsen data developed by Cabletelevision Advertising Bureau.

# Questions for Review and Discussion

## Chapter 1

### Multiple Choice

1. The problem that plagued the early Nielsen Audimeter and rendered unacceptable graphic records of listening behaviors was
   A. Paper recording tape was undependable
   B. Power outage
   C. Difficulty in gaining family acceptance
   D. Too many types of receivers in use
   E. B and D

2. The coincidental telephone method was first used by which rating service?
   A. Cooperative Analysis of Broadcasting (CAB)
   B. A.C. Nielsen
   C. C.E. Hooper
   D. "Crossley ratings"
   E. Arbitron

3. The first meter device for the purpose of providing audience listening behaviors was originally conceived and a patent was held by
   A. Nielsen
   B. RCA
   C. C.E. Robinson
   D. Robert Elder
   E. Woodruff

4. The first real estimate of the total number of radio ownership was provided in 1930 by
   A. Daniel Starch for NBC
   B. 1930 census
   C. CAB
   D. C.E. Hooper
   E. None of the above

5. Significant elements favoring the coincidental telephone interview method over the 24-hour recall interview included
   A. Simplicity of questions
   B. Immediacy element

C. Elimination of all but a limited noncompletion problem (busy signals and refusals)

D. A and B

E. All of the above

6. The first radio researcher to claim national projectable ratings was
    A. Hooper
    B. Nielsen
    C. Crossley
    D. Roslow
    E. None of the above

7. Which of the following questions was *not* one used in CAB field interviewing?
    A. When sets were in use
    B. Who listened
    C. What programs and stations were heard
    D. What commercials were remembered
    E. What programs were preferred

8. The CAB's final downfall was due to the consistent CAB-Hooper difference in coincidental telephone technique results. Which of the following was *not* a factor in explaining the 20% higher ratings reported by Hooper?
    A. The CAB opening question was found to be biased
    B. The Hooper interviewer waited for six rings before classifying a home unoccupied and not listening; where as the CAB interviewer stopped after 4 rings
    C. CAB used an unsatisfactory system of handling listeners who did not or could not identify the program turned on
    D. CAB and Hooper used different statistical treatments of "busy homes"
    E. None of the above

9. Hooper's formula used to project national ratings and audience figures was
    A. U.S. Hooperating X U.S. Diary ratings
    B. U.S. Diary ratings/U.S. Hooperatings
    C. U.S. Hooperatings/U.S. Diary ratings
    D. U.S. Hooperatings—U.S. Diary ratings
    E. None of the above

## True/False

1. National projectable audience ratings was what Nielsen, Hooper, and Crossley ultimately strived for.

2. Although audience mail indicated significant audience response to early radio programming, it was found unsystematic and therefore inconclusive because much of it was in response to 'hyping'.

3. The first study of Hooper to merge diary and coincidental interview ratings was able to provide U.S. audience figures in terms of number of individual listeners.

4. The CAB was eventually taken over by a membership corporation of the Association of National Advertisers (ANA) with Crossley remaining to perform the actual survey work.

5. The CAB first introduced the daypart method of audience listening in order to reduce memory loss.

6. U.S. Hooperatings were widely accepted as national projectable ratings.

7. The Nielsen philosophy of audience surveying was that measurement should be an observation of specific action by consumers, rather than answers to questions where human elements could influence results.

8. Hooper attempted to produce projectable audience figures by the merging of the 24-hour telephone recall technique and the diary technique.

9. The meter that is now known as the Nielsen Audience had its beginnings with Elder and Woodruff.

## Fill in the Blank

1. The increased market in local radio ratings was due to the _____ and the _____.

2. Nontelephone homes become a major concern in radio ratings because they present the problem of _____.

3. The Cooperative Analysis of Broadcasting (CAB) radio rating service originally used the _____ data collection technique.

## Short Answer

1. Hooper analysed audience behavior on data that yielded what information?

2. Hooper's telephone coincidental service was plagued by what two serious problems?

## Chapter 2

### Multiple Choice

1. Controlled Mail Ballot used techniques such as
   A. Follow up on nonresponders after 1 month
   B. Small gift with first mailing
   C. Personal follow up phone call to the respondents
   D. Adequate instructions
   E. B and D only

2. Some of the early radio diary studies revealed
   A. Audience profile of other media use
   B. Audience turn over ratios, composition and ability to chart audience flow from program to program
   C. Audience recall of sponsorship of programs
   D. Self-reported like or dislike of particular programs
   E. All of the above

3. The controlled mail ballot was first used by
   A. NBC
   B. ARB
   C. CBS with Industrial Surveys
   D. Pulse
   E. Hooper

4. Which of the following is a problem with the diary technique?
   A. Self-administered and therefore people can commit errors in program time, program name, channel number or call letters
   B. Listeners can forget to record all listening or make entries well after the listening takes place
   C. Errors of commission, where the respondents fill in the diary ahead of time or after the fact
   D. Diary keepers want to please or "look good," a conditioning elements that can influence their entries
   E. All of the above

5. The first radio cummulative survey of individual listeners ever conducted was
   A. Sindlinger Telephone Recall
   B. Nielsen Radio Index (NRI)
   C. CRAM
   D. RADAR
   E. None of the above

6. Personal interviews were eventually adopted by CBS over mail question-naires because
   A. Obtained a more representative sample
   B. Obtained more information and were more accurate
   C. They were cheaper to conduct
   D. A and C
   E. A and B

7. Random-digit dialing was initially used in which radio study?
   A. CRAM
   B. Arbitron
   C. Nielsen Radio Index
   D. Hooperatings
   E. RADAR

8. Statistical Research Inc. (SRI) contributed important improvements to the RADAR project. These included
   A. High response rate
   B. centrally supervised telephone interviewing using rigid supervisory controls of daily recall interviews
   C. Random-Digit Dialing
   D. A and B
   E. All of the above

9. Which of the following was *not* a reason why Nielsen eventually pulled out of local and network radio measurement?
   A. Problems with measuring radio audiences accurately
   B. Skyrocketing growth of TV
   C. Diminishing public interest in radio
   D. TV research was cheaper to conduct
   E. A and D

10. Response rate is highest when using which method of sample selection?
    A. Cluster
    B. Convenience
    C. Quota
    D. Probability
    E. None of the above

11. A problem with the Birch technique of unaided telephone recall interview is
    A. Unanswered telephone numbers present a serious biasing factor
    B. Memory loss factor tends to depress overall listening levels
    C. Respondents want to impress interviewer so they intentionally give false listening habits

    D. A and B

    E. All of the above

12. Throughout the past history of radio ratings, aside from Birch, several services used the telephone recall method originally used by Crossley at CAB. Some of these were

    A. Hooper

    B. Arbitron and Trace

    C. Burke and Sindlinger

    D. All of the above

    E. None of the above

13. Which radio rating service initially used computer-assisted telephone interviewing (CATI)?

    A. Burke

    B. TRAC-7

    C. RAM

    D. Birch

    E. RADAR

14. The Burke Broadcast Research methodology weaknesses included

    A. Did not use true random-digit dialing

    B. CATI System had many glitches

    C. Weekly cumulative audience estimates were based on a separate set of interviews during which seven day recall was employed

    D. Burke had very little expertise and experience with the telephone recall technique

    E. A and C.

15. The radio rating service that offered flash ratings available within 90 hours of data collection was

    A. Birch

    B. RAM

    C. RADAR

    D. TRACE

    E. Burke

16. Which radio rating service offered coincidental technique in order to obtain a measure of automobile ratio listening?

    A. Hooperatings

    B. Sindlinger

    C. RADAR

    D. Trace

    E. None of the above

17. The rising demand for "people data" forced Nielsen to use which form of data collection other than the meter?
    A. Roster recall technique
    B. Diary
    C. Telephone coincidental
    D. Personal coincidental
    E. B and C

18. What factors eventually lead to the NSI decision to abandon radio?
    A. Discontinuance of quarter-hour ratings
    B. Declining radio listening levels
    C. Increasing number of radio stations
    D. Basic radio listening patterns were changing due to the advent of automobile and portable receivers
    E. All of the above

19. The Sindlinger national radio service included which of the following services?
    A. Measured out-of-home as well as in-home listening
    B. Unit of measurement used was households
    C. Larger and continuous sampling
    D. A and C
    E. All of the above

## True/False

1. Arbitron improved their services throughout the 1970s and 1980s by solving ethnic response problems, by using RDD to bring nonlisted telephone subscribers into the sample and by replacing monthly surveys with quarterly ones.

2. Random-digit dialing employs telephone directory generated telephone numbers.

3. The CBS Industrial Surveys, which determined station listening patterns, eventually led to the experimentation with diaries to obtain program listening data.

4. The diary technique rates on an equal level with the coincidental and the meter in terms of accuracy.

5. Random-digit dialing produces a statistically random sample and ensures that unlisted and newly connected subscribers are included in the sample.

6. The rapid growth of television was one of the developments that slowed the implementation of the personal radio diary.

7. The first national diary study sampled housewives and included a diary of not only listening behavior but other activities such as cooking, cleaning, and shopping.

8. The mailable tape audimeter, used by Nielsen, permitted great improvement in speed of reporting at reduced costs.

9. The Nielsen Station Index (NSI) included both radio and TV audience measurement.

10. Nielsen's measurements of household listening by meter and Sindlinger's measurements of personal listening by telephone recall showed high correlation, that is, their results were just about the same.

11. Although Hooper's coincidentals were limited to in home listening in telephone households, they did offer more demographic detail than Pulse ratings.

## Fill in the blank

1. The _____was recognized by Nielsen as an important technological advancement in the area of ratings production and service.

2. The Sindlinger system of dealing with non-responses was the _____ system where all numbers are dialed six times on a scheduled day, and, if no answer, the number is dialed on the same day of the week two weeks later.

3. Unaided telephone recall technique was used by _____.

4. The roster recall technique (aided recall) was first used by _____ and was known as _____.

## Short Answer

1. What were the factors that can be attributed to the steady decline of Pulse in the 1970s?

2. Which factors can be attributed to the lack of use of the telephone coincidental as an ongoing data collection technique in radio? In which ways does it play an important role in the ratings field?

3. Discuss the contributions of the Cumulative Radio Audience Measurement (CRAM) study?

## Chapter 3

### Multiple Choice

1. The first instantaneous TV meter service was launched by:
   A. Nielsen
   B. Arbitron
   C. Hooper
   D. AGB
   E. None of the above

2. In the early TV years, Nielsen used which report as the standard measure of program popularity under relatively equal competitive conditions?
   A. National Audience Composition Report (NAC)
   B. NTI Planners Report
   C. Multi-Network Area Report (MNA)
   D. NTI Cable Status Report
   E. None of the above

3. One of the greatest changes in the Nielsen Television Index occurred in 1983 and was the
   A. Addition to the sample of 450 new households of which 150 were cable subscribers
   B. Rating of programs less than 5 minutes in duration
   C. The Automated Measurement of Line Ups (AMOL)
   D. The introduction of the Storage Instantaneous Audimeter (SIA)
   E. A and C

4. The National Audience Composition (NAC) was first devised in order to
   A. Test diary methods of data collection
   B. Furnish demographic data not produced by a meter
   C. Keep up with ARB audience demographic services
   D. A and B
   E. None of the above

5. Possible disadvantages of the peoplemeter are
   A. Daily presence of buttons to push could become a boring chore
   B. Could create security problems
   C. Could condition people's viewing patterns
   D. Recruitment rates could be further evoded
   E. All of the above

6. Advantages of the AGB service over the Niesen (NTI) service are
   A. Lower cost meter operation
   B. Larger national sample with significant savings.
   C. A thoroughly tested electronic meter system with integrated peoplemeters, eliminating all diary adjustments, limitations, and costs
   D. A and C
   E. All of the above

7. The first overnight coincidentals in the TV ratings business were furnished by
   A. Birch
   B. Nielsen
   C. Arbitron
   D. Trendex
   E. Hooper

8 Sieler of the ARB supported the diary method of data collection over the Hooper coincidental because
   A. The diary was more economical because it measured every quarter hour of the week
   B. The diary was faster in terms of compiling and distributing data in report form
   C. The diary provided many analytical possibilities of household meter records
   D. A and C
   E. All of the above

9. The Arbitron TV meter service folded due to
   A. Technical problems with the meters
   B. Sample deterioration
   C. Diaries were a more accurate method of collecting audience viewing behavior data
   D. A and B
   E. All of the above

10. Which of the following was *not* an innovation by Arbitron in TV ratings development?
    A. Area of Dominant Influence (ADI) concept
    B. Spanish language diary
    C. Designated Market Area (DMA) concept
    D. Projection of person estimates
    E. Simultaneous sweeps

11. People meters, a household push button device that allows each family member to indicate when he/she is viewing, are used by which rating service?
    A. Nielsen
    B. AGB Research PLC
    C. Telepulse
    D. A and C
    E. A and B

12. Which of the following TV rating services used a viewer diary plus asked for demographic information and opinions of program and commercials watched?
    A. Arbitron
    B. Telerad
    C. Telepulse
    D. Videodex
    E. None of the above

13. The Sindlinger Television Service offered which elements for their TV rating service?
    A. Meter method of data collection
    B. Demographic breakdowns based on interviews with individuals
    C. Roster recall survey technique
    D. Qualitative data
    E. B and D only

## True/False

1. Telepulse's major deficiency was its geographical limitation to metropolitan areas.

2. The first crude TV ratings were a postcard program listing, arranged for mail-back with boxes for viewers to check which programs they had viewed.

3. The Differential Survey Technique (DST) uses heavy monetary premiums to induce cooperation in younger households so that ethnic response rates parallel those for whites.

4. Tanner Electronic Survey Tabulation (TEST) used a system of electronic computers that received the transmitted signal from reporter units attached to a sample of home receivers.

5. Hooper was initially enthuasiastic about the emergence of television and immediately initiated a TV ratings service.

6. In 1973, Nielsen's Storage Instantaneous Audimeter (SIA) provided day-after ratings for local market services in Los Angeles and New York and 48-hour ratings for national network TV shows.

7. A systematic sample was built into NTI to ensure that no homes remained in the sample for over three years.

## Fill in the Blank

1. Tanner Electronic Survey Tabulation (TEST) folded because _____ and _____.

2. The first and foremost syndicator to employ diaries was _____

3. The Differential Survey Technique (DST) was introduced by Arbitron in 1982–1983 in order to draw more _____and _____into the sample.

4. The Total Telephone Frame (TTF) was introduced by Nielsen Station Index (NSI) in order to use both listed and unlisted telephone numbers by the use of _____.

## Short Answer

1. How does the SIA (Storage Instantaneous Audimeter), created by Nielsen, collect data? How quickly are local figures and network ratings available?

2. A current competitor of the Nielsen NTI service is AGB-Research PLC. What does the AGB service offer over and above the NTI service?

## Chapter 4

## Multiple Choice

1. To establish the degree of validity, what two factors must be considered?
   A. Sample size and operational errors
   B. Definition of audience and nonresponse errors
   C. Criteria for validity and sample size
   D. Definition of audience and criteria for validity
   E. None of the above

2. Any sample survey may include which of the following types of error?
   A. Nonresponse error
   B. Operational errors
   C. Errors made in field work
   D. A and C
   E. All of the above

3. When looking closely at the technical aspects of rating methodologies one must know that
   A. All ratings are estimates
   B. Ratings are used primarily to predict future performance
   C. All ratings have some degree of sampling error
   D. A and C
   E. All of the above

4. Which instrument is used most often in ratings methodologies today?
   A. Meters
   B. Self-administered diaries
   C. Coincidental telephone survey
   D. A and B
   E. None of the above

5. Which of the following is *not* an advantage of the telephone coincidental interview?
   A. Probability samples of all telephone households is achieved by random-digit dialing
   B. No memory factor is involved
   C. Only average audience data are obtained
   D. Quality of sampling and interviewing are highly controlled
   E. High response rate

6. The most independent interviewer is the
   A. Telephone interviewer calling from their own home
   B. Personal interviewer
   C. Mall intercept interviewer
   D. Telephone interviewer from centralized interviewing call-out center
   E. None of the above

7. Which of the following is *not* true of the ISR Telephone Coincidental Technique?
   A. Its cost is the same as the normal coincidental
   B. It is used often
   C. It is recognized as the preeminent measurement "standard value" or "reality yardstick" by which other techniques can be tested
   D. Use of rigid routine for multiple calls and follow up interviews
   E. A and B

8. Which technique has overcome the possible bias introduced by growing numbers of unlisted telephone households?
   A. Personal interviewing using quota sampling
   B. Use of latest published telephone directory
   C. Random-digit dialing
   D. Cluster sampling
   E. "Random-digit type samples"

9. Which of the following is *not* a strength of the open-ended personal radio diary?
   A. Provides a record of listening in cars, office and other work places in addition to the home
   B. Response rate is around 40% on the average
   C. Direct demographic sample is not tied to the household size
   D. Weekly cummulative ratings are provided
   E. B and C

10. Nielsen Audience Composition service (NAC) used what type of instrument?
   A. Daily diary
   B. Audilog
   C. Recordimeter
   D. Audimeter
   E. B and C

11. Which of the following are true of the RADAR methodology?
   A. After household is determined and a list of all household members is obtained, the person to be part of the sample is selected by random procedure
   B. Initial telephone contact with predesignated person is made by the interviewer one a week before the survey period begins
   C. A premium gift is sent to the respondent
   D. Calls are made to the respondent each day at an agreed upon time
   E. All of the above

12. Which of the following is *not* an element of the telephone recall survey?
   A. Greater effort is necessary to maintain respondent interest and minimize nonresponse
   B. Average interview lasts about two to three minutes
   C. Probing is crucial to jog interviewees memory
   D. Biasing comments by interviewers are difficult to control except in centralized interviewing
   E. None of the above

13. Households difficult to reach by telephone are generally
    A. Urban
    B. More affluent
    C. Younger
    D. A and C
    E. B and C

14. An important goal of the RADAR instrument was to
    A. Report results speedily
    B. Minimize the expense of the data collection procedure
    C. Yield valid weekly cummulative data that were truly projectable
    D. Produce more accurate data because memory factor was involved
    E. None of the above

15. The function of the NAC is to produce
    A. Audience composition for viewing households as determined by the NTI audimeter
    B. Household rating levels
    C. Cumulative data
    D. A and B
    E. All of the above

16. The housing units in Arbitron's meter parent sample are selected by use of
    A. "Half-open interval" form of area probability sampling
    B. Random-digit dialing
    C. Geographic clustering
    D. Total telephone frame
    E. B and C

## True/False

1. Validity is the degree to which the sample measurement will produce the same results that would be obtained by a complete census utilizing the same methodology under exactly comparable conditions.

2. The principle advantage of the coincidental personal interview over the telephone coincidental is that it covers only telephone households.

3. Nonresponse errors are errors that can occur because not all selected households or persons are actually reached or heard from.

4. Sampling error can be measurable only if non-probability sampling is employed.

5. When selecting a household member to be interviewed over the telephone, if you talk to the person who answers the phone it is guaranteed that there will be an under-representative sample of men and an over-representative sample of teens.

6. The recordimeter is an electrical device that is attached to a TV receiver and flashes a light signal (accompanied by a buzzer—which may be turned off) every 15 minutes to remind viewers to make entries in the Audilog.

7. The personal roster recall technique was developed by Birch in 1980.

8. A major strength of the electronic meter instrument is that every type of measurement can be covered; from average minute and quarter hours to daily, weekly, or four-week cumulative household ratings.

9. A major deficiency of the NAC service is that the conditioning of respondents is always a possibility, especially when the panel household become 'experts'.

10. Samples for the Weekly TV Household Diary technique used by both Arbitron and Nielsen are drawn from telephone directories.

11. A major difference between Nielsen and Arbitron services is that Nielsen interviewers operate from supervised call-out centers and Arbitron handles only a limited portion of its interviewing from a central location, while the remainder is done by field staff working at home.

12. The meter methodology offers the most complete information and the closest to accuracy of any technique in regular use.

13. RADAR approaches true probability samples more closely than any other measurement of individual media exposure.

14. As a substantially less complex methodology than the coincidental, the telephone recall decreases the need for care and quality control.

15. The telephone recall survey involves a telephone interview in which the respondent is asked to recall all radio listening or television viewing for an entire week.

16. The classic assumption that a "no answer" (after four to six rings) meant no one was at home and thus there was no listening or viewing has been proved correct repeatedly by ISR surveys.

17. Arbitron and Nielsen use basically the same incentive and follow-up procedures to induce ethnic household members to respond.

18. An increase in the sample size will decrease the standard error.

19. For most sampling plans, to reduce a standard error by 50 percent requires a doubling of the sample size.

20. Arbitron uses "open-ended" household diaries for TV and "closed-ended" personal diaries for radio.

21. The major aspect of the instrument is that it is the key to the validity of the measurement.

22. An example of an ideal sample frame is the latest telephone directory.

23. When using a probability sample and a fixed design, statistical sample error for ratings is a function of sample size and is not determined by the size of the market of the population measured.

24. Ratings analysts must work with trends and rolling averages of ratings because a single observation is not enough information to tell the whole story of audience response to a particular program.

## Fill in the Blank

1. A major weakness of the personal roster recall methodology is that the sampling procedures involve _____, which reduces statistical efficiency of the survey.

2. Industry researchers lean strongly toward the _____ as a yard stick or criterion for evaluating the effectiveness of other techniques.

3. Nielsen employs a probability sample for national and local meter services based on _____.

4. The NAC survey is an ongoing _____ operation.

5. Random-digit dialing has brought about somewhat _____ cooperation rates.

6. _____ rating service is the latest proponent of the telephone recall technique.

7. In the telephone recall technique, ignoring 'no answers' will eliminate the more 'not at home' people and produce an _____ bias in ratings.

## Short Answer

1. Briefly discuss the types of biases inherent in personal interviewing.

2. What are the four factors that make up a methodology?

3. Compare and contrast the ISR and conventional coincidental telephone procedures. How are no-answers, busy lines, and refusals handled by each methodology?

4. List the major strengths and weaknesses of the conventional telephone coincidental. In which specific ways can its weaknesses be improved?

5. Briefly describe the major strengths and weaknesses of the telephone recall technique. Why is it not able to produce any acceptable weekly cummulative data?

6. What are the four basic elements of the weekly TV household diary (closed-ended) instrument?

7. Briefly discuss the strengths and weaknesses of the personal roster recall methodology. To what degree is interviewer bias a problem in this technique?

## Chapter 5

## Multiple Choice

1. Which nationally syndicated qualitative rating service has been in existence since 1958 and uses a mail survey of a 1500 sample of U.S. TV households?
   A. American Research Bureau
   B. Vox Box
   C. TVQ
   D. Prizm
   E. None of the above

2. What two specific indices of program appeal does the Television Audience Assessment, Inc. (TAA) advocate for development and validation?
   A. Program appeal, star appeal
   B. Program appreciation, star appeal
   C. Program appreciation, program impact
   D. Program involvement, program impact
   E. None of the above

3. Frank/Greenberg Interest-Based Segmentation of TV Audiences
   A. Measured a broad range of physical, intellectual, and cultural interests using 18 categories
   B. Studied how people with different patterns of interest and needs

make use of TV rather than studying the relationship between demographic variables and viewing behavior
C. Used questions that were also directed at viewing behavior and how TV fits into viewers' daily lives
D. B and C
E. All of the above

4. Which of the following are *not* data produced by the Simmons Market Research Bureau (SMRB)?
   A. Magazine audience measurements
   B. Information of TV viewing, radio listening, and newspaper reading
   C. Product use data
   D. Viewer like or dislike of a particular program
   E. None of the above

5. The 'ZIP-market cluster' concept assumes that
   A. People with similar cultural backgrounds and circumstances will 'cluster'
   B. The homogeneous demographic character of a neighborhood is self-perpetrating
   C. The heterogeneous demographic character of a neighborhood is self-perpetrating
   D. A and B
   E. None of the above

6. Which of the following was the qualitative data service that was used to obtain consumer profile data that could be related to radio ratings?
   A. VALS
   B. Qualidata
   C. Simmons Market Research Bureau
   D. Scarborough
   E. B and C

7. TVQ provides commercial industry decision makers with what factor?
   A. Awareness measures of national commercial programming
   B. Awareness measures of nationally broadcast commercials
   C. Viewers' overall program evaluations for programs they know along a 5-point scale
   D. A and B
   E. A and C

8. Percy's Vox Box
   A. Employs a meter that records set usage
   B. Provides opportunity for viewers to record their responses automatically by pushing a button

C. Has a precise logging system for local programs that provides the opportunity for rating commercials

D. A and B

E. All of the above

9. Which qualitative rating service worked directly with the Corporation for Public Broadcasting (CPB) in order to develop a ratings system to serve the interests of noncommercial station programmers?

A. Arbitron

B. Performer Q

C. Vox Box

D. TVQ

E. None of the above

10. Networks, stations, and ad agencies have never been enthusiastic about syndicated qualitative research because

A. Properly analyzed and interpreted quantitative ratings can give many answers to questions about quality

B. There is more confidence in findings derived from actual viewing behavior patterns than from many qualitative measurements that rely on verbalizations of peoples' attitudes and opinions

C. Networks, stations, agencies, and producers conduct extensive special qualitative research on individual shows

D. B and C

E. All of the above

11. Which of the following was *not* an element of the 1982 pilot study conducted by the TAA?

A. Demographic, psychographic, and life-style profiles of programs and networks

B. The relationship between viewers reactions and program recall and comprehension

C. Viewer reaction to programs in terms of satisfaction, loyalty, attentiveness, and involvement

D. How TV viewers select programs and what differences exist between cable and broadcast

12. In the qualitative ratings field, the "quality of the viewing experience" explores which of the following?

A. The viewers expectations, needs, and attitudes toward the viewing experience in order to determine how and why certain programs are viewed

B. What characteristics of programs produce high degrees of attention, satisfaction, and loyalty

C. The viewers' subjective evaluation of the program
D. A and B
E. A and C

## True/False

1. The TAA pilot study used specially designed one-day viewing diaries that were used by respondents to record their watching of 6 P.M. to midnight programs each day for two weeks.

2. In order for qualitative syndicated surveys to be useful, media planners at agencies and advertisers must use the service data as an input requirement for buying.

3. According to Beville, "qualitative" has three principle meanings in audience measurement. These are Quality of individual program appeal, Quality of audience, and Quality of viewing experience.

4. Prizm claims that the 40-point life-style segmentation system is strong enough to explain, yet cannot predict consumer behavior.

5. Networks and others use the TVQ index primarily to spot new high scoring programs that have not achieved widespread exposure.

6. According to the Corporation for Public Broadcasting (CPB) study, 8 of the top 10 of the regularly scheduled "information" and "useful" programs were public television programs.

7. TV Factor Ratings were developed as a diagnostic tool to determine the sources of viewer satisfaction (or dissatisfaction) with individual TV programs.

8. The major effect of the TAA pilot study was that panelists reported being less attentive to and less critical than normal of programming watched.

9. The 1982 pilot study conducted by TAA used only commercial networks and cable networks in the sample.

10. Mediamark Research Inc. (MRI) uses Arbitron's Area of Dominant Influence definition that makes possible separate major market data (local data).

11. Quantiplex supplied the TV market with viewer and consumer ratings (VAC) that defined which programs attract what types of purchasers in what numbers.

## Fill in the Blank

1. ZIP-Market Clusters are _____and were conceived by _____.

2. VALS (Value and Lifestyle Program) segments the national population into nine basic groups which make up four composite groups called _____, _____, _____, and _____.

3. The Vox Box device consists of two rows of buttons, one for _____ and the other for _____.

## Short Answer

1. TAA (Television Audience Assessment, Inc.) describes itself as a non-profit corporation engaged in the development of a new form of program ratings for cable and broadcast TV. Taking into account viewer attitudes and behavior, what two goals does it aspire to?

2. Briefly describe the types of ratings that can be useful in qualitative research.

3. Compare and contrast the local market qualitative product use services in terms of survey methods, number of product categories, when surveyed, sample size, and reporting units. What are the strengths and weaknesses of each?

## Chapter 6

### Multiple Choice

1. The failure of diary reporting in cable audience measurement was due to
   A. Lack of strong identity associated with various cable networks
   B. The remote control tuning potential frequently associated with cable makes fast switching around from channel to channel much easier
   C. Cable diaries do not have the capability to produce cumulative data
   D. B and C
   E. A and B

2. Which of the following is *not* a characteristic of the Cable Mark Probe (ELRA Group) report?
   A. Reports trends in subscriber response to cable programming and consumer interest in new types of cable service
   B. Reports measured cable penetration

    C. Reports measured cable viewership

    D. Uses individual programs as the basic units of analysis

    E. C and D

3. Which of the following techniques used in the CAMS study produced results closest to the coincidental yardstick in determining number of persons using TV (PUT)?

    A. Seven-day household daypart diary

    B. Seven-day personal daypart diary

    C. Seven-day unaided telephone recall

    D. Seven-day aided telephone recall

    E. Standard Nielsen Station Index diary

4. The Arbitron Two-Way Cable/Cable Diary Test was designed to answer which of the following questions?

    A. Is diary based measurement appropriate for Cable viewing?

    B. Can a cable diary be developed in order to educate cable diary keepers and improve their ability to report all set use?

    C. Is telephone aided recall appropriate to measure viewing on local cable systems?

    D. A and C

    E. All of the above

5. The Television Audience Assessment (TAA) study highlights many viewing patterns of the cable television audience. Which of the following is *not* a new pattern?

    A. High Audience turnover

    B. Reduced channel loyalty

    C. Planned viewing

    D. Reduced commercial exposure

    E. Numerous distractions

6. Highlights from the TAA study show that cable subscribers

    A. Have strong interest in sports and movies

    B. Have strong interest in news, arts, and social concerns

    C. Find cable programming more appealing and involving than broadcast programs

    D. A and C

    E. All of the above

7. The fundamental differences between cable and commercial broadcasting are

    A. Cable is a subscriber medium, broadcast TV is 100% advertising supported medium

    B. Cable is a capital and labor intensive business, broadcasting is not

C. Cable suffers as an advertising and marketing medium from its low penetration of major metropolitan areas

D. Cable is not licensed by the FCC to operate in a competitive manner; they are monopolies franchised by local governmental units to operate in prescribed limited geographical areas

E. All of the above

8. Arbitron supplies local ratings for individual cable networks and superstations based on

A. System-specific diary data drawn from a sample of 500 in-tab diaries per report

B. A record of viewing for five minutes or more by a minimum of 20 percent of TV households during survey week

C. Composite data from all franchises within its ADI

D. A and C

E. B and C

9. Results of the Arbitron Two-Way Cable/Cable Diary Test showed that

A. When the standard diary data were compared to the Two-Way Cable data, diary results were underreported

B. When the standard diary data were compared to the Cable Diary, response rate was higher using cable diary than with the standard diary

C. When telephone aided recall data were compared to Two-Way Cable data, no meaningful comparisons were available

D. A and C

E. All of the above

10. The TAA program appeal ratings show that Americans enjoy television. The average appeal score of over 250 programs rated in the study was:

A. 65

B. 90

C. 73

D. 91

E. 86

11. Which of the following is *not* a Network Cable Rating service?

A. NTI Cable Status Report

B. Marquest Cable Ratings

C. Cable Mark Probe

D. National Cable/Non-Cable Report

E. Nielsen Pay Cable Report

12. Results of the CAMS Study confirmed which of the following?

A. The standard household diary understates cable-originated program ratings

B. Coincidentals can accurately measure cable-originated program audiences

C. Audience for cable program originations are difficult to measure

D. B and C

E. All of the above

## True/False

1. Cable TV was developed originally in the 1940s as an extension of broadcast station coverage and provided viewers satisfactory station reception in distant or difficult terrain situations.

2. Because local cable franchise areas represent political rather than marketing areas, systematic measurement is difficult to achieve.

3. The TAA program appeal index measures the degree of intellectual and emotional stimulation a program gives its viewers.

4. By far, the most meaningful cable rating activity has been produced at the local level.

5. "Narrowcasting" is the concept of providing specialized services to selective audiences that advertisers would seek and be willing to pay premium prices to reach.

6. National advertiser interest is high among the majority of cable systems and therefore national advertisers are pushing for ratings measurement in even the smallest population units.

7. The most startling of all the CAMS results was that none of the six techniques tested were able to measure audiences to cable-originated programs correctly.

8. According to the TAA study, programs vary more in their general appeal than in their emotional and intellectual impact on viewers.

9. Warner-Amex QUBE research shows that even though there is appeal in the concept of a lot of channels, the subscriber has ultimately decided that 'more is not necessarily better.'

10. The Nielsen Individual Cable Network Monthly pocketpieces are reports designed to produce ratings based on the particular cable network population, and they contain whatever information the network and the sample limitations dictate.

## Fill in the Blank

1. A major problem with local measurement of cable franchises is the _____ in channel capacity between systems, which makes regularization of program schedules and local promotion next to impossible.

2. The validation tool used in the CAMS study was _____.

3. The validation tool used by the Arbitron Two-Way Cable/Cable Diary test was _____.

4. According to the TAA study the greater the emotional and intellectual stimulation offered by a show, the more viewers report _____

## Short Answer

1. The CAMS (Cable Audience Methodology Study) design tested six methodologies capable of determining both broadcast and cable viewing. Discuss the design of each method and classify each as to which technique (diary or telephone recall) was employed.

2. Discuss the design flaws of the CAMS study and list the questions that the CAMS report found essential to answer before any improvement can be made in the accuracy of cable audience measurement.

3. What are the four methods involved in the Arbitron/Two-Way Cable/Cable Diary Test? Which test markets were used, how was the research sample selected, and what special methodological procedures were used in this study?

4. What are the important milestones that the television cable industry has passed in recent years?

## Chapter 7

## Multiple Choice

1. The single initial household rating of a network program is meaningless unless what other factors are known?
   A. Time period it was scheduled in
   B. Its share
   C. Its competition

QUESTIONS FOR REVIEW AND DISCUSSION

    D. Lead in and lead out

    E. All of the above

2. The affiliate benefits from strong network rating performance in which of the following ways?

    A. Higher rates made possible for commercial positions that the affiliate can sell in and around network shows

    B. Overall audience buildup and flow

    C. Networks give strong affiliates additional airtime to sell locally

    D. A and B

    E. All of the above

3. Which of the following reports represent the only syndicated measurement for the 200 + U.S. television markets?

    A. Arbitron's AID

    B. National Audience Demographic report

    C. 'Sweeps reports'

    D. Nielsen dailies

    E. None of the above

4. Which of the following on-line computer system helps users to develop rating information for specific syndicated programs under various competitive conditions?

    A. Arbitron AID

    B. NSI's Nielsen Plus

    C. Arbitron TAPP

    D. Maximizing Media Performance (MMP)

    E. None of the above

5. Broacast ratings first began being published in the trade and the public press by

    A. C.E. Hooper

    B. TV Guide

    C. Nielsen

    D. CAB

    E. None of the above

6. What two factors have played a major role in keeping local radio a viable medium?

    A. Reach and frequency

    B. Reliable weekly cumes and day part averages

    C. Computerization of data and reliable weekly cumes

    D. More cooperation from ethnic listeners and specific ethnic reports

    E. None of the above

7. Radio ratings would naturally be lower than TV household ratings because
    A. TV measures a people universe
    B. Radio measures a household universe
    C. Radio measures a people universe
    D. A and B
    E. None of the above

8. Which of the following is *not* a function of TV station representatives?
    A. Help TV stations sell its announcements to national advertisers
    B. Are well equipped with ratings-wise and computer-competent research and sales staffs
    C. Respond to an agency request for spot 'availabilities' in terms of gross rating points, reach, and frequency
    D. Help TV stations sell its announcements to local advertisers
    E. None of the above; they are all functions of a TV station rep

9. The Nielsen (NTI) national TV ratings pocketpiece does *not* provide which of the following information?
    A. Overall TV usage versus previous year
    B. TV usage by time periods and dayparts
    C. Person audience estimates for 19 age/sex categories
    D. Program type averages
    E. None of the above; they are all provided by the Nielsen pocketpiece

10. The most important data output report that reveals the most detailed analysis of television viewing in print is
    A. Nielsen's Program Cumulative audiences
    B. NTI pocketpiece
    C. National Audience Demographics report (NAD)
    D. NTI's Market Section Audiences report
    E. The Nielsen 'overnights'

11. Which of the following is widely used by television networks to promote TV audiences?
    A. Magazine
    B. Billboard
    C. Radio
    D. Newspaper
    E. All of the above

12. Which of the following rating services provides audience measurement of PBS?
    A. Nielsen
    B. AGB Research PLC
    C. Arbitron

    D. A and C

    E. All of the above

13. Local radio ratings are frequently an exclusive service of which of the following ratings companies?

    A. Statistical Research Inc.

    B. TVQ

    C. Arbitron

    D. Nielsen

    E. None of the above

14. Which of the following rating services rates interconnected radio networks?

    A. Arbitron Radio

    B. Nielsen

    C. RADAR

    D. A and C

    E. None of the above

15. The most valuable data of interconnected radio network ratings is compiled by

    A. Arbitron Radio

    B. RADAR

    C. Nielsen

    D. Radio networks themselves

    E. None of the above

16. Which of the following is not a reason why the advertisers themselves have no financial interest in the conduct of rating services today?

    A. Advertisers are content to accept the existing ratings as a reasonable guide

    B. Results of numerous validation studies

    C. The existence of the Electronic Media Rating Council as an independent monitoring agency

    D. Relatively high caliber of broadcast measurement data versus direct mail measurement give advertisers confident faith in the numbers used

    E. All of the above

17. Which of the following are counter programming strategies used to break into a block of solidly popular evening programs on a competing network?

    A. Special guest stars used on the opener

    B. Scheduling devices such as hour-long intros for new half-hour series

    C. Inaugurating the series against other than the regular competition

    D. A and B

    E. All of the above

## True/False

1. 'Dailies' are the ratings for prime time programs broadcast the night before.

2. Network program schedules (on all three networks) account for close to 75 percent of all U.S. prime-time viewing.

3. The final network schedule is based solely on ratings.

4. The procedure dictated by the upfront prime-time market involves national advertisers and agencies submitting a plan request to each network with the network responding with detailed program schedules, quarterly audience projections, estimated CPM for total households and target demographics.

5. Although overall rating position is influenced strongly by network programming, stand out local stations contribute audience muscle to their networks.

6. Local independent television stations usually gain audience share with diaries in comparison to meters and therefore are strong supporters of the diary.

7. Program hyping during sweep weeks is of direct benefit to the network because its best programming—and hence, best ratings—occur during this time.

8. When rating services annually rank both ADI and DMA markets, it is significant for stations in markets that are close to breakpoints used in allocating spot budgets.

9. Arbitron AID and NSI's Nielsen Plus use station rating data to provide local stations the opportunity to offer advertisers announcement packages to meet the particular audience target needs.

10. Both TV and Radio programming and selling are based on individual programs of each medium.

11. Compared to TV, radio rates are very low and permit advertisers to achieve heavier frequency and substantial reach by scattering commercials over stations and dayparts.

12. Post analysis serves the agency and advertiser by showing how close to original target objectives the actual performance was.

13. Target Aid is a combination of Arbitron audience data and Donnelley's Cluster Plus and Simmon's product service and brand purchaser profiles.

14. A major use of local rating reports is for advertisers to keep a close eye on what the competition is doing.

15. The 'effective frequency' concept maintains that the effective threshold is five announcement exposures.

## Fill in the Blank

1. Networks furnish _____when the planned schedule of announcement does not attain the required rating level; these will raise the _____and the _____and _____of the schedule to a satisfactory level.

2. Both Arbitron ADI and Nielsen DMA produce 200+ nonduplicated market areas that are _____and _____.

3. Radio audiences are measured and reported solely on the basis of _____, whereas television is a _____medium.

4. Because of the number of stations per market, many radio rating comparisons are made on a _____.

5. Advertisers and their agencies make their media plans based on _____ and _____.

6. The buying strategy used by agencies that dictates purchasing commercial positions on all three networks during the same quarter hour is called the _____.

7. Many agency media departments have turned to combining and integrating _____and _____in order to give their clients 'their best shot'.

## Short Answer

1. Hollywood movie and program producers and independent syndicators are significant users of network and local market rating reports. Discuss which ways these users work with the rating reports.

2. The sale of network television time takes place in what three stages?

## Chapter 8

## Multiple Choice

1. Which of the following is *not* one of the national criticisms of broadcast ratings?
   A. Ratings are not accurate

      B. Ratings are biased

      C. Ratings are misleading

      D. Ratings are misused

      E. None of the above; they are all criticisms of broadcast ratings.

2. Lack of cooperation or response by chosen sample members leads to the suspicion that

      A. Nonrespondents may not be represented by respondents

      B. There exists serious nonresponse error or bias

      C. There would be no difference in data received from respondents and those that might have been received from nonrespondents

      D. B and C

      E. A and B

3. Reasons for ratings differences can be attributed to

      A. Definitional differences

      B. Sample frame differences

      C. Universe differences

      D. B and C

      E. All of the above

4. According to Beville, 'hyping' can be better controlled by

      A. Disclosing unusual contests and prizes and on-the-air promotion activity of individual stations in ratings books

      B. Use of Nielsen NTI national data to alert buyers to the ratings effects of sweeps-weeks network hyping efforts

      C. Deeming all ratings affected by hyping as biased and inappropriate for making sound media buys

      D. A and B

      E. B and C

5. In broadcast audience surveys, conditioning occurs when

      A. Panel members unconsciously change their viewing or listening behavior.

      B. Ratings are affected by waves of extraordinary programming and promotion

      C. Panel members consciously try to affect ratings by claiming more viewing or listening to certain programs and stations than are their favorites

      D. A and C

      E. All of the above

6. A 1982 nationwide Roper Organization survey showed that

      A. Television outdraws radio and newspapers combined as a person's primary news source

B. Newspapers outdraw television and radio combined as a person's primary news source

C. Electronic broadcasting make up over 80 percent of respondents' choice for news source.

D. A and C

E. None of the above

7. Poor response rates of ethnic groups is due largely to
   A. Suspicion
   B. Illiteracy
   C. High incidence of non-listed telephone numbers
   D. Protection of privacy is important to the ethnic groups
   E. All of the above

8. Some of the most cited ways of how ratings are misused include which of the following?
   A. They lead to the cancellation of quality shows
   B. They result in programs appealing to the lowest common denominator
   C. They result in the distortion of news judgment and lead to scheduling of lurid and sensational news stories and investigative reporting
   D. They encourage the imitation of current program successes and discourage 'truly creative' efforts
   E. All of the above

## True/False

1. The average American looks to TV primarily for serious, involving entertainment.

2. According to Beville, to change the ratings, it is not necessary to revise the rating technique; what must change is the taste of the audience, which will then accept changed programming.

3. To cope with poor response rates from ethnic groups, rating services have used weighting of diaries and special field procedures to raise cooperation.

4. Whereas 'hyping' is directed at increasing audiences during rating periods, 'rigging' aims to boost ratings by manipulating the survey itself.

5. A sample of 500–1000 Nielsen households can accurately reflect the viewing patterns of 80 million U.S. television households.

6. As sample size diminishes, so does the amount of sampling error.

7. Rating services came about when advertisers demanded an accurate feedback mechanism that could measure audience behavior.

## Fill in the Blank

1. Advertisers originally initiated broadcast ratings because they realized the potential _____of radio.

2. The ratings user must understand the _____limitations attached to ratings and that ratings are merely _____.

3. Research shows that television is the most popular _____.

## Short Answer

1. Discuss how critics and proponents alike believe that ratings are misused. How do broadcasters themselves feel about that way the ratings are used?

2. What are some of the possible antidotes to hyping?

3. In which ways have ratings been rigged in the past? What is the policy on network or station personnel's participation in rating surveys?

## Chapter 9

## Multiple Choice

1. The publication of the "Recommended Standards for Radio and Television Audience Size Measurements" was the result of which industry committee?
   A. Advertising Research Foundation (ARF)
   B. Special Test Survey Committee of the NAB
   C. Magnuson committee
   D. Monroney committee
   E. None of the above

2. Which of the following is *not* a responsibility of the Electronic Media Ratings Council?
   A. The EMRC must accredit all reasonable applications for Council accreditation
   B. Evolve and determine minimum criteria and standards for broadcast audience measurement services
   C. To secure for the broadcast industry and related users audience measurement services that are valid, reliable, effective, and viable.
   D. A and C
   E. A and B

3. Which of the following is *not* an advantage of a private independent competitive rating firm?
   A. The firm is objective
   B. Ratings are more credible and valuable
   C. Ability to make quick decisions
   D. Presence of commercial competition
   E. Start up costs to launch a new rating service are relatively low

4. The California action toward TVQ is an example of which type of attempted control of rating services?
   A. Private independent competitive ratings firm
   B. Non-profit cooperative organization
   C. Private firms under contract to industry group
   D. Government control
   E. None of the above

5. During the Harris committee hearings, the FCC policy on rating services stated that broadcasters
   A. Must act responsibly in using ratings
   B. Must take reasonable precautions to ensure validity
   C. Must refrain from quoting portions of surveys out of context leaving false and misleading impressions
   D. A and C only
   E. All of the above

6. In order to be accredited by the Electronic Media Ratings Council, rating services must
   A. Supply complete information to the Rating council
   B. Submit to audits by the council but are not required to pay for the audits
   C. Submit to audits by the council and pay for full costs of the audits
   D. Apply one year in advance so that the council can monitor both past and present services
   E. A and C

7. Problems with a non-profit cooperative ratings organization versus private competitive firms are
   A. Major decisions are reached too slowly
   B. How the power and costs will be distributed between opposing broadcaster and customer interest
   C. Incentive for improvement is relaxed
   D. Amount of capital needed for a new service to succeed is too large and too great a risk
   E. All but D

8. Which of the following was *not* a recommendation of the Harris committee report of 1966?

   A. The enactment of legislation providing for government regulation of broadcast audience measurement activities was highly advisable

   B. Support by the federal government should be provided for research relative to sampling techniques and statistical measures

   C. Information coordination relative to ratings complaints must be achieved between industry groups like the Electronics Ratings Council and the FCC and FTC

   D. The federal government should be concerned with the reliability of ratings because improper measurements and ratings can affect the broadcasters ability to produce quality broadcasting in the public interest

   E. A and B

## True/False

1. Both the FTC and the FCC conducted hearings and investigations of rating service practices.

2. The Broadcast Ratings Council was established to conduct methodological research to answer questions raised at Harris hearings and to develop improvements in the techniques and audience measurement.

3. Rating Council accreditation relies on mandatory compliance and cooperation of the individual rating services.

4. Audit reports are used by the Electronic Ratings Council to evaluate rating services qualifications for continued accreditation and are publicly released.

5. A major advantage of the system where private rating firms are under contract to an industry group is that the survey organization can concentrate on service and on technological improvement that may help it get a contract renewal.

6. The major government role in ratings now is its potential for intervention which seems to assure continued and effective industry discipline.

## Fill in the Blank

1. In response to the Harris committee hearings, the _____ said it would take vigorous action against any broadcaster whose claims based on surveys are 'false and deceptive'.

2. The first specific government effort to look at the matter of broadcast ratings was initiated in a letter to ratings services by _____.

3. The establishment of the Broadcast Ratings Council was directly due to the results of the _____.

4. Adovcates of government controlled rating services believes that ratings should not be in the hands of private individuals because _____ can affect results.

5. The establishment of a non-profit cooperative organization is seen in the U.S. in the form of _____and in Canada in the form of _____.

## Short Answer

1. Discuss how the Rating Council's monitoring of rating services has affected methodology procedures, sample error estimates and rating reports.

2. Discuss the recommendations made by the Harris committee report of 1966.

3. What were some of the significant developments made by constant monitoring of ratings services by the Electronic Media Rating Council?

## Chapter 10

### Multiple Choice

1. Which of the following is *not* a cable measurement problem?
   A. Cable networks are new
   B. Channel numbers have not been ingrained in the viewers mind
   C. Programs are generally low rated and not memorable
   D. Viewers are more upscale and don't like to complete diaires
   E. B and C

2. An industry-financed and industry-governed rating service has *not* been a reality in the U.S. because of what factors?
   A. Legal
   B. Managerial
   C. Acceptability
   D. Financial
   E. All of the above

3. Which of the following is *not* an essential element of basic needs of buyers and sellers of broadcast advertising?
   A. CPM
   B. Percentages
   C. Reach
   D. Frequency
   E. None of the above

4. People based ratings were found essential for radio because of what reasons?
   A. In-home competition of television
   B. Increasing out-of-home opportunities presented by car radios and protable AM/FM sets
   C. There was increased emphasis on demographics
   D. A and B
   E. All of the above

5. Which rating service provided the first potential for using cumulative (unduplicated) data?
   A. RADAR
   B. Hooperatings
   C. Nielsen Radio Index
   D. Arbitron
   E. None of the above

6. Which rating service initiated the four-week sweep concept?
   A. Nielsen
   B. Sindlinger
   C. RADAR
   D. Arbitron, originally called ARB
   E. None of the above

7. ADIs and DMAs have been adopted as:
   A. Market and media units of measurement for sales quotas, advertising appropriations, and othermarketing distributions.
   B. FCC regulatory guidelines
   C. Radio and newspaper geographic unit of audience measurement
   D. All of the above
   E. None of the above

## True/False

1. ADIs and DMAs are unduplicated station market areas, where counties are assigned to market areas based on fixed standards of viewing performance.

2. A major problem with industry non-profit research groups was that they were unable to produce crucial decisions.

3. What ratings numbers are said to be in total population terms they are numbers that are projected from percentages.

4. Projectable ratings can be of limited use to station management for tracking trends and evaluating programming and format changes.

5. Studies show that unlisted telephone households tended to use television and radio somewhat less than their listed counterparts.

6. Cumes became especially significant in radio as proliferating station competition and declining quarter hour ratings changed the nature of the medium.

7. Rating service costs today are paid for largely by advertisers and their agencies.

8. The most accurate tool for measuring cable network and local audiences at the household level is the diary.

9. By the close of 1984, Nielsen pulled ahead of Arbitron in the instantaneous meter service.

10. Nielsen uses the Differential Survey Technique (DST) to bring ethnic response up to non-ethnic levels.

## Fill in the Blank

1. While radio used the individual as the unit of measurement, television embraced the _____measurement.

2. Cumulative ratings contributed two dimensions to radio. These are _____ and _____.

3. Delivery schedules for diary services improved steadily and numerical accuracy was gained due to the expansion of _____in the ratings field.

4. The two independent industry committees set up by the NAB to study the accuracy of the diary and the meter were _____and _____.

5. Qualitative ratings services such as TAA and Vox Box give advertisers and agencies some measure of commercial _____ and _____.

## Short Answer

1. Discuss how legal financial, and managerial factors have influenced and dampened any industry-financed and industry-governed rating service in the U.S.?

2. What three significant findings about rating services have evolved in the past 50 years of ratings history?

## Chapter 11

### Multiple Choice

1. Which of the following will *not* be a technological change in present television broadcast services?
   A. Low power television stations (LPTV)
   B. Stereo sound to TV broadcasts
   C. Better picture quality
   D. Two-way viewer interaction
   E. None of the above

2. Video cassette recorders have which of the following amenities?
   A. Home video photography tape
   B. Immediate time shift
   C. Recording for retention
   D. B and C
   E. All of the above

3. The one-way video information service that consists of a catalogue-like series of pages of information receivable on home TV sets is
   A. Videotex
   B. Two-Way Cable
   C. Teletext
   D. Video discs
   E. None of the above

4. Teletext pages can reach the household set in which of the following ways?
   A. Via a cable channel
   B. By use of verticle blanking intervals (VBIs) in present TV transmission
   C. By separate telephone line connections
   D. B and C
   E. All of the above

5. Major videotex interest in the U.S. has involved
   A. Newspapers and local telephone companies
   B. Major m icrocomputer companies
   C. Retail outlets
   D. Merchandising associations
   E. All of the above

6. Which of the following ratings services inaugurated in the U.S. moved the ratings industries toward peoplemeters?
   A. Nielsen
   B. AGB Research PLC
   C. Arbitron
   D. A and B
   E. All of the above

7. Which of the following factors has complicated the measurement of VCR users?
   A. VCR time shifting
   B. Remote control device
   C. VCR fast forward button
   D. A and C
   E. All of the above

8. Two-way cable measurement must be looked at on which levels?
   A. Its effect on HUT
   B. Its effect on PUT
   C. Service usage
   D. A and C
   E. All of the above

## True/False

1. QUBE service has been proven to be uneconomical and not worth the capital expense involved in studios, equipment and cable lines.

2. Videotex and two-way cable provide entertainment driven programming rather than information based programming.

3. Subscription Television (STV) and Multipoint Distribution Service (MDS) are technologies that are being outclassed by cable services and other newer technologies.

4. *Piracy* is a term used to explain satellite dish users receiving such programs as HBO, Showtime, and other cable networks with no program charges.

5. In Direct Broadcast Service (DBS), a stronger signal mean that household receiving dishes must be enhanced to the 8-foot level.

6. One-way cable's growing acceptance in large market areas is predicted to produce a viable and strong advertising medium capable of delivering true national audiences.

7. A threatening competitor of cable is the multichannel multipoint distribution service (MMDS) which can be installed for considerably less money and in less time.

8. There is little industry support for the concept of people meters.

9. Teletext, Videotex, and home computers are all examples of services and usages not directly relevant to broadcast advertising measurement procedures.

10. Due to the favorable pilot results toward cable programming, TAA (Television Audience Assessment, Inc.) will develop additional studies to ascertain program appreciation and program impact.

## Fill in the Blank

1. Installation costs of Satellite Master Antenna Television (SMAT) are by far much _____than what is required by cable.

2. Of all different ways the VCRs serve their owners, _____ continues to be the major use of VCRs.

3. A major drawback of the video disc is that it lacks the _____and _____; uses of the VCR.

4. The_____has greatly intensified local telephone company interest in cable, teletext, videotex, home shopping and home banking services.

5. The lack of economical _____will seriously delay the marketing testing of teletext.

6. The people meter is currently being tested to replace the _____ to measure audience _____.

## Short Answer

1. Discuss the socioeconomic factors that directly affect the future of new broadcasting technologies. Have the new technologies grown at the rate that was predicted for them by the year 1990?

2. One way cable audience measurement has been extremely difficult to accomplish. Discuss the major obstacles that must be dealt with before cable audience measurement will be successful.

3. What are the common characteristics of STV, SMATV, MDS, MMDS, and DBS? Which will flourish and which will gradually lsoe out? In which ways do these services pose less difficult problems than cable audience measurement?

4. What are the principal future needs of audience measurement and rating services as proposed by industry executives and the EMRC?

# Answers

## Chapter 1

### Multiple Choice

1. B. Power outage, p. 21
2. C. C. E. Hooper, p. 11
3. C. C. E. Robinson, p. 17
4. B. 1930 census, p. 3
5. E. All of the above, p. 11
6. A. Hooper, p. 22
7. D. What commercials were remembered, p. 4
8. A. The CAB opening question was found to be biased, p. 10
9. E. U.S. diary ratings programs were converted to U.S. cooperatings by ratio between coincidental and diary ratings in 94 cities, p. 15

### True/False

1. True, p. 25
2. True, p. 3
3. False, p. 16
4. True, p. 6
5. True, p. 8
6. False, p. 22
7. True, p. 24
8. False, p. 15
9. True, p. 18

### Fill in the Blanks

1. Emergence of many local radio stations, growth of spot radio, p. 23
2. An unrepresentative sample, p. 8
3. 24-hour telephone recall interview, p. 4

### Short Answer

1. p. 13
2. pp. 14–15

## Chapter 2

Multiple choice

 1. E.  B and D only, pp. 29–30
 2. B.  Audience turn over ratios, composition, and ability to chart audience flow from program to program, p. 30.
 3. C.  CBS with Industrial Surveys, p. 29
 4. E.  All of the above, p. 28
 5. C.  CRAM, p. 43
 6. E.  A and B, p. 30
 7. E.  RADAR, p. 44
 8. E.  All of the above, pp. 44–45
 9. D.  TV research was cheaper to conduct, p. 37
10. D.  Probability, p. 45
11. E.  All of the above, p. 49
12. C.  Burke and Sindlinger, p. 53
13. B.  TRAC-7, p. 55
14. E.  A and C, p. 57
15. B.  RAM, p. 58
16. D.  Trace, p. 58
17. B.  Diary, p. 36
18. E.  All of the above, pp. 36–37
19. D.  A and C, p. 40

True/False

 1. True, p. 47
 2. False, p. 44
 3. True, p. 30
 4. False, p. 28
 5. True, p. 44
 6. True, p. 45
 7. True, p. 29
 8. True, p. 35
 9. True, p. 36
10. False, p. 42
11. False, p. 33

## Fill in the Blank

1. Computer, p. 35
2. "Call-back, feedback," pp. 40–41
3. Sindlinger, p. 39
4. Rowlow, Pulse, p. 32

## Short Answer

1. p. 33
2. p. 39
3. pp. 43–44

## Chapter 3

## Multiple Choice

1. B. Arbitron, p. 68
2. C. Multi-Network Area Report (MNA), p. 71
3. A. Addition to the sample of 450 new households of which 150 were cable subscribers, p. 72
4. B. Furnish demographic data not produced by a meter, p. 73
5. E. All of the above, p. 76
6. E. All of the above, p. 76
7. D. Tendex, p. 64
8. D. A and C, p. 65
9. D. A and B, p. 69
10. C. Designated Market Area (DMA) concept, p. 70
11. E. A and B, p. 75
12. D. Videodex, p. 77
13. E. B and D only, p. 80

## True/False

1. True, p. 79
2. True, p. 62
3. True, p. 70
4. False, p. 79 and 81
5. False, p. 62
6. True, p. 72
7. False, p. 72

## Fill in the Blank

1. Costs were high, only share of audience figures could be produced, p. 81
2. Arbitron, p. 65
3. Blacks, Hispanics, p. 70
4. Random-digit dialing, p. 74

## Short Answer

1. p. 72
2. p. 76

## Chapter 4

### Multiple Choice

1. D. Definition of audience and criteria for validity, p. 85
2. E. All of the above, p. 86
3. E. All of the above, pp. 86 and 89
4. B. Self-administered diaries, p. 90
5. C. Only average audience data are obtained, p. 85
6. B. Personal interviewer, p. 90
7. E. A and B, p. 97
8. C. Random-digit dialing, p. 102
9. B. Response rate is around 40% on the average, pp. 116–117
10. E. B and C, p. 112
11. E. All of the above, p. 107 and 108
12. B. Average interview lasts about 2 to 3 minutes, p. 104
13. E. B and C, p. 105
14. C. Yield valid weekly cummulative data that was truly projectable, p. 107
15. A. Audience composition for viewing households as determined by the NTI audimeter, p. 114
16. A. "Half-open interval" form of area probability sampling, p. 120

### True/False

1. False, p. 84 and 86
2. False, p. 126
3. True, p. 86
4. False, p. 86
5. True, p. 105

6. True, p. 112 and 113
7. False,p. 122
8. True, p. 121
9. True, p. 115
10. False, p. 110
11. True, p. 111
12. True, p. 121
13. True, p. 108
14. False, p. 106
15. False, p. 104
16. False, p. 101
17. False, p. 89
18. True, p. 92
19. False, p. 93
20. False, p. 89
21. True, p. 90
22. False, p. 91
23. True, p. 92
24. True, p. 92

## Fill in the Blank

1. Clustering, p. 125
2. Coincidental telephone interview, p. 85
3. Geographic area representation, p. 119
4. Panel, p. 113
5. Lowered, p. 110
6. Birch, p. 104
7. Upward, p. 106

## Short Answer

1. pp. 86–87
2. p. 88
3. pp. 100–101
4. p. 103
5. pp. 106–107
6. pp. 109–110
7. p. 125

## Chapter 5

### Multiple Choice

1. C. TVQ, p. 132
2. C. Program appreciation, program impact, p. 151
3. E. All of the above, p. 150
4. D. Viewer like or dislike of a particular program, p. 136
5. D. A and B, p. 138
6. B. Qualidata, p. 139
7. E. A and C, p. 143
8. E. All of the above, p. 145
9. A. Arbitron, p. 146
10. E. All of the above, pp. 134–135
11. B. The relationship between viewers reactions and program recall and comprehension, p. 152
12. D. A and B, p. 147

### True/False

1. True, p. 152
2. True, p. 157
3. True, p. 134
4. False, p. 138
5. True, p. 144
6. True, p. 147
7. True, p. 15
8. False, p. 154
9. False, p. 152
10. True, p. 137
11. True, p. 139

### Fill in the Blank

1. Homogeneous groups each with its own distinct neighborhood lifestyle, PRIZM, p. 138
2. Need driven, outer directed, inner directed, integrated, p. 139
3. Channel selection, recording qualitative response, pp. 144–145

## Short Answer

1. p. 151
2. p. 133
3. p. 142

## Chapter 6

## Multiple Choice

1. E. A and B, pp. 163–164
2. D. Uses individual programs as the basic units of analysis, p. 166
3. C. Seven day unaided telephone recall, p. 171
4. E. All of the above, p. 174
5. C. Planned viewing, p. 177
6. A. Have strong interest in sports and movies, p. 179
7. E. All of the above, p. 161
8. E. B and C, p. 168
9. E. All of the above, pp.175–176
10. C. 73, p. 178
11. B. Marquest Cable Ratings, pp. 164–166, 168
12. E. All of the above, pp. 172–173

## True/False

1. True, p. 160
2. True, p. 167
3. False, p. 178
4. False, p. 164
5. True, p. 162
6. False, p. 167
7. True, p. 171
8. False, p. 179
9. True, p. 181
10. True, p. 165

## Fill in the Blank

1. Disparity, p. 167
2. Large scale telephone coincidental, p. 171

3. Two-say cable measurement, p. 174
4. Enjoying the program, p. 179

## Short Answer

1. p. 170
2. pp. 173–174
3. pp. 174–175
4. p. 182

## Chapter 7

## Multiple Choice

1. E. All of the above, p. 188
2. D. A and B, p. 194
3. C. 'Sweeps reports', p. 199
4. C. Arbitron TAPP, p. 200
5. D. CAB, p. 215
6. A. Reach and frequency, p. 205
7. C. Radio measures a people universe, pp. 202–203
8. D. Help TV stations sell its announcements to local advertisers, p. 201
9. E. None of the above, they are all provided by the Nielsen
10. C. National Audience Demographics report (NAD), p. 189
11. C. Radio, p. 196
12. A. Nielsen, p. 197
13. C. Arbitron, p. 204
14. D. A and C, pp. 203–204
15. B. RADAR, pp. 203–204
16. D. Relatively high caliber of broadcast measurement data versus direct mail measurement give advertisers confident faith in the numbers used, p. 216
17. E. All of the above, p. 190

## True/False

1. False, p. 187
2. True, p. 190
3. False, p. 191
4. True, p. 192
5. True, p. 195

6. False, pp. 198–199
7. False, p. 194
8. True, p. 199
9. True, p. 200
10. False, p. 202
11. True, p. 203
12. True, p. 207
13. True, p. 205
14. True, p. 212
15. False, p. 207

## Fill in the Blank

1. 'Make-good' announcements total gross rating points, net reach, frequency, p. 192
2. Mutually exclusive, additive, p. 198
3. Individual diaries, household, p. 203
4. Rank order basis, p. 203
5. Product needs, budget provided, p. 207
6. Roadblock, p. 208
7. Planning, research, p. 208

## Short Answer

1. pp. 212–213
2. p. 192

## Chapter 8

### Multiple Choice

1. E. None of the above; they are all criticisms of broadcast ratings, p. 223
2. E. A and B, p. 225
3. E. All of the above, p. 227
4. D. A and B, p. 230
5. D. A and C, p. 233
6. D. A and C, p. 238
7. E. All of the above, p. 226
8. E. All of the above, pp. 234, 236

## True/False

1. False, p. 235
2. True, p. 233
3. True, p. 226
4. False, p. 231
5. False, p. 224
6. False, p. 224
7. True, p. 219

## Fill in the Blank

1. Advertising power, p. 221
2. Sample error, estimates, p. 224
3. Leisure activity, p. 239

## Short Answer

1. pp. 235–237
2. p. 229
3. pp. 231–232

## Chapter 9

### Multiple Choice

1. A. Advertising Research Foundation (ARF), p. 242
2. A. The BRC must accredit all reasonable applications for Council accreditation, p. 248
3. E. Start up costs to launch a new rating service are relatively low, p. 252
4. D. Government control, p. 256
5. E. All of the above, p. 245
6. E. A and C, p. 248
7. E. p. 254
8. A. The enactment of legislation providing for government regulation of broadcast audience measurement activities was highly advisable, p. 246–247

## True/False

1. False, p. 243
2. True, p. 247
3. False, p. 248
4. False, p. 249
5. True, p. 253
6. True, p. 255–256

## Fill in the Blank

1. FTC, p. 245
2. Senator Magnuson, p. 243
3. Harris committee hearings, p. 247
4. Profit motive, p. 255
5. Audit Bureau of Circulation, Canadian Bureau of Broadcast Measurement, p. 253

## Short Answer

1. pp. 249–25
2. p. 242
3. pp. 249–250

## Chapter 10

## Multiple Choice

1. D. Viewers are more upscale and don't like to complete diaries, p. 269
2. E. All of the above, pp. 259–260
3. B. Percentages, p. 261
4. D. A and B, p. 263
5. C. Nielsen Radio Index, p. 264
6. D. Arbitron, originally called ARB, p. 265
7. D. All of the above, p. 267

## True/False

1. True, p. 267
2. True, p. 260

3. True, p. 261
4. False, p. 261
5. False, p. 264
6. True, p. 264
7. False, p. 261
8. False, p. 264
9. False, p. 267
10. False, p. 265

## Fill in the Blank

1. Meter household, p. 263
2. Reach, frequency, p. 264
3. Computerization, p. 266
4. CONTAM, COLTRAM, p. 268
5. Exposure, impact, p. 269

## Short Answer

1. pp. 259–260
2. p. 258

## Chapter 11

## Multiple Choice

1. D. Two-way viewer interaction, p. 272
2. E. All of the above, p. 276
3. C. Teletext, p. 279
4. E. All of the above, p. 280
5. A. Newspapers and local telephone companies, p. 281
6. D. A and B, p. 285
7. D. A and C, p. 287
8. D. A and C, p. 288

## True/False

1. True, p. 281
2. False, p. 280
3. True, p. 273

4. True, p. 278
5. False, p. 279
6. False, pp. 273–274
7. True, p. 278
8. False, p. 285
9. True, p. 289
10. False, p. 290

## Fill in the Blank

1. Lower, p. 275
2. Time shifting, p. 276
3. Recording, time shifting, p. 276
4. Breakup of AT&T, p. 282
5. Home decoders, p. 280
6. TV household diary, demographics, p. 285

## Short Answer

1. pp. 283–284
2. p. 286
3. p. 288
4. p. 290

# BIBLIOGRAPHY

## Books

Barnouw, Erik. *The sponsor: Notes on a modern potentate*. New York: Oxford University Press, 1978.

Blankenship, Albert. *Professional telephone surveys*. New York: McGraw-Hill, 1979.

Carnegie Commission on the Future of Public Broadcasting. *A public trust*. New York: Bantam Books, 1979.

Chappell, Mathew N., & Hooper, C. E. *Radio audience measurement*. New York: Stephen Daye, 1944.

Deming, W. Edwards. *Sampling design for business research*. New York: Wiley, 1960.

Fletcher, James F., et al. *Handbook of radio and TV broadcasting: Research procedures in audience, program and revenues*. New York: Van Nostrand Reinhold, 1981.

Frank, Ronald E., & Greenberg, Marshall G. *The public's use of television: Who watches what and why*. Beverly Hills, Calif.: Sage Publications, 1980.

Halberstam, David. *The powers that be*. New York: Knopf, 1979.

Kaatz, Ronald B. *Cable: An advertiser's guide to the new electronic media*. Chicago: Crain Books, 1982.

Lumley, Frederick H. *Measurement in radio*. Columbus: Ohio State University Press, 1934.

Mehling, Harold. *The great time-killer*. Cleveland: World Publishing, 1982.

Metz, Robert. *CBS: Reflections in a bloodshot eye*. New York: Playboy Press, 1975.

Naples, Michael J. *The effective frequency: the relationship between frequency and advertising effectiveness*. New York: Association of National Advertisers, 1979.

Nye, Frank W. *"Hoop" of hooperatings: The man and his work*. Norwalk, Conn.: Privately published, 1957.

Poltrack, David F. *Television marketing: Network/local/cable*. New York: McGraw-Hill, 1983.

Weaver, David H. *Videotex journalism: Teletext, viewdata, and the news*. Hillsdale, N.J.: Lawrence Erlbaum Associates, 1983.

Williams, Bill. *A Sampler on sampling*. New York: Wiley, 1978.

Winner, Roger D. & Dominick, Joseph R. *Mass media research—an introduction*. Belmont, Calif.: Wadsworth Publishing, 1982.

## Articles, Periodicals, and Reports

Achenbaum, Alvin A. *"Effective Exposure," A New Way of Evaluating Media.* Paper read at the Winter Meeting, Association of National Advertisers, February 3, 1977, New York.

"Actors Fighting TVQ Influence." *Television Digest*, April 16, 1984.

American Research Bureau. "The Influence of Non-Cooperation in the Diary Method of Television Audience Measurements." Beltsville, Md.: American Research Bureau, 1963.

Adams, Anthony. "Life-Style Research: A Lot of Hype, Very Little Performance." *Marketing News*, May 14, 1982, Sect. 2, p. 5.

Advertising Research Foundation. "Biases in the 1961 Television Audience Profile Salt Lake City–Ogden–Provo Television Market, A Survey by American Research Bureau." New York; Advertising Research Foundation, 1965.

———. "Comparison of the Nights at Home Formula with Estimates from Six Calls." New York: Advertising Research Foundation, 1961.

———. "Electronic Test of in-Home TV Viewing Among Those Families Who Fail to Respond to the Doorbell." New York: Advertising Research Foundation, Arrowhead Study No. 8, 1968.

———. "Recommended Standards for Radio and Television Program Audience Size Measurements." New York: Advertising Research Foundation, 1954.

———. "Toward Better Media Comparisons: A Report of the Audience Concepts Committee." New York: Advertising Research Foundation, 1961.

Arbitron Ratings Co. "Arbitrends: Computer Delivered Radio Market Information." New York: Arbitron Ratings Co., undated.

———. "Cable: Two-Way Cable/Cable Diary Test, A Summary of Findings." New York: Arbitron Ratings Co., 1983.

Audits and Surveys, Inc. "Feasibility Study of Telephone Measurement of Radio Using Varying Numbers of Interviews per Person." Study conducted under sponsorship of Radio Advertising Bureau and National Association of Broadcasters, June–September, 1977. New York: Audits and Surveys, Inc., Survey Division.

BBM Bureau of Measurement. *"What Do Broadcast Audience Diaries Really Measure?"* Paper read to Advertising Research Foundation Conference by representatives of Canadian BBM headed by Peter R. Jones, President, November 11, 1975, New York.

Beville, Hugh M., Jr. "The ABCD's of Radio Audiences." *The Public Opinion Quarterly*, Vol. 4, No. 2, June 1940, pp. 195–206.

———. "How Will Home Cassette Players Affect Ratings?" Paper Read at Radio and Television Research Council meeting, November 14, 1977, New York.

———. "Social Stratification of the Radio Audience." Princeton, N.J.: Office of Radio Research, 1939.

———. "Surveying Radio Listeners by Use of a Probability Sample." *Journal of Marketing*, October 1949.

———. "VCR Penetration: Will It Surpass Cable by 1990?" *Television/Radio Age*, July 9, 1984, p. 27.

"Cable on the Firing Line: The Cable Television Summit Conference." Proceedings of conference sponsored by *Television Digest*, October 27, 1983, Washington, D.C.

Cabletelevision Advertising Bureau and National Cable Television Association. "Cable Audience Methodology Study," conducted by A.C. Nielsen, Inc., 1983.

"California Senate Sends TVQ Bill on to Assembly." *Daily Variety*, June 15, 1984.

Chappell, Mathew N. "Factors Influencing Recall of Radio Program." *Public Opinion Quarterly*, Spring 1942.

Claritas Corporation. "PRIZM, Geodemographic Market Segmentation and Targeting." Arlington, Va.: Claritas Corporation, 1982.

Columbia Broadcasting System. "The CBS Listener Diary, an Area Measurement of Station and Program Listening." New York: Columbia Broadcasting System, July 1948.

———. "Does Radio Sell Goods?" A laboratory measurement of the sales effectiveness of radio broadcasting based on an enquiry conducted by Professor Robert F. Elder of the Massachusetts Institute of Technology. New York: Columbia Broadcasting System, September 1931.

Committee on Interstate and Foreign Commerce, U.S. House of Representatives. "Evaluation of Statistical Methods Used in Obtaining Broadcast Ratings." House Report No. 193. Washington, D.C.: U.S. Government Printing Office, 1961.

———. "Broadcast Ratings." Report submitted by Oren Harris, Chairman, Special Subcommittee of Investigations, January 13, 1966. Washington, D.C.: U.S. Government Printing Office, 1966.

Committee on Local Television and Radio Audience Measurement. "A Study of Television Usage in Four Local Markets, Final Report, Spring 1972." Westfield, N.J.: Statistical Research, Inc.

Committee on National Television Audience Measurement. "How Good Are Television Ratings?" Results of CONTAM studies 1, 2, and 3. Martin Mayer, February 1966.

———. "How Good Are Television Ratings? (continued . . .)" Report on CONTAM study No. 4, presented at Annual Conference, Advertising Research Foundation, October 14, 1969.

———. "Television Ratings Revisited . . . A Further Look at TV Audiences." Results of CONTAM studies 5 and 6. New York: Television Information Office, November 1971.

Cooper, Stanford L. "Random Sampling by Telephone: An Improved Method." *Journal of Marketing Research*, Vol. 1, No. 4, November 1964, pp. 45–48.

Corporation for Public Broadcasting. "Boston (WGBH) Field Testing of a Qualitative Television Rating System for Public Broadcasting." Washington, D.C.: Corporation for Public Broadcasting, Office of Communications Research, June 1981.

———. "Proceedings of the 1980 Technical Conference on Qualitative Television Ratings—Final Report." Washington, D.C.: Corporation for Public Broadcasting, 1980.

Crossley, Archibald M. *"The Public Wants."* Princeton, N.J.: Unpublished manuscript, March 1979.

Dahlin, Robert. "Commentary on the Unpredictability of Readers." *The Christian Science Monitor*, November 4, 1984.

Demby, Emanuel H. "Two Decades Later: Psychographics." *Marketing Review*, American Marketing Association, New York Chapter, May/June 1984, p. 17.

Dimling, John A. "Why Existing Methodologies?" New York: Advertising Research Foundation Key Issues Workshop, Researching the Electronic Media II, December 15, 1983.

Electronic Media Rating Council. "Maintaining Rating Confidence and Credibility." New York: Electronic Media Rating Council, June 1983.

Glasser, Gerald J., & Metzger, Gale D. "National Estimates of Nonlisted Telephone Households and Their Characteristics." *Journal of Marketing Research*, Vo. XII, August 1975, pp. 359–61.

———. "Random Digit Dialing as a Method of Telephone Sampling." *Journal of Marketing Research*, February 1972, pp. 59–64.

"Group W Schedules Trial for Teletext." *Advertising Age*, July 9, 1984, p. 3.

Gupta, Udayan. "COMP-U-CARD Has Head Start in Electronic Marketing." *Electronic Media*, March 21, 1984, p. 13.

"High Sights, Low Visibility." Interview with Thomas Wyman. *Broadcasting*, March 26, 1984, p. 42.

Hooper, C. E. "How Adequate Is the Telephone Sample for Obtaining Radio Program Ratings?" January 1941.

Hooper (C. E.) Inc. "U.S. Hooperatings, Winter 1948."

"Instantaneous Rating System Claim Made by West Coast Agency Executive." *Broadcasting*, April 23, 1956, p. 50.

"IRTS Brings Big Names Together." Report on 12th Annual Faculty/Industry and College Conference of the International Radio and Television Society. *Broadcasting*, February 6, 1984.

James, Watson S. "The New Electronic Media: An Overview." *Journal of Advertising Research*, August/September 1983.

Jursek, Philip D. *"An Analysis of Broadcast Audience Measurement: Recent Government Investigations and Methodology Research, with an Assessment of the Current State of the Art."* Ph.D. dissertation, Wayne State University, 1970.

Kahan, Hazel. *"Means Are Meaningless, or Variance Is the Name of the Game."* Paper read at a meeting of the Cable Television Administration and Marketing Society, August 10, 1983, San Diego.

———. *"The Cable Subscriber Speaks: Channels, Choice, and Chaos."* Paper read at an Advertising Research Foundation Workshop, Researching the Electronic Media, December 15, 1983.

Keller, Paul. "Media Buyer's View of ARMS Report." *Media/Scope*, February 1967.

Klein, Paul F. "TV Program Creation and Broadcast Research: Conflict or Harmony?" New York: American Marketing Association, April 13, 1981.

Krugman, Herbert. "Why Three Exposures May Be Enough." *Journal of Advertising Research*, No. 6, 1972, p. 11.

"Lee Rich and Lorimar on a Roll." *Broadcasting*, May 5, 1980, p. 48.

Lindsey, Robert. "The Man Who Plots CBS's Climb Back to the Top." *New York Times*, Jan. 27, 1980.

Lumley, F. Hillis. "Habits of the Radio Audience." *Journal of Applied Psychology*, XVII, 1933, p. 29.

Myers, Lawrence Jr. *"An Examination of Television Audience Measurement Methods and an Application of Segmented Analysis to the Telephone Interview Method."* Ph.D. dissertation, Syracuse University, 1956.

McNiece, Jill. "Cable Ops Place Bets on Multichannel MDS." *Multichannel News*, December 12, 1983, p. 40.

Mayer, Martin. "How Good Are Television Ratings?" New York: Television Information Office, February 1966.

———. "The Intelligent Man's Guide to Broadcast Ratings." New York: Advertising Research Foundation, 1962.

Maxwell, Robert. "Pay TV Demands New Research Techniques." New York: Radio/Television Research Council, November 28, 1983.

McDowell, Edwin. "CBS Strives to Retain Lead." *New York Times*, January 11, 1979.

Mediamark Research, Inc. "Focus on the MRI Advantage, MRI Plan for 1982 Reports." New York: Mediamark Research, Inc.

Metzger, Gale D. "A Plea to End Sloppy Research." *Advertising Age*, October 26, 1981, p. 52.

Nagel, Madeline. "Media Diversity Challenges Today's Ad Agencies." *Advertising Age*, Aug. 18, 1980.

"Name of the Game." *Broadcasting*, February 13, 1984, p. 67.

Newman, W. Russell. *"Communications Technology and Cultural Diversity."* Paper read at San Francisco meeting of American Sociological Assocation, September 1982.

National Association of Broadcasters. "How Good Is the Television Diary Technique?" Report of a study by Statistical Research, Inc. in consultation with Committee on Local Television and Radio Audience Measurement. Washington, D.C.: National Association of Broadcasters, 1976.

———. "A Plan for the Evaluation of Audience Measurement Methods." Washington, D.C.: National Association of Broadcasters, 1951.

———. "Recommended Standards for the Preparation of Statistical Reports in Broadcast Audience Measurement Research." Washington, D.C.: National Association of Broadcasters, 1969.

———. "Standard Definitions of Broadcast Research Terms." Washington, D.C.: National Association of Broadcasters, 1967.

National Broadcasting Company. "CRAM: Cumulative Radio Audience Method." New York: National Broadcasting Company, 1966.

Newspaper Advertising Bureau. "Trends in TV Commercial Recall, 1965–1981." New York: Newspaper Advertising Bureau, 1982.

Nielsen, Arthur C. "Television Audience Research for Great Britain." Chicago: A. C. Nielsen Company; Oxford: A. C. Nielsen Company Limited, 1955.

O'Hanlon, Tom. "What Does This Man Want?" *Forbes*, January 30, 1984

Politz, Alfred, & Simmons, Willard. "An Attempt to Get the 'Not at Homes' into the Sample without Callbacks." *Journal of American Statistical Association*, XLIV (1944), p. 10.

"Qualitative Research: Is There a Light at the End of the Tunnel?" *Television/Radio Age* June 25, 1984, p. 75.

"Qualitative TV Rating Study Shows Viewer Attitudes Toward Programs." *Beyond the Ratings*, Vol. 5, No. 5, May 1982.

Radio Advertising Bureau. "All Radio Methodology Study, September 1966." RAB-sponsored study conducted by Audits and Surveys, Inc. under review by Advertising Research Foundation.

Radio Advertising Representatives. "Polyphase—Radio Listening and Some Problems in Its Meaning." Study conducted by National Analysts, Philadelphia, 1967.

Rubens, William S. "A Guide to TV Ratings." *Journal of Advertising Research*, Vol. 18, No. 1, February 1978.

———. *"The Role of Media on Democratic Policy."* Paper read at the National Decisions Program Seminar, Political Science Department, University of Pennsylvania, October 1983.

Salmans, Sandra. "Cable Operators Take a Bruising." *New York Times*, March 4, 1984, Section 3, p. 1.

Schwartz, Tony. "An Intimate Talk with William Paley." *New York Times* Magazine, December 28, 1980.

Seiler, James M. "Ratings on Individual Basis Are Urged." *Broadcasting*, May 12, 1947.

Sindlinger & Company. "Radio Activity: A Report Outlining the Methods and Procedures for Sindlinger's Daily and Continuous Radio Activity That Measures and Reports the Complete Mobility of the Radio Advertising Medium." Norwood, Pa.: Sindlinger & Company, 1962.

Simmons (W. R.) & Associates, Inc. "Evaluating Television Measurement Systems." Report to the 14th Annual Conference, Advertising Research Foundation, October 15–16, 1968.

"Slow Liftoff for Satellite-to-Home TV." *Fortune*, March 5, 1983.

Small, Collie. "The Biggest Man in Radio." *The Saturday Evening Post*, November 22, 1947.

"Sorting Out DBS Proposals." *Broadcasting*, January 16, 1984, p. 48.

Stanton, Frank N. *"A Critique of Present Methods and a New Plan for Studying Listening Behavior."* Ph.D. dissertation, Ohio State University, 1935.

Starch, Daniel. "A Study of Radio Broadcasting Based Exclusively on Personal Interviews with Families in the United States East of the Rocky Mountains." New York: National Broadcasting Company, April 1928.

Statistical Research, Inc. "Special Studies of Television Audiences in the New York Metropolitan Area, Final Report, June 1973." Westfield, N.J.: Statistical Research, Inc.

———. "Study of Television Usage in the New York Metropolitan Area." Westfield, N.J.: Statistical Research, Inc., 1971.

Swerdlow, Joel. "The Ratings Game." *Washington Journalism Revue*, October 1979.

Steiner, Gary A. "The People Look at Commercials: A Study of Audience Behavior." *Journal of Business*, April 1966, pp. 272–304.

"TCI Buys Pittsburgh System." *Television Digest*, March 26, 1984, p. 6.

Television Audience Assessment, Inc. "Appeal and Impact: A Program Ratings Book." Cambridge, Mass.: Television Audience Assessment, Inc., 1983.

———. "Audience Attitudes and Alternative Program Ratings: A Preliminary Study." Cambridge, Mass.: Television Audience Assessment, Inc., October 1981.

———. "The Audience Rates Television." Executive Summary. Cambridge, Mass.: Television Audience Assessment, Inc., 1983.

———. "Involvement with Television Programs: A Literature Review." Boston: Television Audience Assessment, Inc., 1984.

———. "Methodology Report." Cambridge, Mass.: Television Audience Assessment, 1983.

———. "The Multichannel Environment." Cambridge, Mass.: Television Audience Assessment, Inc., 1983.

————. "Program Impact and Program Appeal: Qualitative Ratings and Commercial Effectiveness." Boston: Television Audience Assessment, 1984.

————. "Technical Appendix." Cambridge, Mass.: Television Audience Assessment, 1983.

Television Information Office. "Trends in Attitudes Toward Television and Other Media: A Twenty-Four-Year Review." Report by the Roper Organization, Inc. New York: Television Information Office, 1983.

"Trying to End the Flow of Good Money After Bad in DBS." *Broadcasting*, January 9, 1983, p. 128.

"USCI Reveals High Cost of DBS." *Television Digest*, February 27, 1984, p. 6.

Whalen, Bernie. "Cable's Home Penetration Rate Keeps Rising, But New Competitors Could Fragment Market." *Marketing News*, November 25, 1983.

"The Wired World of Anthony Oettinger." *Harvard Magazine*, May–June 1982, p. 36.

Yuspeh, Sonia. "Slamming Syndicated Data." *Advertising Age*, May 17, 1984, p. M-46.

Zeisel, Hans. "CAB and Hooper, an Investigation of the Coincidental Telephone Interview." New York: McCann-Erickson, Inc., Central Research Department, May 1946.

# Index

# About the Author

## HUGH MALCOLM BEVILLE, JR.

Because of his long and productive career, Mal Beville is often termed "the dean of broadcast research." Joining NBC as a statistician in 1930, he participated in forming the Research Department and rose to Vice President for Planning and Research in 1958. In 1966 Mal began a six-year teaching stint at Southampton College. In 1972 he resigned his full professorship and served ten years as Executive Director of the Broadcast Rating Council (now the Electronic Media Research Council). Since 1982 he has concentrated on writing and consulting. He has written and spoken extensively about peoplemeter development and problems.

Beville holds a 1930 B.S. in Business Administration from Syracuse University and an M.B.A. with distinction from NYU in 1966. His NBC research career involved numerous rating service developments as well as industry committees dealing with broadcast research issues. As NBC's representative to the Advertising Research Foundation for fifteen years, he served as a member of the Technical Committee, the Board and Executive Committees, and numerous ad hoc groups.

Beville was a founding member of the American Association of Public Opinion Research and served as President of both the Market Research Council and the Radio/Television Research Council. His speeches and articles on electronic media ratings are widely hailed for their insightful and clear analyses. In 1986 he was honored by the Market Research Council by selection to the Research Hall of Fame. Thus joining George Gallup, Arthur C. Nielsen, Sr., and C. E. Hooper, whose pioneering contributions to the rating field are highlighted within this volume.

407

# DATE DUE